Transfer of movables
in German, French, English and Dutch law

To my parents

Transfer of movables
in German, French, English and Dutch law

PROEFSCHRIFT

ter verkrijging van de graad van doctor aan
de Universiteit Maastricht,
op gezag van de Rector Magnificus,
Prof. dr A.C. Nieuwenhuijzen Kruseman
volgens het besluit van het College van Dekanen,
in het openbaar te verdedigen
op vrijdag 14 januari 2000 om 16.00 uur

door

Lars Peter Wunibald van Vliet

Ars Aequi Libri
Nijmegen 2000

Promotores:
Prof. mr J.H.M. van Erp
Prof. dr B.A. Rudden (University of Oxford)

Beoordelingscommissie:
Prof. mr G.R. de Groot (voorzitter).
Prof. mr G.E. van Maanen
Prof. dr R. Schulze (Westfälische Wilhelms-Universität, Münster)

ISBN 90-6916-353-5

NUGI 691/692/697

Cover design: L.P.W. van Vliet/J. van Winden, Ars Aequi Libri
front photograph: Old Quad, Brasenose College, Oxford
back photograph: Toren, Oud-Gouvernement, Law Faculty, Maastricht
both photographs © L.P.W. van Vliet

Preface

The preface of this book enables me to depict briefly how the thesis came into being and, more importantly, to thank the people who helped me accomplish the project. When I was reading law at Maastricht University Professor Wolfgang Mincke and Professor Caroline Forder gave me the opportunity to study German and English property law. In her tutorials on property law Caroline Forder excited my interest in English property law. In a very stimulating way she supervised a paper I wrote about land registration in Dutch and English law. Her dedication and zeal impressed me very much.

In this time Professor Gerrit van Maanen (Maastricht University) introduced me to Professor Bernard Rudden (Brasenose College, Oxford), who very generously offered his assistance. Writing the paper I conceived the idea of writing a doctoral thesis on the various systems for the transfer of property. The University of Maastricht gave me the opportunity to start work on the project from September 1993, under the supervision of Professors Mincke and Rudden.

The years of research are a time I look back on with great satisfaction. It is a period in which I have always worked with pleasure and inspiration. Wolfgang Mincke introduced me to 19th century German pandectism and its culmination in the famous *Allgemeiner Teil* by Andreas von Tuhr. Furthermore, he showed me his wisdom and peculiar view of life.

I have many cherished memories of the innumerable discussions Professor Rudden and I had in Brasenose college and via electronic mail. Like fencers we duelled in a sportive, even chivalrous way. After the fight one of us admitted defeat, or, in some cases, we decided on a suspension of arms. The fights, in which I often lost, produced thoughts and questions which, back in Maastricht, occupied my mind for months and were a rich source of inspiration. The time and effort Professor Rudden spends on supervising his pupils is an example of academic dedication. I thank him warmly for the many years of continuous support.

After Wolfgang Mincke had returned to Germany Professor Sjef van Erp (Maastricht University) took over Wolfgang's duties as supervisor (*promotor*) in December 1997. He gave me valuable advice how to distribute the material over the different chapters and how to complete the project. Moreover, it is a great pleasure to discuss legal problems with Sjef.

Professor Spruit (Utrecht University) was so kind as to help me with chapter 7 on the history of the *iusta causa* requirement and other historical parts of the book. I am greatly indebted to him. Many thanks also to Professor Paul Jackson (University of Reading), Peter Smith (University of Reading), Roger Smith (Magdalen College, Oxford) and William Swadling (Brasenose College), who have been very helpful by answering all sorts of questions about English property law and sending me photocopies of articles and case law which were not available in Dutch libraries.

I am equally indebted to Professors De Groot (Maastricht University), Van Maanen and Schulze (University of Münster, Germany) for their willingness to be members of the examining committee (*beoordelingscommissie*). Gerrit van Maanen gave me some valuable suggestions as to textual revision. And, as chairman of the department of private law René de Groot always showed his special interest in the progress of the project in a very encouraging way.

It is very important to any piece of academic research to have quick access at any time to books and articles in the library. I spent quite some time in the Maastricht Jesuit collection. Derk van Gestel, guardian of this collection of old imprints, has always been prepared to do something extra, for example giving me access beyond the very limited opening hours. I have to mention Mrs Marianne Roelofs here as well, who works at the library of Utrecht University. She helped me photocopy articles I needed and checked references I forgot to write down. Their generous help saved me from a lot of delay. The time-consuming correction of the text was done largely by Peter Smith, and partly by Caroline Forder.

A special word of acknowledgement for my parents, who followed the project with great interest. Their constant attention has been very supportive. Having read private law himself my father often asked me penetrating questions on my research. I will never forget the long discussions accompanied by marvellous Italian and French wines. It is them that I dedicate this book.

And finally, a more down-to-earth remark. The manuscript was closed in December 1998. Until September 1999 I have been able, to a limited extent, to make alterations.

Maastricht, 20 September 1999

Contents

6 Gift from hand to hand

7 *Iusta causa traditionis*

8 The three systems compared. A common core?

Abbreviations

ABGB	Allgemeines Bürgerliches Gesetzbuch
AC	Appeal Cases
AcP	Archiv für die civilistische Praxis
Afr.	Africanus
AJCL	The American Journal of Comparative Law
All ER	All England Law Reports
All ER Rep	All England Law Reports Reprints
ALR	Allgemeines Landrecht für die Preußischen Staaten
App. Cas.	Appeal Cases
Barn. & Ald.	Barnewall & Alderson
BGB	Bürgerliches Gesetzbuch
BGE	Entscheidungen des Schweizerischen Bundesgerichts
BGH	Bundesgerichtshof
Bull.	Bulletin des arrêts de la Cour de Cassation
BW	Burgerlijk Wetboek
C.	Justinian's Codex
CA	Court of Appeal; Cour d'Appel
Cass. civ.	Cour de Cassation, chambre civile
Cass. com.	Cour de Cassation, chambre commerciale
Cass. req.	Cour de Cassation, chambre des requêtes
CC	Code Civil
Cels.	Celsus
Ch.	Chancery Division (1891-)
Ch.D	Chancery Division (1875-1890)
CLJ	Cambridge Law Journal
Co. Rep.	Coke Reports
D.	Digest; Recueil Dalloz
D.P.	Dalloz Périodique
D.S.	Recueil Dalloz-Sirey
E&B	Ellis & Blackburn
fn.	footnote
Gai.	Gaius' Institutes
HGB	Handelsgesetzbuch
HL	House of Lords
HR	Hoge Raad der Nederlanden
Inst.	Justinian's Institutes
J	Justice
Jav.	Javolenus
JBL	Journal of business law
Jher. Jahrb.	Jherings Jahrbücher für die Dogmatik des bürgerlichen Rechts
j°	juncto
Jul.	Julianus
JZ	Juristenzeitung

KB	King's Bench
Law Com.	Law Commission
LJ	Lord Justice
Lloyd's Rep.	Lloyd's List Law Reports
LMCLQ	Lloyd's Maratime and Commercial Law Quarterly
LQR	The Law Quarterly Review
LT	Law Times Reports
Marc.	Marcellus
MLR	Modern law review
Ner.	Neratius
NJ	Nederlandse Jurisprudentie
NJB	Nederlands Juristenblad
NJW	Neue Juristische Wochenschrift
OJLS	Oxford Journal of Legal Studies
OR	Obligationenrecht
pr.	principium
Parl. Gesch	Parlementaire Geschiedenis
Parl. Gesch. Inv.	Parlementaire Geschiedenis Invoeringswet
Paul.	Paulus
PCC	Palmers Company Cases
QBD	Queens Bench Division
Rdnr.	Randnummer (marginal number)
Rev. trim. dr. civ.	Revue trimestrielle de droit civil
Rev. trim. dr. com.	Revue trimestrielle de droit commercial
SALJ	South African Law Journal
Scot. Law Com.	Scottish Law Commission
SGA	Sale of Goods Act 1979
S&S	Schip en schade
Stra	Strange
Taunt.	Taunton
TLR	Times Law Reports
Ulp.	Ulpianus
Vent.	Ventris
Ves. Sen.	Vesey senior
Vorbem.	Vorbemerkungen
WM	Wertpapiermitteilungen
WPNR	Weekblad voor privaatrecht, notariaat en registratie
ZEuP	Zeitschrift für Europäisches Privatrecht
ZGB	Zivilgesetzbuch
ZSS Rom	Zeitschrift der Savigny-Stiftung für Rechtsgeschichte, romanistische Abteilung

Concise glossary

causa: **see** *iusta causa traditionis*

constitutum possessorium
> A transfer of possession in which the transferor remains in actual control of the thing. The transferor turns his *possessio* into *detentio* holding the thing for the acquirer.

Defect of will
> A legally relevant shortcoming in the will of someone making a legal act, for example someone entering into a contract under the influence of mistake, fraud or duress.

Detentio
> The holding of a thing for another, respecting the other's rights over the thing.

(Iusta) causa (traditionis)
> Valid legal ground underlying the transfer of ownership.

Possessio
> The holding of a thing for oneself.

Possession
> In legal English the term 'possession' is used as an umbrella term covering *possessio* as well as *detentio*. Note, however, that unless stated otherwise I will use the term 'possession' as equivalent to *possessio*.

Real agreement
> A legal act in which the transferor declares to transfer ownership and the acquirer declares to accept ownership of the thing.

Tradition/*traditio*
> The transfer of *possessio*.

Traditio brevi manu
> A transfer of possession to someone who is already in actual control of the asset. The acquirer's *detentio* is then turned into *possessio*.

Traditio ficta
> A form of transfer of possession in which possession is transferred simply by agreement without any physical handing over being needed.

Traditio vera
> A transfer of possession which involves a physical handing over.

Introduction

Someone agrees to buy a beautiful series of antiquarian books, the *Opera Omnia* by Hugo Donellus. He tells the seller he will come round to collect the books in about a week's time. The seller insists that he pay in advance by crediting the seller's bank account. So he does, but when the buyer arrives at the bookshop it appears that the business has been declared bankrupt. Does he own the books so that the liquidator has to surrender the books to him, or should the buyer claim as an unsecured creditor in the bookseller's insolvency?

Another example: under the influence of a fundamental mistake the owner of a painting sells the painting to an art dealer for a price which is much too low. The contract is avoided and the entire transaction should now be undone. However, while the painting is still hanging in the art dealer's gallery the buyer is declared bankrupt. Certainly, the seller is able to claim the return of the painting. But does he own the painting so that he may revindicate or will he be treated as an unsecured creditor?

The answer to these questions depends on the transfer system applied: Dutch law may answer the question in one way, while French law may give the opposite answer to the same question.

Looking for similarities

The book will examine in detail the three main types of transfer system: the consensual system, the causal tradition system and the abstract tradition system. In doing so it will concentrate on the transfer of movable tangible things. The subject of negotiable instruments will be left out. So too will the creation of security rights by way of transfer and the transfer of equitable ownership in goods by declaration of trust. Quite a few practical differences will be encountered. Still, it is striking to see how much these transfer systems have in common, not only as to the practical results but even in theory, on a dogmatic level. Via a systematic and historical analysis of the systems I have tried to reveal elements that all transfer systems have in common. Such an effort is the more important now that the European Union officially aspires to harmonization of the private law systems in Europe.

The legal systems chosen

The choice of countries has been made so as to represent the main distinctions between the different transfer systems. French law and the English Sale of Goods Act have a so-called consensual transfer system whereas the English common law, Dutch and German law have a tradition system. Moreover, in one of these legal systems, German law, the transfer system is abstract rather than causal. In addition to these technical differences there is the distinction that English law is not based on Roman law and the so-called learned law of the continent, the common legal tradition that started in the Middle Ages when Justinian's Digest was rediscovered. Often this divide between common law and civil law is seen as a complicating factor in harmonizing European private law.

Structure of the thesis

As to the structure of comparative research there is the troubling question of choosing between two different methods of approach: a division into legal systems, that is to say, a successive treatment of the countries or, alternatively, a division into legal problems so that as to each technical problem the countries are treated simultaneously. Yet, although one has to make a choice between these approaches there are sometimes good reasons not to observe the choice too rigidly.

To emphasize the internal structure of each transfer system I have opted for a division into legal systems. Of course, within the description of a certain legal system a lot of references and shorter or larger remarks on other legal systems are needed to explain the legal system in question, to give it a 'perspective'.

After an introduction into the different types of transfer system and some general concepts and principles (chapter 1) German law is treated in chapter 2. Because of the German emphasis on dogmatics we shall find a lot of delicate distinctions and concepts which will be useful also for an accurate description of the other legal systems. Hence its placement in front. In chapter 3 French law, the prototype of the consensual transfer system, follows. Next, in chapter 4, English law will be treated: the English Sale of Goods Act 1979 and the English common law. The Sale of Goods Act 1979 has a transfer system similar to the French system. Yet the similarity is somewhat obscured by the fact that the structure of the Sale of Goods Act differs from that of the French consensual transfer system. The similarities appear only after having analysed the French system. For that reason the chapter on English law follows the French chapter. Last in line is Dutch law (chapter 5), a legal system which has been influenced by French as well as German law. In the beginning of the 19th century it was influenced mainly by the French *Code Civil* and the French legal tradition. From the second half of that century, however, the influence of German law became more and more important. Accordingly the Dutch chapter had to be placed at the end.

On two points I found it necessary to deviate from the country per country approach. The description of the different legal systems is followed by two chapters treating a subject which is common to all or at least some of the legal systems and which therefore is treated better in a separate chapter where the legal systems can be analysed simultaneously. Sticking to the country per country approach would be impossible or lead to an inelegant repetition. The first of these chapters (chapter 6) is about the gift from hand to hand, an informal gift executed by handing over of the subject matter. It poses a dogmatic problem common to all legal systems involved, despite the distinction between consensual and tradition systems. Chapter 7 will analyse the historical background of the *iusta causa traditionis*, the requirement that every transfer should be based on a legal ground. It tries to show when and why the distinction between causal and abstract transfer systems emerged.

It may surprise some of the readers to find an historical chapter at the end of a thesis rather than in the beginning. The reasons are the following. First of all, the historical account is not a general introduction to the different transfer systems. It confines itself to just one dogmatic problem: the divide causal/abstract. Secondly and more importantly, the account is not necessary to understand each individual transfer system. On the contrary, a good understanding of these transfer systems and their practical consequences is needed to understand the historical account. The reason why this chapter is preceded by the chapter on the gift from hand to hand is that F.C. von Savigny used the example of the gift from hand to hand as one of his arguments for developing the abstract transfer system.

In chapter 8, the final chapter, it will appear that the main differences between the transfer systems, the divide consensual/tradition and causal/abstract are not at all unbridgeable, as is often thought. The consensual and the tradition systems have some very important features in common. And the analysis in chapter 7 leads me to the conclusion that there is no good reason to choose between only two interpretations of the *iusta causa traditionis*: the two extremes of the abstract and causal system. Many other interpretations are feasible.

Looking at the length of the various chapters one will notice that the chapters on German law and English law are much larger than the ones on Dutch and French law. The main reason for these differences is twofold. First, dogmatic problems common to German and Dutch law have been treated extensively in the chapter on German law so that the chapter on Dutch law can often suffice itself with a shorter description of the problem and a reference to the relevant pages of the German chapter. The extensive treatment on possession is a good example of this. Secondly, in both the German and the Dutch chapter there is a large part about the transfer of possession and the various ways in which the transfer can be made (*traditio vera* and different forms of *traditio ficta*) and the problems created by this requirement. Within the German chapter it even accounts for three quarters of the chapter. In consensual transfer systems such as France the transfer of possession is not a requirement for transferring ownership. For that reason the chapter on French law is substantially shorter. On the other hand, as English law has two different transfer systems, the Sale of Goods Act and the common law, both of which will be set out in detail, this chapter will obviously be much larger than the French chapter.

German legal literature

When glancing through the different chapters the reader will notice that throughout the book I have very often referred to German literature. As to the chapters which are not about German law this slight preponderance of German legal literature requires some explanation.

In the first decades of the 19th century German legal theory started to flourish under the influence of the Historical School, 'founded' by Gustav Hugo (1764-1844) and especially Friedrich Carl von Savigny (1779-1861). Within a few decades the importance of German legal theory had gained so much that it exercised an enormous influence on other European legal systems. It even had a considerable influence on the legal theory of some non-German speaking countries.[1] This period of flourishing continued until the 1930s. During the 19th century representatives of the Historical School developed many legal concepts that now form essential elements of the private law of various European countries. The creation of new concepts was stimulated greatly by the fact that the legal theory of the Historical School was not based on a recent codification.[2] It was based on the *Corpus Iuris Civilis*, the main part of which is formed by the Digest (*Digesta* or *Pandectae*, hence the name 'pandectists' and 'pandect science'), a collection of classical Roman law texts made in the 6th century AD by order of Justinian, emperor of the East-Roman empire. Taking such a completely outdated and imperfect text as a basis of legal science rules out literal interpretation, a form of interpretation that suffocates any attempt at creating new concepts.

Andreas von Tuhr and Martin Wolff

But even after having explained the predominance of German literature in the thesis the large amount of references to Andreas von Tuhr and Martin Wolff might surprise.

In the beginning of the 20th century Andreas von Tuhr (1864-1925)[3] wrote a large three volume treatise on the *Allgemeiner Teil* (General Part) of the German civil code. Having been educated during the *gemeines Recht* (he was a pupil of the pandectist Ernst Immanuel Bekker (1827-1916)) he forms a bridge between the *Pandektenrecht* and the *Bürgerliches Gesetzbuch*. His book is the most elaborate and,

---

1   Especially the Dutch *Burgerlijk Wetboek* of 1992 has been strongly influenced by the German *Bürgerliches Gesetzbuch*, and indirectly by the 19th century German *Pandektenrecht* or *gemeines Recht*. Yet German law not only influenced other civil law systems such as France and The Netherlands, but also common law systems such as England and the United States, though in a much smaller degree. As to England cf. the works of F. Pollock, for example his *Principles of contract* and *A first book of jurisprudence*). As to the United States cf. O.W. Holmes' *The common law*. The German influence is also noticeable in their letters: see Holmes-Pollock letters, ed. by M. DeWolfe Howe, Cambridge (Massachusetts) 1941.

2   The *Pandektenrecht* dominated legal teaching in the German universities, even in countries such as Prussia that had a codification (*Allgemeines Landrecht für die preußischen Staaten*, 1794). Savigny taught the *Allgemeines Landrecht* only for a few years, and in doing so he used the system and concepts of the *Pandektenrecht* so that the local codification was as it were 'pandecticized'. See P. Koschaker, Europa und das römische Recht, 4th ed., Munich/Berlin 1966, p. 263 et seq.; F.C. von Savigny, Landrechtsvorlesung 1824, Drei Nachschriften, Erster Halbband, Ius Commune Sonderhefte, vol. 67, 3.1, ed. by Chr. Wollschläger et al., Frankfurt a/M 1994, p. XXIV et seq.

3   See A.B. Schwartz, Andreas Von Tuhr, Vortrag gehalten im Zürcherischen Juristenverein, Zurich 1938.

despite its age, the most authoritative on the subject. The abundance of detail and depth of treatment are really astonishing. So is Von Tuhr's ingenuity.

Of equal importance is Martin Wolff (1872-1953). From the early 20th century his *Sachenrecht* has been the leading German book on property law. The last (10th) edition appeared in 1957. It was updated by Ludwig Raiser in collaboration with Martin Wolff. It is still regarded as one of the most authoritative books on German property law.[4] Its treatment of dogmatical problems and the historical background of concepts is unrivalled.

Translation of non-English material

All citations in languages other than English have been translated into English. This applies also to articles of non-English legal codes: where an exact understanding of the text is essential the original text has been quoted together with its translation. In principle the texts have been translated into the English legal language. However, in some cases I opted for terms from other legal systems, such as Scots law, either for reasons of accessibility or because the term in question is a better translation of a certain civil law concept. As to the Dutch, French, German and Swiss civil codes recent translations have been published over the last few decades.[5] Under the editorship of Alan Watson an English translation of Justinian's Digest was made.[6] Although some of these translations are of excellent quality I have still preferred in all cases to make my own translation. The main reason for this choice was to ensure internal coherence between the citations and the text of the book. Only this method guarantees that throughout the book equivalent technical terms are translated into the same English terms.

---

4   See D. Medicus, Martin Wolff (1872-1953), Ein Meister an Klarheit, in: H. Heinrichs, H. Franzki, K. Schmalz and M. Stolleis (eds.), Deutsche Juristen jüdischer Herkunft, Munich 1993, p. 549.

5   P.P.C. Haanappel and E. Mackaay, Nieuw Nederlands burgerlijk wetboek, Het vermogensrecht, Deventer/Boston 1990. As the authors decided to translate the Dutch civil code into the English legal language of Quebec this translation can be used only with care when translating into the legal language of England. J.H. Crabb, The French civil code, Littleton (Colorado)/Deventer 1995. I.S. Forrester, S.L. Goren and H.-M. Ilgen, The German civil code, South Hackensack (New Jersey) 1975. I. Williams, S. Wyler and B. Wyler, The Swiss Civil Code, 2 vols., Zurich 1987.

6   A. Watson (ed.), The Digest of Justinian, 4 vols., Philadelphia (Pennsylvania) 1985.

1 Concepts and principles of the law of property

1 Introduction

Before examining in detail the transfer of movables in German, French, English and Dutch law, we will first have a look at two distinctions commonly made to characterize transfer systems: the distinction between tradition systems and consensual systems, and the one between causal and abstract systems. The description of these dividing lines will represent the traditional view. In the course of the next chapters we will see that both distinctions and the various transfer systems they entail are in fact no more than different starting points. As a result of far-reaching exceptions to the principles involved the differences between the transfer systems are much smaller than the opposing starting-points would make one believe at first glance.

In addition, I will outline a few principles that can be found in a certain form and to a certain extent in the law of property of many legal systems, principles which are important for a lucid analysis of the various transfer systems. In later chapters, where the transfer systems are set out in detail, I will try to examine if and to what degree the various principles here described can be found in the laws of these countries.

2 The first dividing line:
the tradition system and the consensual system

If I sell my bicycle to a friend, does he become owner of the bicycle immediately? In a consensual transfer system he does: ownership in principle passes the moment the contract of sale is made. It is therefore often said that in a consensual system the contract itself transfers ownership of the thing to the buyer. The principle that consensus about the contract suffices to pass ownership is called the *solo consensu* rule. In a tradition system, on the other hand, the transfer of ownership in principle requires *traditio*, that is to say, transfer of the possession of the thing. In addition to the transfer of possession, it is commonly said, a tradition system requires a separate legal act aimed specially at transferring ownership: the real agreement. It is said that unlike a consensual system a tradition system distinguishes between on the one hand the underlying legal act that obliges to transfer ownership and on the other hand the subsequent legal act which effectuates the transfer. Whereas in a consensual system the contract, that is, consensus between the parties suffices (hence its name), in a tradition system the contract merely calls into being an obligation to transfer the thing sold. In the latter system ownership will pass only after the legal act of transfer and *traditio* have taken place.[1] Making this distinction between

---

1   In English law the separate legal act of transfer may be called conveyance. It is a legal term used in English land law.

contract and transfer is in Germany referred to as the *Trennungsprinzip* (the principle of distinction).

Yet, in chapter 3 and 4 we shall see that the principle of consensualism, the *solo consensu* rule, is confined to specific existing things. Where the goods sold are generic or future goods, ownership cannot pass the moment the contract is made. What is more, the *solo consensu* rule applies only to the transfer of the thing, not to the transfer of the money due in exchange. So, the rule does not apply to the buyer.

3 The second dividing line: abstract and causal transfer systems

In our example of my selling my bicycle the contract of sale is said to be the *causa traditionis*, the legal ground for the transfer. The *causa traditionis* makes clear what the legal reason for the transfer of ownership is: sale, barter, or a gift for example. Suppose now that one of the parties has entered into the contract under the influence of a mistake. According to Dutch, German, English and French law the party influenced by the mistake has under certain circumstances the power to annul or avoid the contract, that is to say, to render the contract void. Avoidance of the contract has retroactive effect: having been avoided the contract is deemed never to have existed. In a consensual system, where the contract of sale itself is said to pass ownership, it is obvious to assert that avoiding of the contract will inevitably lead to ownership reverting to the seller with retroactive effect. Moreover, if the contract is void from the outset, it has never been able to transfer ownership. So, in a consensual system it seems as if the transfer of ownership necessarily depends on the validity of the contract. Such a transfer system that needs a valid *causa traditionis* is called a causal system.

In a tradition system the act of transfer is considered as a distinct legal act. Having made the distinction between the underlying contract, which serves as *causa traditionis*, and the transfer, a legal system is confronted with the question how the latter act relates to the former one. Does invalidity of the underlying contract affect the validity of the transfer? Legal systems in which the validity of the transfer does depend on a valid *causa traditionis*, the Dutch system for example, are called causal tradition systems. If in such systems the obligatory contract is void or has been avoided with retroactive effect, the transfer is invalid and either ownership has never passed (in the case of a void contract) or it is deemed never to have passed to the buyer (where the contract has been avoided). The seller is then able to claim back the bicycle on the basis of his ownership. In legal systems based on Roman law he would be said to have an action of revindication (*rei vindicatio*).

In German law, on the other hand, the act of transfer is independent of the validity of the obligatory contract. Systems like the German are called abstract transfer systems because the validity of the transfer is judged abstractly of, that is, independently of the contract. The invalidity of the obligatory contract has no effect on the validity of the transfer; the transfer will stay valid even if the legal act that obliged to make the transfer is void or has been avoided. Yet, where there is no valid *causa traditionis* the transfer, though valid, leads to an unjustified enrichment of the buyer. It obliges him to undo his enrichment by retransferring the thing to the seller. It is a transfer similar to the first transfer and it should accordingly fulfil all requirements every transfer should meet. The *causa traditionis* of the retransfer is the buyer's obligation ex unjustified enrichment.

If the contract of sale is avoided the entire transaction should be reversed: the money, if already paid, should be paid back to the buyer, and the bicycle should return to the seller. This applies to a causal system as well as to an abstract system. However, as we can see the way in which the transfer of ownership is reversed differs. Whereas in a causal system ownership of the bicycle reverts automatically to the seller when the contract is avoided, in an abstract system the validity of the transfer will not be affected. Here the buyer has an obligation ex unjustified enrichment and the seller a correlative personal right to the retransfer of ownership.

Yet, this difference, however important, should not be overestimated. The difference will normally be limited to the transfer of the thing. As to the money paid to the seller all three systems, the causal tradition system, the abstract tradition system and the consensual system, cope with a similar problem: apart from rare exceptions the money will have been mixed with the rest of the buyer's money rendering the money paid unidentifiable. As a result the money cannot automatically revert to the buyer after avoidance of the contract.

4 Insolvency

The difference between having a real or rather a personal right is important especially in the case of insolvency. Let us take the example of the sale of a movable. The seller has entered into the contract under the influence of a defect of will, for example duress. As the transaction does not correspond to his true will the seller has the power to avoid the contract of sale. Where the thing has already been delivered avoidance will oblige the buyer to return the thing to the seller.

In an abstract transfer system the seller merely has a personal right to the retransfer of the thing. As a result the seller does not have any priority in the buyer's insolvency: he is an ordinary unsecured creditor. In a causal system, on the other hand, the seller will in principle be able to claim back the thing relying on his right of ownership, which will normally revert to him as a result of the avoidance. When ownership reverts to the seller the thing does not form part of the buyer's goods available for realization and satisfaction of the buyer's debts. It should be returned to its owner by the liquidator or trustee in bankruptcy. For that reason it is often said that a causal system gives a better protection against insolvency of the other party.

We should bear in mind, however, that the protection against insolvency of the other party is rather imperfect. Firstly, the seller's protection against the buyer's insolvency is limited by a few exceptions: as the protection depends on the transferor's ownership the protection is no longer available when for some reason it is impossible for ownership to revert automatically to the transferor. To give an example, the transferor's action of revindication may be frustrated when the transferee has sold the object to a bona fide third party: if available third party protection will deprive the original owner of his right of ownership. The reverting of ownership to the transferor may also be barred as a result of original acquisition, for example when the thing has been mixed with identical assets in the hands of the transferee (*confusio* and *commixtio*), or if the thing has been used to make a new thing (*specificatio*) or if it has been attached to another thing (*accessio*).

Secondly, in German, Dutch and French law the protection is in principle offered only to the transferor of the thing. The buyer, who has a duty to pay for the goods, is not given a similar protection against the seller's insolvency. The reason is the different nature of the assets both parties have to transfer: a thing and money.

What exactly is a payment of money? Surely it involves the transfer of money to the seller. But what is money? I am going to confine this explanation to continental law, as English law uses a broader and less exact definition of ownership and property. Mostly the buyer is allowed to pay by transferring coins and banknotes. These are movable objects capable of being owned.[2] Accordingly such a payment can be regarded as a transfer of ownership of coins and banknotes. When the contract has been avoided also the payment, a legal act, is void. As a result the coins and banknotes may be revindicated, provided they have not been mixed with other monies so as to make them unidentifiable.[3] The problem for the payor is that usually the monies will be so mixed: only in rare exceptions will the money be kept separate or will the numbers of the banknotes be registered. Normally the buyer will have lost ownership of the money because of the principle of specificity.[4] He has to rely on a personal claim ex unjustified enrichment. What is more, nowadays payments are often made by transferring money from one bank account to the other. Here Dutch, German and French law do not regard the payment as a transfer of ownership: money in a bank account is not regarded as an asset capable of being owned. Strictly speaking no one owns the money in his bank account: it is merely a personal claim of the client against his bank. Such a payment can never be revindicated. So, in all three transfer systems the creditor of a money claim will rank as an unsecured creditor.

Some Dutch and German authors have proposed to give the payor a protection similar to the one given to the transferor of a thing. They came up with a new legal concept which in German literature is referred to as the *Geldwertvindikation*, literally

---

2 Wolff/Raiser, p. 233; F.H.J. Mijnssen, Geld in het vermogensrecht, Deventer 1984, p. 5.
3 Mijnssen, Geld in het vermogensrecht, p. 20-23; W.A.K. Rank, Geld, geldschuld en betaling, (thesis Leiden) Deventer 1996, p. 97; HR 9 September 1949, NJ 1950, 595 (*Houtappel/De Hoofdgroep Verzekering et al.*).
4 See § 5. Sometimes co-ownership of the money may be a solution, but such a co-ownership can arise only if it is known exactly which banknotes and coins have been mixed. As the principle of specificity applies also to co-ownership all banknotes and coins that are co-owned should be identified. Only in rare cases will the principle of specificity be complied with, for example where monies have been put together in a cash-box. Cf. chapter 4, § 3.

a revindication of the value of money, an idea that has had only a few advocates.[5] It would have involved a right of ownership of money somewhat similar to an English beneficial interest in money.[6] Mixing of the money would not destroy the payor's ownership, nor would paying the money into a bank account and drawing on the account. The object of the right of ownership would be liable to a continuing process of substitution: when banknotes are paid into a bank account a claim against the bank is substituted for the banknotes. When banknotes are mixed a right of co-ownership in the mixed amount would be substituted for ownership of the original banknotes.[7]

Still, although the proposal is worth careful consideration it will never achieve a 'fair' treatment of all the insolvent's creditors. Nor will opting for an abstract transfer system. Therefore the choice whether to adopt the causal transfer system, the abstract system or another system should be determined on the basis of systematic arguments, not by taking into account the transferor's and transferee's protection against insolvency of the other party. A suitable protection cannot be achieved simply by opting for a certain type of transfer system.

5 Specificity, absolute effect and the concept of right *in re*

The two main principles of property law are the principle of specificity and the principle of absolute effect. As we will see in this paragraph both principles are based on the definition of the right *in re* (real right). According to the principle of specification rights *in re* such as ownership and limited real rights can exist only with respect to specific things. Real rights cannot exist in a quantity of unspecified goods. As a consequence, if a real right is transferred or a limited real right is granted, it must be established to which specific things the legal act relates. A contract for the sale of unspecified goods of a certain sort and amount is valid, but ownership cannot pass to the buyer before certain goods are specified as the goods to be transferred to the buyer.

The requirement can be explained by looking at the nature of the right *in re*. In my opinion a right *in re* consists of two fundamental elements. First it forms a relationship between a person (natural or legal) and a certain identified asset. A

---

5 It was proposed by among others H.R. Hoetink, Het voorwerp van het zakelijk recht, Indisch Tijdschrift van het recht, vol. 135 (1932), p. 109-136; G.E. Langemeijer, Geld, dat aan een ander toebehoort, in: Rechtskundige opstellen op 2 November 1935 door oud-leerlingen aangeboden aan Prof. Mr. E.M. Meijers, Zwolle 1935, p. 541-554; Harry Westermann, see Westermann, Sachenrecht, vol. 1, Heidelberg 1990, § 30 V. See also Wolff/Raiser, p. 321, fn. 6; A. Stadler, Gestaltungsfreiheit und Verkehrsschutz durch Abstraktion, (*Habilitationsschrift* Freiburg im Breisgau), Tübingen 1996, p. 448 and P. Scholten in NJ 1940, p. 483.

6 For example equitable ownership of money under a constructive trust.

7 In Westermann's proposition the *Geldwertvindikation* would confine substitution to different forms of money (banknotes, accounts etc.) thus excluding tracing into assets other than money, for example a car or painting bought with the money.

right *in re* gives its holder a direct power over the object of his right[8], in contrast with a personal right to the transfer of a thing which merely provides an indirect power over a good by giving its holder a right against the owner of the good. As the right *in re* forms a relationship between a person and an identified asset so that a right *in re* can exist only in respect of certain identified assets, a transfer of such a right must also relate to identified assets. Second, the right *in re* is an absolute right, it has absolute effect, that is to say, in principle it works against everyone: third parties have to respect the right. I will call this the principle of absolute effect.

The problem of identity of goods has received much attention in English law. It has been discussed quite often in English cases. Moreover, in 1995 the English Sale of Goods Act was amended to mitigate some of the unwanted consequences of the principle of specificity. I will therefore discuss the problem of identity in the chapter on English law.

6 The *nemo plus* principle and the requirement of privilege of disposal

The name of the so-called *nemo plus* principle is derived from a sentence in Justinian's Digest, where Ulpianus mentions the ancient Roman rule *nemo plus iuris ad alium transferre potest, quam ipse haberet.*[9] Translated literally it says that nobody can transfer more right than he himself has.

With respect to modern private law it is, however, more precise to say that in order to transfer a thing the transferor must have the privilege to dispose of the thing in question. Mostly, it is true, the owner of the thing will be the person privileged[10] to dispose, but in exceptional cases it may happen that ownership and privilege of disposal do not go hand in hand. Where the owner has been declared bankrupt, for example, the owner no longer has the privilege to dispose of his property and his privilege of disposal is conferred on the trustee in bankruptcy. The latter is then privileged to dispose of another person's property.[11] As a consequence of this requirement an act of disposal executed by a person not having the privilege to dispose is invalid and the intended acquirer of the right does not acquire the right in question.

---

8   H. Rey, Berner Kommentar, Band IV (Sachenrecht), 2. Abteilung (Die beschränkten dinglichen Rechte; die Dienstbarkeiten und Grundlasten), 1. Teilband (Die Grunddienstbarkeiten), Lieferung 1 (Systematischer Teil und Kommentar zu art. 730 und 731 ZGB), Bern 1981, p. 14 et seq.; A. Meier-Hayoz, Berner Kommentar, Band IV (Sachenrecht), 1. Abteilung (Das Eigentum), 1. Teilband (Systematischer Teil und Allgemeine Bestimmungen, Art. 641-654 ZGB), Bern 1981, p. 103 et seq.

9   Ulp. D. 50,17,54.

10 The term 'privilege to dispose' will be explained in chapter 2, § 5. It will be contrasted with 'right to dispose' and 'power to dispose'.

11 The privilege of disposal is required not only to transfer property, it is also needed for instance to grant or transfer a limited real right. It is needed for any change in real rights in an asset.

Such acts of disposal should be marked off sharply from what in German law are called *Verpflichtungsgeschäfte*: legal acts that merely call into being an obligation for example to transfer a thing, but that do not change any real right in respect of the thing.

7 Protection of third parties

German, French, English and Dutch law all acknowledge, although in varying degree,[12] that in certain instances a transfer made by someone who lacks the privilege to dispose should nonetheless be regarded as valid. It may seem that third party protection qualifies the absolute effect of real rights in that the more generous bona fide parties are protected the less absolute real rights are. Does it contradict the above statement that absolute effect is one of the essential elements of every real right? To my mind it does not. Take an example: I lend a book to a colleague. He forgets it is mine and sells it to another. True, I cannot revindicate the book from the bona fide acquirer. The reason is that the latter has acquired ownership of the thing. Does this mitigate the absolute effect of my ownership? Not at all. Mitigation of the absolute effect would mean that my right of ownership works as against everyone except the bona fide acquirer. But, where a bona fide acquirer is given ownership I lose my right of ownership altogether, not only against the third party but as against everyone.[13,14]

8 The principle of priority and the principle of *droit de suite*

As to the order between different limited real rights priority is in principle given to the older of the rights. I will refer to this rule as the principle of priority. Of course, the principle is important only where certain limited real rights are wholly or partly incompatible with each other.

According to the principle of *droit de suite* once a limited real right burdens a certain piece of property it will continue to do so after the asset is transferred to another person, that is to say, the limited right will run with the property burdened. It enables the holder of the right to follow the property into the hands

---

12 English law especially is very reluctant to recognize exceptions to the *nemo plus* principle.

13 See Von Tuhr, Allgemeiner Teil I, p. 208.

14 The absolute effect is truly mitigated where a transfer of ownership is seen as relatively void. If, for example, a thing is sold under the market price defrauded creditors of the transferor may in many legal systems avoid the transaction (the action is often called *actio Pauliana*). The avoidance renders the contract and transfer relatively void, that is to say, the transfer is void against the creditors and valid against everyone else. As a result ownership of the thing seems to be relative. As against the creditors the transferor is still owner, as against others the buyer is the owner.

of every new owner. Hence its name: *droit de suite* (lit.: right to follow).[15] The same notion expressed by the principle of priority for a conflict between two limited real rights is expressed by the *droit de suite* principle for a conflict between a limited real right and a subsequent owner. They both have in common that they protect an earlier real right against any subsequent acquirer of a real right, be it ownership or a limited real right. Both the principle of priority and the principle of *droit de suite* find their explanation in the absolute character of the real right: if a real right works as against everybody, it also works against a subsequent acquirer of a real right. In reality priority and *droit de suite* are not distinct principles but simply special applications of the principle of absolute effect.

9 The principle of publication and the closely related principle of the protection of third parties

Since rights *in re* in principle work as against everybody, these rights should be easy to recognize by third parties. To achieve this the principle of publication requires that every transfer of property and every transfer, granting and release of a limited real right be made known to third parties. Where 'publication' has not been made or is impossible to achieve, third parties are often protected against real rights the existence of which they did not know. The principle of publication and the principle of protection of third parties are closely related in that the need for protection of third parties increases the more unreliable the publication of rights is.

As to immovable property the publication takes place by entering the rights onto a register. There are also special registers for some categories of movables such as ships and aircraft, but as regards most categories of movable property the law has to make use of possession as a means of publication. For that reason tradition systems require that in order to transfer the ownership of a movable possession of the asset should be transferred to the acquirer.

Yet, possession is a very unreliable means of publication: there are many situations in which physical power over a thing does not go hand in hand with ownership of the thing. The owner may have hired or lent the thing to someone else. Moreover, possession can be transferred simply by agreement without any physical handing over being needed (the so-called *traditio ficta*). For a third party it is hard to find out who is the owner of the thing and which limited real rights burden it. As a consequence many legal systems offer an extensive protection to bona fide third parties.

---

15 It is called *zaaksgevolg* and *Folgerecht* in Dutch respectively German law. By the way, it is not comparable to the English term 'tracing'.

2 Transfer of movables in German law

1 An abstract transfer system

1.1 Introduction

In contrast to the Dutch Civil Code[1] the German Civil Code, the *Bürgerliches Gesetzbuch*, does not contain a provision summing up the requirements common to all transfers of property.[2] There are different rules for each sort of asset. For the transfer of immovables and choses in action, for instance, there are special provisions in § 873[3] and § 398 respectively. The rules on the transfer of movables, which will be set out in this chapter, are to be found in § 929 et seq.

Paragraphs 929 et seq. form the general rules on the transfer of movables: they apply to all sorts of movables unless they are excepted by a special provision. Moreover, unlike the provisions of the English Sale of Goods Act, the rules are not restricted to contracts of sale. They apply to the transfer of movables irrespective of which *causa traditionis* underlies the transfer, a sale, barter, gift, unjustified enrichment or another *causa*.

1.2 The tradition system

In German law a contract for the transfer of property cannot in itself bring about the passing of ownership (as is the case in for example English and French law[4]). The tradition system makes a sharp distinction between on the one hand the underlying legal act or fact[5] that obliges to transfer ownership and on the other hand the subsequent legal act effectuating the transfer of ownership. This is referred to as the principle of distinction (*Trennungsprinzip*). In all cases a separate legal act is needed which aims specifically at the transfer of the asset in question. It is called the *Übereignung* (transfer).[6]

The nucleus of this legal act consists in the real agreement (*dinglicher Vertrag*). In this agreement the transferor declares to transfer ownership of a specified asset and the transferee declares to accept ownership of the asset. The requirement of a real agreement means that both parties should agree about the passing of ownership of a particular asset. The agreement need not be made expressly. Usually it will be implicit: it must be clear from the circumstances of the case that the transferor and transferee have a common intention to transfer ownership of the asset involved.

---

1   Article 3:84 BW.
2   Nonetheless such general requirements do exist: for every voluntary transfer of property the transferor and transferee must enter into a real agreement and the transferor must be privileged to dispose of the object. Both requirements will be discussed in this chapter.
3   Unless stated otherwise the paragraphs mentioned in this chapter refer to the *Bürgerliches Gesetzbuch*.
4   England: section 17 and 18 Sale of Goods Act 1979; France: art. 1138 and 1583 *Code Civil*.
5   The legal act can for instance be a contract; a legal fact that requires a transfer to be made can for instance be an obligation *ex delicto* or ex unjustified enrichment.
6   Synonyms are *Übertragung* and *Veräußerung*. The concept of *Verfügung*, however, is much broader: see § 5.1.

As to the transfer of movables the real agreement should in most cases be accompanied by *traditio*, the transfer of possession of the asset. In some instances, however, no additional act is needed so that the real agreement suffices to transfer ownership. As will be explained below, this is the case for example where ownership is transferred by means of *traditio brevi manu* (§ 929, 2nd sentence BGB).

Within the transfer of ownership *traditio* should be seen as a *condicio iuris*. The term denotes a condition required by the law for the validity of a legal act (here: the real agreement), as distinct from a condition attached to a legal act by the parties themselves.[7] The concept of *condicio iuris* enables us to distinguish the nucleus of a legal act, the declaration of will, from additional requirements needed for the validity of the legal act. Very common *condiciones iuris* are for example the capacity to make legal acts[8], privilege of disposal[9], consent of a third party or a formality such as making up a notarial deed. Where movables are transferred the nucleus of the legal act of transfer is the real agreement while the transfer of possession or any substitute formality is a *condicio iuris*. Hence, we can say that the real agreement is more than an indispensable part of the transfer: it *is* the legal act of transfer itself.[10]

1.3 Abstract transfer system

In the German abstract transfer system the validity of the transfer, the *Verfügungsgeschäft*, is considered 'abstract from', i.e. independent of the underlying *causa traditionis*. The transfer is valid and ownership passes whether or not there is a valid *causa* to justify the passing of ownership.

In many instances the transfer will be based upon a legal act obliging to effect the transfer of ownership, a contract of sale for example. When such a contract is voidable, avoidance of the contract, the *causa traditionis*, will cause the contract to fall away with retroactive effect so that it is deemed never to have been valid. This does not affect the validity of a transfer which has been performed on the basis of that contract: ownership passes to the transferee and remains with him, even though the *causa traditionis* has lapsed. Similarly, if the contract has been void *ab initio* or if the parties wrongly assumed that a contract had been made (*causa putativa*), the legal act of *traditio* nevertheless passes ownership.

In a causal transfer system such as the Dutch, on the other hand, a valid transfer always demands a valid *causa traditionis*. As a result ownership cannot pass under a void contract, and, if at the outset ownership has passed under a voidable contract, it automatically reverts to the transferor when the contract is avoided. In Dutch law avoidance of a contract has retroactive effect, so that when the contract is avoided after the transfer has taken place, the *causa traditionis* is deemed never

---

7 See for this concept in general: P. Oertmann, Die Rechtsbedingung, Leipzig/Erlangen 1924 and Von Tuhr, Allgemeiner Teil II, p. 147-152 and III, p. 282.
8 *Geschäftsfähigkeit*.
9 *Verfügungsbefugnis*.
10 More extensive and focusing on Dutch law: chapter 5, § 2.2.

to have existed and accordingly the transferee is considered never to have been owner of the asset.

In consequence, where the contract is void or has been avoided, the transferee will in principle not be able to transfer the asset to a second transferee, as he is not owner of the asset (*nemo plus* rule). Let us have a look at an example to explain the causal system. A sells and transfers an asset to B who in turn sells and transfers it to C. After C has become owner of the thing A finds out that he has acted under the influence of a defect of will and he accordingly avoids the contract. As a result ownership will revert to A. The first transferee, A, is deemed never to have lost his right of ownership and C is deemed never to have become owner of the thing. So, in a causal system defects in the *causa traditionis* may have wide implications on third parties: it makes the first acquirer (here: B) in principle unable to transfer ownership to a second acquirer. Such effects can, however, be mitigated by a rule protecting bona fide acquirers.

By deciding in favour of an abstract system instead of a causal system the German civil code limits the consequences of defects in the underlying legal act, the *Verpflichtungsgeschäft*, to the parties to this legal act, with the result that these defects do not affect a second acquirer. Even though the underlying contract is invalid (i.e. void *ab initio* or avoided) the transfer passes ownership to the first transferee (B in the above example) and thus enables him to transfer ownership of the thing to a third party (C).

Offering this protection to subsequent acquirers the abstract system in itself protects third parties in that it prevents defects in the *causa traditionis* from automatically affecting a subsequent transfer. In the German *gemeines Recht*[11] this effect of the principle of abstraction was of great importance because the *gemeines Recht* did not offer any protection to bona fide third parties against the transferor's lack of privilege to dispose.[12] In the first draft of the *Bürgerliches Gesetzbuch* such a general protection of third parties was lacking as well. In this draft the principle of abstraction still had the function of protecting third parties.[13] In a later stage, however, it was decided to provide for a general third party protection after all. Yet the draftsmen did not draw the conclusion that as a result the principle of abstraction was no longer needed to protect third parties. This protection is clearly superfluous because even if Germany had opted for a causal system the subsequent

---

11 The term *gemeines Recht* (lit: common law) denotes the learned law based on the *Corpus Iuris Civilis*. Mostly, the term is confined to the learned law of the 19th century. In this period the learned law was in force as a subsidiary source of law. Local codes such as the Prussian *Allgemeines Landrecht* (1794), statutes and other laws prevailed. As these primary sources of law varied from region to region the learned common law remained the basis for academic debate.

12 See Wolff/Raiser, Sachenrecht, p. 118 and F. Ranieri, Die Lehre der abstrakten Übereignung in der deutschen Zivilrechtswissenschaft des 19. Jahrhunderts, in: H. Coing and W. Wilhelm (eds.), Wissenschaft und Kodifikation des Privatrechts im 19. Jahrhundert, vol. 2, Frankfurt a/M 1977, p. 102. See also chapter 7. Some protection, however, was offered by the concept of *usucapio* (acquisitive prescription).

13 Together with prescription.

acquirer would have been sufficiently protected.[14] In the case of an invalid or non-existing *causa traditionis* a causal system would prevent ownership from passing to the acquirer. Under § 932 BGB a second acquirer would be protected against the first acquirer's lack of ownership, provided he is in good faith. If under this provision protection is available for him, the second acquirer will become owner of the asset.

Yet the protection given by the principle of abstraction is not only superfluous, it also goes too far. The abstract system itself protects irrespective of good faith: even if the second acquirer knew or should have known that the first transferee had acquired the asset without a valid *causa*, ownership passes to him.

We have seen that a transfer which is not based on a valid *causa traditionis* is nevertheless valid and passes ownership to the transferee. As said before this does not mean that the transfer is inviolable. The transferor, it is true, cannot revindicate the asset, since ownership did not stay with him nor reverted to him. Yet as there is no legal ground for the transfer the transferee is unduly enriched by the transfer. Consequently, the transferee is obliged to undo the transfer and the transferor has a correlative claim to restoration of the enrichment (*condictio indebiti* ex § 812 et seq. BGB). The asset has to be *re*transferred to the transferor. The *causa traditionis* of the latter transfer is the obligation ex unjustified enrichment. The concept of unjustified enrichment thus completes the abstract system by giving the transferor a personal action against the transferee.[15]

In section 2.2, however, we will see that the abstract system is mitigated in some respects. Certain defects which affect the validity of the *causa traditionis* may at the same time affect the validity of the real agreement and thereby the passing of ownership. Moreover, the parties may implicitly or explicitly make the validity of the transfer depend on the validity of the underlying *causa traditionis*. So, we could say that the abstract system is *ius dispositivum*, that is to say, it is a rule which may be set aside by the parties.

2 Transfer of ownership (*Übereignung*)

2.1 Introduction

The first sentence of § 929 BGB reads: 'For the transfer of ownership of a movable it is required that the owner hand over the movable to the acquirer and that both agree about the passing of ownership.' It contains the standard mode of transferring movables. The passage makes clear that the legal act of transfer consists of two elements: a real agreement and *traditio* (*Übergabe*). Later on we will see that in some

---

14 See also Staudinger-Wiegand, 1995, § 929, Rdnr. 27; W. Wiegand, Die Entwicklung des Sachenrechts im Verhältnis zum Schuldrecht, AcP 1990, p. 112 et seq., p. 136; Wolff/Raiser, Sachenrecht, p. 238.

15 W. Flume, Allgemeiner Teil des Bürgerlichen Rechts, vol. 2, Das Rechtsgeschäft, 4th ed., Berlin/Heidelberg 1992, § 12 I 2, p. 156 and 157. See also D. Reuter and M. Martinek, Ungerechtfertigte Bereicherung, Tübingen 1983, p. 77.

instances movables can be transferred without *Übergabe* (by way of *traditio brevi manu, Abtretung des Herausgabeanspruchs* and *constitutum possessorium*). In the real agreement the transferor and the transferee express their common intention to transfer the asset involved. Then, the transfer is completed by *traditio* of the asset (*Übergabe*).[16] An additional requirement for a valid transfer, a condition which is not mentioned in § 929 et seq., is that the transferor should have the privilege to dispose of the asset in question. As said before, all these additional requirements should be seen as *condiciones iuris* of the legal act of transfer, that is, the real agreement.

2.2 The real agreement

As we have seen the real agreement (*dinglicher Vertrag*, in § 929 referred to as *Einigung*) is a legal act in which the transferor declares to transfer ownership and the transferee declares to accept the ownership. It may be made orally or in writing and it may also be made implicitly by conduct. Where the transfer of goods takes place by actual handing over of the goods, there will normally be no express agreement as to the transfer of ownership. In that case the common intention to transfer ownership should be inferred from the parties' conduct and other circumstances.

In order to be effective the real agreement should relate to a specific asset: ownership of unascertained goods cannot exist and as a consequence generic goods cannot be transferred unless it is known exactly which individual assets are to pass to the acquirer. If there is an obligation for the transfer of a certain number of generic goods the appropriation takes place in the real agreement. So, the real agreement has the role of specifying the assets and thus of complying with the principle of specificity. One might think that actual handing over suffices to specify which goods should be transferred to the acquirer. Yet, in many instances a handing over, a *traditio vera*, is not needed. Here we must rely on the real agreement to specify the assets.

Since the making of a real agreement entails two *Willenserklärungen* (declarations of intention), the provisions on *Willenserklärung* in the *Bürgerliches Gesetzbuch* apply to real agreements as well. These provisions are to be found in the *Allgemeiner Teil* (General Part) of the *Bürgerliches Gesetzbuch*, in the paragraphs 116 et seq. The rules contain, among other things, provisions about defects of will (*Willensmängel*: § 119 and 123), illegality (*Gesetzesverstoß*: § 134) and public morality (*Sittenwidrigkeit*: § 138). As a consequence the real agreement may be void or voidable on one of these grounds in the same way as the underlying contract.

That being so, the effects of the principle of abstraction are somewhat mitigated where the defect in question affects the contract as well as the transfer. If a contract has been made under the influence of fraud or duress (*Täuschung* or *Drohung*: § 123)

---

16 In § 3.4, 3.6 and 4.3 we will see that *Übergabe* should not be regarded as equivalent to *traditio vera*. The notion covers all instances of *traditio vera* but also a few cases of *traditio ficta* (§ 854, subs. 2 BGB and *Geheißerwerb*).

the transfer will as a rule be voidable on the same ground. Similarly, where the contract is void for undue influence (§ 138 subs. 2) the transfer is taken to be void as well.[17] Such a parallel defect of will is called identity of defect (*Fehleridentität* or *Fehlerkongruenz*).[18] However, it is not accepted that a defect of will within the contract automatically affects the subsequent transfer as well. *Fehleridentität* is accepted only in rare exceptions. Fraud and duress seem to be the only cases in which identity of defect is commonly accepted. Where the contract has been made under the influence of a mistake (*Irrtum*: § 119), to give an example, the mistake will normally not render the transfer of ownership voidable. The difference seems quite arbitrary. Still, although a contract of sale and its execution (the transfer of ownership) are part of one and the same economic transaction, the legal act of transfer is seen as a 'neutral' act which as a rule cannot be affected by defects of will. This isolation of the transfer from any defects in the underlying contract is often based on the odd argument that a wide application of *Fehleridentität* would erode the principle of abstraction.[19]

As it is a legal act the provisions on conditional legal acts (§ 158-163 BGB) can be applied to real agreements as well. According to these paragraphs a real agreement may be made subject to a suspensive or resolutive condition (*aufschiebende* and *auflösende Bedingung*) or a condition of time (*Zeitbestimmung*, *Befristung*). An example of a transfer subject to a suspensive condition is a transfer with retention of ownership, which is expressly provided for in § 455 BGB. A resolutive condition means that the legal act is valid and effective until the occurrence of some uncertain event. A transfer subject to such a condition passes ownership, but when the condition is fulfilled, the legal act of transfer falls away and as a result ownership reverts to the transferor.[20] The resolutive condition opens the possibility for the parties to stipulate that the real agreement be valid only if and as long as the underlying contract is valid. This enables them to deviate by agreement from the principle of abstraction.[21]

---

17 Staudinger-Wiegand, 1995, § 929, Rdnr. 18 et seq.; Westermann, Sachenrecht, § 4 IV.
18 Cf. chapter 7, fn. 31.
19 Staudinger-Wiegand, 1995, § 929, Rdnr. 18.
20 Ownership does not revert with retroactive effect, but the reversion nonetheless works as against everyone. See § 158-159 BGB and Von Tuhr, Allgemeiner Teil III, p. 319-323.
21 Staudinger-Wiegand, 1995, § 929, Rdnr. 29-31. A similar interdependence between the *causa traditionis* and the real agreement can be obtained when the parties expressly or implicitly consider these legal acts as one integrated legal act in the sense of § 139 BGB. See Staudinger-Wiegand, 1995, § 929, Rdnr. 27. As to the principle of abstraction and its decline see: W. Wiegand, Die Entwicklung des Sachenrechts im Verhältnis zum Schuldrecht, AcP 1990, p. 112 et seq.

3 Possession and the transfer of possession (*Übergabe*)

3.1 The importance of possession

As we have said before the German transfer system is a tradition system. For the transfer of movable property it in principle requires a transfer of possession of the thing to the acquirer. This act is referred to as *Übergabe* (transfer of possession). As possession is a core concept in the transfer of ownership a thorough analysis of this concept will be needed to understand the transfer of ownership itself.

In order to appreciate the modern concept of possession as laid down in the German civil code we should realize that it has two different origins: Roman law and Germanic law.[22] As a result the concept of possession forms an amalgam combining elements of both laws. True, Roman law has had an overwhelming influence on German law, especially since the so-called Historical School founded in the beginning of the 19th century. It was a movement interested in the study of 'pure' Roman law, that is, Roman law of the classical era (the first two and a half centuries AD[23]) and of Justinian's time (6th c. AD). As Justinian's Digests or Pandects formed one of the most important sources of this Roman law the movement was mostly referred to as 'pandectism'. The so-called *Pandektenrecht* formed a secondary source of law in 19th century Germany. It was called the *gemeines Recht* (lit.: common law). Its dominance in legal theory provoked a counter-movement named the *Deutschrechtler* or *Germanisten*, which, translated literally, means 'German law jurists', that is, jurists who study German law. The misleading term refers to the jurists who studied Germanic law and those legal concepts in modern 19th century German law which derived from Germanic law.[24] Through them Germanic law has had a considerable influence on the modern concept of possession in the German civil code.

3.2 Possession

Before discussing the transfer of possession we should have a look at a few distinctions made in German law between different sorts of possession. *Besitz*, which is not defined in the German civil code, divides into *unmittelbarer Besitz* (direct possession) and *mittelbarer Besitz* (indirect possession). Where for instance A, the possessor of a thing, lends the thing to B or deposits it with him, A will

---

22 Germanic law refers to the ancient law of the different Germanic tribes in Europe. It consists mainly in customary law. Germanic law should be distinguished from German law, the modern law applied in Germany.

23 Kaser I, p. 2.

24 Prominent *Germanisten* were for example Von Gerber, O. von Gierke, Brunner and Heusler. For the same reason 19th century German book titles can be very misleading. Books titled *Römisches Recht* or *Pandekten(recht)* etc. describe not only classical and Justinianian Roman law but also the *gemeines Recht*. Titles such as *Deutsches (Privat)recht*, on the other hand, do not describe the German law in force during the 19th century but rather the Germanic institutions, many of which were no longer applied, or applied only as modified by Roman and/or canon law.

remain possessor of the object. Yet, B will also become possessor of the thing. A's possession does not shift to B, but a second instance of possession arises with B. Both A and B are now possessor of the object.

To distinguish between the two forms of possession B is called the *unmittelbarer Besitzer* (direct possessor), since he has actual power over the object. A, on the other side, is said to have *mittelbarer Besitz* (indirect possession): he possesses the object not directly but rather via B[25], who holds the thing respecting A's possession.[26]

At the same time another distinction can be made. B, who acknowledges and respects A's possession, holds the object for A. Accordingly he is said to have *Fremdbesitz*; A, who holds the thing for himself, has *Eigenbesitz*. As laid down in § 872 BGB an *Eigenbesitzer* is 'a person who holds a thing as if it belongs to him.'[27]

Under the influence of Germanic law the *Bürgerliches Gesetzbuch* altered the meaning of the term *Besitz* greatly: whereas 19th century German legal science, the pandectism, distinguished between *possessio* and *detentio*,[28] now German law uses a uniform word to refer to both concepts. In pandectistic law the *possessor* held the thing for himself, the *detentor* held the thing for another.[29] Since someone holding a thing for another was not regarded as a possessor he could in principle not use

---

25 In these instances B is often called a *Besitzmittler*.

26 § 868 BGB provides the following: 'If someone possesses a thing as a usufructuary, pledgee, *Pächter* (a certain kind of lessee), *Mieter* (another kind of lessee), depositary or in a similar relationship, under which he is as against another person entitled or obliged to have possession for a certain time, the other person has possession as well (indirect possession).'

27 In Savigny's theory possession consists of two elements: actual power over the object and the will to possess the thing for one's own benefit (*Besitzwille, animus possidendi*). See: F.C. von Savigny, Das Recht des Besitzes, 7th ed., ed. by A.F. Rudorff, Vienna 1865, p. 109-110 and 121). It accords with the traditional view of the jurists of the *Usus Modernus Pandectarum*: see H. Coing, Europäisches Privatrecht, vol. 1, p. 280. The latter element has been fiercely and successfully disputed, among others by Jhering in his book *Der Besitzwille* (Jena 1889, repr. Aalen 1968).
Some of the criticism expressed is still valid: also in modern German law the *animus possidendi* cannot be applied as a criterion to distinguish *Eigenbesitz* from *Fremdbesitz*, as there are instances in which a person is possessor of an object without being aware of it. To give a standard example, the recipient of a letter is possessor of it even if he does not know that the letter has been put in his letter-box. However, the *Bürgerliches Gesetzbuch* has not been able to replace the criterion by a better one. It rather avoids giving any criterion. The *Bürgerliches Gesetzbuch* does not require any will to possess and leaves it to doctrine and case law to decide whether any such will is needed (see W. Schubert, Die Entstehung der Vorschriften des BGB über Besitz und Eigentumsübertragung, Berlin 1966, p. 89).

28 Note, however, that Roman law did not know *possessio* as a clearly defined technical term. What is more, the term *detentio* was unknown altogether. See Kaser I, § 94 II 2 and Kaser II, § 239 II.

29 This pandectistic distinction deviates slightly from Roman law in that Roman law itself did not confine the term *possessio* to persons who held the object for themselves. In some instances it gave possessory interdicts (possession protected by the *praetor*) to persons who clearly held for another. The main examples are the pledgee, a person who held a thing by way of *precarium* (see chapter 3, fn. 20), a *sequester* (safe-keeping a thing which was the subject-matter of litigation) and the holder of the right of *emphyteusis* (a form of lease of land). See Kaser I, p. 388-389; F.C. von Savigny, Das Recht des Besitzes, p. 119-121. Thus, the criterion of holding for oneself or holding for another was not always decisive for the divide *possessor/detentor*. Still, these instances may be regarded as exceptions created for historical reasons.

possessory interdicts (remedies) to protect or regain his actual power over the thing. If, for example, A has lent a book to B and the book is stolen by C, the borrower has no action in Roman law to reclaim the book. Since he has no *possessio* but mere *detentio* he will have to ask the owner to revindicate the book.

In adopting the Roman view pandectistic law neglected a development in Germanic and canon law aimed at protecting the *detentor*'s legal position. According to Germanic law both the *possessor* and the *detentor* had possession (*Gewere*): the *possessor* had *Eigengewere* and the *detentor beschränkter Sachgewere*.[30] Moreover, possibly influenced by the Germanic *Gewere*[31] medieval canon law extended the scope of the canonistic possessory remedies far beyond their original scope of protecting the *possessor*'s power over the object. From the 12th century canon law offered the so-called *actio spolii*, the canonistic action for the return of the thing, to every *detentor*.[32] The *Bürgerliches Gesetzbuch* continues this Germanic and canonistic tradition. The consequence of the German civil code having created the umbrella term *Besitz*[33] is that both *Eigenbesitzer* and *Fremdbesitzer* now enjoy the protection of § 858-869 BGB, the former possessory interdicts. Oddly, in this respect modern Dutch law codified the Roman situation: possessory remedies are not available to a *detentor*, a *houder*, (art. 3:125 subs. 1 BW). As a modern legal system must give the *detentor* some action to protect his legal position the Dutch *detentor* may use a general delict action (*onrechtmatige daad*) to protect his position (art. 3:125 subs. 3 BW), an inelegant way to repair an obvious shortcoming.

In part, though, this change in German law is no more than cosmetic: despite having a uniform term *Besitz* the *Bürgerliches Gesetzbuch* still distinguishes between a person who holds a thing for himself and a person who holds the thing for someone else. The former *possessor* and *detentor* are now referred to as *Eigenbesitzer* and *Fremdbesitzer*. Since the umbrella term *Besitz* may cause some confusion among lawyers who retained the romanistic terms, such as Dutch lawyers, I shall instead refer to the terms *possessio*[34] and *detentio* where necessary to avoid misunderstandings.

---

30 O. Gierke, Deutsches Privatrecht, vol. 2 (Sachenrecht), Leipzig 1905, p. 215. Note, however, that the meaning of the term *Gewere* is not exactly similar to the concept of possession. Still, being a fact and a right at the same time, *Gewere* is to a large extent comparable to possession, and in the 19th century it was generally regarded as similar to possession. I therefore feel free to simplify things and translate the term with 'possession'.

31 Wolff/Raiser, p. 21.

32 C.G. Bruns, Das Recht des Besitzes im Mittelalter und in der Gegenwart, 1848 (repr. Osnabrück 1965), p. 229-231; Gierke, Deutsches Privatrecht, vol. 2, p. 248, fn. 7; G. Wesenberg/G. Wesener, Neuere deutsche Privatrechtsgeschichte, 4th ed., Vienna/Cologne 1985, p. 18-19. The term *actio spolii* derives from the word *spoliatio* (robbery), but it applied to every loss of possession contrary to the possessor's will (e.g. fraud, duress).

33 See the survey by Kipp in Windscheid/Kipp, Lehrbuch des Pandektenrechts, 9th ed., vol. 1, p. 783. In the last two editions of Windscheid's famous book, both of which are edited by Kipp, the editor has added to Windscheid's descriptions of the *gemeines Recht* a concise description of the same subject as treated in the German civil code, and an analysis of distinctions and similarities between the old and new law.

34 Cf. fn. 29 *supra*.

Apart from *Eigenbesitz* and *Fremdbesitz* a third notion should be discussed: the *Besitzdiener* (*Diener* meaning servant). This person has neither *Eigenbesitz* nor *Fremdbesitz*; he has actual power over an object without having any form of possession over it. He helps the real possessor (called *Besitzherr*) in exercising the latter's possession. Using the terminology of the *gemeines Recht* he is a *detentor*, he has mere *detentio*, he is merely holding the object concerned.[35] It is the only form in which the *detentio* still survives in modern German law alongside the Germanic umbrella term *Besitz*. *Besitzdienerschaft* arises in certain cases of subordination.[36] Par. 855 BGB provides: 'Where a person exercises actual power over a thing for another person in the latter's household or business or in a similar relation, under which he has to follow the latter's instructions, only the other person has possession.' The subordinate person (*Besitzdiener*) exercises his superior's possession in the latter's interest. Under § 860 he has the power to defend his superior's possession against any interference by third parties to the same extent as the superior himself (§ 859).

Although it is hard to find an exact translation of the terms I will call *Besitzdienerschaft* subordinate possession, the *Besitzdiener* a subordinate possessor and the *Besitzherr* a superior possessor.[37] When comparing subordinate possession to the terms *possessio* and *detentio* we can see that the *Bürgerliches Gesetzbuch* split up the concept of *detentio* to form *Fremdbesitz* on the one hand and *Besitzdienerschaft* on the other hand.

3.3 Possession: a fact or a right?

I would here like to touch on an old controversy about whether possession may pass to another person by derivative acquisition. Where a person acquires possession derivatively he acquires the very same possession that before belonged to another person. The acquirer is then said to derive his possession from his predecessor. In the opposite instance, called original acquisition, a person acquires something that has never belonged to another person and has been created only in his hands.

The answer to the controversy depends on whether you regard possession as a bare fact or rather as a right. If you consider possession to be a mere fact, it cannot be transferred, as you cannot transfer a fact, transfer meaning the *legal act* of

---

35 Kaser, Römisches Privatrecht, 16th ed., Munich 1992, § 19 V; R. Sohm, Institutionen des römischen Rechts, 13th ed., Leipzig 1908, p. 416-417.

36 Similarly in English law a servant who has actual control over his master's things is regarded as having mere custody of them rather than possession. Possession remains with his master. See D.R. Harris, The concept of possession in English law, in: A.G. Guest (ed.), Oxford essays in jurisprudence, Oxford 1961, p. 69, at p. 78.

37 The only disadvantage of the term is that it might suggest subordinate possession to be a special kind of possession, whereas the subordinate possessor has no possession at all.

transfer. If, on the other hand, you see it as a right, it is tenable to contend that possession is indeed transferable.[38]

In his famous book *Das Recht des Besitzes* Savigny asserted that possession should be regarded as a mere fact.[39] From this he drew the conclusion that possession could be acquired only originally. He denied the possibility of derivative acquisition of possession, such as a transfer of possession.[40,41] In his view possession could be acquired only by *Apprehension*, a term which normally denotes physically taking hold of an object so as to become its possessor.[42] Yet, in several instances, for example in the case of *traditio ficta*, Roman law does not require such a physical *apprehensio* for the acquisition of possession. To explain these cases Savigny had to change the definition of *apprehensio* to mean the *opportunity* to exercise physical power over an object, rather than the power itself.[43] Rather than giving the acquirer physical power the fictitious *traditio* then gives him the opportunity to gain that power by getting hold of the object. Savigny's book had an enormous success and in the following decades his view became generally accepted and dominated

---

38 Having seen this it surprises that Strohal who, as we will see, demonstrated clearly that possession can be transferred so that the new possessor continues possession of his predecessor, nevertheless holds the opinion that possession is not a right. See his essay *Der Sachbesitz nach dem BGB*, Jher. Jahrb. vol. 38 (1898), p. 1 et seq., at p. 63-66.

39 Das Recht des Besitzes, § 5 and 6, especially p. 55-59. Yet, Savigny is not always consistent. On p. 250 he says that the transfer of possession cannot be seen as a *juristische Handlung*, a legal act. This is logical if you consider possession as a mere fact. However, on p. 245 he acknowledges that the transfer of possession may be conditional, referring to Jul. D. 41,2,38. In this case the acquirer at first gets *detentio*, holding the thing for the transferor. After the condition has been fulfilled his *detentio* will change into *possessio* (apparently a suspensive condition is meant). This cannot be reconciled with Savigny's overall theory because only a legal act may be conditional. It is unimaginable for a factual act to be conditional. Moreover, sometimes Savigny uses the term *Recht des Besitzes* (right of possession): see for example p. 246, 248, and above all, the title of the book. In § 5 he says that possession is a fact and a right at the same time: 'Demnach ist er Factum und Recht zugleich, nämlich seinem Wesen nach Factum, in seinen Folgen einem Rechte gleich...' (So it [i.e. possession] is fact and right at the same time, in essence a fact, according to its consequences akin to a right...). Yet, he does not draw any conclusions from this double nature of possession: in most of the book he regards possession as a mere fact.

40 Von Savigny, Das Recht des Besitzes, p. 44 and 324.

41 Yet Bekker demonstrates that Savigny contradicts his own theory: in *Das Recht des Besitzes*, p. 355, fn. 4, Savigny mentions the transfer of possession by a *pupillus* (a minor who could bind himself by legal act only with his *tutor*'s permission). The minor may give the object to another so that he loses possession and the latter obtains possession, but this should not be regarded as a transfer of possession, as this would require the minor's will which he is deemed not to have. Referring to Ulp. D. 41,2,29 Savigny says: 'However, *alienare* possessionem [to transfer possession] means to lose possession so that it constitutes a legal succession. Yet succession is impossible because it depends on the *animus* [the intention] of the former possessor.' (Allein *alienare* possessionem heisst so den Besitz verlieren, dass darin eine juristische Succession liegt, diese aber ist unmöglich, weil es dabei auf den *animus* des vorigen Besitzers ankommt.). See E.I. Bekker, Das Rechts des Besitzes bei den Römern, Festgabe an Johann Caspar Bluntschli, Leipzig 1880, p. 312, fn. 1.

42 Von Savigny, Das Rechts des Besitzes, p. 206-207.

43 Das Rechts des Besitzes, p. 205 et seq., especially p. 211. He had to acknowledge, however, that an act of *apprehensio* sufficient for a *traditio* could be insufficient for a unilateral *apprehensio*, that is a taking without the former possessor's permission. See p. 240-241.

the debate about possession in the German speaking countries.[44] In 19th century Germany possession has since been generally regarded as a mere fact.[45] Only from the latter half of the 19th century was this view challenged again and the controversy revived.[46]

As we shall see there are several clear indications that already in Roman law possession, which in primitive legal systems is often regarded as no more than a fact, had developed into a right. Or, at least, in some important respects it was treated as a right. As a result of this process the word *possessio* got a double meaning: possession as a fact, that is, power over an object, and possession as a right, the rights and actions available to the possessor to defend his position. Sometimes the first element dominates, sometimes the second. Roman jurists occasionally use the term *ius possessionis* to denote the right of possession as distinct from the fact of having physical power over the object.[47] However, they normally do not distinguish between the two meanings.[48]

Nor does modern German law, even though the double meaning of the concept was clearly demonstrated in the last decades of the 19th century by among others Bekker and Strohal[49]. These jurists recognized that possession is not just a fact but that it should also be seen as a real right. The view accorded with Germanic law which distinguished actual power over an object and the right of possession. In this law someone could have a right of possession (*Gewere*) even if he had no physical power over the thing.[50] *Gewere* therefore was a right.[51] In the beginning of the 20th century this distinction between possession as a fact and possession as a right was adopted by a number of important authors[52] and became the prevailing

---

44 Cf. E.I. Bekker, Das Rechts des Besitzes bei den Römern, Festgabe an Johann Caspar Bluntschli, Leipzig 1880, § 2 and 32; E. Strohal, Succession in den Besitz nach römischem und heutigem Recht, Graz 1885, p. 14.

45 See for example G.F. Puchta, Pandekten, 11th ed. edited by A.F. Rudorff, Leipzig 1872, § 126 and 130; A. Randa, Der Besitz nach österreichischem Rechte, 4th ed., Leipzig 1895, § 3; Windscheid/Kipp, Lehrbuch des Pandektenrechts, 9th ed., § 148, p. 734 and 744 (see however § 148 fn. 11 and 12 which demonstrate that Windscheid's opinion is untenable); H. Dernburg, Pandekten, vol. 1, Allgemeiner Teil und Sachenrecht, 7th ed. (with assistance of J. Biermann), Berlin 1902, § 169 and 177.

46 Brinz seems to have been the first to revive the controversy and assert the possibility of derivative acquisition of possession. See Strohal, Succession in den Besitz, p. 24, who refers to Brinz' *Lehrbuch der Pandekten*, 1st ed. 1857 p. 55 et seq. In later editions of his book Brinz mitigated his view. See 3rd ed. vol. 1, § 135. The controversy is extensively treated in Strohal's book and as to modern German law in V. Bruns, Besitzerwerb durch Interessenvertreter, Tübingen 1910, especially § 4. See also Windscheid/Kipp, Lehrbuch des Pandektenrechts, vol. 1, § 153, fn. 10. See also Randa, Der Besitz nach österreichischem Rechte, § 3.

47 Bekker, Das Recht des Besitzes bei den Römern, p. 333-340.

48 Bekker, p. 334-335.

49 Succession in den Besitz, p. 40.

50 O. Gierke, Deutsches Privatrecht, vol. 2 (Sachenrecht), p. 195-196 and 213-214.

51 Gierke, Deutsches Privatrecht, vol. 2, p. 214; Wolff/Raiser, p. 20-21.

52 F. Endemann, Lehrbuch des bürgerlichen Rechts, vol. 2 (Sachenrecht - Familienrecht), 7th ed., Berlin 1900, § 25. Von Tuhr, Allgemeiner Teil I, p. 137-138. K. Hellwig, Lehrbuch des deutschen Civilprozeßrechts, vol. 1, p. 206-207. K. Cosack/H. Mitteis, Lehrbuch des bürgerlichen Rechts, vol. 2, 7th-8th ed., Jena 1924, § 4. L. Enneccerus, Lehrbuch des bürgerlichen Rechts, vol. 1, erste Abteilung,

view.[53] Martin Wolff, the leading German author on property law in the 20th century, makes a comparable distinction between three different meanings of possession: firstly, physical power over a thing, secondly, any circumstance without physical power which the legal system nevertheless treats as equivalent to physical power and, thirdly, all rights and remedies connected with the physical power or its equivalent.[54]

Still their thoughts are not generally followed in modern German law. It seems that the modern view is divided over the problem and that a number of authors have returned to the old theories of Savigny *cum suis*.[55] A similar development can be found in Dutch law. Much earlier than in German law it was acknowledged by some authors that possession had a double meaning. In 1828 Van Hall[56] suggested to distinguish between possession as a fact and the right of possession, a thought adopted by Diephuis.[57] However, as in German law, a number of modern Dutch authors have returned to the opinion that possession is no more than a fact, although they seem to be a minority.[58]

Einleitung, Allgemeiner Teil, 6th-8th ed., Marburg 1911, § 73; O. Gierke, Deutsches Privatrecht, vol. 2 (Sachenrecht), Leipzig 1905, p. 213-214; Julius von Gierke, Bürgerliches Recht, Sachenrecht, 2nd ed., Berlin 1928, p. 6, fn. 1.

53 Enneccerus, Allgemeiner Teil, § 73, nr. 3.

54 Wolff/Raiser, § 3. He adds the following explanation: 'Der Besitz erscheint hierbei nicht als Summe der rechtlichen Wirkungen des Besitztatbestandes, sondern als deren Quelle. Wie zwischen die eigentumsbegründenden Tatsachen und die einzelnen Befugnisse des Eigentümers das 'Eigentum' tritt, als Folge jener Tatsachen, als Quelle dieser Befugnisse, so schaltet sich hier zwischen den Besitztatbestand und die einzelnen Rechte des Besitzers 'der Besitz' selbst als deren Mutterrecht. Nur diese Vorstellung veranschaulicht befriedigend die Übertragbarkeit und Vererblichkeit des Besitzes; von ihr aus erscheinen die Ansprüche des früheren Besitzers als Ausflüsse eines den Besitztatbestand überdauernden gegenwärtigen Besitzrechtes.'
('Here possession is not the sum of the legal effects of factual possession, but rather their source. As 'ownership' stands in between the facts giving rise to ownership and the various privileges of the owner, it being a consequence of those facts and the source of these privileges, so here 'possession' comes in between the factual possession and the privileges of the possessor forming their motherright. Only this conception clarifies properly why possession can be transferred and inherited. Moreover, in this view the claims of a former possessor should be regarded as consequences of a present right of possession which outlasts the factual possession.') The last sentence refers to someone who has lost actual power over the thing and who is given a remedy to claim back actual power over the thing (§ 862 BGB).

55 See for example Westermann, Sachenrecht, § 8,4; Schwab/Prütting, Sachenrecht, § 6; Baur/Stürner, Sachenrecht, § 9 V 1. For a different view see for example Ernst Wolf, Lehrbuch des Sachenrechts, § 2.

56 F.A. van Hall, Dertig vragen omtrent bezit en bezitregt, volgens het nieuwe Nederlandsche Burgerlijke Wetboek, Bijdragen tot Regtsgeleerdheid en Wetgeving, 1828, p. 118 et seq.

57 G. Diephuis, Het Nederlandsch burgerlijk regt naar de volgorde van het burgerlijk wetboek, vol. 3, 1st ed., Groningen 1846, nr. 96, 104 and 246-48.

58 See for example J.L. den Dulk, de zakelijke overeenkomst, (thesis Groningen 1979) Alphen a/d Rijn 1979, p. 103-104; J.H.A. Lokin, Bezitsverschaffing en bezitsoverdracht, in: T. Hartlief et al. (eds.), CJHB (Brunner-Bundel), Deventer 1994, p. 245 et seq., at p. 256. The double meaning is acknowledged by among others Beekhuis (Asser/Beekhuis, vol. 1, 10th ed., Zwolle 1975, p. 88-89), Mijnssen and Schut (Bezit, levering en overdracht, p. 9 et seq. and Asser/Mijnssen/De Haan, nr. 140-142) and Snijders and Rank-Berenschot (Goederenrecht, nr. 144).

Nonetheless, the view that possession is a mere fact disregards the true nature of the concept of possession as laid down in the *Bürgerliches Gesetzbuch*. There are many indications that in modern German law possession cannot be regarded as a mere fact, that it is also a right.[59] Because of its double character possession has always escaped attempts at defining the concept. Possession tends to obscure any concept in which it plays a part, such as *traditio*, the transfer of possession. A massive amount of books and articles have been written about it: the concept of possession was one of the favourite subjects of the 19th century German jurists. A lot of interesting thoughts can be found here. Yet, because of the double nature of possession, being a fact and a right at the same time, none of these publications has been able to solve the problem whether possession is a fact, a right or something in between. To my mind it is impossible to solve the problem. Still, it is very fruitful to distinguish between the two characters of possession.

The following examples taken from the text and system of the German civil code clearly show that possession is more than just a fact. Where needed I will refer to Dutch law, as it shares most of the dogmatic problems of possession with German law.

Protection of possession

If the thing in his possession is taken away, or the enjoyment of his possession disturbed otherwise, the possessor may use special actions to defend his position or to claim the thing back (*Besitzschutz*, § 858-869 and § 1007 BGB)[60]. They derive from classical Roman law that provided a similar protection by offering a number of interdicts (*interdicta*).[61]

Par. 862 BGB protects the possessor against any intrusion on the enjoyment of his possession. Par. 861 and § 1007 give the possessor whose possession has been taken away a claim for the return of the object. The actions of § 861 and 862 are given to every possessor, even a wrongful possessor, i.e. a possessor having no right to possession based for example on a real or personal right. The protection of possession aims at a peaceful settlement of conflicts. Wrongful possession ought to be ended not by self-given authority but rather by judicial proceedings. For that reason self-given authority (*Eigenmacht*) is in principle forbidden.

The double character of possession can be seen especially in § 861, the claim for the return of the thing. What is the claim based on? As to § 862 this question is easy to answer: the action to defend possession is based on possession. Yet, what is the claim ex § 861 based on? It is often said to be a claim for the return of possession given to someone who has lost possession. It is understandable that in such a view one is inclined to say that the claim cannot be based on possession, for that is the very thing the plaintiff has lost. Therefore the claim is sometimes said to be based on the plaintiff's former possession. But this cannot be true. Every right

---

59 Yet, the view that possession is also a real right does not necessarily entail that it enjoys the same protection as all other real rights. Its protection is limited: possession is a weak right.
60 In Dutch law art. 3:125 BW.
61 Kaser I, § 96.

of action is based on a present material right: the material right is the cause, the right of action its effect.[62] A former right is no right and therefore cannot give rise to a present right of action. Whereas a right may outlast its right of action (compare for example the *naturalis obligatio*),[63] the reverse, the right of action outlasting its right, is impossible.[64]

The confusion is caused by the double nature of possession: a fact and a right. To my mind the paragraph should be explained as follows. Although the possessor has lost possession regarded as a fact, that is, physical control over the thing, he has not yet lost possession regarded as a right. It is this right of possession, curtailed by the loss of physical control, which gives the possessor a right of action for the return of the thing.[65] As Martin Wolff puts it the claims of a former possessor should be regarded as consequences of a present right of possession which outlasts the factual possession[66], a thought expressed already by Diephuis in 1846.[67,68]

Oddly, the person who took over physical control of the thing, the thief for instance, is also possessor of the thing. Are there now two possessors of the same thing? Jurists have been saying for hundreds of years that *compossessio plurium in solidum*, possession exercised by more people over the same thing, is impossible.[69] Nonetheless, there is no valid reason why *compossessio* should be impossible. More rights of possession may exist over the same thing, as long as they differ in rank:[70] the first possessor's right of possession prevails over the second possessor's right of possession. The second right of possession works against everyone except the first possessor. The second possessor, if possessing wrongly, must return the thing to the first possessor, even if the latter is not the owner. The second possessor cannot answer the claim for the return of the thing by referring to a third party's right of ownership, the *ius tertii*. Although the first possessor's right is not the strongest right, it is still better than the second possessor's right. The different ranks of possession may be compared to the English concept of 'right to possession': the

---

62 This was acknowledged already by Accursius' *Glossa Ordinaria*. See gloss *actio autem* on Inst. 4,6, pr.: 'Nam obligatio est causa & mater actionis' (For the obligation is the cause and mother of the action).

63 See § 4.4.

64 As to the terms 'material right' and 'right of action' see § 4.4.

65 Cf. Wolff/Raiser, p. 19.

66 Wolff/Raiser, § 3. See fn. 54 *supra*.

67 Diephuis, Het Nederlandsch burgerlijk regt naar de volgorde van het burgerlijk wetboek, vol. 3, Groningen 1846, nr. 246-48.

68 Sometimes Roman law uses the term *ius possessionis* to indicate the right of possession as distinct from the fact of physical control. Unfortunately the concept is often referred to by the shorter but very confusing term 'possession' making it extremely difficult to analyse which of both meanings was intended. Bekker warned against the misunderstandings caused by the double meaning of possession and urged that a sharp distinction should be made between possession as a fact and possession as a right. See E.I. Bekker, Das Rechts des Besitzes bei den Römern, Festgabe an Johann Caspar Bluntschli, Leipzig 1880, p. 149 et seq., 333-334, § 30-31, p. 358 et seq.

69 They based their adage on Paul. D. 41,2,3,5: '...plures eandem rem in solidum possidere non possunt...' (it is impossible for several persons to possess the same thing in its entirety).

70 Cf. J.C. van Oven, De bezitsbescherming en hare functies, thesis Amsterdam, Amsterdam 1905, p. 127; Asser/Beekhuis I (Zakenrecht), 12th ed., Zwolle 1985, nr. 205.

above difference between the two rights would in English law be expressed by saying that the former has a better right to possession of the thing.[71]

Indirect possession

Another indication that possession has developed into a right is the existence of indirect possession (*mittelbarer Besitz*)[72]. It is often said that an indirect possessor has possession which he exercises via the direct possessor. When the owner leases an object to another, he does not lose possession of it. Rather he continues to possess, but without physical control over the asset. A primitive legal system regarding possession as direct physical control over the asset cannot acknowledge such a form of possession. In this example there is clearly no physical control. The 'control via the lessee' does not give the lessor physical power over the object. A system allowing this kind of possession acknowledges that possession is a right, which therefore may continue while its holder has no physical control.

Inheritance[73]

When a possessor of an object dies his heir automatically acquires possession of the object, even if he is unaware of this and living far away from the object (§ 857 BGB)[74]. He acquires the deceased's possession, that is to say, his possession is not

---

71 For the comparable English rule see *Armory v. Delamirie* (1722) 1 Stra 505, [1558-1774] All ER Rep 121; *Jeffries v. Great Western Railway Co.* (1856) 5 E&B 802. See also Williams, Principles of the law of personal property, p. 49, 52; Bell, Modern law of personal property, p. 77-78. Gordley and Mattei claim that this so-called doctrine of relative title is not the result of centuries of English case law, as is generally thought, but that it was developed by Sir Frederic Pollock. See J. Gordley and U. Mattei, Protecting possession, AJCL 1996, p. 293 et seq, at p. 301-305 and 326-27.

   To a certain extent the English concept of 'right to possession' resembles the German *Recht zum Besitz* (right to possession). The *Recht zum Besitz* denotes the right to be in actual physical possession, a right which may be based on ownership, a limited real right, a personal right etc. When for example the owner has lent a thing to another for a certain period the owner cannot claim it back before the time agreed upon is over: the borrower can bar this claim by setting up his right to possession (§ 986 BGB). Moreover, when the owner transfers ownership of the thing to another while the borrower is still using the thing (§ 931 BGB) the new owner cannot revindicate the thing from the borrower before the time agreed upon by the first owner, the lender, has lapsed: the right to possession works against everyone (§ 986 subs. 2). The concept of an absolute right to possession is based on Germanic law rather than Roman law. See Wolff/Raiser, p. 325. Dutch law, on the other hand, does not acknowledge the concept. The borrower would have to surrender the thing to the owner. In Dutch law the borrower's 'right to possession' is purely contractual (based on the contract of loan for use) and has no absolute effect. After all, contracts work between the contracting parties only. It is the Roman law rule. However, exceptions have been made for lease (*huur* and *pacht*): art. 7A:1612, respectively art. 34 Pachtwet.

   Despite the similarities it seems that the *Recht zum Besitz* does not fully correspond with the English 'right to possession'. True, often the English right to possession will be based on ownership, a limited real right or a personal right. Yet it may also originate simply in possession itself. The German right to possession, on the other hand, can never be based on mere possession as this would destroy the distinction between the right *of* possession and the right *to* possession.

72 *Middellijk bezit* in Dutch law.

73 Cf. Wolff/Raiser, § 3 III and § 12 I 4.

74 Cf. art. 880 BW, art. 3:116 BW and art. 4.5.1.1. subs. 1 BW.

new but it is the very same possession the deceased himself exercised. The heir is said to succeed in the deceased's possession. Inheriting possession is a derivative acquisition of possession, as distinct from an original acquisition in which case new possession is created. The rule is of Germanic origin: in Germanic law possession passed to the heir immediately after the possessor had died, even before the heir had acquired physical control.[75]

Acquisitive prescription

The above distinction between original and derivative acquisition is important for acquisitive prescription (*usucapio, Ersitzung*, § 937-945 BGB): if a prescription period was running in favour of the deceased, the heir continues this period. That is to say, because his right of possession is not new, because he acquires the deceased's right of possession the heir need not start a new prescription period (§ 943).[76] To give an example, as to movables the prescription period is ten years (§ 937). If six years after he acquired possession the possessor dies, his heir acquires ownership of the thing after only four years.[77]

Also when possession is voluntarily transferred *inter vivos* the acquisition of possession is called derivative. As a result a prescription period running in favour of the transferor may be continued by the acquirer (§ 943).[78] If a possessor who is not owner of the thing sells the thing to another person and transfers possession to the buyer, the latter may continue the prescription period, provided he meets all requirements for acquisitive prescription, most importantly good faith.[79] In both instances, inheritance and transfer *inter vivos*, the acquirer is regarded as succeeding in his predecessor's right of possession (*Rechtsnachfolge*, succession in a right).

Extinctive prescription

The continuation of a prescription period is also recognized in the case of extinctive prescription of the revindication. The concept of extinctive prescription refers to what in English law is called limitation of actions. The action of revindication will be statute barred within 30 years (§ 195 BGB). After the prescription of the revindication the owner will no longer be able to revindicate his property as against the person to whom the action of revindication related, for example the first thief. As under German law a new action of revindication arises against each new possessor, in principle a fresh period of 30 years will start as against every new

---

75 Gierke, Deutsches Privatrecht, vol. 2, p. 194-195; Wolff/Raiser, p. 21. Cf. the adage *le mort saisit le vif*.
76 Cf. art. 3:102 subs. 1 BW.
77 Provided, of course, that all other requirements for acquisitive prescription are met. In Roman law and modern Dutch law the heir is deemed to be in good faith or in bad faith if the deceased was in good or bad faith respectively. See Paul. D. 41,4,2,19; Inst. 2,6,12; J.H.A. Lokin, Prota, 3rd ed., Groningen 1993, p. 183. See as to Dutch law art. 3:116 BW; Asser/Mijnssen/De Haan (1992), nr. 208 and 495. So, the heir inherits not only possession but also the quality of being in good or bad faith. German law deviated from this by requiring the heir to be in good faith himself. See Windscheid/Kipp, vol. 1, p. 939; Wolff/Raiser, p. 262.
78 Cf. art. 3:102 subs. 2 BW.
79 See for this example Wolff/Raiser, p. 262.

possessor of the asset. Yet, § 221 BGB provides that where the new possessor continues the possession of the former possessor the time of prescription which elapsed in favour of the former possessor is subtracted from the period running in favour of the new possessor (*accessio temporis*).[80] However, the 'accession of time' applies only if the new possessor can be seen as continuing the right of possession of its predecessor: there must be a succession in a right (*Rechtsnachfolge*).[81]

In both instances, acquisitive and extinctive prescription, the *accessio temporis* demonstrates clearly that German law recognizes the concept of *Rechtsnachfolge* (succession is a right), that is, derivative acquisition of possession.[82] The concept of *Rechtsnachfolge* is also mentioned in § 858 subs. 2, § 861, subs. 2, § 862, subs. 2 and § 999, subs. 1 BGB.

3.4 Transfer of possession (*Übergabe*)

Now, as set out above, in principle a valid transfer needs *Übergabe*, a transfer of direct or indirect possession of the asset. Possession may be transferred by handing over the object, or by giving the acquirer physical power over the object otherwise. These two ways of meeting the requirement of *Übergabe* are set out in § 854 BGB. According to § 854 subs. 1 BGB possession may be acquired by obtaining actual power over the thing. Yet in some cases possession may be transferred by a mere agreement. According to § 854 subs. 2[83] an agreement suffices if the acquirer is able to exercise actual power over the object. A classical example is sawn wood lying in a forest. If the acquirer has access to the forest giving him the possibility of exercising physical power over the wood an agreement suffices to transfer possession. It is an example of *traditio ficta*, a transfer of possession without any physical act and without the parties even being in the presence of the things involved. It is nonetheless regarded as an instance of *Übergabe*.

For the sake of clarity we should note that although both are called *Einigung* (agreement) the agreement mentioned in § 854 subs. 2 is different from the real

---

80 Par. 221 BGB: 'If a thing with regard to which a real right of action (*dinglicher Anspruch*) is available, comes into the possession of a third party by way of succession in a right (*Rechtsnachfolge*) the time of prescription which elapsed during the possession of the predecessor benefits the successor.'

81 Oddly, the first judgment on § 221 BGB explaining what amounts to a succession in the right of possession is a judgment by an English court: *City of Gotha and Federal Republic of Germany v. Sotheby's and Cobert Finance S.A.* (High Court, Queens Bench Division, Case nrs. 1993C and 1997 G), lexis-nexis.

82 Windscheid/Kipp, vol. 1, p. 794; Wolff/Raiser, p. 262. Also in Roman law the heir may continue a prescription period which was running in favour of the deceased. It was called *successio in possessionem* (succession in possession) (Ner. D. 41,3,40). Of course pandectists such as Puchta had to recognize this succession in possession when writing about acquisitive prescription: see Pandekten, § 156. Yet he thereby contradicts his opinion that possession is a mere fact and not a right. See Pandekten, § 126 and 130.

83 § 854 subs. 2, reads: 'Die Einigung des bisherigen Besitzers und des Erwerbers genügt zum Erwerbe, wenn der Erwerber in der Lage ist, die Gewalt über die Sache auszuüben.' (For the acquisition of possession an agreement between the possessor and the acquirer suffices, if the acquirer is able to exercise power over the thing).

agreement required in § 929: the former aims at transferring possession, the latter at transferring ownership.

3.5 Is the transfer of possession a legal act?

The examples mentioned in section 3.3 justify the conclusion that possession is not only a fact but also a right. May we therefore draw the conclusion that the transfer of possession is a legal act? After all, the transfer of a right is a legal act.

Windscheid (1817-1892), who had an enormous influence on the drafting of the German civil code,[84] answered the question as follows: 'Since publication of the 6th edition the idea of succession in possession has been disseminated further. The starting-point of the idea is the view that possession is a right... Indeed, if possession is a right rather than a factual relationship it cannot be disputed, for reasons of logic, that this right may be transferred; but the question is whether in separating possession from its factual foundation Roman law had progressed up to this point.'[85] Windscheid himself persisted that possession is a pure factual relationship.[86]

As we will see in section 6 answering the question is important when the transferor or the transferee wishes to make use of an agent for the transfer of possession. For, in principle the concept of agency can be applied to legal acts only. But again, answering the question is complicated by the double nature of possession. When possession is transferred by *traditio vera*, that is actual handing over of the thing, possession is usually seen as a fact more than as a right. On the other hand, in the case of *traditio ficta*, where possession is transferred by mere agreement, possession is regarded mainly as a right.

As a consequence the answer is different for both types of *traditio*. The transfer of possession by agreement mentioned in § 854, subs. 2 BGB is generally seen as a legal act.[87] On the other hand, the actual handing over in § 854, subs. 1 BGB is not regarded as a legal act. It is rather seen as a factual act, a *Realakt*. The transfer of possession is said to be aimed solely at a factual result, namely another person's actual power over the object.[88]

---

84 He was one of the most prominent members of the first drafting commission. Furthermore, in the second half of the 19th century Windscheid's *Lehrbuch des Pandektenrechts* was the most influential book about the *gemeines Recht*. See P. Koschaker, Europa und das römische Recht, 4th ed., Munich/Berlin 1966, p. 103-104; W. Schubert, Die Entstehung der Vorschriften des BGB über Besitz und Eigentumsübertragung, Berlin 1966, p. 19. This gradual influence has been even more important than his direct influence in making the first draft of the *Bürgerliches Gesetzbuch*.

85 Lehrbuch des Pandektenrechts, 9th ed., § 153, fn. 10 (p. 766).

86 Windscheid/Kipp, Lehrbuch des Pandektenrechts, vol. 1, § 148, 149 and especially § 150.

87 Westermann, § 13 III 2; Wolff/Raiser, p. 40; Von Gierke, vol. 2, p. 234 et seq.; Flume, Das Rechtsgeschäft, p. 750. Von Tuhr disagrees: see Allgemeiner Teil II, p. 110. He calls this transfer of possession a *Rechtshandlung*, which means an act that contains a declaration of will directed towards a factual result. Any legal consequences of the act will occur irrespective of the party's intentions. For that reason it should be distinguished from the concept of legal act, which is called *Rechtsgeschäft*.

88 Westermann, § 13 II; Von Tuhr, Allgemeiner Teil II, p. 110; Flume, Das Rechtsgeschäft, p. 110.

Still, the law is far from consistent here. Martin Wolff shares the general view that *traditio vera* cannot be avoided for defect of will and that a minor may transfer possession to another minor. But he adds that if the will to transfer lacks, for example because possession is transferred by a lunatic, there is no transfer of possession but only a loss of possession for the transferor and an original acquisition of possession for the acquirer.[89] To my mind this is the key to a solution: the transfer of possession, that is a derivative form of acquisition, needs the will of both parties to transfer, respectively acquire possession. If such a will is lacking the agreement is void and does not pass possession. However, possession as a fact nevertheless passes, provided the acquirer gets physical power over the asset. Possession as a right, on the other hand, remains with the 'transferor'. Similarly, where the agreement has been avoided for a defect of will possession as a right in principle reverts to the transferor, but possession as a fact stays with the acquirer if he has got physical power over the thing.[90] The acquisition in this case is not derivative but original.[91]

3.6 *Geheißerwerb*[92]

Geheißerwerb is a special form of *Übergabe* often used where there is a chain of buyers. Let us take the following example. A, the supplier of goods, has sold the goods to B, a merchant, who in his turn has sold the goods to C. A is still the owner and possessor of the goods. For practical reasons the three parties agree that A should hand the goods over directly to C. Now, A could of course transfer ownership of the goods directly to C. When doing so C will acquire ownership from a person other than his seller, and B will never become owner of the goods, not even for an imaginary second. Commonly, though, the parties will prefer ownership to pass via B, that is, 'through the chain', so that each buyer receives ownership from his seller.[93] A will normally not be familiar with the terms of the contract between B and C: there might be a retention of ownership clause

---

89 Wolff/Raiser, p. 40.
90 Gierke, Deutsches Privatrecht, vol. 2, p. 235. The same opinion can be found in Dutch law. If a prescription period was running in favour of the transferor he continues this period after the transfer of possession has been avoided. He does not need to start a new prescription period, even though the transferee has been in possession until the avoidance. For as a result of the avoidance the transferor is deemed always to have had the right of possession. The transferee is deemed never to have had more than factual possession. Cf. Asser/Mijnssen/De Haan, nr. 192.
91 Note, however, that this may have unforeseen consequences for acquisitive prescription: in principle a prescription period running in favour of the transferor may be continued by the acquirer only where the acquisition of possession is derivative. Still, for practical reasons the law may in certain cases allow an *accessio temporis* (addition of time) even where there is no succession in possession. See also Asser/Mijnssen/De Haan, nr. 192.
92 This subject is most extensively dealt with by M. Martinek: Traditionsprinzip und Geheißerwerb, in AcP 188 (1988), p. 573-648 and by F.-J. Kolb: Geheißerwerb, Eine Positionsbestimmung im Spannungsfeld zwischen Traditionsprinzip und Verkehrsbedürfnis, (*Dissertation* Mainz) Frankfurt a/M 1997.
93 Martinek, Traditionsprinzip und Geheißerwerb, p. 599.

(*Eigentumsvorbehalt*) in this contract.[94] A direct transfer from A to C would frustrate such a clause.

The first requirement for a transfer of ownership, the real agreement, will not cause any problem: A will make a real agreement with B, and B in turn will make another real agreement with C. The obstacle is the second requirement: the transfer of possession. It would be impractical if it were necessary for A to transfer possession to B and for B to transfer possession to C. Although the text of § 929 suggests that a transfer of possession is required between every transferor and his acquirer, the parties can nonetheless make a valid transfer via B without having to hand the goods over to B. The result can be reached by using the notion of *Geheißerwerb* (lit.: acquisition to order). If B orders A to transfer possession of the goods directly to C and A follows this order (*Geheiß*), A is deemed to have transferred possession to B and B to C so that the requirement of *Übergabe* mentioned in § 929 is complied with, as between A and B and also as between B and C. As a result ownership passes from A to B and from B to C. It will have been with B for an imaginary second only. So, the requirement of *Übergabe* is fulfilled even though there has been no transfer of physical possession from A to B and from B to C.[95]

Previously I have stated that *Übergabe* in principle means the transfer of direct or indirect possession. However, these instances of *Geheißerwerb* are regarded as amounting to *Übergabe* even though there is no transfer of physical possession between the transferor and the transferee. *Geheißerwerb* is not seen as a substitute for *Übergabe* but rather as a special form of *Übergabe*.[96] How do we reconcile this? Should we adapt our definition of *Übergabe*?

When German law says that possession is transferred from A to B and from B to C, although the object is physically handed over from A to C, it means that the right of possession is transferred from A via B to C whereas the fact of possession, that is physical possession, is given directly to C. So, it is a form of *traditio*, not a substitute for *traditio*. Yet, as physical possession does not follow the chain it should be seen as a *traditio ficta*. Still, to my mind it is confusing to stretch the meaning of *Übergabe* to cover cases of *traditio ficta* as well.

---

94 Martinek, p. 599 and 615.

95 For other instances of *Geheißerwerb* see Martinek's article. In English law something resembling *Geheißerwerb* was acknowledged in *Four Point Garage Ltd. v. Carter* [1985] 3 All ER 12.

96 The same result (a transfer of ownership to C via B without having to transfer direct possession via B) can also be reached by making use of one of the traditional substitutes for *Übergabe*, namely *constitutum possessorium* (§ 930), a concept that will be discussed in § 4.3. *Constitutum possessorium* means that A agrees with B to become *Besitzmittler* for B. As a result B will receive indirect possession and, if A has the power to dispose, ownership of the asset as well. Subsequently B will be able to transfer his possession and ownership to C in exactly the same way.

Be that as it may, regarding *Geheißerwerb* as a form of *Übergabe* in the sense of § 929 has the advantage that the protection of third parties given by § 932 is applicable to *Geheißerwerb* cases as well (see Wolff/Raiser, p. 254-255). On the other hand, § 932 does not apply to a transfer by way of *constitutum possessorium*. Neither will § 933 give any protection, as it requires that the transferee have acquired direct possession from the transferor. In this case the transferor is B whereas C acquires his possession from A.

4 *Übergabe* substitutes

4.1 Introduction

Where the § 929 requirement of *Übergabe* would be impractical, *Übergabesurrogate* (substitutes for *Übergabe*)[97] may be used: according to § 929 2nd sentence, § 930 and § 931 in certain circumstances *Übergabe* is not required for a transfer of ownership. Yet, the requirement of *Einigung* (real agreement) will under no circumstances be subject to exception, not even when an *Übergabe* substitute is used. *Einigung* is an indispensable element of every voluntary transfer (*Übertragung*) of assets.

4.2 *Traditio brevi manu*

The *Übergabe* substitute mentioned first in the *Bürgerliches Gesetzbuch* is the so-called *traditio brevi manu* laid down in the second sentence of § 929. The provision reads: 'If the acquirer is in possession of the thing, the real agreement about the passing of ownership will suffice.' So, it makes *Übergabe* redundant in these cases. To give an example, the owner of a book has lent it to someone, and now intends to sell and transfer it to the borrower. If § 929 2nd sentence did not exist, the borrower would first have to give the book back in order to enable the owner to transfer possession of the book to the borrower. The *traditio brevi manu* makes it possible to skip the requirement of *Übergabe* here.

Generally the transferee will have acquired possession from the transferor. However, in German law *traditio brevi manu* is not confined to these cases. It can be used whatever way the transferee has acquired possession. Moreover, it is irrelevant whether the transferee has direct or indirect possession of the object.[98]

Under the *gemeines Recht traditio brevi manu* was seen as a special form of *traditio*, not as a substitute for it. Here *traditio brevi manu* was limited to cases in which possession had been transferred by the transferor. Physical transfer of power was not required because it had already taken place: prior to the *traditio brevi manu* the transferor had made the transferee *detentor* of the thing.[99] Yet, under the *Bürgerliches Gesetzbuch* it is no longer correct to see *brevi manu* as a special form of *traditio*, as § 929 2nd sentence applies also to cases where the transferee has acquired possession otherwise. Hence the treatment of *traditio brevi manu* in the chapter on *Übergabesurrogate*.

---

97 The term does not mean that the substitutes for *Übergabe* never entail a transfer of possession. If it does entail a transfer of possession it should be regarded as a form of *traditio ficta*, because every *traditio*, also a *traditio ficta* is transfer of possession.

98 Wolff/Raiser, p. 241.

99 A. Randa, Der Besitz nach österreichischem Rechte, mit Berücksichtigung des gemeinen Rechtes, des preußischen, französischen und italienischen, des sächsischen und züricherischen Gesetzbuches, 4th ed., Leipzig 1895, p. 426, fn. 35.

4.3 *Constitutum possessorium* (*Besitzkonstitut*)

Where the transferor and transferee want the former to stay in possession after the transfer, *Übergabe* can be replaced by *constitutum possessorium*.[100] When using this method of transferring possession the acquirer is made indirect *Eigenbesitzer* (*possessor*) of the object and the transferor, who previously was *Eigenbesitzer*, is changed into *Fremdbesitzer* (*detentor*), holding the object for the acquirer. As here *Eigenbesitz* (*possessio*) is transferred from the transferor to the acquirer the German *constitutum possessorium* could be regarded as a form of *traditio ficta*. Other examples of *traditio ficta* are *Geheißerwerb* and the transfer of possession by mere agreement (§ 854 subs. 2).[101] *Constitutum possessorium* could be called the opposite of *traditio brevi manu* in that the transferor's *Eigenbesitz* is changed into *Fremdbesitz* whereas *traditio brevi manu* turns the acquirer's *Fremdbesitz* into *Eigenbesitz*.[102]

To illustrate, if the parties agree that after the transfer of ownership the transferor will hold the thing in safe keeping for the acquirer or that the transferor will remain in possession as a borrower, they may transfer possession without any actual handing over being needed. In such cases *Übergabe* can be replaced by creating a *Besitzmittlungsverhältnis* (ground for *Fremdbesitz*). Par. 930 reads: 'If the owner is in possession of the thing, *Übergabe* may be replaced by the owner and the acquirer creating a legal relation under which the transferee acquires indirect possession.'

It is in dispute whether or not the ground for *Fremdbesitz* (the *causa detentionis*) should be specified, that is to say, whether or not it should be possible to infer from the parties' words or conduct which specific *causa detentionis* they have agreed upon: a loan for use, a lease, a deposit or another legal relation creating *Fremdbesitz* (*Besitzmittlungsverhältnis*).[103] In his book *Die Lehre vom Rechtserwerb durch Tradition*[104] (1867) Exner attacked the then prevailing view which did not demand any specific *causa detentionis*. For a *constitutum possessorium* to be valid Exner required a specific legal relationship between the transferor and transferee which was able to justify why the transferor retained actual power over the object. It is called the requirement of a concrete *constitutum possessorium*, whereas the opposite

---

100   The term *constitutum possessorium* as a *terminus technicus* may have been introduced by Andreas Tiraquellus (1488-1558) in his monograph *De iure constituti possessorii Tractatus*, Paris 1549.

101   It is strange to see that both *Besitzkonstitut* and *Geheißerwerb* involve a fictitious transfer of possession (a transfer of the right of possession without any physical handing over) but that nonetheless the second is regarded as a form of *Übergabe* whereas the first is not.

102   In the 17th and 18th century *constitutum possessorium* was sometimes seen as a form of *traditio brevi manu*. See J. Biermann, Traditio ficta, Stuttgart 1891 (repr. Amsterdam 1968), p. 235.

103   See in general Ph. Heck, Grundriß des Sachenrechts, 3rd ed., Tübingen 1930 (repr. Aalen 1994), p. 500-503; K.W. Kolbe, Die Wirksamkeitsvoraussetzungen des constitutum possessorium nach der Pandektistik, (*Dissertation* Frankfurt a/M) s.l. 1957; Staudinger-Wiegand, 1995, § 930, Rdnr. 14 et seq. Advocates of the *causa detentionis* requirement do, however, concede that the specific *causa* need not be valid.

104   A. Exner, Die Lehre vom Rechtserwerb durch Tradition nach österreichischem und gemeinem Recht, Vienna 1867.

view in which a *causa detentionis* need not be indicated is said to suffice itself with an abstract *constitutum possessorium*. Exner's view was not to be accepted generally, but until today German law has been divided over the question.[105]

Among the various reasons brought forward in support of the concrete *causa detentionis* the most important were the following three. First, the requirement of a concrete *causa detentionis* was said to be in accordance with Roman law: in almost all passages about *constitutum possessorium* the *causa detentionis* is clearly indicated. The Roman texts give specific examples, such as a usufruct or hire. The argument, however, does not convince. Apart from the fact that historical arguments can never be decisive, it should be stressed that the Roman texts do not have the same level of abstraction as the German *Pandektenrecht*. Far from it, Roman lawyers tend to explain by giving examples, not by abstract formulations. Hence, from the fact that many cases of *constitutum possessorium* are illustrated by examples we cannot infer that Roman law demanded a concrete legal ground as a requirement for validity. Moreover, the most famous text on *constitutum*, Cels. D. 41,2,18, pr., has been formulated very abstractly without reference to any specific legal relationship.

Another argument for demanding a concrete *causa detentionis* is the fear that an abstract *constitutum* will undermine the tradition system. Clearly this applies to all forms of *traditio ficta*, not only to the *constitutum possessorium*. Besides, it is hard to see how the requirement of a concrete *causa detentionis* would mitigate the undermining of the tradition system. Most probably authors using this argument believe that the requirement of a *causa detentionis* would reduce the number of cases in which ownership is transferred by way of *constitutum possessorium*, a thought which seems unlikely to me.

Thirdly, the requirement is believed to prevent simulated legal acts. In this view the specific legal ground makes plausible that the parties have a genuine will to transfer ownership. The argument was especially important at the end of the 19th century when the concept of *fiducia cum creditore* (a kind of mortgage on movables)[106] was controversial.[107] Opponents of *fiducia cum creditore* claimed that *constitutum possessorium* enabled a debtor to reduce invisibly his creditworthiness by alienating parts of his estate while retaining in actual possession of the objects,

---

105   Following Exner's view, which had been adopted by Windscheid among others (Wind-scheid/Kipp, Lehrbuch des Pandektenrechts, vol. 1, § 155, fn. 8a-c,) the first and second drafting commission of the *Bürgerliches Gesetzbuch* demand such a specific legal ground, but the reasons for doing so are not explained. See Mugdan, vol. 3, p. 54 (*Motive*) and p. 625 (*Protokolle*). The German Supreme Court (the *Bundesgerichtshof* and its predecessor the *Reichsgericht*) does not take a clear position in this matter. See Staudinger-Wiegand, 1995, § 930, Rdnr. 15.

106   The transaction, *Sicherungsübereignung*, which is now accepted as valid, involves a transfer of ownership to a creditor. The transfer is executed by way of *constitutum possessorium* so that the debtor may continue to use the objects concerned.

107   R. Johow, Entwurf eines bürgerlichen Gesetzbuches für das Deutsche Reich, Sachenrecht, Begründung, vol. 2, Berlin 1880, p. 756-758, published in: Die Vorlagen der Redaktoren für die erste Kommission zur Ausarbeitung des Entwurfs eines Bürgerlichen Gesetzbuches, Sachenrecht, vol. 1 (Allgemeine Bestimmungen, Besitz und Eigentum), ed. by W. Schubert, Berlin/New York 1982.

thus defrauding his creditors. Yet, again the requirement of a specific legal ground is unable to prevent these fraudulent acts. When a debtor is prepared to defraud his creditors by pretending a genuine transfer of ownership it is not difficult for him to pretend in addition a specific *causa detentionis*.[108]

4.4 Assignment of the *Herausgabeanspruch*

A third *Übergabe* substitute is laid down in § 931: 'If a third person is in possession of the thing, *Übergabe* may be replaced by the owner assigning to the acquirer his *Herausgabeanspruch* (claim to the return of the thing).'

The *Herausgabeanspruch* may have two different origins. If the owner is in indirect possession of the thing, the *Herausgabeanspruch* to be transferred originates in the legal relationship between the owner/indirect possessor and the direct possessor who holds the object for the former. This legal relationship, the so-called *Besitzmittlungsverhältnis*, gives rise to a claim as against the direct possessor for the return of the object (*Herausgabeanspruch*). Under a loan contract or a right of usufruct, for instance, the owner has a claim and the borrower or the usufructuary a correlative duty to give the object back to the owner in due course. According to German legal science it is this claim that should be transferred to the acquirer. According to the *Bundesgerichtshof* (the German Supreme Court) § 870 BGB[109] applies here: by transferring this *Herausgabeanspruch* the owner's indirect possession is transferred to the acquirer.[110] It is merely a complicated way of saying that the owner should transfer his indirect possession to the acquirer.

So, in the above instance a transfer of possession is needed in order to transfer ownership. Although the transferee acquires indirect rather than direct possession it is a true *traditio*. It is odd to see that nevertheless this act of transferring possession is not seen as *Übergabe* but as an *Übergabe* substitute.

If, on the other hand, the owner has no possession at all, for example because of loss or theft, *Übergabe* can be replaced by assigning the *Herausgabeanspruch* ex § 985: the revindication. At least, this is what the text of § 931 seems to suggest. The following will show us that the true meaning is quite different.

The *Anspruch*

In order to grasp the meaning of the word *Herausgabeanspruch* and consequently the meaning of § 931 BGB we should analyse thoroughly the concept of *Anspruch* in general. The concept was developed by Windscheid[111] on the basis of classical

---

108   Ph. Heck, Grundriß des Sachenrechts, p. 501-502.

109   Par. 870 reads: 'Indirect possession can be transferred by assigning to the acquirer the claim for the return of the thing (*Anspruch auf Herausgabe*).'

110   BGH 21-4-1959, NJW 1959, p. 1536 et seq. See also Wolff/Raiser, p. 245 and Baur/Stürner, p. 585.

111   In his book *Die Actio des römischen Civilrechts vom Standpunkte des heutigen Rechts*, Düsseldorf 1856 and the book *Die Actio, Abwehr gegen Dr. Theodor Muther*, Düsseldorf 1857, which he wrote as a reply to Th. Muther's *Zur Lehre von der römischen Actio, dem heutigen Klagrecht, der Litiscontestation und der Singularsuccession in Obligationen, eine Kritik des Windscheid'schen Buchs 'Die Actio des römischen Civilrechts vom Standpunkte des heutigen Rechts'*, Erlangen 1857. All three books have been

Roman law. It has eventually been adopted by the *Bürgerliches Gesetzbuch* and has since formed an essential part of the German private law system.

In its classical period the Roman private law system was based on a collection of *actiones*.[112] To begin legal proceedings a person had to turn to the *praetor* first to be given an *actio*. The *praetor* had to examine whether there was a suitable *actio* for the case submitted to him. In exceptional instances he could create a new *actio* if he thought fit. When the plaintiff had been granted an *actio* he could subsequently bring his case before a *iudex* (judge) whose task it was to consider the evidence and decide the dispute on the basis of the *actio* concerned. The system of *actiones* did not draw a clear distinction between substantive law and civil procedure: in fact the concept of *actio* belonged to both areas of law. The *actio* indicated the possibility to obtain a judgment against the defendant and at the same time, tacitly though, the material right that had to be enforced.[113] In addition the word was used to indicate the proceedings before the judge.[114]

Only many centuries later was it perceived more clearly or at least expressed more straightforwardly that the possibility of bringing a case before a court and getting a judgment logically presupposed having a material right against the defendant in the first place. Once jurists became more aware of this a separation between substantive law and procedural law could begin to develop. It is not known in which century the distinction was introduced into legal science[115], but the *Glossa Ordinaria*[116] already made a distinction between the obligation and the corresponding *actio*, calling the *obligatio* the *causa et mater actionis* (cause and mother of the action).[117] Nowadays in many civil law countries the distinction is well-established and the term to indicate the material right is 'subjective right'.

Now that the material right has been separated from its *actio* we can distinguish the following three concepts: right, right of action and the action itself. The right of action denotes the possibility to have a right enforced in court against the defendant's will. It is distinguished from the underlying material or subjective right (in German: *subjektives Recht*) which it is designed to protect and strengthen. 'Right'

reprinted in one volume, Aalen 1984.

112   H. Coing, Zur Geschichte des Begriffs 'subjektives Recht', in: H. Coing, Zur Geschichte des Privatrechtsystems, Frankfurt a/M. 1962, p. 36.

113   Kaser/Hackl, Das römische Zivilprozeßrecht, 2nd ed., Munich 1996, p. 234-35.

114   Kaser/Hackl, Das römische Zivilprozeßrecht, p. 236. For other meanings of the term *actio*, that are not relevant in this context, see: H. Heumann and E. Seckel, Handlexikon zu den Quellen des römischen Rechts, 11th ed., Jena 1907 (repr. Graz 1971), p. 9 and 10.

115   There are many different theories about this development. See for a brief overview Coing, Zur Geschichte des Begriffs 'subjektives Recht', R. Feenstra, Ius in re, Leiden/Zwolle 1979 and F. Wubbe in: Paulys Realencyclopädie der classischen Altertumswissenschaft, neue Bearbeitung begonnen von G. Wissowa, Supplementband X, Stuttgart 1965, columns 333-343.

116   Gloss *actio autem* on Inst. 4,6, pr.: 'Nam obligatio est causa & mater actionis' (For the obligation is the cause and mother of the action).

117   Cf. H. Coing, Zur Geschichte des Begriffs 'subjektives Recht', p. 40. See also R. Feenstra, Ius in re, p. 12, fn. 51 and literature mentioned there.

is related to 'right of action' as cause to effect.[118] The 'action', finally, refers to the proceedings before the court and is purely a concept belonging to civil procedure (*Prozeßrecht*). The 'right of action' somehow forms the bridge between the subjective right and the action, between substantive law and civil procedure.

Windscheid's concept of Anspruch
In the middle of the 19th century Windscheid published a book[119] about the *actio* in Roman law in which he emphasized the double meaning of the term *actio* in classical Roman law, showing that it indicated not only the right of action but also the subjective right itself. He proposed to introduce into German legal science the concept of *Anspruch* with the intention, if I understand him correctly, to capture the double meaning of the Roman law term *actio* in a German legal concept.[120] Whatever Windscheid's original intention the concept of *Anspruch*, together with its ambiguous meaning, became generally accepted in German legal science of his time, despite some sharp criticism.[121] It was introduced into the *Bürgerliches Gesetzbuch* and lead to a number of inconsistencies as a result of its double meaning.

The need to distinguish right and right of action[122]
Commonly right and right of action go hand in hand. Yet the difference between the concepts appears where the holder of a right cannot bring an action, for example because he did not have a right of action from the outset or because his right of action has prescribed.

To give an example of the first group of cases, the promise of a fee to a marriage broker (§ 656) and gaming and betting (§ 762 et seq.) do not give rise to a right of action. Still they do bring about an obligation. In these instances the obligation is called a *naturalis obligatio*[123], which means an obligation without right of action. The right is unenforceable, but if the debt is nonetheless paid, it cannot be claimed back ex unjustified enrichment, since the debt was owed.

The second example is prescription of the *Anspruch* (§ 194 BGB). The paragraph reads: 'The right to claim that someone should perform or should not perform a

---

118   There are some rights of action, however, that are not based on any subjective right at all. See W.H. Heemskerk, Vorderingsrecht en rechtsvordering, Deventer 1974, p. 8 et seq.

119   Die actio des römischen Zivilrechts vom Standpunkte des heutigen Rechts, Düsseldorf 1856.

120   Die actio des römischen Zivilrechts, p. 1-7.

121   O. von Gierke, for example, raised the objection, which was only to be expected, that the new term *Anspruch* was no more than a modern word for the Roman *actio* (see: Der Entwurf eines bürgerlichen Gesetzbuchs und das deutsche Recht, Leipzig 1889, p. 40). The concept was also disapproved of by Th. Muther (Zur Lehre von der römischen Actio) and H. Dernburg, Pandekten, 7th ed., Berlin 1902, vol. 1, p. 86, fn. 7; Dernburg, Das bürgerliche Recht des Deutschen Reichs und Preußens, vol. 1 (Die allgemeinen Lehren), Halle 1902, § 42.

122   See also J. Esser, Einführung in die Grundbegriffe des Rechtes und Staates, Vienna 1949, § 77 and B. Rehfeldt, Einführung in die Rechtswissenschaft, Berlin 1962, § 15.

123   In German it is called *Naturalobligation*: Staudinger-Reuter, 1995, § 656, Rdnr. 11; Staudinger-Engel, 1996, Vorbem. §§ 762-764, Rdnr. 3.

certain act (*Anspruch*) is subject to prescription.' Again, we should keep in mind the *Anspruch*'s double meaning. After a certain period of prescription the *Anspruch* is no longer enforceable against the debtor's will. The *Anspruch* does not lapse[124] but the defendant is given an *exceptio*[125] (defence) to bar the plaintiff's *Anspruch*. If the debtor nevertheless performs his obligation, he cannot claim his performance back (§ 222), since he was obliged to perform. In addition the creditor may in certain circumstances seek fulfilment of his unenforceable right by a set-off (*Aufrechnung*) against a counter-claim (§ 387-390), at least as far as personal rights are concerned. Here prescription blocks only the creditor's possibility to have his right enforced in court against the defendant's will (right of action); it does not affect the subjective right itself. Therefore *Anspruch* in § 194 must denote the right of action.

With this in mind it is rather confusing to read § 222 and § 223 BGB. Sentence 2 of § 222 provides: 'What has been done in satisfaction of an *Anspruch* which has prescribed, cannot be reclaimed...' Then in § 223, first sentence, we can find the following passage: 'If the *Anspruch* was secured by a mortgage...' In these two passages the word *Anspruch* must indicate the subjective right, since a right of action cannot be performed and cannot be burdened with a limited right. A subjective right, however, can.

The *dinglicher Anspruch* ex § 985

In the following it will become apparent why this rather extensive analysis of the concept of *Anspruch* was necessary. In the above we concentrated on the *schuldrechtlicher* (personal) *Anspruch*, the *Anspruch* that springs from an obligation. An *Anspruch*, however, may also originate in a real right (*dinglicher Recht*) and is then called a *dinglicher Anspruch*. The *Herausgabeanspruch* ex § 985 is an example of such an *Anspruch*. A *dinglicher Anspruch* comes into being the moment the real right is violated. If a thing is stolen, for instance, the owner is given an *Anspruch* as against the thief for the return of the thing.

Here again the notion of *Anspruch* is used in the two different meanings set out above. On the one side *Anspruch* indicates that the owner can go to court to have his right of ownership enforced against the defendant's will (right of action: the revindication). On the other side, the notion of *Anspruch* is used to denote the claim against the thief for the return of the object. Unlike the right of action the latter claim is not distinct from the *subjektive Recht* of ownership: it embodies the right of ownership, it is a concretization of the *subjektive Recht*.

Once more, the difference becomes apparent when the *Herausgabeanspruch* is barred because of prescription.[126] The owner will not be able to have his right enforced in court against the defendant's will. Yet, the prescription does not affect his right of ownership and consequently the possessor is still under a duty to

---

124   Staudinger-Peters, § 194, Rdnr. 23.
125   The creditor can still bring an action, but if the debtor invokes his *exceptio*, he cannot be compelled to pay.
126   Here the prescription period is 30 years (§ 195 BGB).

return the stolen object.[127] If the thief returns the object he cannot claim it back when afterwards he thinks better of it: he has no right over the thing.

The true meaning of § 931

Now the following question arises: what is really meant when § 931 BGB says we should transfer the *dinglicher Herausgabeanspruch*? Is it the right of action or the subjective right itself?[128] If it is the subjective right it would be more straightforward to say that the subjective right should be transferred, rather than its *Herausgabeanspruch*. On the other side, if the right of action is meant, German law has chosen for an illogical solution: in order to transfer its cause (the subjective right) the result (the right of action) should be transferred.

It is quite possible that nonetheless the drafting commissions had in mind the right of action. For, in the 19th century it was generally accepted that a right of action[129] could be transferred.[130] This applied to the revindication as well: it could be transferred independently of the underlying right of ownership. If the revindication was assigned, ownership did not immediately pass to the assignee. Only when the assignee got hold of the object did he acquire ownership.[131] Paragraph 931 may have been drafted in accordance with this former theory of the *gemeines Recht*.[132]

Be that as it may, it is nowadays generally acknowledged that a right of action, such as the revindication, cannot be transferred, at least not independently of the right of ownership.[133] As Von Tuhr expressed it, the revindication is an indispensable safeguard of ownership which the owner cannot transfer without simultaneously giving up his right of ownership.[134] The passing of the revindication to the acquirer should not be seen as a prerequisite for the transfer of ownership but rather as a consequence of it: the right of ownership itself is transferred and as a result the revindication passes to the acquirer.

Since reading the term *Herausgabeanspruch* as the right of action would be illogical, we should assume that in these cases *Herausgabeanspruch* stands for the

---

127 Acquisition of ownership by way of prescription (§ 937) applies to possessors in good faith only.

128 From the *Motive* and *Protokolle* we can infer that here the right of action, the revindication, should be transferred. See Mugdan, vol. 3, p. 222 and 628.

129 It was usually called transfer of the *Klage*: see L. Arndts von Arnesberg, Lehrbuch der Pandekten, 10th ed., Stuttgart 1879, § 112. The word denoted the right of action. After Windscheid's concept of *Anspruch* became more and more established *Klage* was gradually replaced with *Anspruch*: see for example Windscheid/Kipp, vol. 2, § 337.

130 Perhaps this theory was also a result of the difficulty to distinguish between right and right of action.

131 Windscheid/Kipp, vol. 2, § 337 (especially fn. 1 and sub 4).

132 See for example K.H. Neumayer, Die sogenannte Vindikationszession (§ 931 BGB) im dogmatischen Spannungsfeld zwischen Übereignung und procuratio in rem, in: K. Kuchinke (ed.), Rechtsbewahrung und Rechtsentwicklung, Festschrift für Heinrich Lange zum 70. Geburtstag, Munich 1970, p. 305-324, at p. 318-320.

133 Staudinger-Wiegand, 1995, § 931, Rdnr. 13-16 and Staudinger-Gursky, 1993, § 985, Rdnr. 3; Münchener-Quack, § 931, Rdnr. 18 and Münchener-Medicus, Vorbem. § 985, Rdnr. 5.

134 Von Tuhr, Allgemeiner Teil I, p. 266.

right of ownership. As a consequence, in the second group of § 931 cases, in which the owner has no possession of the thing, ownership is transferred merely by *Einigung*, the real agreement between the transferor and transferee.[135] So, the *Einigung* needs to regard the passing of ownership only. The parties' will need not regard the assignment of the revindication as well.[136]

Apart from this historical and theoretical argument there is a practical argument for this interpretation as well. Namely it offers a solution for the transfer of things without possessor. Literally § 931 requires that a third person be in possession of the thing. Yet it is generally accepted that it applies also to cases where no one is in possession of the thing, for example because of loss.[137] In such instances assignment of the revindication will be impossible, as there is no revindication. The transfer of ownership will nonetheless be possible, as it takes place simply on the basis of the *Einigung* between transferor and transferee. The practical need of this lies in the transfer of stolen or lost objects that are insured. Under many insurance policies the beneficiary must transfer ownership of the object to the insurance company, in exchange for the benefit. Par. 931, as interpreted in this way, enables the owner to execute the transfer simply by making a real agreement.

We have reached the following conclusions. Where the owner is in indirect possession, he should transfer his indirect possession. If he has no possession at all, it will suffice for him to make a real agreement with the acquirer.

5 Privilege to dispose (*Verfügungsbefugnis*)

5.1 The privilege to dispose and its sources

Another condition for a valid transfer, though unmentioned in § 929 BGB, is that the transferor should have *Verfügungsbefugnis*.[138] The term *Verfügung* in the German civil code is an extension of the word *Veräußerung* (transfer, *alienatio*)[139] and derives from 19th century legal science.[140] Late 19th century pandectism used the term *Verfügung* as an umbrella term covering not only the transfer (*Veräußerung*) of ownership or another asset (such as a claim or a limited real right) but also the creation, alteration or release of a limited real right.[141] Accordingly the word *Verfügungsbefugnis* indicates the legal privilege to transfer a certain asset, to burden it with a limited real right, to release a right, or to change the contents of a

---

135   Wolff/Raiser, p. 246; Westermann, § 42 II 4b; Baur/Stürner § 51 F II 2.
136   Wolff/Raiser, p. 246; Von Tuhr, Allgemeiner Teil I, p. 266, fn. 105.
137   Staudinger-Wiegand, 1995, § 931, Rdnr. 17; Münchener-Quack, § 931, Rdnr. 11.
138   Münchener-Quack, § 929, Rdnr. 108.
139   Von Tuhr, Allgemeiner Teil II, § 54, fn. 1.
140   See W. Wilhelm, Begriff und Theorie der Verfügung, in: H. Coing and W. Wilhelm (eds.), Wissenschaft und Kodifikation des Privatrechts im 19. Jahrhundert, vol. 2, Frankfurt a/M 1977, p. 213 et seq.
141   For other examples of *Verfügung* see Von Tuhr, Allgemeiner Teil II, § 54, I.

right.[142] When discussing the transfer of assets it can be translated with 'privilege to dispose'.

Yet, the term 'privilege' is somewhat vague, to say the least. It is impossible to give a clear definition of the terms *Befugnis* and *Recht*, nor is it possible to indicate any difference between the terms. So, why not translate the term *Verfügungsbefugnis* with 'right to dispose'? The reason is the following. The translation may give the impression that the holder of the right is fully entitled to dispose of the asset. However, having a privilege does not necessarily entail having the right to use the privilege in every individual case. A person may have the privilege to dispose while in the particular circumstances being under a duty not to make use of the privilege. To give an example, the owner of a thing who sells the thing twice and transfers to the second buyer, has the privilege to transfer to the second buyer: he is able to make a valid transfer to the latter. Yet, as against the first buyer he is under a duty not to exercise his privilege in this way. So, the question whether or not a person has *Verfügungsbefugnis* is considered irrespective of the circumstances in which or the person to whom the transfer is made.

The privilege to dispose can originate in three different sources only, which are ownership, a legal act or a special statutory provision.[143] Normally the owner of the asset alone has the privilege of disposing of the asset. Ownership entails the privilege to dispose; it is one of the privileges belonging to the right of ownership. In exceptional cases, however, a statutory provision may take away this privilege and confer it on another person. For example, if the owner is declared bankrupt the privilege to dispose of his property is taken away from him and given to an *Insolvenzverwalter*. The bankrupt remains owner of his assets. Yet, to prevent him from dealing with his assets and to enable the *Insolvenzverwalter* to realize the assets, the bankrupt's privilege to dispose is transferred to the *Insolvenzverwalter* (§ 80 subs. 1 *Insolvenzordnung*[144]).

The example we have just seen shows us that a special statutory provision can be the source of the privilege to dispose. In this case the statutory provision is § 80 subs. 1 *Insolvenzordnung*: it gives a non-owner a privilege to dispose. Another example of a statutory provision offering a privilege to dispose is § 1242 BGB that enables the *Pfandgläubiger* (the pledgee) to sell the pledged goods.

A privilege to dispose can also originate in a legal act. As long as the owner himself has the privilege to dispose he may grant a similar privilege to another person, so that this person is able to make a valid transfer without having ownership. Under § 185, subs. 1 BGB, a non-owner can validly make a transfer if the owner has granted permission in advance (this permission is called *Einwilligung*) or afterwards (in which case it is called *Genehmigung*). In the second instance the transfer is void at the outset, but becomes valid if the owner subsequently gives his permission (see § 185, subs. 2). By granting this permission,

---

142   See Von Tuhr, Allgemeiner Teil II, p. 238.
143   Cf. as to Dutch law L. Groefsema, Bevoegd beschikken over andermans recht, (thesis Groningen 1993) Deventer 1993, ch. 3.
144   Statute of 5 October 1994, which came into force 1 January 1999.

in advance or afterwards, the owner confers on the non-owner a privilege to dispose (*Verfügungsbefugnis*). Yet, the owner's privilege to dispose will stay unimpaired: the non-owner receives a duplication of the owner's privilege to dispose.[145]

As an example of granting such a privilege by legal act we can have a look at security rights on trading stock. If goods have been sold and transferred under a retention of ownership clause so that ownership will pass only when the goods are fully paid for, the buyer will in principle be unable to transfer the goods to his customers before he has paid for them. As trading in these goods will render the money needed to pay for the goods, it is common practice for the seller to allow the buyer to sell and transfer the goods to third parties in the ordinary course of business.[146] This permission gives the trader a privilege to dispose of the goods that still belong to the seller.[147] Similarly the pledgee of goods may permit the pledgor to sell and transfer the goods free of the right of pledge. It gives the pledgor a privilege to dispose of the pledgee's right of pledge. The moment the pledgor transfers the goods he releases the right of pledge.

5.2 *Einwilligung* is not a form of agency

The legal notion of *Einwilligung* and *Genehmigung* in § 185 should be distinguished from the notion of *Stellvertretung* (§§ 164 et seq. BGB). In the case of *Stellvertretung* (direct agency) a person, the agent (*Vertreter*), performs a legal act on his principal's account and in name of the principal (*Vertretener*). The agent does not become party to the legal act himself. The legal consequences of the act (any rights, duties etc. arising from it) will affect the principal only. For that reason this form of agency is called direct agency (*unmittelbare Stellvertretung*).[148] The principal is deemed to have performed the legal act himself. If therefore the agent sells any goods as an agent for the principal, a contract of sale will come into being between the principal and the third party buying the goods. Accordingly, the principal will have the seller's rights and duties, whereas the agent will have no rights and duties whatever under the contract of sale, since he is not a party to the contract.

---

145   The permission and consequently the non-owner's privilege of disposal is always related to a specific asset. See Flume, Das Rechtsgeschäft, p. 904. This can be explained by bearing in mind that the permission of § 185 duplicates the owner's privilege of disposal. As set out in ch. 1, § 5 the right of ownership, which the privilege of disposal is part of, forms a relationship between a person (natural or legal) and a specific object. Since the non-owner's privilege of disposal is simply a reproduction of the owner's privilege, the non-owner's privilege must relate to a specific object as well.

146   The latter expression means, among other things, that the buyer should sell the goods at market value.

147   Palandt-Heinrichs, 56th ed., Munich 1997, § 185, Rdnr. 9; Münchener-Schramm, § 185, Rdnr. 34.

148   Also called *offene* (disclosed) *Stellvertretung*.

In principle these consequences occur only when it is apparent to the third party that the agent acts in his principal's name: agency should be disclosed.[149] It should be clear from the agent's declarations or from the circumstances of the case that the agent is acting in his principal's name and does not have the intention to bind himself. If agency is not so disclosed, the agent is deemed to act in his own name. In such a case the agent's intention not to act in his own name but rather in his principal's name is irrelevant and will therefore not be taken into account (see § 164 subs. 2).

If the agent executes a legal act on his principal's account, acting, however, in his own name or without disclosing the agency, the agent himself becomes party to the legal act performed: rights, duties etc. arising from the legal act will be the agent's. This undisclosed form of agency, used for example by the *Kommissionär*[150] (undisclosed commercial agent), is no *Stellvertretung* in the sense of the *Bürgerliches Gesetzbuch*. To distinguish it from real *Stellvertretung* it is called *mittelbare Stellvertretung*[151] (indirect agency). *Einwilligung* as well as *Genehmigung* allow the non-owner to transfer the asset in his own name.[152] The transaction may be on behalf of the owner and on the owner's account, but the transfer itself takes place in the non-owner's name. Hence the non-owner is regarded as the person who transfers the asset. He, not the owner, is the party to that legal act.[153] The transfer will affect the owner only in that he will lose his right of ownership as a result.

An agent, on the contrary, makes a transfer in his principal's name. True, the agent can also be said to have been granted permission, but this is a different sort of permission. It is a privilege to represent his principal (*Vertretungsbefugnis*).[154] He is authorized by the owner (the principal) to make certain legal acts, a sale and transfer for instance, in the principal's name. The principal is deemed to have performed the sale and transfer himself. For this reason the legal acts are directly binding upon the principal. The agent, on the other hand, is not bound by the acts. The legal acts and their consequences are attributed to the principal. Since the principal is regarded as having made the legal act himself it is unnecessary for the agent to have a privilege to dispose. The agent does not need this privilege; it suffices for him to have a privilege to represent, that is, the privilege to bind the

---

149 An exception to this principle of disclosure is the so-called *verdecktes Geschäft für denjenigen den es angeht* (unrevealed legal act for whom it concerns). The concept denotes direct agency for an undisclosed principal. This undisclosed agency is valid provided that it is indifferent to the third party whom he contracts with. When the legal act is a cash purchase, the principal will be party to the contract even though the agent did not make clear that he acted for his principal. See Larenz, Allgemeiner Teil, p. 604-605 and Flume, das Rechtsgeschäft, p. 767 et seq.

150 See § 383 *Handelsgesetzbuch*.

151 It is also called *verdeckte* (undisclosed) *Stellvertretung*.

152 Flume, Das Rechtsgeschäft, p. 902 and 904.

153 Flume, Das Rechtsgeschäft, p. 904.

154 See also Von Tuhr, Allgemeiner Teil II, p. 374.

principal. By representing his principal the agent, so to speak, makes use of the principal's privilege to dispose.[155]

5.3 Power to dispose

Above the notion of *Verfügungsbefugnis* has been described as the privilege to dispose of an asset. At the same time, however, the definition had to be restricted by pointing out the limited sources from which a privilege to dispose can arise. The question whether or not a person is privileged to dispose depends on a few factors only. The privilege can stem from ownership, legal act or a statutory provision. A person who is privileged to dispose has the ability to dispose. One could say he has a power to dispose. The privilege to dispose always gives a power to dispose.

However, in exceptional cases a person may be capable of transferring an asset even though he has no privilege to dispose. In principle the transfer is invalid when made by a person not having a privilege to dispose. Yet, under certain conditions a bona fide acquirer is protected against the transferor lacking the privilege to dispose (see § 932 et seq. BGB). If a third party is so protected the transfer is nonetheless valid. Here the transferor has the capacity to transfer, although he has no privilege to dispose. I would suggest calling this ability to transfer a 'power to dispose'.[156]

Using the word 'power to dispose' as described above offers a uniform term for every instance in which a person has the ability to make a valid transfer, whether or not he has the privilege to do so. Furthermore it shows more clearly a characteristic which the transfer to a bona fide third party and the transfer under § 185 have in common. In both situations a non-owner is given the power to transfer another person's asset. In the former instance, however, the transferor has in addition a privilege to dispose.

Another advantage of using the notion of 'power to dispose' is that it enables us to give a sharp analysis of the transfer to a bona fide third party, an analysis which applies not only to German law but also to Dutch law. In certain circumstances

---

155   Cf. Hellwig, Wesen und subjektive Begrenzung der Rechtskraft, Eine prozessuale Abhandlung mit Beiträgen zum bürgerlichen Recht, insbesondere zur Lehre von der Rechtsnachfolge und der Verfügungsmacht des Nichtberechtigten, Leipzig 1901, p. 100-101.

156   The notion of 'power of disposal' should not be confused with the German expression *Verfügungsmacht*. Although it may seem to indicate a power to dispose, it is generally regarded as synonymous with *Verfügungsbefugnis*. I would nevertheless suggest using the term *Verfügungsbefugnis* to indicate the privilege to dispose and the term *Verfügungsmacht* to indicate the power to dispose. In Dutch the appropriate equivalents would be *beschikkingsbevoegdheid* and *beschikkingsmacht*.

Hellwig does make a distinction between the two terms, though a distinction slightly different from the one I suggest. See: Hellwig, Wesen und subjektive Begrenzung der Rechtskraft, p. 96 et seq. See also: Hellwig, Lehrbuch des Deutschen Civilprozeßrechts, vol. 1, Leipzig 1903, p. 275; Crome, who does not distinguish between the two terms says that where the third party is protected the transferor has *Verfügungsmacht* and is *befugt* (privileged) to dispose of the thing. See C. Crome, System des deutschen bürgerlichen Rechts, vol. 1 (Einleitung und Allgemeiner Teil), Tübingen/Leipzig 1900, p. 314.

these legal systems protect a bona fide acquirer of a movable against the transferor not being privileged to dispose of the asset. If, for instance, a borrower sells and transfers the thing he has borrowed to a third party the buyer may acquire ownership (German law, § 932 BGB; Dutch law, art. 3:86 subs. 1 BW).

It is unsettled whether the second buyer acquires ownership originally or derivatively.[157] One thing is certain: under a special statutory provision protecting the bona fide acquirer the owner loses his ownership and the bona fide third party becomes the new owner. But does the third party derive his ownership from someone else? If so, from whom? Or does he acquire a new right of ownership?[158]

To my mind there are good reasons to claim that it is a real transfer, i.e. a derivative form of acquisition.[159] First, § 932 BGB and art. 3:86 subs. 1 BW protect only against the transferor not being privileged to dispose. That is to say, these provisions will give the bona fide third party ownership only if all other requirements for a valid transfer have been met. The provisions do not cure shortcomings such as voidness, defects of will, incapacity[160] or defects in the transfer of possession. Original acquisition, on the other hand, would cure all shortcomings whatever. Of course, if it is no transfer these defects cannot be of any influence.

Second, original acquisition gives the acquirer a new right. As the old right of ownership lapses so will any limited real rights burdening that right. Is this what § 932 and art. 3:86 subs. 1 intend? It appears not. The purchaser's protection depends on his good faith. If the purchaser of a thing was unaware of a limited real right burdening the thing he will be protected under § 936 BGB or art. 3:86 subs. 2 BW. To give an example, the owner sells a thing which is burdened with a limited real right invisible to the buyer. If the buyer is in good faith and all other requirements for protection have been met he will acquire the thing free of the burden. Let us now take the following example. A bona fide buyer does not know that the seller is a non-owner, but he does know that the thing he wishes to buy is burdened with a right of pledge. If he were to acquire originally he would acquire the thing free of the charge, although he knew of it. Obviously, this solution would not accord with the intention of third party protection. The third party should be protected only against the rights he did not know and should not have known. All

---

157 Von Tuhr, Allgemeiner Teil II, p. 52; Schwab/Prütting, Sachenrecht, § 35, VIII. For an overview of Swiss, French and German opinions about the question see: F. Guisan, La protection de l'acquéreur de bonne foi en matière mobilière, (thesis Lausanne) Lausanne 1970, p. 175-178.

158 J.C. van Oven regards it as an instance of original acquisition: Praeadvies over causa en levering, The Hague 1924, p. 108 and 116-117.

159 The view that this acquisition is derivative is shared by Von Tuhr, Allgemeiner Teil II, p. 52 et seq.; Crome, System des deutschen bürgerlichen Rechts, vol. 1, p. 313-14; Dernburg, Das Bürgerliche Recht des deutschen Reiches und Preußens, vol. 1, p. 316 (Dernburg's arguments, though, are not very clear); Hellwig, Wesen und subjektive Begrenzung der Rechtskraft, p. 96-105; Martin Wolff, Das Recht zum Besitze, Berlin 1903, p. 11.

160 *Geschäftsunfähigkeit* or *handelingsonbekwaamheid*.

other rights should survive the third party's acquisition. Yet, this solution is possible only if the third party's acquisition is regarded as derivative.[161]

We now see that under § 932 and art. 3:86 a non-owner who has no privilege to dispose makes a valid transfer of assets belonging to another person in the same way as a non-owner under § 185 transfers the owner's asset (in the latter case with the owner's consent of course). In these instances the positions of transferor and predecessor in a right,[162] which normally go hand in hand, are separated: the predecessor of the acquirer is the owner, while it is the non-owner who performs the legal act of transfer and therefore is the transferor. Through the legal act of transfer performed by the non-owner an asset passes directly from the owner to the third party.[163]

5.4 Right, privilege and power to represent

Within the concept of agency a distinction can be made between the right, the privilege and the power to represent. Although this subject is a digression it is interesting to have a short look at it because it forms an extra argument for making the distinction between right, privilege and power to dispose. It demonstrates that the distinction has a broader use and that it may be applied also beyond the concept of transfer.

For a valid act of agency the agent must have the privilege to represent the principal: he should have, as it is called, *Vertretungsbefugnis* or *Vertretungsmacht*[164], which I will translate with 'privilege to represent'. This privilege may have various origins. It may be conferred on the agent by the principal, in which case the privilege is called *Vollmacht*. It can also be based on the articles of association of a juridical person or directly on a statutory provision.[165]

The privilege to represent should be distinguished from the underlying legal relationship between the principal and his agent on which the privilege is based, the so-called inner relationship (*Innenverhältnis*). The inner relationship, which indicates the purpose for which the privilege has been granted may impose duties on the agent to make use of the privilege in a certain way or determine to which extent and in which way the agent is authorized to use the privilege. Yet, any limitation of the right to represent will work only as between the principal and his agent. The limitations do not determine the scope of the privilege so granted. The privilege may exceed the internal authorization: the agent may have the privilege to represent although he is, as against the principal, under a duty not to use the

---

161 Cf. Hellwig, Wesen und subjektive Begrenzung der Rechtskraft, p. 102.
162 In the case of succession in a right (*Rechtsnachfolge* or *rechtsopvolging*) the previous holder of the right is called *Rechtsvorgänger* or *rechtsvoorganger*, the subsequent holder *Rechtsnachfolger* or *rechtsopvolger*.
163 Cf. Hellwig, Wesen und subjektive Begrenzung der Rechtskraft, p. 103-104.
164 Like *Verfügungsbefugnis* and *Verfügungsmacht* both terms are commonly treated as identical.
165 For example parents and guardians derive their privilege to represent from a statutory provision. Cf. § 1629 (parents) and § 1793 (*Vormund*, guardian of a minor).

privilege in this manner. When, for instance, the agent is instructed to sell a certain thing at the best price and he sells it for a considerably lower price, he acts contrary to his duty, his authorization. He has no right to represent in this case. However, in principle the legal act falls within the scope of his privilege to represent and is therefore binding upon the principal.[166,167]

It is often said that the internal relationship determines what the agent is allowed to do (the *Dürfen*), whereas the privilege determines what he is able to do (the *Können*). Be that as it may, defining the privilege as the ability or capacity to represent would be misleading. The privilege, it is true, determines the ability as against the general public to represent the principal, but as against certain persons the scope of this ability is even broader, so that the agent is able to bind his principal although he has no privilege to do so.

When the agent exceeds his privilege to represent or when he has lost or has never had the privilege, a situation which is called *Vertretung ohne Vertretungsmacht* (agency without privilege to represent), a bona fide third party will in some cases be protected against the agent's lack of privilege. If the pretence of the agent being privileged to represent can be imputed to the principal (on the basis of fault or risk[168]), the legal act performed will often be binding on the principal.[169]

Thus, where protection is available for the bona fide third party, the agent is able to bind his principal, even though he has no privilege to represent him. He could be said to have a power to represent. This distinction between privilege and power to represent is parallel to the distinction I suggested earlier between the privilege and the power to dispose: a person not having the privilege to dispose may still be

---

166   Larenz, Allgemeiner Teil, p. 616.
167   For the history and development of the distinction between *Mandat* (which determines the right to represent) and *Vollmacht* (the privilege to represent) see W. Müller-Freienfels, Die Abstraktion der Vollmachtserteilung im 19. Jahrhundert, in: Coing and Wilhelm (eds.), Wissenschaft und Kodifikation des Privatrechts im 19. Jahrhundert, vol. 2, p. 144 et seq. In German law the distinction between the right and the privilege to represent was elaborated in the second half of the 19th century by, among others, Jhering, Goldschmidt, Brinz and Laband. See Müller-Freienfels, p. 158-164.

The distinction aims at protecting third parties against unusual limitations in the agent's right to represent which they should not expect. In most cases third parties will have no knowledge of such limitations. To protect them it should be impossible for the principal to set up these limitations to third parties. For that reason the restrictions work only as between the principal and agent. Case law, though, has accepted some exceptions to this rule: if the third party is aware of the agent acting contrary to his principal's instructions and interests, the instructions may still prevent the agent from binding his principal. See Müller-Freienfels, p. 198 et seq.

168   An example: if an employee has been appointed to a certain function a bona fide third party may assume that the employee has the privilege to represent needed to fulfil his function properly. The employer cannot set up unusual limitations within the *Vollmacht* to the third party: they are for the employer's risk. See Palandt-Heinrichs (1997), § 173, Rdnr. 21.
169   See §§ 170, 171 and 172 BGB; see also Larenz, Allgemeiner Teil, p. 628, 636, 639 and 641. The concept of *Vertretung ohne Vertretungsmacht* offers additional protection next to the rule that certain restrictions of the agent's right to represent cannot be set up against third parties.

able and therefore have the power to transfer an asset if the third party acquirer is protected.[170]

Clearly, *Vertretungsbefugnis* or *Vertretungsmacht* cannot be defined as the ability to represent. Such a definition, which can be found in many German textbooks, would turn the common expression *Vertretung ohne Vertretungsmacht* into a contradiction in terms. It would seem to say: the agent is able to bind his principal even though he has no ability to do so. However, when distinguishing between the terms privilege and power, the expression makes sense and tells us the following: the agent may have the power to bind his principal even where he has no privilege to do so.

6 *Traditio* by agents

6.1 The dogmatic problem

The subject of agency offers a good illustration of the practical consequences of the current theories on possession. As we have seen modern German law holds that in most cases the transfer of possession should not be seen as a legal act. As agency is possible only in regard to legal acts, this view seems to rule out the possibility to use an agent for the *traditio* of movables.[171]

Yet, not every form of *traditio* is ruled out by this opinion. Where possession is transferred by mere agreement (the *traditio ficta* mentioned in § 854 subs. 2) there is no problem, since the agreement needed is regarded as a legal act. Similarly agency is possible where *Übergabe* substitutes are used: also here the act of transfer consists exclusively of one or more legal acts: the real agreement, which is required for any transfer of property, and in some instances an additional legal act. When the transfer is executed by way of *traditio brevi manu* (§ 929 subs. 2) the real agreement suffices. Under § 930 (*constitutum possessorium*) in addition a *Besitzmittlungsverhältnis* should be created. And § 931, finally, requires in some cases assignment of a *Herausgabeanspruch*. All these requirements are legal acts; there is no 'factual act' needed, such as the transfer of physical possession. Consequently, in all these instances agency can be used.

On the other hand, *traditio vera* (§ 854 subs. 1) is regarded as a *Realakt* or *Rechtshandlung*, that is to say, a factual act rather than a legal act. As a result agency in the strict sense of the word (*Stellvertretung*) is impossible here. The unavailability of agency is a conclusion that logically follows from the view that the transfer of possession is a factual act, a view that in its turn is a logical conclusion from the

---

170 I would suggest to use the terms *Vertretungsbefugnis* to indicate the privilege to represent and the term *Vertretungsmacht* to indicate the power to represent. Dutch equivalents would be *vertegenwoordigingsbevoegdheid* and *vertegenwoordigingsmacht*.

171 As consensual transfer systems like French law and the English Sale of Goods Act do not require a transfer of possession the problem occurs only in tradition systems. For that reason the concept of agency will be discussed only in regard to German and Dutch law.

definition that possession is a fact. Yet, the conclusion is unnecessary and wrong, as I have shown above. A distinction should be made between possession as a fact and possession as a right. Moreover, the conclusion turns back a long-standing tradition: already in classical Roman law possession could be transferred and acquired through free persons,[172] a viewpoint which was recognized also in the German *gemeines Recht* which regarded these instances as agency.[173] In addition, ruling out agency in the transfer and acquisition of possession is difficult to reconcile with the concept of *constitutum possessorium* in § 930 of the German civil code, which has often been regarded as a case where the transferee acquires possession through the agency of the transferor.[174,175]

---

172   Kaser I, p. 393. F. Schulz, Classical roman law, Oxford 1951 (repr. Aalen 1992), p. 438-39. In classical law the free person had to be a *procurator*. In Justinianian law possession could be acquired through any free person. See Inst. 2,9,5.

173   Windscheid/Kipp, Lehrbuch des Pandektenrechts, vol. 1, § 155; Dernburg, Pandekten, vol. 1, § 180.

174   See for instance Azo, Summa Codicis, on C. 7,32, ed. Pavia 1506, (repr. Turin 1966, p. 276): 'Thus possession is acquired through whoever is in possession in my name.' (Item quaeritur [possessio] per quemcumque qui meo nomine sit in possessione.). See also *Glossa Ordinaria*, gloss *ministerio* on D. 41,2,18, pr. In Cels. D. 41,2,18, pr., the famous text in which Celsus describes the *constitutum possessorium*, the following is said: '...I cease to possess and I make another person possessor through my service. And indeed, to possess and to possess in another's name are not the same thing: for possessor is the person in whose name something is possessed; the procurator renders service to another's possession' (...desino possidere et alium possessorem ministerio meo facio. nec idem est possidere et alieno nomine possidere: nam possidet, cuius nomine possidetur, procurator alienae possessioni praestat ministerium). Among the glossators the view that *constitutum* amounts to agency is prominent but not generally accepted. Cf. W.M. Gordon, Studies in the transfer of property by traditio, Aberdeen 1970, p. 107-109. The view seems to have been dominant among the commentators (cf. Gordon, p. 147-148). In the *gemeines Recht* of the 19th century it was generally recognized. Cf. Windscheid/Kipp, vol. 1, § 155. Note that in Roman law agency was still unknown. True, possession could be acquired through a procurator, but only later was this regarded as an instance of agency. For that reason the translation of D. 41,2,18, pr. by J.A.C. Thomas (in A. Watson (ed.), The Digest of Justinian) may be misleading: it translates *ministerio meo* with *through my agency* and *alienae possessioni praestat ministerium* with *provides the agency of another's possession*, thus wrongly conveying the impression that Roman law recognized agency as a technical concept. De Zulueta translates these passages with *through my instrumentality* and *supplies the instrumentality for the possession of another*. See F. de Zulueta, Digest 41,1 & 2, Oxford 1950 (repr. Aalen 1979), p. 97.

175   The concepts of *constitutum possessorium* recognized by the Dutch civil code in art. 3:115 sub a is a strong indication that also in Dutch law possession may be acquired through an agent. Yet in Dutch literature hardly anything has been written about the problem. Some leading authors acknowledge without any further explanation that an agent can be used for the transfer and acquisition of possession. See for example Mijnssen in Asser/Mijnssen/De Haan, nr. 219, and Reehuis in Reehuis/Heisterkamp, Goederenrecht 1994, nr. 300 and 304, who seems to share this view. However, they do not expressly draw the conclusion that in this view the transfer of possession must be regarded as a legal act.

6.2 Using *Besitzdiener* or *Besitzmittler*

To solve this problem which German theory got itself into it had to find other means to reach the same result. Accordingly it created something akin to agency: the use of *Besitzdiener* and *Besitzmittler* to transfer possession.[176] Whenever you would need to use an agent to transfer or acquire possession, you may instead order another person to participate in the transfer as a *Besitzdiener* or *Besitzmittler*. The transfer of possession by or to a *Besitzdiener* or *Besitzmittler* will be attributed to the principal for whom he acts.

The transferor may instruct one of his employees, who has actual power over the asset, to hand the asset over to the transferee. Since the employee, a *Besitzdiener*, is merely exercising his superior's possession without himself being possessor the superior is deemed to have transferred his possession personally. Similarly, when the object is handed over to one of the acquirer's subordinates possession is deemed to have been transferred to the superior, while the subordinate has become a mere *Besitzdiener*.

Furthermore the transferor and transferee can use a *Besitzmittler* in the process of transferring possession. A transferor who has indirect *Eigenbesitz* may instruct his *Besitzmittler*, the direct *Fremdbesitzer*, to hand the object over to the transferee. If the *Besitzmittler* follows the instructions and passes the object to the acquirer this legal act is attributed to the indirect possessor so that it is regarded as *Übergabe* by him.[177] Similarly the acquirer may instruct a person to accept possession of an object as *Besitzmittler* for him with the result that the acquirer receives indirect possession.[178] This is regarded as *Übergabe* to the acquirer. Moreover, the above instances may be dovetailed so that both transferor and acquirer make use of their own *Besitzmittler* or *Besitzdiener*. To give an example: A, the owner and possessor of a car, who has lent the car to B, needs to transfer possession of the car to his buyer C. The buyer does not want to use the car himself but plans to lease it to D. Accordingly he instructs the seller A to hand the car over directly to D, the lessee. A on his turn will have to instruct his *Besitzmittler* B to hand the car over to D. Thus, in fact B hands the object over to D, but it is regarded as a *traditio* between A and C.[179]

---

176 Von Tuhr, Allgemeiner Teil III, p. 373; Windscheid/Kipp, Lehrbuch des Pandektenrechts, vol. 1, p. 788 and 789; Westermann, § 14.

177 M. Martinek, Traditionsprinzip und *Geheißerwerb*, AcP 188 (1988), p. 588-589.

178 It should be marked that creating a *Besitzmittlungsverhältnis* (*Besitzmittler* relation) between the transferor and the acquirer does not amount to *Übergabe*, but is rather seen as an *Übergabe* substitute (*constitutum possessorium*, § 930 BGB).

179 In this example B, the transferor's *Besitzmittler*, transfers immediate *Fremdbesitz* to D, the acquirer's *Besitzmittler*, B and D being two distinct persons. It should not be confused with the situation in which the transferor's *Besitzmittler* is changed into the acquirer's *Besitzmittler*: the latter example does not amount to an *Übergabe* within the meaning of § 929, but is rather the substitute for *Übergabe* mentioned in § 931. See Wolff/Raiser, Sachenrecht, p. 235.

Let us examine two possible instances: an 'agent' acting on the transferor's side and an 'agent' acting on the acquirer's side.[180] And let us assume that in both cases a *traditio vera* of the object is needed. In the first instance, in which the agent is acting for the transferor, the agent will have actual control over the object being a *Besitzdiener* or a *Besitzmittler*. An employee of a company, for example, delivering goods to its customers, is regarded as a *Besitzdiener*. If ordered so by his principal, the *Besitzherr*, to deliver the goods to the customers and the agent acts accordingly, the principal, as we have seen, is deemed to have transferred possession himself.[181]

In the second instance the transferee orders his agent to accept possession of the thing for him. When the agent acts according to the order and accepts possession for the transferee, the latter will become possessor. The agent, who has actual power over the thing, will become a *Besitzdiener* if he is a subordinate of the principal, and a *Besitzmittler* if he is not.

Oddly, in German law these are not seen as instances of agency in the strict sense of the word, i.e. *Stellvertretung*[182], although they have similar legal consequences: in reality the transfer of possession is performed by an 'agent' for the benefit of the transferor or transferee, yet it is deemed that *Eigenbesitz* (*possessio*), passes directly from the transferor to the acquirer. Why not call this agency? Just because of a certain dogmatic definition of possession? The example of *traditio* by agents demonstrates clearly that the transfer of possession should be regarded as a legal act. In excluding the possibility of agency German law again fails to distinguish possession as a fact from possession as a right. When making this distinction the cases of agency can be explained as follows. Physical possession is transferred via the agent, yet the right of possession passes directly from the transferor to the transferee. That is to say, a factual act performed by the agent has a legal effect, the *traditio*, which is attributed to the principal.

---

180 Of course the transferor and transferee can both use an agent at the same time.
181 Likewise, if by order of the indirect possessor the direct possessor of an object, the *Besitzmittler*, a lessee for instance, hands the object over to a third party, the indirect possessor is deemed to have transferred possession to the third party.
182 Von Tuhr, Allgemeiner Teil III, p. 372; Westermann, § 14.

3   The French transfer system

1 Introduction

1.1 Consensual transfer system

French law has a consensual transfer system. It is said that the contract itself transfers ownership of the thing to the acquirer. This is often referred to as *effet translatif des obligations* (translative effect of obligations). It presupposes, of course, that the transferor is owner of the asset or that he has been given permission by the owner to make the transfer. Unlike in English law the principle of consensualism is not confined to contracts of sale: it applies to all contractual obligations, as we can learn from the general formulation of articles 711 and 1138 of the *Code Civil*. For specific types of contract the principle is restated in articles 938 (*donation*, gift), 1583 (*vente*, sale) and 1703 (*échange*, barter). Article 1138, though, is commonly considered as the principal article in which the *solo consensu* rule is laid down. It reads as follows: 'The obligation to transfer a thing is performed by the sole consensus between the contracting parties. It makes its creditor owner and places the thing at the latter's risk the moment it ought to have been transferred, even if a transfer of possession has not taken place,...'[1] In article 1583 the principle is concentrated on the contract of sale: 'It [the contract of sale] is performed between the parties, and ownership is acquired by the buyer as against the seller the moment they have agreed about the thing and the price, even if the thing has not yet been delivered or the price not yet been paid.'[2] *Traditio*, transfer of possession, is not required: in principle mere consensus suffices.

However, the *solo consensu* rule is subject to some very important exceptions. First of all, the *solo consensu* principle is confined to specific goods. Where generic goods are sold ownership cannot pass at the moment the contract is made. Moreover, the rule applies only to specific goods that are in existence at the moment the contract is made: ownership of future goods is excepted from the *solo consensu* rule. As a

---

1   Art. 1138: 'L'obligation de livrer la chose est parfaite par le seul consentement des parties contractantes. Elle rend le créancier propriétaire et met la chose à ses risques dès l'instant où elle a dû être livrée, encore que la tradition n'en ait point été faite,...'

The term *parfaite* may derive from the Roman law term *perfectus*. In Roman law a contract of sale (*emptio venditio*) was said to be *perfecta* (definitive) in principle when there was agreement about the object and the price. See Paul. D. 18,6,8 and Kaser I, p. 552-553 and Zimmermann, The law of obligations, p. 284. At the moment the contract was *perfecta*, commonly the moment the contract was made, the risk of the goods passed to the buyer: from that time accidental loss or deterioration of the goods sold was at the buyer's risk. Yet, ownership did not pass until possession had been transferred to the buyer (*traditio*). Pothier also uses the term *parfait* to denote the moment when risk passes. See for example his *Traité du contrat de vente*, part 4, nrs. 307-312, Œuvres de Pothier, vol. 3, Paris 1847, p. 123 et seq.

2   Art. 1583: 'Elle est parfaite entre les parties, et la propriété est acquise de droit à l'acheteur à l'égard du vendeur, dès qu'on est convenu de la chose et du prix, quoique la chose n'ait pas encore été livrée ni le prix payé.' Article 1703, which is about the passing of ownership in the case of barter, simply refers to the article on sale.

result, in commerce, where most sales are for an amount of generic goods, the *solo consensu* rule applies only in the smaller number of cases: existing specific things.

Another important mitigation of the *solo consensu* rule, one which is normally overlooked, is that the rule applies only to the obligation to transfer ownership of the thing (*obligation de livrer*). Consequently a contract of sale is self-executing only on the side of the seller. The buyer's obligation to pay for the thing cannot be self-executing.[3]

1.2 Identity of goods

As the *solo consensu* rule is confined to specific goods it is important to know when goods are regarded as specific or rather generic. The first category consists of goods the identity of which is exactly known, for example the sale of certain antique furniture or a painting. All goods that are not specific can be called generic goods. Typically generic goods are for example wheat, coal and oil: goods that are sold in certain quantities. It is normally irrelevant to the buyer which wheat or oil he receives, as long as it meets the quality standards he is entitled to expect under the contract.

At first sight, the distinction between specific goods and generic goods seems to lie in the nature of the goods themselves, specific goods being of a unique nature and generic goods being goods that are not unique and can therefore be replaced by other goods with exactly the same characteristics. However, in reality the question whether goods are specific or generic does not depend on their nature but on the contract between the parties. Goods which most people consider to be generic can be specific to others. It simply depends on what the parties have agreed.

Let us take as an example the sale of a Bösendorfer piano. Someone who cannot hear the difference in sound between pianos of the same type does not care which piano is eventually delivered to him, as long as it is of the right type and colour. In this contract the piano is regarded as a generic thing. Yet, someone who does notice the difference will select a certain piano and insist on delivery of that specific Bösendorfer. Here the piano is a specific thing.

In English law the category of generic goods divides into wholly unascertained goods and quasi-specific goods.[4] To give an example, if there is a contract for the sale of 25 tons of wheat of a certain quality which the seller is entitled to draw from any source available to him the goods are wholly unascertained. Where, on the other hand, the parties have agreed that the contract goods should be taken from

---

3 This reduces the *effet translatif des obligations* to one side of the transaction only, as Professor Rudden asserted in one of our discussions. Besides, it should be noted that most payments are made from one to the other bank account, in which case the concept of ownership does not apply. As to money the concept of ownership applies only to banknotes and coins. Yet, even if the contract stipulates that the buyer should pay in banknotes and coins ownership of the money cannot pass before certain banknotes or coins are identified as the means of payment.

4 See chapter 4, § 3.1.

a specified source, for example a specified silo containing 100 tons, the goods are called quasi-specific. These are *generic* goods to be taken from a *specified* source.

The distinction between wholly unascertained and quasi-specific goods is useful to French law as well. The importance lies in the way these goods may become specified. If the source of the goods has been specified the seller is not allowed to deliver goods drawn from another source. When in the above example there are two buyers, the first buying 75 tons and the second 25 tons, 75 tons should be removed and appropriated to the first contract. Because of the reduction of the bulk the remaining goods (25 tons) become identified without any act of individualisation being needed. For it is certain that these goods should be transferred to the second buyer. The quantity left matches exactly the quantity sold, and the seller is not allowed to deliver other goods. Similarly the quantity in the silo may decrease as a result of loss or damage. If there is a contract for the sale of 25 tons of wheat to be taken from a silo containing 100 tons, and water damages 80 tons in the silo the remaining 20 tons become identified as a result of exhaustion. In English law these instances of individualisation by reduction of quantity are called appropriation by exhaustion. So whereas wholly unascertained goods always require individualisation by the transferor and transferee, quasi-specific goods may become ascertained by exhaustion, without (but not against) the parties' consent.

1.3 The principle of specificity

The exception to the *solo consensu* rule that ownership of generic goods cannot pass at the moment the contract is made can be logically explained. Like the law of property of the Netherlands, Germany and many other European legal systems French property law is based on the principle of specificity.[5] According to this principle real rights can exist only in relation to specific assets. The rule applies to ownership as well as to limited real rights. It must always be known to which specific asset a real right relates. Ownership of a quantity of goods can exist only if it is known which specific assets are subject to the right of ownership. Consequently the transfer of ownership is impossible if it is unknown which specific goods are to be transferred to the acquirer. As the problem of identity of goods and the principle of specificity have given rise to an amendment of the English Sale of Goods Act 1979 the question and its theoretical foundation will be discussed in detail in chapter 4.

2 Real agreement in French law

It is traditionally said that in French law the contract itself transfers ownership of the thing to the acquirer (*effet translatif des obligations*). Still, for various reasons which I will explain below I think it would be useful to apply the concept of real

---

5   Cf. for instance C. Larroumet, annotation on Cour d'Appel de Paris, 14 October 1997, D 1998 J 91.

agreement also to the French transfer of ownership. Yet, before analysing the systematic arguments in support of the real agreement we should examine the history of the French transfer system, as it illustrates the gradual metamorphosis from a tradition system to a consensual system. It will reveal that the contrast between tradition systems and consensual systems is far less sharp than is usually thought. Moreover, the survey of this development could be used as an extra argument, though not a decisive argument, for accepting the concept of real agreement in French law.

2.1 History

Before the Napoleonic *Code Civil* from 1804 French law required a *traditio* for the transfer of immovable as well as movable property.[6] The requirement applied to the whole of France, even though French law did not form a uniform system in this period. French law consisted of two different legal systems. In the south of France Roman law was the dominant source of law. These regions were called *pays de droit écrit* (regions of written law), *écrit* indicating that the law was to be found in Justinian's *Corpus Iuris Civilis* and the writings of learned jurists.[7] As a matter of course the *traditio* requirement applied in these regions, since the requirement was Roman law.[8] Yet, a comparable requirement applied in the north of France, where customary law predominated and where Roman law was used only as a last resort (*pays de droit coutumier*, regions of customary law).[9] In these regions the transfer of land required a procedure called *investiture réelle* (real investiture).[10]

Now, the *traditio* requirement was gradually being eroded as in many instances a true transfer of direct possession (*tradition réelle*) was no longer needed. Often a simple declaration that possession had been transferred replaced the actual transfer that was required originally.

As far as Roman law is concerned the *traditio* requirement was considerably mitigated already in classical Roman law (the first two and a half centuries AD[11]). In this period forms of *traditio* were acknowledged in which no transfer of direct

---

6   Mazeaud/Chabas, Leçons de droit civil, vol. II, 2, Biens: droit de propriété et ses démembrements, Paris 1989, p. 324.

7   See R.C. van Caenegem, An historical introduction to private law, Cambridge 1992, p. 27.

8   Paul. D. 41,1,31, pr: 'Numquam nuda traditio transfert dominium, sed ita, si venditio aut aliqua iusta causa praecesserit, propter quam traditio sequeretur'; Kaser I, p. 416-417. See also Pothier, Traité du droit de domaine de propriété, part 1, ch. 2, section 4, and Traité des obligations, part 1, ch. 2, article 2, Œuvres de Pothier, vol. 9, p. 168 et seq. and vol. 2, p. 70 et seq.

9   As to the order of the different sources of law in these regions, see: H. Kooiker, Lex scripta abrogata, De derde Renaissance van het Romeinse recht, Deel I, De uitwendige ontwikkeling, (thesis Groningen 1996) Nijmegen 1996, p. 161 et seq.

10 J. Brissaud, Manuel d'histoire du droit privé à l'usage des étudiants en licence et en doctorat, nouvelle édition, Paris 1935, p. 308.

11 Kaser I, p. 2.

possession[12] took place: *constitutum possessorium* and *traditio brevi manu*, as they were later to be named.[13] From the period of the glossators these forms of *traditio ficta* have been disseminated over the continent alongside the Roman law requirement of *traditio*. As a result, in the south of France the requirement of *traditio* did not necessarily involve a transfer of direct possession.

Also in the north of France, the *pays de droit coutumier*, forms of *tradition feinte* were developed.[14] The procedure of *investiture*, that originally had to take place in the presence of the land, was simplified by substituting for the land itself a symbol representing the land, for example a clod of earth.[15] As a result it was no longer needed for the transfer to be executed on the land.[16] Later, during the feudal period, the transfer of feudal lands had to be executed before the lord or his court. The procedure was called *dessaisine-saisine* or *devest-vest*: the transferor, who was a vassal (tenant), returned the land to his *seigneur* (lord) who then granted it to the transferee, the new vassal.[17]

Particularly for the transfer of immovable property forms of fictitious *traditio* were being used on a large scale in pre-civil code law. It had become an established practice for notaries to include falsely in the contracts for the sale of land a passage declaring that possession had been transferred from the seller to the buyer.[18] These passages were called *clauses de dessaisine-saisine*[19] or *clauses de devest-vest*. A similar method was to write in the contract a clause that possession had been transferred

---

12 Later the commentators (13th-15th century) called such a form of *traditio* 'fictitious' (*traditio ficta*). See: Biermann, Traditio ficta, Stuttgart 1891, p. 71. To prevent misunderstandings note that Biermann uses the term post-glossators to denote this group of jurists. See for this terminology F. Wieacker, Privatrechtsgeschichte der Neuzeit, 2nd ed., Göttingen 1967, p. 81. The French equivalent of *traditio ficta* is *tradition feinte*.

13 W.M. Gordon, Studies in the transfer of property by traditio, Aberdeen 1970, ch. 1 (*constitutum possessorium*), ch. 2 (*brevi manu*) and ch. 3 (*longa manu*). Note, however that it is controversial whether or not Roman law recognized *constitutum possessorium* already in its classical period. The arguments pro and contra are described in ch. 1 of Gordon's book. At any rate, there is no doubt that *constitutum possessorium* was acknowledged in Justinianian law (6th century). For an account of the development of the different forms of *traditio ficta* from classical Roman law until the end of the *Usus Modernus Pandectarum*: see Biermann, Traditio ficta, and Gordon.

14 Pothier, Traité du droit de domaine de propriété, part 1, ch. 2, section 4, article 1, § 6, nr. 212-213, Œuvres de Pothier, vol. 9, p. 173-174; Brissaud, p. 335.

15 Brissaud, p. 309.

16 Later, as a result of Roman law influence, *tradition per cartam* was acknowledged, in which a chart represented the land: see Brissaud, p. 315.

17 J. Brissaud, p. 317. The term *saisine* was originally comparable to possession (see Brissaud, p. 250 et seq.). In the 13th century, however, *saisine* was turned into a real right (inferior to ownership though): a person who had been in possession for one year acquired *saisine* (see Brissaud, p. 264-265; C.G. Bruns, Das Recht des Besitzes im Mittelalter und in der Gegenwart, Tübingen 1848 (repr. Osnabrück 1965), p. 362-364). Most land in the north of France was feudal, but there was also *allodium*, free land not subject to the feudal system. For the transfer of these lands: see Brissaud, p. 321-322.

18 See P. Viollet, Histoire du droit civil Français, 3rd ed., Paris 1905 (repr. Aalen 1966), p. 655-656; Brissaud, p. 335 et seq., particularly p. 339.

19 The noun *saisine* or the alternative *seisine* derives from the verb *saisir*, to get hold of, to take possession of. Accordingly the term means possession. Cf. the English term 'seisin' and 'livery of seisin': chapter 4, fn. 102.

by way of *constitutum possessorium*.[20] Domat even held that, if such a clause was not expressly stipulated, it should nonetheless be deemed to be made tacitly, an opinion that would diminish even further the importance of a *tradition réelle*'.[21] Most probably these *constitutum* clauses originated in late medieval Italy where a similar practice had developed for notaries to include such clauses in contracts for the sale of immovables.[22]

Thus, in the period prior to the *Code Civil* the *traditio* requirement had been severely eroded, in the *pays de droit écrit* as well as in most of the *pays de droit coutumier*. The practical result of the widespread use of fictitious *traditio* was the following: in the larger part of France, the regions were these clauses were common practice, ownership of land passed when the contract of sale was made. We can now see that the decision made in the *Code Civil* to let ownership pass the moment

---

20 Viollet, p. 656. The clauses had different names. Sometimes it was simply referred to as *clause de constitut*. Often the *constitutum possessorium* took the form of the seller remaining in direct possession of the object as a usufructuary; it was then called a *clause de rétention d'usufruit* (clause to retain a usufruct). Another name frequently used is *clause de précaire*. See also Pothier, Traité du droit de domaine de propriété, part 1, ch. 2, section 4, article 1, § 6, Œuvres de Pothier, vol. 9, p. 172-173. In Roman law the term *precarium* denotes a loan at will, that is, a loan which may be terminated by the lender at any moment. Yet, in French pre-*Code Civil* law the term *precarium* or *précaire*, in Roman law just one of many instances in which someone holds a thing for another, was used to indicate every instance where someone holds a thing for another (i.e. *detentio*): every person holding a thing for another is said to have *possession précaire*. See Merlin, Répertoire, vol. 28 at *précaire*. See also literature mentioned by C.G. Bruns, Das Recht des Besitzes, p. 445, fn. 1. Note, however, that in Roman law the holder by way of *precarium* enjoyed the protection of possessory interdicts and was therefore seen as a possessor.

21 J. Domat, Les loix civiles dans leur ordre naturel, Paris 1723, Livre I, titre 2, section 2, nr. 8 (he calls it a *clause de précaire*). When accepting this view one in effect abolishes the *traditio* requirement. Yet, it is doubtful whether Domat intended to do so. Traditionally Domat is said to adhere to a consensual transfer system. In his *Loix Civiles* there are passages suggesting that in the case of sale the contract itself passes ownership without *traditio* being needed, for instance Livre I, titre 1, section 1, nr. 8 and titre 2, section 1, nr. 2. Both texts state that sale is accomplished by mere agreement without payment of the price or delivery of the thing being needed. These passages are often quoted to demonstrate that Domat adhered to the consensual system. However, in both instances Domat refers to passages from the *Corpus Iuris* which make clear that consensus suffices to create the *contract of sale* (Inst. 3,22, pr.; Inst. 3,23, pr.; Paul. D. 18,1,1,2). The passages do not say anything about the moment when ownership passes. In addition, in Livre I, titre 2, section 2, nr. 10 Domat unequivocally says that transfer of possession is needed to transfer ownership. He even refers to C. 2,3,20: ownership is transferred by *traditio* and by acquisitive prescription, not by mere agreement (traditionibus et usucapionibus dominia rerum, non nudis pactis transferuntur). On the other hand, there is a passage in Livre III, titre 7, section 3, nr. 2 where Domat seems to say that in the case of sale ownership may pass before the transfer of possession. Cf. Gordon, Studies in the transfer of property by traditio, p. 182, footnote 2. Perhaps Domat simply uses the term possession to mean actual power over the object.

22 In one of his *consilia* Bartholomaeus Socinus (1436-1507) writes that it is a well-established practice for notaries to include such clauses into contracts for the sale of immovable property. He even adds that if the clause has been left out this should probably be seen as a mistake which should not prejudice the parties. See B. Socinus, Consiliorum seu potius responsorum Mariani Socini ac Bartholomaei filii senensium..., 4 vols, Venice 1579, vol. 4, Consilium LV, Rdnr. 11 (*in fine*). See also Gordon, Studies, p. 142.

the contract is made, was not a great change; it was merely the formal acknowledgement of a common practice.

Even so, as to movable property the provisions meant a considerable change, since, despite the availability of fictitious forms of *traditio*, the *ius dispositivum* rule still required a *tradition réelle* for ownership to pass. That is to say, unless the parties agreed otherwise ownership of a movable did not pass when the contract was made.

In addition to the widespread use of *tradition feinte* clauses in the sale of land there was another influence in favour of the *solo consensu* principle. Two important representatives of the natural law school, Grotius and Pufendorf, held that according to natural law ownership could be transferred by a mere agreement and that the requirement of *traditio* was only positive law.[23] Still, this view has never been generally accepted in France: Pothier, for example, rejected it and persevered with the *traditio* requirement (in the form of a *tradition réelle* or *feinte*, of course).[24]

As we have just seen the *solo consensu* principle corresponds with the old practice of the transfer of land. To emphasize this similarity Portalis, one of the draftsmen of the *Code Civil*, wrote in a description of the *Code*'s 'motives' (*exposé des motifs*) that a contract for the transfer of ownership contains a certain *tradition civile* (fictitious *traditio*) which performs the transfer of rights.[25]

Yet, it is not clear what the above passage means; it could even be called misleading. Literally it means that every contract of sale is deemed to contain a

---

23 H. Grotius, De iure belli ac pacis, 2,6,1 and 2,8,25, Amsterdam 1712; S. Pufendorf, De iure naturae et gentium, 4,9,5 et seq., specially § 8, Amsterdam 1704. Grotius 2,8,25: 'Atqui supra diximus, ad dominii translationem naturaliter traditionem non requiri;' (Yet, above we have said that according to natural law *traditio* is not required for the transfer of ownership;).

    Pufendorf 4,9: in § 6 he writes that the question whether or not *traditio* is needed, can be solved by making a distinction between ownership regarded as a moral quality and, on the other hand, ownership considered as being combined with possession. Then in § 8 he concludes: 'Hisce positis adparet, omnino per sola pacta transire posse dominium, prout id consideratur nude tanquam qualitas moralis, & prout abstrahit à possessione: verum prout illud etiam aliquid physicæ facultatis intelligitur continere, per quam statim actu exerceri queat, præter pacta etiam traditionem requiri. Id quod non ex jure positivo, sed ex ipsa naturali ratione fluit.' (This being said it is evident that ownership can pass simply by mere agreement when it is considered merely as a moral quality and when it abstracts from possession. On the other hand, when it is considered to contain also some physical power by which ownership can be instantly used, in addition to the agreement *traditio* is required. This does not follow from positive law, but rather from natural reason itself).

24 Pothier, Traité du droit de domaine de propriété, part 1, ch. 2, section 4, article 4, Œuvres de Pothier, vol. 9, p. 186 et seq.

25 Locré, Législation civile, commerciale et criminelle, ou commentaire et complément des codes Français, vol. 7, Brussels 1836, p. 71. The term *tradition civile* has the same meaning as the term *tradition feinte*. It derives from the term *traditio civilis* which was used by some of the commentators to denote forms of *traditio ficta*. See: Biermann, traditio ficta, p. 73. The relevant passage reads: 'Par la seule expression de notre volonté nous acquérons pour nous-mêmes, et nous transportons à autrui les choses qui peuvent être l'objet de nos conventions. Il s'opère par le contrat une sorte de tradition civile qui consomme le transport du droit,...' (By mere expression of our will we acquire and we transfer to another the things that can be the object of our agreements. As a result of the contract a kind of *tradition civile* takes place which completes the transfer of the right,...).

tradition feinte and that as a result ownership passes the moment the contract is made. Bufnoir refers to this passage to support his view that in modern French law the *traditio* requirement is still being upheld, though in a hidden form.[26] As additional evidence he draws attention to the text of article 938 of the *Code Civil*. The exact wording of the article, which is about gifts, can be understood only by keeping in mind Portalis' remark on the *tradition civile*. Article 938 reads: 'A gift, if duly accepted, will be performed by the mere consensus of the parties; ownership of the things donated will pass to the donee without *another traditio* being needed.' [italics added][27] Bufnoir holds that from these two passages it can be concluded that there must be an earlier tradition that is deemed to be executed tacitly. In his opinion this must be the *traditio* that from Roman times until the *Code Civil* has been a requirement for the transfer of goods.

The theory sounds plausible. Yet, to my mind, the *tradition* that is supposed to be a tacit element of every transfer cannot be the *traditio* in its old form, that is to say, a *traditio* requiring a transfer of possession. For, if modern French law still required a transfer of possession, even if only a fictitious *traditio*, the owner who does not have possession would be unable to transfer ownership. But according to modern French law it is possible for an owner without possession to transfer ownership under article 1138, as Bufnoir himself says.[28] The *Code Civil* abolished the requirement of *traditio* altogether: neither a *tradition réelle* nor a *tradition feinte* is needed.

So, Bufnoir seems to contradict himself when he states that *tradition* is still required but a transfer of possession is not needed. What is more, even the passage by Portalis which Bufnoir relies on becomes incomprehensible when a transfer of possession is not required. Most probably Portalis did not intend to say that a transfer of possession is still needed and his reference to the old *tradition civile*, the fictitious transfer of possession, was meant only to stress that the *Code Civil* did not require a transfer of direct possession (*tradition réelle*), a result that under the old French law could be reached only by making a *tradition civile*. In that case the confusing last words of article 938 CC could simply be an unfortunate choice of words by jurists whose way of thinking was still strongly influenced by the old conceptions.

Be that as it may, Bufnoir's theory can be saved by distinguishing two elements within the act of transfer: the real agreement and, on the other side, the transfer of possession. An important difference between the two elements is the following: the second element, the transfer of possession, is not an essential part of a transfer and can consequently be missed. Under article 3:95 *Burgerlijk Wetboek* and § 931 *Bürgerliches Gesetzbuch*, for example, it is possible for an owner to transfer ownership without having possession of the object. The transfer of possession to the

---

26 C. Bufnoir, Propriété et contrat, 2nd ed., Paris 1924, p. 45 et seq.
27 Article 938 CC: 'La donation dûment acceptée sera parfaite par le seul consentement des parties; et la propriété des objets donnés sera transférée au donataire, sans qu'il soit besoin *d'autre tradition*.' [italics added]
28 On p. 46.

acquirer is intended merely to make known the passing of ownership and thus comply with the principle of publicity. For that reason it is not essential to the transfer itself. The first element, however, is indispensable, because it contains the parties' will to the transfer of ownership of a particular object: it *is* the legal act of transfer. What the *Code Civil* abolished was the second element, the transfer of possession. The concept of real agreement, however, is not influenced by this abolition. One could contend that this concept is still alive in French law.

Despite the above analysis Portalis' remark remains inexplicable. He describes the contract of sale as containing a kind of *tradition feinte*, whereas the *Code Civil* went further than abolishing only the requirement of a *tradition réelle*: as we have just seen it eliminated the requirement of *traditio* altogether, real as well as fictitious *traditio*. Of course, interpreting *tradition civile* as meaning 'real agreement' would render Portalis' statement sound and logical, but it is very unlikely that Portalis had the concept of real agreement in mind. This concept was still unknown when the *Code Civil* was drafted. It was created by the German jurist Savigny after the *Code Civil* had been promulgated. The earliest documents in which Savigny's concept of the real agreement can be found date back to 1815/16.[29]

We can therefore say that Portalis' statement is most probably a slip of the tongue, a result of Portalis describing the new law with the old terminology, accustomed as jurists at that time were to the pre-*Code Civil* concepts. Consequently, Portalis' statement as well as the last words of article 938 CC cannot serve as an historical argument in favour of acknowledging the real agreement. Yet, it is important to see that neither does the abolition of the *traditio* requirement form an obstacle to accepting the real agreement. The change in the transfer system cannot have had the intention to abolish or exclude the real agreement, as the real agreement was not yet known as a concept.

As we have seen in this section the history of Roman and French law shows us a gradual transformation from a tradition system to a consensual system. As to immovable property the *Code Civil*'s consensual system was no more than a formal confirmation of a long established practice. Of eminent importance in this transformation was the concept of fictitious tradition: when a tradition system allows possession to be transferred merely by the consensus of the parties it in fact accepts that ownership can be transferred by the mere consensus of the parties.

2.2 Systematic arguments

While there are no historical arguments for acknowledging the real agreement, there are enough systematic reasons for accepting the concept, as we will see below.

---

29 Felgenträger, Friedrich Carl v. Savigny's Einfluß auf die Übereignungslehre, Leipzig 1927, p. 34 et seq. Savigny needed the concept for the abstract transfer system he devised. See chapter 7, § 4.1 *in fine*. Yet, although it was developed for an abstract system it has an important function in causal systems as well, as we shall see in this section.

Contract for the transfer of generic goods

In Dutch and German law the real agreement has two closely related functions. First of all, it contains the parties' will to transfer and, secondly, it pinpoints, if the assets are not yet identified, the exact objects that have to be transferred to the acquirer. As it expresses the parties' will to transfer we can expect to find the real agreement in every voluntary transfer, even in English and French law, where the term is not used.

It may be objected that in a consensual transfer system the real agreement is superfluous because the contract which obliges to transfer already contains both parties' will to transfer. Selling a thing entails transferring it to the buyer. As a consequence, from the seller's entering into a contract of sale it can be inferred that he is also willing to transfer the thing. The objection is correct, but it is correct only as regards the transfer of specific and existing goods.

As we have seen, the parties' will to transfer ownership of a certain amount of generic goods does not suffice to let ownership pass. True, for the contract of sale to be valid it suffices if the sort, quality and quantity of the goods is known (*déterminé*, determined) or at least can be determined on the basis of the contract (*déterminable*, determinable) (article 1129 CC).[30] Ownership, however, passes only when certain goods are identified as the goods to be transferred.[31] The act of ascertaining the contract goods is called *individualisation*. Unlike in English law it is not known whether or not appropriation requires both parties' consent. Some authors contend that goods can be appropriated unilaterally by the seller. Yet, the buyer's right to reject non-conforming goods[32] demonstrates that the buyer's consent is indispensable. Both parties should agree about which specific goods are to be transferred to the acquirer. The will to transfer, as already expressed by the contract, has to be focused on certain identified assets. This consensus about the transfer of specific things is called the real agreement.

Retention of ownership

Seller and buyer may agree a so-called retention of ownership clause (*clause de réserve de propriété*). It has the effect that ownership of the goods sold passes to the buyer only if the full purchase price has been paid. Ownership of the goods remains with the seller even after physical delivery of the goods to the buyer's premises.

The absence in French legal theory of a second legal act aimed specifically at the transfer of ownership once led the French Supreme Court (*Cour de Cassation*) to hold that, where the parties have agreed a retention of ownership, the contract itself has been made under the suspensive condition of full payment.[33] This view would entail that all legal consequences of the contract, such as the seller's obligation to deliver the object and the buyer's obligation to pay, would be suspended. Clearly,

---

30 Mazeaud/Chabas, Vente et échange, 7th ed., Paris 1987, p. 125.
31 Mazeaud/Chabas, Vente et échange, p. 124 and 182-183.
32 See *infra*, p. 87-88
33 Cass req 21 July 1897, D.P. 1898.1.269.

this would be undesirable and would not correspond with the parties' intentions. Most probably these consequences were not intended by the *Cour de Cassation*. Nonetheless it is an example of failing to make a clear distinction between the sales contract and the transfer of ownership.[34] Whatever the *Cour de Cassation* in the above decision really had in view, currently the retention of ownership clause is seen as a condition suspending only the passing of ownership.[35]

As we have seen in chapter 2, § 2.2 in German law it is explained by saying that the suspensive condition is attached to the real agreement. The contract then obliges the seller to make a real agreement which depends on a suspensive condition. That is to say, the *duty* to make the real agreement is unconditional; the condition of full payment is attached solely to the real agreement itself.[36]

In a causal system, however, another explanation is possible, whether it be a tradition system or a consensual system.[37] It may be argued that in French law, for instance, the condition is not attached to the transfer (i.e. the real agreement) but rather to the seller's obligation to make the transfer.

Attaching the condition to the contract itself would suspend all legal effects of the contract. Yet, attaching it to the seller's obligation to transfer suspends only one

---

34 Note that in the decision appealed against the *Cour d'Appel* of Grenoble held that '...par ce contrat Schönher [the appellant] a entendu suspendre la livraison des métiers vendus jusqu'à payement complet du prix et ne se dessaisir de sa propriété qu'après en avoir reçu l'équivalent par le payement de la somme totale en versements successifs et fractionnés;...' (under the contract Schönher intended to suspend the *livraison* of the weaving looms sold until full payment of the purchase price and intended not to transfer his ownership before having received the equivalent through payment of the total sum in successive instalments). See D.P. 1898.I.269. So this court, whose decision was upheld by the *Cour de Cassation*, did not attach the suspensive condition to the contract of sale. Rather it said that the *livraison* was suspended. This term certainly does not denote the actual delivery of the goods, since the goods were already delivered to the buyer. Most probably it means, together with the expression *dessaisir de sa propriété*, the transfer of ownership seen as a legal act, that is to say, the real agreement.

35 Cass com 20 November 1979, D. 1980 IR 571, Rev. trim. dr. com. 1980, p. 43. See also Cass com 8 February 1994, arret n° 396, published in Lexis-nexis; Cour d'Appel of Nancy 19 December 1985, D.S. 1986 J 246; Cour d'Appel of Douai 10 December 1992, n°-role 835/92, published in Lexis-nexis. See also Mazeaud/Chabas, Vente et échange, p. 208-209. This view is also laid down in the statute number 85-98 of 25 January 1985 (Redressement et liquidation judiciaires) concerning insolvency. Article 121, 2nd subs., as changed by statute nr. 94-475 of 10 June 1994, expressly provides that the retention of ownership clause subjects the passing of ownership to the condition of full payment: '...une clause de réserve de propriété subordonnant le transfert de propriété au paiement intégral du prix...'.

36 § 455 BGB: 'Hat sich der Verkäufer einer beweglichen Sache das Eigentum bis zur Zahlung des Kaufpreises vorbehalten, so ist im Zweifel anzunehmen, daß die Übertragung des Eigentums unter der aufschiebenden Bedingung vollständiger Zahlung des Kaufpreises erfolgt und daß der Verkäufer zum Rücktritte von dem Vertrage berechtigt ist, wenn der Käufer mit der Zahlung in Verzug kommt' (Where the seller of a movable has retained ownership until full payment of the purchase price, it should, in any case of doubt, be assumed that the transfer of ownership is performed under the suspensive condition of full payment of the purchase price and that the seller has the right to terminate the contract for breach of contract when the buyer defaults on payment of the price).

37 In an abstract transfer system, on the other hand, the first analysis is the only possible one, because defects in the *causa traditionis* do not affect the validity of the transfer.

of the contract's effects. As long as the condition has not been fulfilled the suspended obligation does not form a valid and effective *causa* for the transfer of ownership. In consequence, ownership does not pass before the seller's obligation to transfer has become fully effective, i.e. upon full payment of the purchase price.[38]

So, according to the first analysis the condition suspends the transfer rather than the obligation to transfer. In the second analysis the condition suspends the obligation to transfer and in result the passing of ownership. Since in the second instance no real agreement is needed, the retention of ownership clause cannot be used to prove the existence, or at least the usefulness, of the real agreement. On the other hand, it is important to note that it is not an argument against the real agreement.

Transfer without prior contract

The French consensual system presupposes a prior contract in which the parties have expressed their will to transfer ownership of a certain asset. When the obligation to transfer is based on another *causa traditionis*, for example *payement de l'indu* (*solutio indebiti*, undue payment; article 1376 CC), ownership does not pass immediately after the obligation has arisen. In these cases an act of transfer is needed in which the parties agree about the passing of ownership of specific assets. In other words, a real agreement is needed.

Yet, even if there is a contract, the contract does not necessarily contain an obligation to transfer ownership. Some contracts come into being only as a result of the transfer of ownership. Unlike in the case of consensual contracts mere consensus between the contracting parties does not suffice to create these contracts. In addition to consensus a 'real' element such as the transfer or delivery of a thing is required. To distinguish them from consensual contracts they are called real contracts.[39] To our discussion of the real agreement only those real contracts are interesting which involve a transfer of ownership. Two of them are contracts that were already known as real contracts to classical Roman law[40]: *mutuum* and *depositum irregulare*. The third is the gift from hand to hand.[41] As a matter of course a transfer of ownership made in order to form a real contract cannot be based on a contractual obligation.

---

38 For Dutch law this analysis is put forward by Vriesendorp, who in his thesis cannot apply the first analysis because he contends that, at least as to most categories of movables, the real agreement is superfluous. See R.D. Vriesendorp, Het eigendomsvoorbehoud, (thesis Groningen) Deventer 1985, p. 22-26.

39 This category of contracts derives from Roman law and is called real contract because the contract comes into being *re* (=by means of a thing). That is to say, the contract comes into being only when an object is handed over or, as the case may be, ownership transferred. The name real contract, however, was unknown to Roman law as a *terminus technicus*.

40 Kaser I, p. 530 (*mutuum*) and 536 (*depositum irregulare*). The other Roman real contracts did not involve a transfer of ownership but merely a handing over of an object: *depositum* (safe-keeping), *commodatum* (loan for use) and *pignus* (pledge).

41 This contract will be treated separately in chapter 6.

Mutuum (prêt de consommation)

Mutuum (in French *prêt de consommation* or *prêt de consomption*; in English 'loan for consumption') is the transfer of fungible goods, for example money, to the borrower imposing on the latter the duty to return to the lender in due time goods of the same sort, quality and quantity (article 1892 CC).[42] Where there is *commodatum* (*prêt à usage*, article 1875 CC) the borrower is under a duty to return the very same goods lent to him; ownership of these goods remains with the lender. On the other hand, *mutuum* is intended to give the borrower the right to consume the goods. For that reason *mutuum* requires a transfer of ownership of the goods to the borrower (art. 1893 CC).

In classical Roman law[43] as well as in modern French law[44] the contract of *mutuum* is said to come into existence only when the goods have been transferred to the borrower. The transfer of ownership is a prerequisite for the creation of the contract. There is no obligation to transfer ownership before the contract is made and the contract comes into existence as a result of ownership being transferred to the borrower.

How do we explain this transfer of ownership? The consensual transfer system has no answer to this. It presupposes a contractual obligation to transfer which is then executed immediately. As we have seen article 1138 CC provides that an obligation to transfer is performed immediately without *traditio* being needed. Ownership is supposedly transferred *par effet des obligations* (by obligations). In the case of a *contrat réel*, however, there is no such obligation.

The passing of ownership is not preceded by a contract in which both parties' will to transfer ownership of the assets is expressed. As this declaration of will is essential for every transfer the parties still have to meet this requirement. When possession of the object is transferred to the borrower the parties should make an agreement in which they demonstrate their will to transfer ownership of that particular asset. This is the very definition of the real agreement.

Originally, in ancient Roman law, the contract of *mutuum* was gratuitous, a contract to assist neighbours and friends.[45] When in a later period in Roman law *mutuum* was also used for commercial loans, a method had to be found to stipulate interest payment. The *mutuum* being gratuitous in origin, the obligation to pay

---

42 As to money a transfer of ownership takes place only where coins and banknotes are concerned. Yet, nowadays the money is given mostly by a transfer from one bank account to the other. Here the bank transfer is the 'real' moment. Besides, it is not always necessary for the lender to transfer the money or other fungibles to the borrower. Already in classical Roman law the requirement of handing over was gradually relaxed. In Roman law the owner of a thing could create a *mutuum* by ordering someone to sell the thing and keep the money as a loan. In this case the *mutuum* arises when the seller receives the money (the so-called *contractus mohatrae*). Kaser I, p. 531.

43 Kaser I, p. 530.

44 Planiol/Ripert, vol. 11, p. 465. Mazeaud/Chabas, Principaux contrats, 2e partie, p. 889 and 897-898.

45 Kaser I, p. 170; A. Watson, The evolution of law, Oxford 1985, p. 9-10.

interest could not be incorporated into the *mutuum* contract itself. To stipulate interest one had to enter into an additional contract: the *stipulatio*.[46] Often the entire legal act, the loan for consumption and the interest payment were included into the *stipulatio*.[47] But the two contracts, *mutuum* and *stipulatio* of interest were never integrated into one contract and *mutuum* kept its original form.

The contract came into being only when the object in question was transferred to the borrower. An agreement to make a *mutuum*, a so-called *pactum de mutuo dando* was not binding, unless made in the form of a *stipulatio*.[48] In modern French law, however, a promise to make a loan at interest is binding. Where the *mutuum* is gratuitous the requirement of transferring ownership in order to create the contract can be explained as a requirement protecting the owner against binding himself impetuously (cf. the contract of gift).[49] Yet, when the contract is for consideration there is no reason for such protection. According to French law a prospective lender can bind himself by contract to make in due time a contract of *mutuum* with the prospective borrower.[50] The *pactum de mutuo dando* is called an *avant-contrat* (pre-contract), as it precedes the contract of *mutuum*. In the case of a loan of money (*prêt d'argent*) it is often called *ouverture de crédit* (opening of credit).[51] French law allows the parties in this case to bind themselves by contract without any transfer of ownership being needed.

In reality the real contract loses its 'real' character when accompanied by a binding pre-contract: the pre-contract is a true contract which is binding without a transfer of ownership. Regarding the pre-contract and the *mutuum* together as one legal act, one can see that in reality the *mutuum* has become a consensual contract obliging the lender to transfer ownership. In Dutch[52], German[53] and Swiss law[54] the *mutuum* contract is now finally recognized as a consensual contract, i.e. a contract coming into existence by mere consensus of the contracting parties. Yet, despite the recognition of a binding pre-contract in French law the two legal acts, pre-contract and *mutuum*, are not merged into one contract. The transfer of ownership is a prerequisite for the creation of *mutuum*. Moreover, as regards gratuitous loans there is no reason to alter this.

---

46 A Roman contract formed by oral question-and-answer which could be used for any type of transaction. Definition by Watson: The evolution of the law, p. 150.

47 Presumably the date and place of repayment had to be included into the *stipulatio* as well. See Kaser I, p. 532.

48 Kaser I, p. 531, footnote 9.

49 See M.-N. Jobard-Bachellier, Existe-t-il encore des contrats réels en droit Français? Ou la valeur des promesses de contrat réel en droit positif, Rev. trim. dr. civ. 1985, p. 1 et seq.

50 Mazeaud/Chabas, Principaux contrats, 2e partie, p. 889 and 909.

51 Mazeaud/Chabas, Principaux contrats, 2e partie, p. 909.

52 Art. 7.2.1.1. BW (not yet in force).

53 Although the text of § 607 BGB is most probably based on the view that *Darlehen* is a real contract, the *Darlehen* is now generally seen as a consensual contract. See Münchener/Westermann, Vorbem. § 607, Rdnr. 7.

54 Art. 312 OR.

However, this is overtly in conflict with article 1138 CC according to which ownership passes immediately when the contractual obligation to transfer arises (here the moment the pre-contract is made). Apparently, the pre-contract, which is a true and binding contract creating an obligation to transfer, does not suffice here.

Two additional legal acts are needed in order for ownership to pass. First, the pre-contract should be followed by the parties transferring possession of particular assets. So, apparently the ancient *traditio* requirement survived the promulgation of the *Code Civil*. *Tradition réelle* or *feinte* is needed whereas article 1138 CC intended to abolish the *traditio* requirement for the transfer of ownership, at least so it seems considering the general formulation of art. 1138. Secondly, there should be a transfer of ownership of these identified things. The transfer can be effected only by the parties declaring their will to transfer ownership, in other words, by a real agreement.

Depositum irregulare

As the concept of real agreement can help explain the *mutuum* contract, so can it explain the *depositum irregulare*, another real contract where ownership is transferred (*dêpot irregulier*). In the case of normal *depositum* goods are handed over for safe-keeping obliging the depositee to return in due time the same objects to the depositor, who remains owner of the objects. The *depositum irregulare*, however, involves the transfer of ownership of the objects deposited and, like *mutuum*, obliges the depositee merely to return goods of a the same sort, quality and quantity. Originally, in classical Roman law, *depositum irregulare* could be used only for the deposit of money.[55] But in modern French law it can be used for all sorts of fungible goods.

Like *mutuum* the *depositum irregulare* is a real contract coming into existence only when ownership is transferred to the depositee. Since the transfer is not based on any obligation, the transfer should be based on a real agreement in which the parties express their will to transfer ownership of certain identified assets.

Delivery of defective goods and non-conforming goods

Where generic goods have been sold and the goods delivered do not conform to the contract requirements, the buyer has the right to reject the goods. This applies to goods of a different quality as well as to goods with an apparent defect (*vice apparante*). The rejection of such a tender does not necessarily entail the termination of the contract (*résolution*). If the time for delivery has not yet expired the buyer has the right to make a second tender and so to cure his first defective tender. Accordingly, the buyer is under a duty to accept the new tender. On the other hand, if time has expired, the buyer may terminate the contract. Yet, he may also demand specific performance (*exécution de la vente*, execution of the sale). If he opts for the latter, the seller is under a duty to make a second tender. The right to reject non-conforming goods without simultaneously terminating the contract applies to

---

55 Kaser I, p. 536.

commercial sales (*ventes commerciales*) as well as normal sales (*ventes civiles*).[56] It is called *refus* (rejection) or, in the case of commercial sales, *laissé pour compte* (lit.: the leaving on account of).

Clearly, ownership of the rejected goods should remain with the seller, and, if ownership has already passed to the buyer, ownership should revert to the seller. Making use of the concept of real agreement it is possible to give a simple explanation of what happens to the ownership of the non-conforming goods. We should distinguish two instances: rejection upon delivery and rejection after delivery. If on delivery the buyer notices the defect of the goods, he may refuse to accept the delivery (*refuser de prendre livraison*) by refusing to make the real agreement needed for the transfer of ownership. Ownership then has never passed to the buyer. If, on the other hand, ownership has already passed and the buyer has a short time to inspect the goods, he may within this time reject the goods by avoiding the real agreement. This causes ownership to revert automatically to the seller.[57]

The rejection of non-conforming goods cannot be satisfactorily explained by the traditional French view that the contract itself passes ownership. A rejection of goods which maintains the contract of sale requires making a distinction between two different legal acts: the contract, which obliges to make a transfer of ownership, and the transfer itself. Rejection of goods avoids only the transfer of the goods.

Goods that have yet to be manufactured
Where an object is sold that has yet to be manufactured ownership does not pass at the moment the contract is made. The *solo consensu* principle of article 1138 CC does not apply here. In principle ownership and risk pass to the buyer when the object is finished. And, according to the *Cour de Cassation*,[58] it is finished when it is in such a state that it can be delivered by the seller and accepted by the buyer. The object should be in the state agreed upon by the parties.[59]

Yet, it is not always easy to tell if the object has reached the point of completion. The criterion is far from clear. Of course the object should answer to the description in the contract. But even this is too vague. How do we know whether the object meets the contract requirements? Should the manufacturer decide, or the commissioner?

---

56 J. Huet, Traité de droit civil, Les principaux contrats spéciaux, Paris 1996, p. 210, fn. 232.
57 An alternative theory would be to say that the formation of the real agreement is deferred until the time for rejection has lapsed. Rejection should then be regarded as a refusal to make a real agreement. If the time for refusal expires unused, this should be seen as a tacit acceptance of the real agreement. It is unknown which of both theories is right, as we do not know who is owner of the goods during the time between delivery on the one hand and rejection or acceptance on the other hand. The question, though, is very important because also in French law the quality of owner determines the risk of insolvency and the risk in the goods.
58 Cass civ 1 August 1950, S. 1951.1.100; Cass civ 12 July 1976, arret n° 1.123, published in Lexis-nexis; Cass civ 15 November 1989, arret n° 1482, published in Lexis-nexis.
59 See Mazeaud/Chabas, Vente et échange, p. 187 and 215-216.

In 1900 the *Cour de Cassation* had the opportunity to decide this question in a case between the famous painter Whistler and Lord William Eden.[60] The latter had commissioned Whistler to make a portrait of Lady Eden. Whistler started working and made a painting that fully met Lord Eden's expectations. However, ultimately Whistler refused to deliver the painting and showed the painting on an exposition at Champ de Mars in Paris. The *Cour de Cassation* held that where a painting has been commissioned ownership passes only when the artist hands the painting over to the client and the latter approves of the painting. Until that moment the artist remains the 'master of his work'.[61] So, where a work of art is commissioned both parties should agree to the passing of ownership. In other words, they should make a real agreement about the transfer of ownership.[62]

3 Causal transfer system

The question whether the French transfer system is causal or abstract is not discussed in French law. When the *Code Civil* was drafted the terms 'causal' and 'abstract' to indicate different transfer systems were not yet known. It seems that the question whether the transfer system in the *Code* should be causal or abstract did not interest the draftsmen. Nor do modern French textbooks mention the question.[63]

Nevertheless, it is not difficult to see that the French transfer system is causal. As in the traditional French view the contract itself transfers ownership it follows that the contract must be valid in order to be able to pass ownership. For, a void contract is unable to pass ownership. And, if a voidable contract is avoided ownership of the thing, which has passed to the acquirer, reverts to the transferor. Since avoidance has retroactive effect the contract is deemed never to have been valid. Consequently it is taken that ownership and, because of the *res perit domino* rule[64], risk of accidental loss or damage have never passed to the acquirer.[65]

---

60 Cass civ 14 March 1900, D. 1900.1.497.
61 Not only did the *Cour de Cassation* hold that ownership of the painting had not passed, it also held that the artist could not be forced to deliver the painting. In other words, in these cases the judge is not willing to order specific performance. The client has to content himself with damages.
62 The judgment in *Whistler/Eden* gives the impression that in these instances the pre-*Code Civil* requirement of *traditio* has revived.
63 Cf. chapter 7, especially § 5.
64 The rule means that the owner of a thing bears the risk of accidental damage or loss. See for this rule: Malaurie and Aynès, Cours de droit civil, Les contrats spéciaux, 10th ed., Paris 1997, p. 185-187. Although the wording of the rule is based on Roman law (Cf. C. 4,24,9) the French application of the adage does not accord with Roman law, in which risk normally passed the moment the contract of sale was made. See fn. 1.
65 Cass civ 6 December 1967 (Bull. civ., I, nr. 358) discussed by J. Chevallier in Rev. trim. dr. civ. 1968, p. 708-709.

4 Transfer of movables in English law

1 Two different transfer systems

In the 13th century English law required for every transfer of movables delivery of the object, that is, transfer of possession. A similar rule applied to the transfer of immovable property. There was a unitary transfer system that can be called a tradition system. In later times, however, two exceptions to the delivery rule came into being: at the end of the 13th century it was accepted that a gift could be made by deed rather than by delivery,[1] and gradually in the course of the 15th century it became acknowledged that in the case of sale ownership of the thing passes to the buyer when the contract is made even if the thing has not yet been delivered to the buyer. It is the birth of the *solo consensu* rule in English law. When the law of sales was codified at the end of the 19th century the *solo consensu* rule was laid down in the Sale of Goods Act 1893. It was subsequently adopted in the Sale of Goods Act 1979 which to a large extent is similar to its predecessor.

The acknowledgement of these exceptions entailed the end of a unitary transfer system. However important the sales contract may be in a modern society, from an historical point of view the *solo consensu* principle is a mere exception to the delivery principle: the ancient common law rule of delivery was not replaced with the *solo consensu* principle. As a result there are now two different transfer systems: the consensual transfer system for gifts by deed and for contracts of sale, and on the other hand the tradition system, which applies to all other transfers. Accordingly, the current chapter consists of two separate parts, the first dealing with the sale of goods, the second with the delivery principle. Moreover, in part B of this chapter an historical survey will examine how the *solo consensu* rule developed.

A) TRANSFER BASED ON SALE

2 Introduction

2.1 The *solo consensu* rule

As regards the sale of goods the provisions on the transfer of ownership are to be found in sections 16 to 26 of the Sale of Goods Act 1979 (SGA).[2] According to section 17 the moment when ownership[3] of the goods passes to the buyer depends

---

1 Both kinds of gift will be discussed in part B of this chapter.
2 Unless stated otherwise 'Sale of Goods Act' or 'SGA' refers to the Sale of Goods Act 1979.
3 Here and in all other provisions the Sale of Goods Act uses the word 'property'; it means ownership. See R.M. Goode, Proprietary rights and insolvency in sales transactions, London 1985, p. 4. As the word 'property' in English law is also used to denote the object of a right of ownership (the asset one owns), I prefer to use the term ownership to indicate the right over the object. For the meaning of 'ownership' see A.M. Honoré, Ownership, in: A.G. Guest (ed.), Oxford essays in jurisprudence,

on the intention of the parties to the contract. If no intention appears the *ius dispositivum* rules in section 18 will apply. It is in this section that the principal rule can be found. Rule 1 of this section reads as follows: 'Where there is an unconditional contract for the sale of specific goods in a deliverable state the property [i.e. ownership] in the goods passes to the buyer when the contract is made, and it is immaterial whether the time of payment or the time of delivery, or both, be postponed.' So, the starting-point is ownership passing to the buyer the moment the contract is created. No *traditio* is needed, that is to say, it is not necessary to transfer possession of the object to the buyer. Ownership passes *solo consensu*, simply as a result of the consensus between the parties.[4] As with French law it is presupposed that the transferor is either the owner of the asset or has been authorized by the owner to sell and transfer the thing.[5]

However, the English *solo consensu* principle is subject to the same exceptions we have previously seen in French law. The *solo consensu* rule is confined to existing specific goods.[6] This excludes all generic and future goods. In addition, the principle applies only to the transfer of the thing, not to the transfer of the money due under the contract.

2.2 The risk of insolvency and the risk in the goods

In the English Sale of Goods Act as well as in the French *Code civil* ownership determines the risk of insolvency and the risk of accidental loss of the goods. As to the first risk, a buyer who has paid in advance but has not yet become owner of the goods bears the risk of the seller's insolvency. If, on the other hand, ownership passes to the buyer before the goods are paid for, the seller bears the risk of the buyer's insolvency. Ownership also determines the risk of accidental loss or deterioration of the goods for which neither seller nor buyer is liable. Normally, according to the rule *res perit domino* (the thing perishes on the owner's account) the risk of accidental loss or deterioration of the thing is linked to ownership of the

---

Oxford 1961, p. 107 et seq. See also Williams, Principles of the law of personal property, who treats the terms 'property' and 'ownership' as equivalent, though favours the term 'ownership' (*passim*, but especially ch. 1). T.B. Smith, however, regards the terms 'property' and 'ownership' as distinct concepts: T.B. Smith, Property problems in sale, Tagore law lectures, London/Calcutta 1978, p. 50.

4   As we will see in this chapter a large category of obligations is excepted from the *solo consensu* principle: monetary and other generic obligations.

5   Goode, Commercial law, p. 449.

6   The Sale of Goods Act defines a contract of sale to divide into 'sale' and 'agreement to sell'. The first refers to a contract of sale which passes ownership immediately when the contract is made. The second indicates all other instances, that is, the instances in which ownership does not immediately pass. See s. 2 and 61(1) SGA. The term sale is therefore applicable only to specific things. I shall not always follow this terminology: unless stated otherwise I shall use the words 'contract of sale', 'contract to sell', 'sales contract' and 'sale' as synonyms so as to accord with the similar use of these terms in other chapters of the book. See A.G. Guest et al. (eds.), Benjamin's Sale of Goods, 5th ed., London 1997, § 1-025 to 1-029.

thing[7], unless the parties agreed otherwise.[8] Where goods are lost while at the buyer's risk, the buyer has to pay the purchase price despite the loss.

3 Identity of goods[9]

3.1 Specific, quasi-specific and unascertained goods

To indicate the extent in which the goods are identified English law distinguishes between specific, quasi-specific and wholly unascertained goods. Goods which are not specific are called unascertained or generic goods. The latter category divides into wholly unascertained goods and so-called quasi-specific goods. Generic goods are termed quasi-specific if the seller and buyer have agreed that the contract goods should be taken from a specified source, for instance the sale of 4 million tons of brent oil out of a named vessel containing 200 million tons. Here the seller is not allowed to deliver brent oil from another source, even if the quality is the same. If the oil is lost because of an accident the seller is not allowed nor under a duty to deliver oil from another source: it is no longer possible to perform the contract.[10] As we shall see below the fact that generic goods have to be taken from a specified source entails that special appropriation rules apply.

3.2 The co-ownership regime of sections 20A and 20B

In 1995 a reform of the Sale of Goods Act gave fresh attention to one of the most fundamental problems of property law: the problem of identity of assets. Where unascertained generic goods have been sold ownership cannot pass to the buyer until goods have been earmarked as the assets to be transferred to that buyer (appropriation). This rule, which can be found in section 16 of the Sale of Goods Act 1979, is still in force, though in 1995 it has been modified for the sale *ex bulk*, as the requirement of identification was considered to be too restrictive in such instances.

The identity problem is not unique to English law: Dutch, French and German law as well as many other continental legal systems know a similar identification requirement within their law of property. Dutch, German and French law, for example, founded their property law systems on this requirement. Accordingly they all had to make special statutory regimes to cope with cases in which goods lose

---

7   Section 20 SGA. See for the *res perit domino* rule: Goode, Commercial law, p. 225 and chapter 9. See for the identical French rule: Malaurie and Aynès, Cours de droit civil, Les contrats spéciaux, 10th ed. Paris 1997, p. 185-187. Although the adage is based on C. 4,24,9 the English and French application of the adage does not accord with Roman law. See chapter 3, fn. 1; Kaser I, p. 552-553.

8   See s. 20(1) SGA; Malaurie and Aynès, p. 186.

9   Cf. L.P.W. van Vliet, Identity matters, in: P. Jackson and D.C. Wilde (eds.), The reform of property law, Aldershot/Brookfield USA/Singapore/Sydney 1997, p. 239-253.

10 Goode, Commercial law, p. 218-220.

their identity as a result of being mixed with other identical goods. The solution they have reached can to some extent be compared with the new provisions in the English Sale of Goods Act.

3.3 *Re Goldcorp Exchange Ltd*

For a lucid example of the practical effects of the identification requirement we can look to the Privy Council case in *Re Goldcorp Exchange Ltd*.[11] In this New Zealand case a company dealing in gold and other precious metals had sold bullion for future delivery to numerous purchasers. The bullion was not appropriated to the individual contracts, but was instead stored *en masse* as part of the company's overall stock of bullion. Subsequently the company became insolvent and a bank holding a debenture secured by a floating charge appointed receivers. The purchasers contended *inter alia* that under the contracts of sale ownership of the bullion had passed to them, so that the bullion purchased was not subject to the bank's charge.

The Privy Council's advice was tendered by Lord Mustill. He based his decision as to whether ownership had passed to the purchasers on section 18 of the New Zealand Sale of Goods Act 1908, which corresponds to section 16 of the English Sale of Goods Act 1893 and 1979. This section provides that where there is a contract for the sale of unascertained goods, no property in the goods is transferred to the buyer unless and until the goods are ascertained. Thus, the purchasers had not acquired ownership of the bullion, since no bullion had been appropriated to their individual contracts. Then Lord Mustill explained the reason why ownership in unascertained goods cannot pass. He said: '...common sense dictates that the buyer cannot acquire title until it is known to what goods the title relates.' 'It makes no difference,' he continued, 'what the parties intended if what they intend is impossible: as is the case with an immediate transfer of title to goods whose identity is not yet known.'[12] To illustrate this he quoted a passage from Lord Blackburn's *Treatise on the effect of the contract of sale*.[13] In this passage Lord Blackburn observes that the rule according to which ownership of generic goods cannot pass before the parties agree as to which specific goods are to be transferred, is a rule 'founded on the very nature of things.'

3.4 **Rights** *in re*

Is this rule really based on 'the very nature of things'? And what then is this 'nature of things'? If we analyse the requirement of identification it will become

---

11 [1994] 2 All ER 806. The question that arose in this case had been dealt with previously several times, but in less clear terms. See for example: *Re Wait* [1927] 1 Ch. 606 and *Re London Wine Co (Shippers) Ltd* [1986] PCC 121.

12 [1994] 2 All ER 814.

13 C. Blackburn, A treatise on the effect of the contract of sale: on the legal rights of property and possession in goods, wares and merchandize, 1st ed., London 1845, p. 122-123.

apparent that it is a consequence of one of the most important principles of property law, namely the principle that ownership, or more correctly, rights *in re* in general, can exist in relation to specific assets only. The object of the right of ownership, or any other right *in re*, must be a specific object. It is the principle of specificity we have previously seen in chapter 1. Although the principle is never mentioned in English legal literature or case law it is not confined to continental legal systems. From various provisions and cases we can deduce that the principle of specificity applies to English law as well.

In order to prevent certain misunderstandings we should pay attention to a question of legal terminology before focusing on the character of the right *in re*. In English legal literature the words right *in rem* and right *in re* are normally used indiscriminately and without giving a proper definition. Many authors understand these concepts as being equivalent and therefore interchangeable. Hohfeld[14], however, makes a clear distinction between the concept right *in rem* and the concept right *in re*. He uses the term right *in rem* to denote the large category of rights that work as against everyone, such as ownership, but also patents and copyrights.[15] This is the group of rights that in German law is referred to as *absolute Rechte* (in contrast with *relative Rechte*, rights *in personam*, that work against one or more definite persons only). The word right *in re*, on the other hand, is used by Hohfeld to indicate rights *in rem* directly concerning a tangible object (*Sachenrechte* or *dingliche Rechte* in German law).[16] Although it is rather confusing to use the words right *in rem* and right *in re* for two different concepts (personally I would prefer the word absolute or universal rights instead of rights *in rem*) it is very important to distinguish clearly between the two concepts: the large group of absolute rights and, within this group, a smaller category of rights relating to certain objects.[17] Nonetheless, it seems that the majority of writers do not follow Hohfeld's distinction and use the term right *in rem* to denote real rights.[18]

Now, to go back to the main discussion: the principle of specificity, according to which rights *in re* can exist in specific assets only, can be explained by examining the nature of the right *in re*. To my mind a right *in re* is composed of two fundamental elements. Firstly, a right *in re* is an absolute right, it has an 'absolute effect', that is to say, in principle it is binding upon everyone: third parties have to respect the right. The second characteristic is that a right *in re* in a certain sense forms a relationship between a person (natural or legal) and an object[19]: a right *in*

---

14 W.N. Hohfeld, Fundamental legal conceptions as applied in judicial reasoning, New Haven 1964 (repr. Westport, Connecticut 1978).

15 See p. 73-74 and 85; part of this group is also, among other things, the right of every person that nobody should commit a battery against him, or the right of privacy (p. 74 and 85).

16 P. 86.

17 I will use the term 'right *in re*' to denote rights that directly relate to objects whether corporeal or incorporeal.

18 The term right *in re* is hardly ever used in an English textbook or judgment.

19 In some systems of law (such as German and Swiss law) the object can be tangible only; in others (such as Dutch law) a right *in re* can relate to tangibles as well as intangibles (claims for instance). See also H. Coing, Europäisches Privatrecht, vol. 2, p. 369-370.

re namely gives its holder a direct (actual or potential) power over an object,[20] as opposed to a personal right (right *in personam*) to the transfer of a thing that merely gives its holder an indirect power over the object via the debtor, at least so far as specific performance is available. Both elements are equally important.[21]

The second characteristic, i.e. the right being somehow related to an object, forms the basis for the principle of specificity. It logically entails that a right *in re* can exist in a specific object only. It is also the reason why section 16 of the Sale of Goods Act provides that ownership of unascertained goods cannot pass to a buyer. The character of the right *in re* makes it impossible to be owner of unascertained goods. For, if ownership forms a relationship between a person and a certain thing, it must be known to which specific asset the right relates. This relationship between person and object is in my view the 'very nature of things' to which Lord Blackburn referred.

3.5 A relationship between a person and an object

One could object, as Hohfeld does, that a legal relation cannot exist between a person and an object and that the only legally relevant relations are those between persons. Hohfeld warns against the view that a right *in rem* (which in his system includes rights *in re*) is a right against a thing. According to him all rights *in rem* are in fact against persons: 'To say that all rights, or claims, must avail against persons is...simply another way of asserting that all duties must rest upon persons. The latter is no less obvious than the proposition that all rights must reside in persons.'[22] In his system a right *in rem* forms a bundle of right-duty relations between the holder of the right on the one side and those bound by it on the other side. There are as many right-duty relations as there are people bound by the right *in rem*. The holder of the right has a bundle of similar, though separate, rights against an indefinite number of persons. Hohfeld gives an example of the ownership of land to illustrate this and explains that under the right-duty relation the owner has the right that others should not use the land, and that the latter are under the correlative duty not to use it.

---

20 H. Rey, Berner Kommentar, Band IV (Sachenrecht), 2. Abteilung (Die beschränkten dinglichen Rechte; die Dienstbarkeiten und Grundlasten), 1. Teilband (Die Grunddienstbarkeiten), Lieferung 1 (Systematischer Teil und Kommentar zu art. 730 und 731 ZGB), Bern 1981, p. 14 et seq.; A. Meier-Hayoz, Berner Kommentar, Band IV (Sachenrecht), 1. Abteilung (Das Eigentum), 1. Teilband (Systematischer Teil und Allgemeine Bestimmungen, Art. 641-654 ZGB), Bern 1981, p. 103 et seq.

21 In Von Tuhr's opinion there are rare instances where the second element, the power over the thing, is lacking. As an example he mentions the *servitus altius non tollendi*, a servitude forbidding the owner of the servient land to erect buildings over a certain height. See Von Tuhr, Allgemeiner Teil I, p. 133, fn. 1. It is a purely negative servitude which gives its holder no right to take any positive action in regard to the land, such as using it or selling it in satisfaction of a claim. This view is a result of regarding the relationship between person and thing as *Herrschaft* (power over the thing). Yet to my mind the view is wrong: although this servitude does not entitle the owner of the dominant land to any positive act it still forms a relationship between him and the servient land.

22 P. 76, note 30.

In Hohfeld's system the right *in personam* is composed of the same right-duty relations as one can find in a right *in rem*. The difference, however, between the former and the latter sort of right is that a right *in personam* consists of a definite number of right-duty relations (namely as many relations as there are debtors), whereas a right *in rem* consists of an indefinite number of these relations.

In fact, the right-duty relations formed by the right *in rem* in Hohfeld's system[23] express exactly the same idea as the term absolute or universal effect: both mean that the right in question in principle works against the world.

However, to describe the right *in re* as a bundle of right-duty relations would give an incomplete picture. The right-duty relations merely give the holder of the right *in re* a negative right to exclude others. Yet the owner of a thing, for example, has not only the right to exclude others, to prevent them from using it; in addition he has the positive right to use the object himself. In Hohfeld's theory this right is called a 'privilege' and may exist alongside the right-duty relation. Ownership is not the only right that gives its holder such a privilege: according to Hohfeld in principle all rights *in re* give their holder a privilege to use the object of his right in a certain way and under certain conditions.[24]

Whereas the right-duty relation expresses the idea of absolute effect, Hohfeld's concept of privilege expresses the requirement of specificity. The privilege is related to a specific thing, the object of the right *in re*; it is a privilege over a certain thing. You cannot have the privilege to use or enjoy an asset if it is unknown which specific asset the privilege relates to. Hohfeld avoids calling it a relationship between the holder and the object of the right, but both concepts, Hohfeld's privilege and what I call the second element of the right *in re*, represent the same idea. They both express the notion that a right *in re* in a certain way relates to a specific thing, the object of the right *in re*, and they thereby both give the explanation for one of the most important principles of property law: the principle of specificity. The above shows that this principle flows from the very nature of the right *in re*, whether or not one accepts that legal relationships between persons and objects are possible.

3.6 The amendment of the Sale of Goods Act

As to sales ex bulk the law has changed significantly: the Sale of Goods (Amendment) Act 1995 has created a special statutory regime in sections 20A and 20B giving buyers ex bulk under certain conditions a proprietary interest in the

---

23 Hohfeld calls them 'multital' right-duty relations because of the indefinite number of relations.

24 Some authors who assert that legal relations can exist only between persons say that the right *in re* consists solely in the holder's negative right to exclude others. A prominent adherent of this view was Windscheid: see Windscheid/Kipp, § 38 and fn. 3 *ibidem*. But when overlooking the holder's positive rights over the thing (use or sale) it is almost impossible to explain security rights such as the pledge. These rights give their holder a privilege to sell the thing and use the proceeds to satisfy a claim. How to explain this as a right to exclude others? Cf. Von Tuhr, Allgemeiner Teil I, p. 134. For a detailed description of this controversy see E.B. Rank-Berenschot, Over de scheidslijn tussen goederenrecht en verbintenissenrecht, (thesis Leiden 1992) Deventer 1992, p. 35 et seq.

bulk goods.[25] The proprietary interest takes the form of a right of co-ownership in the bulk.

The reform was induced by the decision in *The Gosforth*[26], a case decided by the Dutch District Court of Rotterdam in 1985. It was a case in which goods that were on board a vessel called 'The Gosforth' had been sold to several buyers. The goods, citrus pulp pellets, had not been appropriated to the individual contracts. Now, although the case was decided on other grounds, which are not relevant here, the President of the court stated, in an *obiter dictum*, that under English law ownership of generic goods cannot pass until they are identified.[27] Of course, there was nothing remarkable about this statement. Nonetheless it once more drew attention to the identification issue in section 16 SGA and led to the Law Commission examining the legal position of buyers ex bulk. In 1989 the English and Scottish Law Commissions issued a consultation paper about the subject.[28] Subsequently, in 1993 they released their final reports[29] which, among other things, contained a list of recommendations to change the law regarding sales ex bulk and a draft bill embodying the changes recommended.

We should bear in mind, however, that the amendment of the Sale of Goods Act is confined to sales ex bulk (see section 20A subs. 1). Thus, if there is no sale ex bulk, section 16 will apply and accordingly ownership will not pass before appropriation of the goods. So, two elements will now play a pivotal role: the definition of the word 'bulk' and, if there is indeed a bulk in the sense of section 20A, the question whether the parties to the contract of sale intended that the goods should be taken from that bulk only. These two elements will determine whether or not the co-ownership regime will apply. The definition of 'bulk', which is now to be found in section 61(1) SGA, is not exactly unambiguous, but from the Law Commission's report we can at least understand that it was intended to exclude the seller's general stock.[30] Apparently in cases like *Re Goldcorp* the co-ownership regime will not apply and the buyers will still have to content themselves with a personal right against the seller.

---

25 Not long before the amendment of the Sale of Goods Act, in *Re Stapylton Fletcher Ltd* [1995] 1 All ER 192, buyers of unascertained goods were given co-ownership of a collection of goods. It was decided that, if the seller has segregated goods from his general stock and appropriated them unconditionally to the buyers collectively, the buyers become co-owners (tenants in common) of those goods. Appropriation to the individual buyers was held not to be necessary.

26 President Arrondissementsrechtbank Rotterdam, 20 February 1985, S&S 1985, 91.

27 S&S 1985, p. 245.

28 Law Com. Working Paper No. 112, Rights to Goods in Bulk (April 1989); Scot. Law Com. Discussion Paper No. 83, Bulk Goods: Section 16 of the Sale of Goods Act 1979 and Section 1 of the Bills of Lading Act 1855 (August 1989).

29 Sale of goods forming part of a bulk, Law Com. No. 215, Scot. Law Com. No. 145.

30 Law Com. Report, p. 18.

3.7 The peculiar consequences of the specificity principle as to sales ex bulk

As regards sales ex bulk the principle of specificity, as applied before the 1995 amendment, gave rise to some odd and quite arbitrary results. Let us take an example. Where the owner of a cargo has sold 500 tons out of a total bulk of 1000 tons, ownership does not pass to the buyer before goods have been appropriated as the assets to be transferred to that particular buyer. This is, as we have seen, the result of the specificity principle. Nevertheless, it is possible for the seller to sell a 50% share in the bulk. In that case ownership of the share passes to the buyer immediately after the contract of sale is made. No appropriation is needed because the share relates to the whole of the bulk and consequently to every item within the bulk.[31] Since the amount of goods is exactly the same, it is hard to see any practical difference. Yet the buyer of a share acquires a proprietary interest whereas the buyer of a certain amount merely has a personal right to delivery of the goods.

If, to give another example, in the first case appropriation has taken place and subsequently the 500 tons, that have now passed to the buyer, are mixed with the remaining bulk, the seller and buyer will become co-owners of the bulk. The buyer does not lose his proprietary interest, even though the goods have lost their identity: his right of ownership is converted into a right of co-ownership (a 50% share) of the bulk. As regards identity of the goods the situation is the same as before appropriation: the goods form part of a larger bulk. Nonetheless, the buyer whose goods have been appropriated and then mixed again, has a proprietary interest, whereas the buyer whose goods have never been appropriated, has to content himself with a personal right.[32]

3.8 Co-ownership under sections 20A and 20B of the Sale of Goods Act

In order to protect buyers ex bulk they are under certain conditions given a proprietary interest in the form of co-ownership of the bulk. For a buyer to become a co-owner it is first of all necessary that the goods form part of a bulk which is identified either in the contract of sale or by subsequent agreement between the seller and the buyer (see section 20A subs. 1 (a)). Obviously it must be known which particular collection of goods the buyer is a co-owner of.[33] Furthermore the regime of co-ownership is limited to those goods which are paid for.[34] However, to acquire co-ownership it is not necessary for the buyer to pay for all the goods bought by him. If only part of the goods have been paid for, the buyer will become a co-owner of that smaller amount. His share will then grow proportionately with every subsequent payment.

31 See § 3.11.
32 Both examples are mentioned in the Law Com. Report on p. 4 and 5.
33 See § 3.11.
34 This requirement reminds one of a similar rule in Roman law (Inst. 2,1,41). See R. Feenstra, Reclame en revindicatie, Haarlem 1949 and R. Zimmermann, The law of obligations, Roman foundations of the civilian tradition, Cape Town/Deventer/Boston 1992, p. 272 et seq.

The buyer's share in the bulk is determined differently from the method normally used in cases of co-ownership. The main rule as to calculating the proportion of the share is to be found in section 20A subs. 3: '...the undivided share of a buyer will at any time be such a share as the quantity of goods paid for and due to the buyer out of the bulk bears to the quantity of goods in the bulk at that time.'

By using this method of calculation section 20A creates a special form of co-ownership, namely co-ownership of a certain amount of goods: the buyer will become co-owner of such number of goods as corresponds with the amount bought and paid for. The normal form of co-ownership, on the other hand, is for a certain percentage rather than a certain amount. If the prepaying buyer were given the normal form of co-ownership, he would profit from an increase[35] in the bulk and lose in case of a reduction[36] of the bulk. Where there is normal co-ownership the relative proportion of the share is fixed, i.e. the percentage remains the same, but the absolute amount it represents fluctuates when the bulk increases or decreases. We can therefore say that the standard form of co-ownership entails a fixed percentage and a variable amount of goods.

Yet this kind of co-ownership is not the most appropriate form to give to buyers ex bulk. The purpose of the co-ownership regime in section 20A is to secure the buyer's rights as to the goods bought and paid for. That being so, it is more suitable to make the buyer co-owner of a fixed amount of goods. To achieve this result the buyer is given a variable percentage that will fluctuate so as to represent at any time the exact amount of goods bought and paid for. That is to say, the relative proportion of the share (the percentage) may vary; the absolute quantity of the share, however, remains the same.

As this special sort of co-ownership, which I will call protective co-ownership, entails a fixed quantity of goods, a supplementary rule is needed to adjust the proportion of the shares in case there are two or more buyers and the quantity of goods bought and paid for exceeds the total amount of the bulk, for instance as a result of overselling, or because some of the goods have perished. Section 20A subs. 4 provides that in the event of such an excess the buyers' shares are 'reduced proportionately so that the aggregate of the undivided shares is equal to the whole of the bulk'.

If, after the buyers' shares have been so reduced, the bulk increases again, we can assume that each buyer's share will increase accordingly, though to a maximum of the amount bought and paid for. Such fluctuations are quite common, especially when the goods are located in a warehouse and they should therefore not be allowed to inflict permanent damage on the buyers' interests. The new goods that top up the bulk should be regarded as intended to replenish the buyers' shares. Normally the bulk will increase as a result of the seller replenishing the bulk, but the increase may also be caused by the avoidance of a contract of sale between the

---

35 For example an increase as a result of the avoidance of a contract of sale or as a result of original acquisition.
36 For instance, when part of the goods perish.

seller and one of the buyers. The buyer's co-ownership, or, if appropriation has already taken place, his right of ownership then falls back to the seller because the contract, which formed the basis for the transfer of ownership, lapses.

Naturally, whenever the bulk contains more than the quantity bought and paid for, the seller himself will also be a co-owner of the bulk. Since his legal interest is subordinate to the buyers' protective co-ownership, his share will be the first to suffer any losses in the bulk and the last to profit from any subsequent increase. To give an example, if from a total bulk of 2000 tons 500 are sold to A and another 500 to B, A and B will, provided they have paid for the goods, both become co-owners of 1/4 (which represents 500 tons). The seller is co-owner of 1/2. If then 500 tons are sold and directly delivered to C, the delivery will affect only the seller's share: the seller and the buyers A and B are now co-owners of 500 tons, all of them holding a 1/3 share in a total bulk of 1500 tons. The example would be the same if 500 tons had perished or had been otherwise lost. As we can see the seller has a rather odd form of co-ownership. Yet it is a logical and necessary complement of the buyers' preferred position; it could be called subordinate co-ownership.[37]

3.9 When does ownership pass?

If the requirements in section 20A are met, the buyer will become a co-owner of the bulk.[38] Even so, when the contract is for the sale of a certain number of goods the seller is obliged to pass ownership of these goods to the buyer. That the buyer has already received a share in the bulk does not suffice. The seller is obliged to transfer individual ownership[39] of a certain number of identified assets. In order to do this appropriation of the goods is needed. As to that nothing has changed. The co-ownership regime is merely a transitional phase designed to protect the buyer in the event of the seller's insolvency. We could see it as a security interest or a peculiar sort of 'buyer's lien' in the form of co-ownership. The moment of appropriation should still be considered as the moment when ownership of the contract goods passes. Accordingly we can assume that this is also the time when the risk passes to the buyer under section 20 of the Sale of Goods Act.

---

37 The situation could be complicated even more if a third party's goods are commingled with the bulk. According to the present law the mixing in principle leads to co-ownership, that is to say, to the normal form of co-ownership. Consequently the two forms of co-ownership will then appear at the same time, the buyers having co-ownership of a certain amount and the third party having co-ownership of a certain percentage. Such an instance is more than just hypothetical: think of appropriation by exhaustion making the remaining buyer owner of the goods, followed by a replenishing of the bulk and the sale of and payment on certain quantities. The first buyer will most probably have normal co-ownership whereas the subsequent buyers will get protective co-ownership. Of course, treating these buyers differently is far from desirable.

38 Though, it should be noted that the new co-ownership regime is *ius dispositivum*: the parties can agree that co-ownership will pass at a later time or they can opt out of the new provisions altogether. See section 20A subs. 2 and the Law Commission's report, p. 20 and 39.

39 As distinct from co-ownership.

3.10 Protective co-ownership in other jurisdictions

Co-ownership for a certain amount rather than a certain percentage can also be found in some civil law systems which have a special statutory regime regarding the collective keeping of shares and bonds. The Dutch *Wet giraal Effectenverkeer*[40] and the German *Depotgesetz*[41], for example, provide for such a form of co-ownership. These statutes allow shares and bonds to be kept and administered *en masse* without any need to register the shares' and bonds' individual registration numbers. For each sort of share or bond a separate depot is created in which the shares and bonds are stored collectively. In an accompanying register is entered how many shares or bonds each client contributed to the depot. The collective depot systems facilitate considerably the administration of the shares and bonds and especially the settlement of transactions. On the other hand, as a result of not registering the individual registration numbers it is impossible for the clients to have ownership of individual shares or bonds. Here again the principle of specificity causes difficulties. Since the objects are mixed together[42] it can no longer be established which individual objects belong to which client: a problem identical with the one we have seen in sales ex bulk. To solve this problem the clients become co-owners of the depot for the amount they contributed. In German law a similar form of co-ownership has been created for the collective storage of goods (*Sammellagerung*).[43]

This form of co-ownership, whose only purpose is to protect as far as possible the depositor's legal position, is sometimes called 'unstable' co-ownership, as the depositor can always require severance and delivery of the quantity he co-owns.[44] Consent of the other co-owners, which would be needed in case of normal co-ownership, is not required in this case.

3.11 A violation of the specificity principle?

The new sections of the Sale of Goods Act, as well as the foreign statutes discussed in section 3.10, have created a peculiar form of co-ownership. As we have seen, normal co-ownership entails a fixed percentage and a variable absolute quantity.

---

40 Wet van 8 juni 1977, Staatsblad 333; see articles 12 and 38.

41 Gesetz über die Verwahrung und Anschaffung von Wertpapieren vom 4. Februar 1937 (Reichsgesetzblatt I 171), in the version of 1 August 1994 (BGBl. I 34); for the co-ownership regime see § 6.

42 The Roman term for this kind of mixture is *commixtio*. See for example: P. Birks, Mixtures, in: N. Palmer and E. McKendrick (eds.), Interests in goods, London/New York/Hamburg/Hong Kong 1993, p. 449.

43 See § 469 *Handelsgesetzbuch* and J. Koller in: Staub, Handelsgesetzbuch, Großkommentar, ed. by C. Canaris, W. Schilling and P. Ulmer, 4th ed., Berlin/New York 1987, § 419, Rdnr. 8; see also § 23 and 30 *Verordnung über die Orderlagerscheine*.

44 J. Koller in: Staub, Handelsgesetzbuch, § 419 Rdnr. 16, 18 and 20; the word 'unstable' co-ownership (*labiles Miteigentum*) is used by P. Liver in: Schweizerisches Privatrecht, Sachenrecht, Erster Halbband, ed. by A. Meier-Hayoz, Basel/Stuttgart 1977, p. 382, fn. 6.

On the other hand, where there is protective co-ownership, the shares are fixed as to their absolute quantity. To reach this result the relative quantity, i.e. the percentage, is always ready to adopt itself so that it represents at any moment the absolute quantity belonging to the different co-owners.

In practice this amounts to ownership of a quantity of unascertained goods, which would clearly be a violation of the specificity principle: it must be known exactly to which assets a real right relates. However, when we examine this form of co-ownership more closely, it will appear that in reality there is no such violation.

In order to understand how the principle of specificity is applied to protective co-ownership we should first examine if this principle is complied with in the case of normal co-ownership. Actually, co-ownership is not an interest different from ownership; it is simply a situation in which a right of ownership belongs to more than one person at the same time. Therefore the principle of specificity should be applied to co-ownership in exactly the same way as to 'individual' ownership. And indeed it is applied the same way: if a collection of goods is owned by one person, he has in fact as many rights of ownership as there are goods.[45] Similarly, where a collection of things is co-owned, the co-owners' shares relate to every single item of the collection, that is to say, every item is co-owned in the same percentage.[46] As to identification there is no difference between normal co-ownership and protective co-ownership.[47] Here as well the shares relate to every item within the bulk. This is in no way changed by the fact that the percentage is prone to constant fluctuation. So, there is no violation of the principle of specificity.

This has important consequences for defending the right of co-ownership against a third party who infringes the right, for example by stealing one of the assets in the bulk. Every co-owner has an independent right to bring an action. If, however, the co-owners' shares were seen as relating not to every single item but rather to a certain amount of assets, such a right of action would be impossible, because the plaintiff would never succeed in proving his right of ownership. It would be impossible for him to demonstrate that his interest related to the very asset in question, even if it were undeniable that the asset came from the bulk which the plaintiff was a co-owner of.

---

45 See for example Wolff/Raiser, Sachenrecht, p. 178 and A. Meier-Hayoz, Berner Kommentar, IV,1,1, p. 75. See also the expression by A. Brinz: 'Eine Sache, Ein Eigenthum' (one thing, one right of ownership) in his *Lehrbuch der Pandekten*, vol. 1, 3rd ed. Erlangen 1884, p. 475.

46 See for instance J. Koller, Staub, Handelsgesetzbuch, § 419, Rdnr. 8 and 14.

47 For a different opinion see S. Zimmermann, Die Sammelverwahrung von Edelmetallen, (*Dissertation* Zurich) Bern 1981, p. 125, fn. 378: 'Verletzt ist jedoch das Spezialitätsprinzip..., da sich das Eigentumsrecht beim Mengeneigentum nicht auf einzelne bestimmte individualisierte Sachen bezieht, sondern lediglich auf eine Teilmenge einer Vielzahl von Sachen.' (Yet the principle of specificity is violated..., since in the case of ownership of a quantity the right of ownership does not relate to single specified things but rather to a smaller quantity of a larger amount of things).

3.12 Protecting ownership against the principle of specificity

The sale ex bulk provisions give us an example of an attempt to escape from some of the undesirable consequences supposedly caused by the principle of specificity. In truth, however, the undesirable effects are not so much caused by the principle itself as by an inflexible application of it.

The principle of specificity in itself is a logical necessity; it flows directly from the definition of the right *in re* as a right working against everyone constituting a relationship between a person and a particular object. Exceptions to this principle cannot be allowed because they would entail changing the definition of the right *in re* and accordingly calling into question the entire property law system.

Yet the fact that the principle of specificity forms a necessary element does not mean that we have to accept all the unwelcome consequences it is supposed to cause. Some of these consequences can be avoided without abandoning the principle, by allowing a more liberal use of real substitution[48] and the concept of co-ownership. Both are able to help a real right survive when the relationship between the right and its object is severed.

Real substitution is able to put in place of the original object a new object that can be considered to have taken over the original asset's position. Consequently, where real substitution has taken place, the real right can last while its object has been changed. This is not a breach of the specificity principle. Before the substitution the right relates to a specific object; after the substitution it still relates to a specific object, namely the new object that has been substituted for the original one. In English law this concept is applied to the trust fund and to the assets burdened with a floating charge. In both instances a right, the beneficial interest and the charge respectively, relates to a certain fund or collection of assets whose components can be replaced automatically with other objects. Tracing, whether at law or in equity, makes use of substitution as well. It allows a real right to subsist where, applying the principle of specificity strictly, the real right would lapse. The use of real substitution could easily be extended to sales ex bulk so as to give a better protection to the co-owning buyers. If the bulk is no longer sufficient to satisfy all co-owners, for instance because the bulk is oversold or because an amount of goods has been withdrawn, the shares will be reduced proportionately (section 20A subs. 4 SGA). Good protection of those buyers who do not insist on immediate delivery of the goods demands that any subsequent replenishing of the bulk should be considered as a substitute to replenish the buyers' shares in the bulk. It should not be possible for the seller to object that he had no intention to replenish the buyers' shares.

The notion of co-ownership can assist where the object of the real right has not disappeared but has been so commingled with other goods that it is no longer possible to determine to which object the right relates. It offers the possibility of replacing the original real right with a share in the commingled mass of goods. In

---

48 In some legal systems this concept is called real subrogation instead.

fact, this is also a form of substitution: the object is changed from the original asset into the entire mass of goods and simultaneously the right itself is changed from individual ownership into co-ownership.

4 Agreement about the passing of ownership: the real agreement

In the third chapter I proposed to introduce the concept of real agreement in French law. The systematic arguments for introducing the concept apply to a large extent to English law as well.

Appropriation of generic goods

In § 3 we have learnt that there is a major exception to the *solo consensu* principle: in order for ownership of generic goods to pass to the buyer it is needed that certain goods be irrevocably appropriated to the contract. The process of appropriation turns the generic goods into identified goods thereby complying with the principle of specificity.[49]

As stated in section 18 rule 5(1) of the Sale of Goods Act the appropriation should take place with the consent of both transferor and transferee. True, the seller or buyer may give his consent in advance, so that the appropriation of the goods seems to have been accomplished unilaterally by one of the parties. After having examined a certain bulk of goods the buyer may decide that the contract goods should be taken from that particular bulk, leaving it to the seller to make the ultimate selection of the goods. In doing so he consents beforehand to the seller's final appropriation. Yet, it would be wrong to infer that it is not vital for both parties to give their consent. Quite the reverse: the other party's consent is essential to any act of appropriation.[50] Appropriation therefore needs an agreement between transferor and acquirer as to which individual goods have to be transferred. Now, if we compare this agreement to the concept of real agreement used in tradition systems it is impossible to see any relevant difference. Both concepts express the need for consensus about the passing of ownership of certain identified assets and are therefore equal.

The reason why this kind of appropriation requires both parties' consent is the following. A voluntary transfer of property depends on the transferor's will.[51] In addition, the acquirer's will to accept the property is needed. As ownership is possible only in relation to identified objects, the transferor's will to transfer and the transferee's will to acquire should relate to identified objects as well. If there are more generic goods than have to be transferred, the parties should concentrate their

---

49 This requirement applies also to the payment of money, though only when banknotes or coins are used. The transfer of banknotes or coins is a transfer of ownership of generic things. Where the payment of money takes another form, the payment cannot be considered as a transfer of ownership because as regards money the concept of ownership is limited to banknotes and coins.

50 Cf. A.G. Guest et al. (eds.), Benjamin's Sale of Goods, 5th ed., London 1997, § 5-073.

51 This is true even if he is under a duty to transfer.

will on certain specified assets. For this reason the selection can never be made by the transferor alone, that is to say, without the acquirer's consent.

Naturally, where there is a contract for the sale of quasi-specific goods, the parallel between the appropriation process and the real agreement is confined to an appropriation performed consciously. If a bulk of 1000 tons of cocoa is sold to A and B, both buying 500 tons, appropriation of 500 tons to A's contract necessarily entails appropriation of the remaining 500 tons to B. The seller's will to appropriate certain goods to A's contract includes his will to appropriate the rest to B's contract.

In contrast, identification of the goods can also take place as a result of an accidental reduction in the number of goods leaving a bulk which is no longer larger than the amount sold to the buyer (appropriation by accident). Of course, such appropriation can take place only when there is one single buyer of the goods. In that instance there is no longer any choice to be made, and, in consequence, the parties' will need no be narrowed. Here through accident the generic goods have become identified.[52]

Transfer without prior contract

There are, however, more reasons for introducing the concept of real agreement in English law. The sale of generic goods is just one of many cases where the *solo consensu* principle does not apply. The most compelling reason for using the concept is that the consensual transfer system presupposes a prior contract. However, a transfer can also be based on a non-contractual obligation, such as unjustified enrichment. Moreover, the transfer may be by way of gift[53]. Of course, these cases fall beyond the scope of the Sale of Goods Act. Yet, taking these into consideration enables us to accentuate a feature common to all transfers *inter vivos* of movables in English law. Since the parties' will is essential for a voluntary transfer, their will to transfer must be present in these instances as well. Yet, here the parties' consensus about the transfer of the asset is not enclosed in any contract. Consequently, there must be an independent agreement in which the transferor and acquirer agree about the transfer of a certain object. This is exactly what the term real agreement represents.

Transfer of future goods

Even within the Sale of Goods Act there are instances in which a real agreement is needed for a sound analysis, for example, where the thing sold has yet to be manufactured: the sale of non-existing future goods. If a work of art, a statue for example, has been commissioned, ownership of the statue does not pass immediately upon work being started.

The parties to the contract may agree that ownership will pass before the object commissioned is finished: according to section 17 SGA ownership passes when the

---

52 Section 18 rule 5(3). Both kinds of appropriation by reduction are called appropriation by exhaustion.
53 In English law a gift is not considered as a contract, because for a contract consideration is needed: a promise is binding only if accompanied by some form of recompense. See part B of this chapter, and chapter 6.

parties intend it to pass. Sometimes in ship-building contracts the parties agree that ownership in the future ship (the keel and everything attached to it) should pass when certain instalments have been paid.[54] By doing so the buyer excludes the risk of the builder's insolvency, accepting at the same time, though, the risk of accidental loss or damage.

Normally, however, the parties do not intend ownership to pass before completion of the object. For that reason section 18 rule 5(1) gives a *ius dispositivum* provision which applies when the parties do not stipulate the moment when ownership should pass: if the thing produced is in a deliverable state and if it is unconditionally appropriated to the contract, ownership passes. But how do we decide when work on the object is finished? Should we leave it to the manufacturer or artist to decide? What if the client does not approve of the object? Does he become owner against his will? Of course, both parties should agree about the passing of ownership. Ownership cannot pass to the client against his will. In other words, apart from the contract, under which the object is commissioned, a real agreement is needed in which the parties agree about the passing of ownership. The appropriation mentioned in section 18 can be regarded as such a real agreement. It needs both parties' consent. If the buyer does not accept the thing, he may refuse to give the consent necessary for a valid appropriation. If, on the other hand, ownership has already passed and subsequently the object turns out to be unsatisfactory the buyer has the right to reject. This right will be discussed below.

Termination for breach and rejection of defective goods

Termination[55] of a contract makes an end to the contract in question. It works *ex nunc*, that is to say, it has no retroactive effect. If ownership of a thing has passed to the buyer before the termination of the contract, the legal ground for this transfer remains intact: after all, unlike in the case of rescission or avoidance, it is not deemed that the contract has never existed. As a result ownership of the thing cannot automatically revert to the seller.[56] This is different when the buyer exercises his right of rejection. Where the thing delivered to the buyer does not

---

54 Benjamin's Sale of Goods, § 5-091. See *McDougall v. Aeromarine of Emsworth Ltd* [1958] 3 All ER 431. Once ownership of the keel has passed to the buyer materials used in the building process and fixed onto the future ship automatically pass to the buyer as a result of *accessio*. See Lord Watson in *Seath v. Moore* (1886) 11 App. Cas. 350, at p. 380.

55 Note that the term discharge is used as a synonym. The term is similar to the Dutch term *ontbinding* (art. 6:265 BW) and the German term *Rücktritt* (§ 327 j° 346 et seq. BGB) or *Wandlung* (§ 462 et seq. BGB, a special form of *Rücktritt* to which § 346 et seq. apply as well). It should be distinguished from rescission or avoidance (these terms are interchangeable), which ends a legal act with retroactive effect, that is, *ab initio*, or *ex tunc*. In the latter case the contract is deemed never to have existed. See *Johnson v. Agnew* [1979] 1 All ER 883, at p. 889(f) per Lord Wilberforce. Cf. Goode, Commercial law, p. 83-84; A.G. Guest et al. (eds.), Chitty on Contract, vol. 1, 27th ed., London 1994, § 24-001 and 24-042. Rescission or avoidance is similar to the Dutch *vernietiging* (art. 3:53 BW) and the German *Anfechtung* (§ 142 BGB).

56 As we shall see in § 5 the transfer system of the Sale of Goods Act can be regarded as a causal transfer system. If it were an abstract system neither termination nor avoidance would revest ownership in the seller, and the question of retroactive effect would be irrelevant.

conform to the contract requirements the buyer has the right to reject the thing. If ownership has not yet passed it prevents ownership from passing to the buyer. If, on the other hand, the buyer has already acquired ownership it revests ownership in the seller.[57] As Goode expresses it, rejection of the goods nullifies delivery.[58] Since normally the risk of accidental loss is linked to ownership, rejection also reverts the risk to the seller.[59] In *McDougall v. Aeromarine of Emsworth Ltd*[60] ownership of a ship which was in the process of being built passed to the buyer on payment of the first instalment. When it was eventually delivered to the buyer he rightfully rejected the ship because it did not meet the contract requirements. Ownership was held to return to the seller as a result.

In *Kwei Tek Chao v. British Traders and Shippers Ltd*[61] Devlin J. explains the reason of this revesting as follows. Ownership of the objects passes to the buyer 'subject to the condition that they revest if on examination he finds them not in accordance with the contract... That means that he gets only conditional property in the goods, the condition being a condition subsequent [= a resolutive condition].'[62]

Using the concept of real agreement the process of rejection may be explained as follows. The legal act of transferring ownership of the thing, i.e. the real agreement, has been made under an (implicit) resolutive condition. It is important to note that the condition is not attached to the entire contract but solely to the transfer. This can be explained only by regarding the transfer of ownership as a distinct legal act, that is to say, by recognizing the real agreement. For a condition cannot be attached to a factual act; it can be attached only to a legal act or part of a legal act such as an obligation arising from a contract. A fact cannot be nullified; a legal act, however, can.

Also when the goods are rejected before ownership in them has passed to the buyer the concept of real agreement can help us explain this. Where generic goods

---

57 *Kwei Tek Chao v. British Traders & Shippers Ltd* [1954] 1 All ER 779 at p. 795-796; *McDougall v. Aeromarine of Emsworth Ltd* [1958] 3 All ER 431 at p. 437; *Tradax Export S.A. v. European Grain & Shipping Ltd* [1983] 2 Lloyd's Rep. 100, at p. 107 (per Bingham J.): '...a clear, unequivocal and bona fide rejection of goods liable to rejection has the effect of preserving or revesting the ownership of the goods in the seller' (see Goode's comment on this case in *Commercial law*, p. 371, fn. 18); *Gill & Duffus SA v. Berger & Co Inc* [1984] 1 All ER 438, at p. 446(g-h). Section 36 SGA provides that the buyer need not return the rejected goods to the seller, that is to say, he need not redeliver them physically to the seller. It suffices if he notifies the seller of the rejection. Note that s. 36 SGA is not about revesting ownership.

58 Goode, Commercial law, p. 362. Here the term 'delivery' most probably denotes the transfer of ownership.

59 See Goode, Commercial law, p. 363; Benjamin's Sale of Goods, § 12-065.

60 [1958] 3 All ER 431.

61 [1954] 1 All ER 779, at 796.

62 A condition precedent, also called suspensive condition, suspends the effects of the legal act to which it is attached until the occurrence of some uncertain event in the future. It does not postpone the creation of the legal act but merely freezes its legal consequences. On the other hand, if the legal act is subject to a condition subsequent, or resolutive condition, occurrence of the uncertain future event causes the legal act's consequences, which have already materialized, to lapse. Before fulfilment of the resolutive condition, however, the legal act is fully effective.

are sold certain goods should be appropriated to the contract as the goods to be transferred to the buyer. The act of appropriation commonly requires agreement between the parties.[63] If the buyer notices the defect before the appropriation is completed the rejection will prevent ownership of the goods from passing to the buyer as a result of the buyer's refusal to assent to the appropriation.[64]

A similar explanation can be used where the amount of goods delivered to the buyer is smaller or larger than the amount contracted for. The buyer may reject such a tender.[65] If he rejects before having assented to the appropriation, no appropriation will take place. On the other hand, when he discovers the shortage only after having assented to the appropriation, he may reject the goods by avoiding the appropriation, i.e. the real agreement. Where too many goods are delivered the buyer may, instead of rejecting the whole tender, opt to reject only the surplus. If he does so, rejection of the surplus will again cause identification problems. As ownership of a certain quantity of unascertained goods cannot exist, ownership of the surplus cannot revert to the seller before a certain amount of goods is separated from the tender and thus identified for re-delivery to the seller. Such a re-transfer also needs a real agreement in which the buyer expresses his will to transfer certain identified assets and the seller expresses his will to accept ownership of them.

Rejection and the seller's right to cure

Rejection does not always lead to the termination of the contract in question. It is true, where generic goods sold are defective and do not correspond to the contract requirements one of the remedies available to the buyer is to terminate the contract.[66] Yet, as it ends the entire contract, termination often does not answer the needs of the contracting parties. In many cases the buyer's and seller's interests are best served by maintaining the contract and rejecting only the goods which have been offered.[67] The buyer may elect for a new transfer of appropriate goods to be made. If he chooses to do so, the contract of sale will remain valid and the seller can make a second tender.[68] In this case both parties agree that the contract should not be terminated and that the seller should have a fresh chance to deliver.

Furthermore, the buyer may even be obliged to accept a new tender against his will. For, in principle the seller has the right to cure, that is, the right to replace the defective goods with a new delivery of conforming goods, as long as the time for

---

63 Agreement is not needed where the goods are appropriated by accident.
64 Cf. M.G. Bridge, The Sale of Goods, Oxford 1997, p. 198.
65 S. 30 subs. 1 and 2. By the way, a buyer who does not deal as consumer may not reject the tender when the shortfall or the excess is so slight that rejection would be unreasonable: s. 30 subs. 2A.
66 Goode, Commercial Law, p. 362.
67 As to the conditions under which rejection is possible, see: Goode, Commercial Law, p. 358-361.
68 In principle the buyer has no right to claim specific performance, that is to say, he is unable to demand that the contract be properly performed and conforming goods be tendered. See Goode, Commercial Law, p. 387-388.

delivery has not yet expired.[69] Making this new tender entails appropriating substitute goods to the contract. Thus a new real agreement is needed, a new legal act of transfer.

The possibility of rejecting a tender without terminating the contract can be explained only when regarding the transfer of ownership as a distinct legal act. Rejection will nullify the transfer of the first tender, i.e. the real agreement which passed ownership in these goods. The second tender needs a second real agreement. It is clear that the *solo consensu* rule cannot apply here: there is no fresh contract to pass ownership to the buyer. The initial contract, after all, remained valid. As it cannot pass ownership of the second tender the passing must have been brought about by another legal act: a real agreement. Although the contract and the transfer will normally coincide they should nevertheless be seen as two distinct legal acts.

Retention of ownership

Section 17 SGA enables the parties to the contract to postpone the passing of ownership and make it depend on payment of the full price. The condition does not affect the entire contract of sale. It suspends the passing of ownership. All other consequences of the contract are independent of payment and arise immediately. That is to say, unless otherwise agreed, the buyer will be obliged to pay and the seller obliged to deliver the object (i.e. transferring direct possession) immediately after the contract has been made.

From a Dutch or German point of view it could be contended that a transfer system which allows a retention of ownership clause[70], must have a real agreement. Recognizing a real agreement in English law enables us to explain the retention of ownership in a way analogous to Dutch and German law. Yet it would be exaggerating to argue that the retention of ownership clause cannot be explained otherwise and that it therefore proves the existence of a real agreement.[71]

The clause can be explained in two ways. The clause could be part of a real agreement, thus suspending the transfer of ownership, but it could also be attached to the obligation to transfer. In the latter case it suspends the seller's obligation to transfer ownership. The obligation does exist, but it will become effective only upon full payment of the purchase price. Until that moment the obligation will remain dormant and accordingly will not form a valid and effective *causa traditionis* needed in the English causal system[72] to let ownership pass. The second theory does not need the concept of real agreement.

---

69 *Borrowman Phillips & Co. v. Free & Hollis* (1878) 4 QBD, 500; *Motor Oil Hellas (Corinth) Refineries S.A. v. Shipping Corporation of India (The 'Kanchenjunga')* [1990] 1 Lloyd's Rep., 391; see: Goode, Commercial Law, p. 363-366.

70 The retention of ownership is also called 'reservation of ownership', 'reservation of title' or, quite imprecisely, 'reservation of the right of disposal'.

71 The same reasoning applies to French law. See chapter 3, § 2.2.

72 See *infra* § 5.

5 A causal or abstract transfer system, or something in between?

The question whether the transfer system in the Sale of Goods Act is causal or abstract or something different is not debated in English case law and legal literature.[73] The terms 'abstract' and 'causal' are not used to denote different transfer systems. What is more, the question behind these terms is unknown as well. It seems to fascinate civil lawyers only. This may be explained to a certain extent by English law not having originated in the continental learned law. As we shall see in chapter 7 the debate about our question was based on texts in Justinian's *Corpus Iuris Civilis*. This collection of texts as interpreted by the learned jurists had an enormous influence on the development of continental law. Since English law has been developed independently of the continental learned law the texts of the *Corpus Iuris Civilis* did not give rise to a discussion in English law about our problem.

Still, although the question is not discussed in English law, the answer can be found by analysing the influence of various defects rendering a contract void, voidable or unenforceable. In this section I will confine myself to the contract of sale. In part B of the chapter we shall see whether a similar analysis can be made for transfers outside the scope of the Sale of Goods Act, where the old common law requirement of delivery still applies.[74]

In English law a contract may be void for example for want of consensus or consideration, mistake as to the identity of one of the contracting parties or mistake as to the subject matter of the contract, or it may be declared void by statute.[75] Strictly speaking a void contract has no legal consequences whatever.[76] As a result there is no valid *causa traditionis* to support the passing of ownership. English law draws the conclusion that ownership cannot pass under a void contract.[77]

As an illustration we can examine the decisions in *Cundy v. Lindsay*[78], *Ingram v. Little*[79] and *Lewis v. Averay*[80], all of which are cases about mistake. In *Ingram v. Little* the plaintiffs advertised their car for sale. The buyer was a rogue acting under a false name. He wanted to take the car with him at once and proposed to pay by cheque. As the plaintiffs did not trust the buyer they initially insisted on cash payment. But using the name of a respectable businessman the buyer persuaded

---

73 Only sporadically it has been discussed. See for example T. Weir, Taking for granted - the ramifications of *nemo dat*, in: M.D.A. Freeman (ed.), Current Legal Problems, vol. 49(II), Oxford 1996, p. 325.

74 See *infra* § 9.

75 See Goode, Commercial law, p. 82.

76 Guest et al., Chitty on Contracts, vol. 1, § 1-023; Goode, Commercial law, p. 82; Halsbury's Laws of England, 4th ed., vol. 9(1), Reissue 1998, Contract, section 6 (Void and illegal contracts, by R.J. Bragg), § 887.

77 L. Crispin Warmington (ed.), Stephen's commentaries on the laws of England, vol. 2, 21st ed., London 1950, p. 147; A.G. Guest et al., Chitty on Contracts, vol. 1, § 1-023.

78 (1878) 3 App. Cas. 459 (HL).

79 [1960] 3 All ER 332.

80 [1971] 3 All ER 907.

them to accept the cheque. Of course, the cheque was dishonoured and the rogue had disappeared. In the meantime he had sold the car to a bona fide third party, Mr Little. The sisters Ingram, the sellers of the car, started proceedings against Little for the return of the car or, alternatively, damages for its conversion.[81] The Court of Appeal held that the contract between the plaintiffs and the rogue was void and that as a consequence ownership of the car had never passed to the rogue. Moreover, it concluded that under the *nemo plus* rule the rogue had never been able to transfer ownership of the car to the bona fide purchaser.[82] The third party had to return the car to the plaintiffs or pay damages.

In his judgment Pearce L.J. clearly set out the consequences of voidness and avoidability: 'The real problem in the present case is whether the plaintiffs were in fact intending to deal with the person physically present who had fraudulently endowed himself with the attributes of some other identity or whether they were intending only to deal with that other identity. If the former, there was a valid but voidable contract and the property passed. If the latter, there was no contract and the property did not pass.'[83]

To a large extent the facts of the other two cases are similar: a rogue fraudulently using the name of a very respectable firm (*Cundy v. Lindsay*) or person (*Lewis v. Averay*) leads someone into selling a thing to him. After the object has been delivered to the buyer it is not paid for and the buyer resells the thing to a bona fide third party. Also in these decisions it was held that a void contract cannot pass ownership.[84] The decisions form an unequivocal proof that the transfer system of the Sale of Goods Act is causal and certainly not abstract.

This view is supported by section 23 of the Sale of Goods Act, a section mitigating the third party effects of avoidance. A voidable contract is a valid contract that can be avoided, i.e. nullified, by one or more of the contracting parties. A contract may be voidable for instance for misrepresentation, duress, undue influence, minority, unsoundness of mind, or it may be voidable under statute.[85]

---

81 The action is comparable, though not similar, to the civil law action of revindication.

82 It should be noted that English law has no general protection of bona fide third parties like § 932 BGB, art. 2279 CC or art. 3:86 BW.

83 [1960] 3 All ER, p. 340(h).

84 The case in *Lewis v. Averay* was exactly the same, the seller being Mr Lewis and the bona fide purchaser being Mr Averay. In his judgement Lord Denning said: 'The real question in the case is whether...there was a contract of sale under which the property in the car passed from Mr Lewis to the rogue. If there was such a contract, then even though it was voidable for fraud, nevertheless Mr Averay would get a good title [i.e. ownership] to the car. But if there was no contract of sale by Mr Lewis to the rogue - either because there was, on the face of it, no agreement between the parties, or because any apparent agreement was a nullity and void ab initio for mistake, then no property would pass from Mr Lewis to the rogue. Mr Averay would not get a good title because the rogue had no property to pass to him. See [1971] 3 All ER, p. 909(j).

    In *Cundy v. Lindsay* Lord Cairns L.C. held the following: '...there was no *consensus* of mind which could lead to any agreement or contract whatever...My Lords, that being so, it is idle to talk of property passing. The property remained, as it originally had been, the property of the Respondents...'. See (1878) 3 App. Cas. p. 465-66.

85 Chitty on Contracts, vol. 1, § 1-024.

The avoidance, also called rescission, renders the contract void and nullifies the legal consequences of the contract. What is more, it does so with retroactive effect, that is to say, after the avoidance the contract is deemed to have been void from the outset.[86] Yet, does avoidance of a contract of sale entail avoidance of the transfer of ownership based on it? An affirmative answer would mean that the transfer needs a valid legal ground, that it is causal.

From section 23 of the Sale of Goods Act it can be inferred that the transfer is indeed avoided. Section 23 protects the buyer against a seller having a so-called voidable title. The seller is said to have a voidable title when he has acquired ownership under a voidable legal act, for example a voidable contract. If B has fraudulently induced the owner, A, to sell and transfer a thing to him the contract of sale is voidable at the option of the original owner; upon avoidance ownership will automatically revert to A. The fraud's ownership hangs by a thread and accordingly his right of ownership, which in section 23 of the Sale of Goods Act is indicated with the term 'title', is called voidable. After the avoidance the fraud is deemed never to have been owner of the object. Consequently he has never been able to transfer ownership to a third party. So, where before avoidance of the contract between A and B the thing is resold by B to C avoidance of the first contract will revest C's ownership in A. Section 23 SGA protects the second buyer (C) against the *nemo plus* rule by laying down that in the above example the fraud is nonetheless able to pass ownership to him provided C is in good faith and has no knowledge of the seller's (B's) title being voidable. The protection is limited to cases where at the moment of sale to the innocent third party the voidable contract has not yet been avoided. If the transfer of ownership were abstract avoidance would never return ownership to the seller. As a consequence, in an abstract system section 23 SGA would be superfluous. So, from the mere existence of section 23 SGA we can infer that the transfer system is causal.

From the above cases and the existence of section 23 SGA we may conclude that a transfer under the Sale of Goods Act needs a valid *causa traditionis* and that it could be called a causal transfer system in continental terminology. As in French law the characterization accords with the traditional view that the contract itself passes ownership.[87]

Against this view the following objection could be made. In the case of an illegal contract ownership can validly be transferred to the acquirer despite the illegality.[88] This is clearly laid down in *Singh v. Ali*[89] and in *Belvoir Finance Co. Ltd*

---

86 Goode, Commercial law, p. 83-84.

87 In chapter 7 we will see that there is no good reason to choose between only two interpretations of the requirement of *causa traditionis*. There may be transfer systems which are neither causal nor abstract. Still, although the case law quoted above was about defects of will I see no reason why the judgments should be confined to voidness for defect of will: the passages are formulated in general terms. So is s. 23 SGA.

88 G.H. Treitel, The law of contract, 9th ed., London 1995, p. 438 et seq.; J. Beatson, Anson's law of contract, 27th ed., Oxford 1998, p. 333 et seq. See, however, Sachs L.J. in *Belvoir Finance* [1970] 3 All ER, p. 668(f).

v. Stapleton[90]. In *Singh v. Ali* a car was sold under an illegal contract. Possession of the car was transferred by the seller (Ali) to the buyer (Singh). Some time later the seller took possession of the car without the buyer's consent and denied ever to have sold it to Ali. The latter brought an action for the return of the car or its value. In the Privy Council advice was tendered by Lord Denning. He held that, although the contract was illegal, it was effective to pass ownership.[91]

So, it is certain that ownership can pass on the basis of an illegal contract. This might induce civil lawyers to assert that in English law a transfer under an illegal contract is an abstract transfer. Still, the objection is unconvincing. Although the consequences of a contract being illegal are far from clear it seems that generally illegal contracts are held to be unenforceable rather than void. That is to say, the contract is valid but it cannot be enforced by the parties.[92] To my mind case law does not allow us to conclude that in spite of the contract being void it is still able to pass ownership. Most probably the decisions in which ownership was held to pass did not intend the illegal contract to be void.

This is an important difference with German law, where an illegal contract is in principle void.[93] It has no legal effects and is therefore unable to serve as a *causa traditionis* for a transfer of property. In German law ownership is nevertheless able to pass under an illegal contract. Yet, the fact that also in English law ownership may pass under an illegal contract has a different reason: the contract is valid and therefore forms a valid legal ground. So, the transfer under an illegal contract fits into the model of a causal transfer system and cannot be used to prove the existence of abstract transfers in English law.

Note, however, that there are instances where it seems as if ownership of money or fungible goods passes to the acquirer although the underlying contract is void, for example where goods are delivered to the acquirer and stored in his silo in which they are mixed with similar goods already belonging to the acquirer. Still, ownership can never be transferred on the basis of a void contract; the passing of ownership in these cases is not the result of a valid transfer (a form of derivative acquisition) but rather the result of the plaintiff's goods being mixed with the defendant's goods making the acquirer owner through original acquisition.[94]

---

89 [1960] 1 All ER 269 (PC). The reasoning has been applied in *Glastnos Shipping Ltd and Continental Chartering & Brokerage Ltd Hong Kong Branch v. Panasian Shipping Corporation and Withers* [1991] 1 Lloyd's Rep. 482, at p. 487.

90 [1970] 3 All ER 664 (CA). Here the Court of Appeal applied the decision in *Singh v. Ali*.

91 Yet Lord Denning said that ownership would pass only if the contract were executed. In this case the contract was held to be executed, since possession of the car had been transferred to the buyer. It is strange to require any physical delivery here, as under the Sale of Goods Act transfer of possession is no requirement for the transfer of ownership.

92 That is to say, the parties have no right of action. Cf. the civil law adage *nemo auditur propriam turpitudinem allegans*.

93 Paragraph 134 BGB.

94 For the same reason cases where money is handed over and mixed with the recipient's own money or cases where money is paid into the payee's bank account are unable to prove that in English law the transfer of ownership is abstract. See § 9 *infra*.

B)   TRANSFER *INTER VIVOS* NOT BASED ON SALE

6 The *traditio* requirement and the origin of its exceptions

In fact, the rules in the Sale of Goods Act as to the passing of ownership, though of immense commercial interest, are merely an exception to the general principle. The general rule is still the ancient common law principle that in order to transfer ownership delivery[95] is needed.

The main example of a case where *traditio* still plays an important role is the gift *inter vivos*.[96] During the 19th century there has been quite some controversy whether or not delivery was needed for a valid gift. In 1819 the Court of King's Bench held in *Irons v. Smallpiece*[97] that a verbal gift requires delivery of the object involved. This view was adopted in many subsequent decisions.[98] Yet, several judgments declined to apply the rule in *Irons v. Smallpiece*, holding that a verbal gift unaccompanied by delivery is valid.[99] The uncertainty was brought to an end only in 1890 by the Queen's Bench's decision in *Cochrane v. Moore*.[100] In an extensive judgment Fry J. analysed thoroughly the old authorities and held that the common law has always required delivery for an oral gift to be valid.

The decision was welcomed by Pollock and Holdsworth as historically correct.[101] In the 13th century the requirement of delivery applied to all transfers of movables. It accorded with the requirement of 'livery of seisin'[102] (transfer of possession) applicable in land law.[103] In later centuries two important exceptions

---

95   Note that here the term delivery has a meaning comparable to the civil law term *traditio*, that is, transfer of possession as a requirement for a transfer of ownership. In English sales law, however, the term is used to denote the physical transport of the object sold, that is to say, bringing the object into the power of the buyer or an agreed third person. In Dutch and German law this is called *aflevering* and *Ablieferung* respectively (see e.g. art. 7:9 BW and § 477 BGB, § 377 and 419 HGB, Staudinger-Honsell, 1995, § 433, Rdnr. 95 and § 477, Rdnr. 37).

96   As to gifts this chapter will be confined to gifts *inter vivos*, i.e. gifts taking effect during the donor's lifetime, as contrasted with the *donatio causa mortis*, the gift taking effect only upon the donor's death (see Nourse LJ in: *Sen v. Headley* [1991] 2 All ER 636). Moreover, it is limited to gifts transferring legal ownership of movable property.

97   (1819) 2 Barn. & Ald. 551.

98   See judgment by Fry in *Cochrane v. Moore* (1890) 25 QBD, p. 57, at p. 61 et seq.

99   See Fry's judgment in *Cochrane v. Moore*, p. 62 et seq.

100 (1890) 25 QBD 57.

101 F. Pollock, Gifts of chattels without delivery, LQR 6 (1890), p. 446 et seq.; W. Holdsworth, A history of English law, vol. 3, 5th ed., London 1942, p. 354 and vol. 7, London 1937, p. 505-509.

102 Like the verb 'deliver' the noun 'livery' derives from the French *livrer* and the Latin *liberare* (to deliver up, to hand over). The word 'seisin/seizin' or the alternative 'sasine' derives from the old-French *seisine* or *saisine* (see chapter 3, fn. 17 and 19). Cf. the English 'seize' and the French *saisir* (to get hold of, to take possession of, etc.).

103 F. Pollock and F.W. Maitland, The history of English law, vol. 2, 2nd ed., Cambridge 1898 (repr., ed. by S.F.C. Milsom, Cambridge 1968), p. 180-181 and p. 210; Pollock, LQR 6 (1890), p. 448. The requirement applied for example to the transfer of a freehold interest (an estate in fee simple or in fee tail).

to the delivery rule have developed: delivery is held unnecessary where either the transfer is based on sale or the transfer takes place by deed (a sealed document).

6.1 Origin of the *solo consensu* rule in sales

From the time of Henry VI's reign (1422-1461) the buyer of a specific[104] thing could sue the seller in detinue[105] and ownership was held to have passed to the buyer prior to delivery of the thing.[106] Before this period the action of detinue was commonly used in the case of wrongful detention of goods. From long time past the action of detinue had been available to bailors against bailees[107] refusing to return the goods[108], that is, against defendants wrongfully possessing goods. If the action of detinue was successful the defendant had the choice either to return the object or to pay to the plaintiff the value of the thing. So, detinue was really an action for the return of the object or its value. In this respect detinue was comparable to the *rei vindicatio* of classical Roman law.[109]

Now, whereas originally detinue was used mainly against bailees, from the time of Henry VI the action of detinue was extended beyond its original scope and granted to the buyer of specific goods. According to Holdsworth it is this extension of the action of detinue which induced the rule that a sale of specific goods passes ownership immediately after the contract is made.[110] For the action of detinue was available to a person entitled to the possession of the thing involved, someone having a right to possession.[111] In this period the right to possession was often referred to as 'property'.[112] Holdsworth argues that because the buyer was

---

104 Note that the buyer's action of detinue, and consequently the *solo consensu* rule, was confined to the sale of specific goods. Also here the principle of specificity applied. See Holdsworth, vol. 3, p. 357; S.F.C. Milsom, Historical foundations of the common law, 2nd ed., London 1981, p. 266; *Orwell v. Mortoft* (1505), in: J.H. Baker and S.F.C. Milsom, Sources of English legal history, Private law to 1750, London 1986, p. 406, at p. 408-409 (judgment by Kingsmill).

105 'Detinue' derives from the Latin *detinere* (to withhold).

106 Milsom, Historical foundations of the common law, p. 266. I have also used part of the manuscript of a book which Prof. J.H. Baker is in the process of writing. I am greatly indebted to him for sending me the chapter *Property in Chattels*. The book will be the 1483-1558 volume of the *Oxford History of the Laws of England*.

107 The term bailee is to some extent comparable to the civil law term *detentor*.

108 See cases in: Baker and Milsom, English legal history, Private Law to 1750, chapter 9.

109 When the *rei vindicatio* proved successful the defendant was not forced to return the object. The judgment was for money (*condemnatio pecuniaria*), not for the return of the thing itself. Its price was estimated by the judge or the plaintiff (*litis aestimatio*). The defendant could relieve himself of the obligation to pay the price by returning the thing to the plaintiff. See M. Kaser/K. Hackl, Das römische Zivilprozeßrecht, 2nd ed., Munich 1996, § 54 IV 1. In Justinianian law the principle of money condemnation was abolished. As a consequence, where a *rei vindicatio* was successful, the defendant could be forced to return the object rather than its value. See P. Jörs, W. Kunkel, L. Wenger, Römisches Recht, 4th ed. by H. Honsell, Th. Mayer-Maly, W. Selb, Berlin etc. 1987, p. 538.

110 Holdsworth, vol. 3, p. 355.

111 As distinct from the right of possession, i.e. having possession and the rights connected to it.

112 Holdsworth, vol. 3, p. 356.

granted the action of detinue, which gave him a right to possession, he was gradually regarded as having ownership. So, in civil law terminology the reasoning was as follows: from the buyer having been granted a revindication it was inferred that he was owner of the goods. This theory is plausible, as it is a common process to infer from a right of action a material, substantive right.[113]

Milsom's theory: constructive delivery

According to Milsom[114] the availability of detinue to buyers may have originated in the use of constructive delivery (*traditio ficta*). Conceding that the evidence is not incontestable, he draws attention to several judgments on sale in which after the contract of sale the goods were said to remain with the seller *salvo custodienda* (retaining custodianship). In some other cases it was said that goods were redelivered to the seller by the buyer, assuming a prior delivery to the buyer. In both instances the seller became bailee for the buyer.[115] In the second instance the redelivery was apparently not to retransfer ownership, but simply to make the seller a bailee for the buyer.

To understand Milsom's theory we should first have a look at the concept of bailment in general. The concept of bailment belongs to the law of property, but it is also closely related to the law of contract, as most bailments are linked to a contractual relationship.[116] It covers, among other things, the loan for use (*commodatum*), hire (*locatio conductio*) and safe-keeping (*depositum*), all of which are accompanied by contractual relationships. If someone hands over a number of containers to a warehouseman for safe-keeping, the former is called bailor, the latter bailee. Apart from their being contracts these bailments contain a property aspect: the bailee is in possession of an asset and exercises his possession for the benefit of the bailor, respecting the bailor's rights in the asset as being superior.[117] In some instances, on the other hand, any contractual aspect is lacking altogether, for example where the finder of a lost object safeguards it for the owner. We can therefore say that the property aspect, the bailee's exercising possession for the bailor, is the essential element in bailment.

Using civil law terminology the bailee's position is comparable with the German *Fremdbesitzer*. He is a true possessor and accordingly has possessory actions to defend his rights and the asset against any wrongful interference by third parties, yet he acknowledges the superior rights of the bailor.

However, the bailor's position is quite different from the position he would have in German law in that he will usually lose his right of possession for the duration

---

113   Cf. chapter 2, § 4.4.
114   S.F.C. Milsom, Sale of goods in the fifteenth century, LQR 77 (1961), p. 257 et seq., at p. 273 et seq.
115   Milsom, however, warns that, although it is very probable that these cases concerned specific goods, there is no evidence for this.
116   See also § 8.4.
117   Normally the bailor will be owner of the asset, but it suffices if the bailor has a better title, i.e. right, to possession than the bailee. The bailee's right should be subordinate to the bailor's right.

of the bailment. In German law, on the other hand, a lender or lessor remains in possession, albeit indirect possession: the lender or lessor is indirect *Eigenbesitzer*, the borrower or lessee direct *Fremdbesitzer*. Only in exceptional cases does English law acknowledge a similar double possession. The bailor will be regarded as having possession if the bailment can be terminated by him at any moment, so that the bailor can be said to have a 'right to immediate possession', 'immediate' meaning 'without delay'. Examples of such bailments at will, as they are called, are a gratuitous loan for use or a deposit where no term has been agreed. In such instances there are two possessors of one and the same asset: the bailor, who has indirect possession, exercising possession for his own benefit, and the bailee having direct possession.

Now, to return to the *salvo custodienda* passages, these clauses were intended to transfer possession, and, as a result, ownership of the thing prior to the physical delivery of the object. It was therefore a *traditio ficta*. As the function of the *salvo custodienda* passages was to transfer possession to the buyer (the future bailor) the choice of bailments was limited to bailments at will, such as a deposit or a loan for use, because in these instances also the bailor has possession. By using such a *salvo custodienda* clause the parties were able to meet the requirement of delivery without a physical handing over being needed. Ownership then passed to the buyer at the moment the contract was made. Accordingly, from that moment the buyer was able to sue the seller in detinue.

If Milsom's thesis is correct there is a striking similarity with the evolution in pre-revolutionary French law that eventually led to the *Code Civil*'s *solo consensu* rule. In French law, we have seen,[118] the frequent use of *constitutum possessorium* in sales of land undermined and eroded the *traditio* requirement. Notarial deeds contained clauses declaring that possession had been transferred, for example by way of *constitutum possessorium* (*clause de constitut*), making the seller detentor for the buyer. As a result, in practice ownership of land passed when the contract of sale was made. In 1804 this practice was codified and extended to cover movables as well.

6.2 Gifts by deed

The second exception to the delivery rule is the gift made by deed, a certain kind of document in writing. Originally any gift, whether made orally or in writing, needed delivery. Yet from the end of the 14th century a gift could validly be made by deed without delivery being required.[119]

The use of a deed is not limited to gifts alone. It has a very wide field of application and can be used to effect many different legal consequences.[120] In

---

118   Chapter 3, § 2.1.
119   J.H. Baker, An introduction to English legal history, 3rd ed., London 1990, p. 433 where Baker refers to *Pynchoun v. Geldeford* (1385) Year Book Hilary 8 Richard II: see fn. 27 there.
120   As a thorough analysis of the transfer by deed would involve a detailed description of English land law, I will treat the subject only briefly.

continental terminology it could be called a declaration of will (*wilsverklaring*, *Willenserklärung*) laid down in a particular form. It is able, among other things, to create obligations and create or transfer interests in goods and land, irrespective of there being any consideration. What is more, it is able to let ownership pass even when the deed does not indicate the *causa*, the legal ground, of the transfer. We can therefore say that a deed allows of an abstract transfer.

7 The gift from hand to hand

One of the main instances where *traditio* is still required is the gift from hand to hand, i.e. a gift by delivery rather than a gift by deed. Before analysing in detail the requirement of *traditio* we should examine another vital element of the gift from hand to hand: the donee's acceptance. It does not suffice to deliver the thing to the donee; in addition the donee should accept the thing and should agree that the transfer is a gift. As a matter of course a person cannot be compelled to accept a gift. Every gift needs the consent of both donor and donee. It is required that they agree about the subject matter of the transfer and about the transfer being without recompense. The donee's will need not be express, though: it may be inferred from the circumstances of the case, such as his behaviour. When the donee receives an object knowing that the donor wishes to give it to him, the donee's acceptance can readily be inferred from his keeping the object and not repudiating the generous gesture.

Yet, if the donee is unaware of the donor's intention to make a gift the situation is different. Can we say that there is a valid transfer to the donee when he does not know of the gift being made? Clearly, a gift against his will is ineffective, but what about a gift absent his will?

In English law the donee is presumed to have accepted the gift even though he is unaware of the gift. There is a long-standing line of authority to this effect, affirmed in *Standing v. Bowring*.[121] In this case the plaintiff, Mrs Standing, a widow, had made a gift to her godson Mr Bowring. She had Consols[122] to the value of £6,000 transferred into the joint names of her and Mr Bowring without him knowing of the transfer. About two years later she remarried and began to regret having made the gift. Her solicitor demanded Mr Bowring to consent to a retransfer of the bonds to Mrs Standing. Only when he got the solicitor's letter did he learn about the gift. He had been unaware of it for more than two years. Mr Bowring refused to cooperate on the retransfer, and proceedings were started to force him to do so. Counsel for the plaintiff contended that the gift was incomplete and that consequently the gift could be revoked as long as it was not made known to the donee.

---

121 (1886) 31 ChD 282.
122 Consolidated Annuities or Consolidated Stock, interest-bearing securities or bonds issued by the British Government which have no maturity (repayment) date. Definition by J.H. Adam, *Longman dictionary of business English*, 2nd ed., Beirut-Harlow 1989, p. 135.

The Court of Appeal held that a gift is valid even though it is not known to the donee and accordingly not expressly accepted by him. Ownership passes to the donee immediately when the gift is made, provided all requirements for a valid gift, other than the donee's acceptance, are met. However, ownership passes to the donee subject to the donee's right of repudiation. If he repudiates the gift ownership of the thing given reverts to the donor.[123] The decision is in accordance with previous cases such as *Butler and Baker's Case*[124], *Thompson v. Leach*[125] and *Siggers v. Evans*[126].

The judgments in *Standing v. Bowring* do not mention why a gift is valid without the donee's acceptance. To find the reason we should resort to the older cases which the Court of Appeal relied on. In *Thompson v. Leach* the point is discussed at length.[127] First Ventris J. noted that a conveyance (i.e. transfer) is a contract (in modern terminology: an agreement) and consequently requires the assent of all parties. Having said this he continued that if the transfer is for the transferee's benefit he is presumed to accept until the contrary appears. '...(F)or the assent of the party that takes, is implied in all conveyances, and this is by intendment of law, which is as strong as the expression of the party, till the contrary appears; stabit p'sumptio [i.e. presumptio] donec probetur in contrarium.'[128] 'Where an act is done for a man's benefit an agreement is implied, till there be a disagreement. This does not only hold in conveyances, but in the gift of goods, 3 Co. 26. A grant of goods vests the property in the grantee before notice.'[129]

8 The *traditio* requirement in the case of gifts

8.1 Introduction

In this section we will examine the different forms delivery may take. As it amounts to a transfer of ownership, delivery requires a real agreement. In addition in most cases *traditio*, a transfer of possession, is needed. As to the latter requirement, however, there are some exceptions. For instance, where statute requires registration for the transfer of certain assets, a gift of these assets will have to meet these requirements rather than the common law requirement of *traditio*.[130] So, we can say that in the case of a gift the transfer of ownership consists of two

---

123   It is unknown whether it reverts with retroactive effect.
124   (1591) 3 Co. Rep. 25a.
125   (1690) 2 Vent. 197.
126   (1855) 5 E&B 367.
127   2 Vent., at p. 202-204.
128   2 Vent. p. 202. The Latin passage means: a presumption shall stand until the contrary has been proven. In Dutch law a similar presumption of acceptance can be found in the new article 7.3.1. subs. 2 BW.
129   2 Vent. p. 203. The reference '3 Co. 26' refers to Butler and Baker's Case.
130   Example: in *Standing v. Bowring* government bonds were transferred by an entry into the books of the Bank of England. See (1886) 31 ChD, p. 287-288, per Cotton L.J.

elements: one permanent element, the real agreement, and in most cases an additional element: a transfer of possession.[131] The English word 'delivery' does not distinguish between these elements and denotes both the real agreement and the *traditio*, or sometimes only one of these elements. For that reason I prefer the romanistic term *traditio* to refer to the transfer of possession.

As a matter of course possession can be transferred by handing over the object in question to the donee, that is to say, by a physical act transferring the donor's direct possession to the donee. As in some instances such an act will be cumbersome or unnecessary, English law recognizes certain kinds of *traditio ficta*, called 'constructive delivery': legal acts which transfer possession without any physical handing over. Moreover, in some cases a real agreement suffices and the common law requires no transfer of possession at all, not even a *traditio ficta*.

Sadly, case law does not offer a clear and complete statement of the *traditio* requirement. Often case law about *traditio ficta* or *traditio symbolica* are not about gifts but have a different context, such as pledge, mortgage or *donatio causa mortis*. True, the delivery requirement applies here as well. Still, this does not necessarily mean that what amounts to a valid delivery to create a pledge will also suffice to make a gift. In *RA Barret & Company Ltd v. Liversey*[132], a case about pledge, Buckley L.J. said: '(I)n this respect [i.e. as to the delivery requirement] it seems to me that a pledge and a gift *inter vivos* are analogous.' After this he applied to a pledge a form of *traditio ficta* allowed for gifts *inter vivos*. The reverse analogy, i.e. applying to gifts a form of *traditio ficta* acknowledged for pledge, may not always be allowed. As we will see in § 8.5, one form of delivery allowed to create a pledge is probably not allowed to perfect a gift: the so-called *constitutum possessorium*. Moreover, in the case of a *donatio causa mortis* the delivery requirement is applied less strictly than in the situation of a gift *inter vivos*.[133] In all, the concept of *traditio* is a highly casuistic part of the law of property and a part, as Roger Smith says, not lacking odd requirements.[134] Now, let us examine which forms of *traditio* are acknowledged to make a valid gift.

8.2 *Traditio vera* without handing over

The classic example of a *traditio vera* without handing over of the object is the handing over of keys. It is sometimes called *traditio symbolica* or symbolical delivery. Handing over of the keys of a safe or warehouse, for example, is regarded as a valid *traditio* of the objects locked away in it.

In *Balding v. Ashley*[135] the respondent, Mr Ashley, who was married with a family, started an affair with Mrs Balding, the appellant. After Mr Ashley's wife

---

131 Dogmatically the real agreement should be distinguished from the transfer of possession. See chapter 2, § 1.2 and chapter 5, § 2.2.
132 Court of Appeal, 6 November 1980, published in Lexis-nexis.
133 R.J. Smith, Property law, London 1996, p. 96, fn. 91, p. 97 and 160.
134 R.J. Smith, Property law, p. 98.
135 Court of Appeal, 27 March 1991, published in Lexis-nexis.

and children had left him, he lived together with the appellant for a few years. Eventually the association ended and Mrs Balding had to leave Mr Ashley's house. She claimed that during their cohabitation Mr Ashley had made a valid gift of a Ferrari motor car to her.

The judge at first instance held that Mr Ashley intended the Ferrari to be a gift to Mrs Balding. The car was registered in the appellant's name and she became a member of the Ferrari Owners Club. In the judge's opinion, however, no sufficient act of delivery had taken place to perfect the gift. The Court of Appeal agreed that the registration process did not amount to an act of delivery, but, at the same time, it held that a handing over of the keys would have sufficed to complete the gift.

According to Anthony Lincoln J. '(i)t is indisputable that if the respondent had handed the appellant the keys to the Ferrari, these circumstances could well constitute the basis for holding that there had been a constructive delivery.' Fox L.J. agreed to this saying '(a)s to the delivery of the keys by the respondent to the appellant, it is, however, a vital issue. It is accepted (quite rightly, I think) by Mr Smith for the respondent that if the keys were handed over there would then be a basis upon which the court could conclude that there was a delivery of the car, but we do not know precisely what evidence was before the judge relating to delivery.' Delivery of goods by handing over the key of a trunk or warehouse, or other means of access to the goods, has been recognized for centuries.[136] However, there was uncertainty over whether or not Mr Ashley's words of gift had indeed been followed by his handing over the keys of the car to the appellant. As the Court of Appeal had no access to all the evidence brought before the judge in first instance, it ordered the case to be remitted to the latter judge to examine if there had been such handing over of the keys.

When a collection of goods has to be transferred *traditio* may take place by handing over one of the objects as a *pars pro toto*. This form of *traditio* was used for example in *Lock v. Heath*.[137] Mr Heath made a gift of a collection of furniture to his wife and handed over one chair as a symbol representing all the furniture. This was considered to be a valid gift of the furniture.

Yet in *Re Cole*[138], a case similar to *Lock v. Heath*, the court held that there had been no sufficient act of delivery, so that the gift was invalid. It was about a gift of furniture between husband and wife. Mr Cole had furnished the new family home in London. During that time Mrs Cole had stayed at Clitheroe, where the family had lived until then. When she came to London Mr Cole showed her the new house. He showed her all the rooms and the new furniture and told her he wanted to give her all the furniture. Some years later Mr Cole was declared bankrupt. The proceedings were between Mr Cole's trustee in bankruptcy and Mrs Cole, the trustee challenging the validity of the gift.

---

136   See for instance *Ryall v. Rowles* (1750) 1 Ves. Sen. 348, at 362 and *Ward v. Turner* (1751) 2 Ves. Sen. 431, at 443. The second case is about *donatio causa mortis*.
137   (1892) 8 TLR 295.
138   [1963] 3 All ER 433.

Had there been an act of delivery accompanying the words of gift? Harman L.J. gives a detailed account of what took place.[139] 'He brought her into the house, took her into a room, put her hands over her eyes and then uncovered them saying "Look". He then accompanied her into other rooms on the ground floor where she handled certain of the articles; next she went upstairs by herself and examined the rest of the house. When she came down again he said: "It's all yours".' Would this be a transfer of possession perfecting the husband's words of gift?

Counsel for Mrs Cole in the words of Harman L.J. 'boldly put forward an entirely novel proposition to the effect that a perfect gift of chattels[140] is constituted by showing them to the donee and speaking words of gift. It is enough, he [i.e. counsel] says, that the donee should be brought to the chattels rather than the chattels to the donee, and that she should be 'near' the chattels (though what degree of proximity is needful remained vague) when the words of gift are spoken.' The difficulty in these instances of gift is that the transfer of possession is invisible: before as well as after the gift both husband and wife have the same degree of physical control over the furniture.[141]

Oddly, the Court of Appeal did not accept the counsel's view and held that there had been no delivery of the furniture. Despite this, the decision in *Lock v. Heath* was approved of.

Is *traditio symbolica* a form of *traditio ficta*?

Sometimes *traditio symbolica*[142] is regarded as an instance of *traditio ficta* rather than *traditio vera*. This opinion is, however, mistaken. Certainly, where the keys of a warehouse are handed over, there is no handing over of the goods themselves. The parties need not even be in the neighbourhood of the warehouse. Yet, it would be wrong to suppose that only a handing over can be regarded as a *traditio vera*. Any act transferring the donor's direct possession to the donee will suffice. And a handing over of keys will do just that.

A clear explanation of this was given by Lord Hardwicke in *Ward v. Turner*[143]: 'It is argued, that though some delivery is necessary yet delivery of the thing is not necessary, but delivery of anything by way of symbol is sufficient: but I cannot agree to that; nor do I find any authority for that in the civil law... Delivery of the key of bulky goods, where wines &c. are, has been allowed as delivery of the possession, because it is the way of coming at the possession or to make use of the

---

139   At p. 435.

140   The term 'chattels' here denotes tangible movable things (so-called choses in possession). Cf. F.H. Lawson and B. Rudden, The law of property, 2nd ed., Oxford 1982, p. 19-20.

141   In these cases Dutch and German law content themselves with a verbal transfer of possession without any physical act (in Dutch law it is sometimes called *traditio sine manu*). See Snijders/Rank-Berenschot, p. 109-110; Wolff/Raiser, § 9.

142   The term *traditio symbolica* or *traditio per symbolum* was most probably created in the course of the 17th century. See Biermann, Traditio ficta, p. 171 et seq.

143   (1751) 2 Ves. Sen. 431, at 443. The passage is cited by Pollock with approval. See Pollock and Wright, An essay on possession in the common law, Oxford 1888, p. 62 et seq., particularly p. 68. Here *Ward v. Turner* and other cases concerning *traditio symbolica* are treated in great detail.

thing, and therefore the key is not a symbol, which would not do.' Of course, the keys are not, as the term *traditio symbolica* suggests, a mere symbol representing the goods locked away. On the contrary, they are the means of access, of control over them. Consequently, handing over of the keys is a *traditio vera*: the direct possession of the goods is transferred to the donee.[144] The term *traditio ficta*, on the other hand, is confined to instances in which there is a transfer of possession but no transfer of direct possession from transferor to acquirer.

8.3 *Traditio brevi manu*

In *Winter v. Winter*[145] a son was in the possession of a barge belonging to his father. He worked on it as a servant to his father. When the father fell ill he made a gift of the barge to the son.[146] From that moment the son used the barge as his own and paid the crew's wages. After the father had died another of his sons, acting as the deceased's executor, challenged the validity of the gift contending there had been no delivery of the barge. The court, however, held that the facts amounted to a valid delivery. There had been a change in the son's possession: the son who first possessed the barge as a servant to his father, now possessed and worked it as an owner. In civil law terminology the son had changed from a *detentor* into a *possessor*.

Is *traditio brevi manu* in English law a transfer of possession?

In *RA Barrett & Company Ltd v. Livesey*[147], a car was pledged, and delivery, required to create a pledge, took the form of a *traditio brevi manu*. Mr Livesey, one of the directors of a small family business, had been given the use of a company car. When the company needed extra cash Mr Livesey was prepared to give a loan provided he was given a pledge on the company car in his possession. I shall quote a passage from Buckley L.J.'s judgment as it raises the question whether *brevi manu* should be regarded as a form of *traditio* at all. 'It is, of course, an essential characteristic of a pledge that the pledgee has possession, actual or constructive[148], of the pledged chattel. Normally a delivery of the chattel to the pledgee is consequently necessary to complete the transaction. Such delivery need not, however, be actual physical delivery: constructive delivery will suffice...Where, however, the chattel is already in the physical possession of the pledgee, no delivery is necessary. The pledgee must, however, establish that his possession has become that of a pledgee, distinct from whatever the nature of his possession previously was. It may be possible to describe such a change of possession as constructive delivery, but I should prefer myself to say that no delivery, actual or

---

144   Pollock and Wright, Possession, p. 68; L.C. Hofmann, Het Nederlandsch zakenrecht, 3rd ed., Groningen/Batavia 1944, p. 235.
145   (1861) 4 LT, 639.
146   This was a gift *inter vivos*, not a *donatio causa mortis*.
147   Court of Appeal, 6 November 1980, published in Lexis-nexis.
148   Mostly the term constructive possession denotes indirect possession.

constructive, is necessary in any case in which at the date of the pledge the subject matter is already physically in the possession of that person to whom delivery would otherwise need to be established.'

Buckley L.J.'s opinion accords with a passage from Pearson L.J.'s judgment in *Re Cole*[149]. Discussing the validity of a gift of an object already in the possession of the donee at the time of the gift Pearson L.J. said: 'In the case of prior delivery, it may not be necessary that the delivery should have been made by the donor; a pre-existing possession of the donee, however it arose, may be sufficient.'

Although *Barrett v. Livesey* is about pledge, which does not involve a transfer of ownership, it raises a general question about the true nature of *traditio brevi manu* in English law. Let us examine a standard example of *brevi manu*: A leases a car to B. After A has delivered the car to B, the latter will have possession of the car as bailee, respecting A's right of ownership. If now A makes a gift of the car to B the character of B's possession will change from possession as a bailee into possession as an owner.

In Dutch law the lessee is regarded as a *detentor* (*houder*) rather than a possessor (*bezitter*), so that a transfer of possession has still to take place. However, in a legal system that does not know the concept of detentorship, such as English and also German law, there is, understandably, an inclination to hold that *brevi manu* is not a transfer of possession, as the acquirer has possession already. For this reason German law, unlike Dutch law, does not consider *brevi manu* as a *traditio ficta* but rather as an exception to the *traditio* requirement.

Still, the above reasoning does not inevitably lead to the conclusion that *brevi manu* cannot be called a transfer of possession. To find out which view is correct we should examine whether it is needed that, prior to the gift, the possessor should have received possession from the donor, so that one can say *traditio* preceded the words of gift. As to German law there is convincing evidence that *brevi manu* cannot be regarded as a transfer of possession: for a valid *traditio brevi manu* (§ 929, subs. 2 BGB) it is irrelevant whether the transferee acquired possession from the transferor or received possession in another way.[150] It seems that the same goes for English law, considering Pearson L.J.'s judgment in *Re Cole* quoted above, where he stresses that it does not matter how the donee got possession of the object.

8.4 Third party in possession as bailee

Would it be possible to make a gift of goods while they are in the possession of a third party who holds the goods as a bailee for the donor? Certainly, the donor will not be able to make a *traditio vera*, i.e. a transfer of direct possession. A *traditio vera* will be possible only after termination of the bailment. Where goods are in the custody of a warehouseman for safe-keeping the donor and donee can agree that the donee is to collect the goods at the warehouse. The gift will then take effect,

---

149   [1963] 3 All ER, p. 439(e).
150   See chapter 2, § 4.2.

that is delivery will take place, when the donee receives the goods from the warehouseman.

However, it may be that the donee wishes the goods to remain in the warehouse, or it may be that the bailment cannot be terminated for a certain time, for example where the thing is hired out. In such instances ownership can be transferred without terminating the bailment, provided that two requirements are met. First, there should be an agreement between the donor and the donee that henceforth the bailee will possess the thing for the benefit of the donee. Secondly, the bailee should agree to this and should indeed begin so to possess the thing.[151] That is to say, the bailee, the third party, should change himself from a possessor for the transferor into a possessor for the transferee. The change is called 'attornment'[152] and results in the acquirer being substituted for the transferor in the bailment relation. The attornment produces the change in the bailee's possession needed to meet the delivery requirement.

Unlike in English law, the Dutch equivalent of attornment (art. 3:115 sub c BW) does not need the third party's assent. In order to transfer possession of the goods it suffices if the transferor and transferee agree about the passing of possession and either the third party acknowledges this passing or one of the parties to the transfer, transferor or acquirer, notifies the passing to the third party. The latter's assent is not needed and the attornment will take place automatically as a result of the notification or acknowledgment, turning the third party into a possessor for the acquirer.

The difference with English law can be explained by examining the consequences of attornment for the contractual relations between the transferor and the third party. When bailment constitutes a contract, as in our example, it is a concept belonging to the law of property as well as to the law of contract. The property aspect, which determines who has possession of the asset, is then inseparably connected with the contractual aspect. The quality of bailor is united with the quality of contracting party within the contract of safe-keeping.

Attornment does more than just change the bailee's possession and render the acquirer bailor. At the same time it takes all contractual rights and duties based on the bailment away from the shoulders of the transferor and passes them on to the acquirer. This is the reason why attornment requires the bailee's consent: it confronts him with a different contracting party. And like in any other case of novation the remaining contracting party should consent to the replacement of his contracting party.[153]

Dutch law, on the other hand, separates the passing of possession from the passing of contractual obligations. The *traditio ficta* of art. 3:115 sub c BW merely transfers indirect possession to the acquirer and makes the third party possessor of the goods for the new owner. As to the contract, however, nothing changes. The

---

151   *In Re Hamilton Young* [1905] 2 KB 786; *Dublin City Distillery v. Doherty* [1914] AC, p. 847-848 and 852; Pollock and Wright, Possession, p. 73; R.J. Smith, Property law, p. 97.

152   Confusingly, the term is used also to denote *constitutum possessorium*.

153   See for this instance of novation G.H. Treitel, The law of contract, 9th ed., London 1995, p. 617-18.

former owner remains the custodian's contracting party: he will be responsible for fulfilling all the contractual duties, such as paying rent for the safe-keeping. As a result, the custodian cannot be confronted against his will with a new debtor, who may be less solvent.[154] In order to substitute within the contract the new owner for the former, a separate legal act is needed: *contractsovername*, a form of novation.

Is attornment by the third party a form of *traditio*?

It is difficult to say whether such attornment constitutes a *traditio ficta* or a *traditio* substitute. Commonly the bailor has no possession of the thing bailed. He will have possession only if he has a right to immediate possession, that is, the right to claim at will that he be given direct possession of the object. In that case both bailor and bailee will have possession: the bailee will have direct possession which he exercises for the benefit of the bailor and the bailor will have indirect possession which he exercises for his own benefit.[155] Now, where the bailor has possession attornment can indeed be regarded as a *traditio*: a transfer to the acquirer of the bailor's indirect possession.[156] If, on the other hand, the bailor has no possession, the act of attornment obviously cannot be seen as a transfer of possession: no possession, not even indirect possession, is transferred. In English terminology it is nonetheless called a form of constructive delivery.

8.5 *Constitutum possessorium*

In principle *traditio* may take place simply by an agreement between transferor and transferee that the former will henceforth hold the asset as a bailee for the acquirer. The asset will then temporarily remain in the custody of the transferor, though his possession will change from possession as an owner into possession as a bailee.[157] It is the inverse of *brevi manu*. By analogy with attornment by a third party also this change of possession is sometimes called attornment.[158] Yet, to prevent confusion I will instead use the civil law term *constitutum possessorium*.

This form of *traditio* was discussed in *Dublin City Distillery v. Doherty*, a case about the pledge of a quantity of whisky. Lord Atkinson, examining different instances of constructive delivery, mentioned the following example: '...it is not disputed that if a vendor who has sold goods should, after the sale has been completed, agree with the vendee to retain the physical possession of the goods, but on such terms that the nature and character of his former possession is changed from that of an owner to that of bailee for the purchaser, that transaction will

---

154 The third party has a lien over the goods in his custody for the payment of, for example, storage rent or repair costs, which can be invoked not only against the contracting party (the former owner) but also against the new owner. This lien is called *retentierecht* (literally: right to retain, or withhold).

155 See § 6.1 *supra*.

156 Cf. Dutch law: art. 3:115 subs. c BW.

157 *Dublin City Distillery v. Doherty*, p. 844 (per Lord Atkinson) and p. 852 (per Lord Parker of Waddington).

158 See for example: Goode, Commercial law, p. 277.

amount to an acceptance and actual receipt of the goods...and necessarily to a good constructive delivery sufficient to create a pledge.'[159]

Next he analysed cases where *traditio* by way of *constitutum possessorium* had been allowed, such as *Elmore v. Stone*[160], a case about the sale of two horses. Here seller and buyer agreed that after the sale the seller, a horse dealer and livery stable keeper, would keep the horses at livery for the buyer. The latter paid for the keeping of the horse. This, it was held, showed that the character of the seller's possession had changed from that of an owner into possession as a bailee.[161]

Again, like attornment by a third party, *constitutum possessorium* can be regarded as a form of *traditio ficta* only if it transfers indirect possession to the acquirer. As explained before, the transferee, who is at the same time bailor, will acquire possession only when he gets a right to immediate possession.

Now, though it is certain that *constitutum possessorium* is a valid form of *traditio*, no case can be found in which it was accepted as a delivery sufficient to perfect a gift. The reason for this is most probably that English law does not easily assume that the donor really wants to make a gift. It is not content with words of gift alone and insists on some act of execution. Hence the requirement of delivery. As Harman L.J. said in *Re Cole*[162] '(t)he English law of the transfer of property, dominated as it has always been by the doctrine of consideration, has always been chary of the recognition of gifts.'

Donner et retenir ne vaut

Perhaps a gift executed by way of *constitutum possessorium* would be regarded by English law as a reliance on mere words of gift, because possession stays with the donor. In chapter 6 we will see that also in French law a gift cannot be made by mere words. In French law a valid gift requires either a written instrument, a notarial deed, or *traditio*.[163] Words of gift are not binding in French law: the donor has the right to think better of it and go back on making the gift.[164] The *traditio* may take the form of *brevi manu* and may also take place while the goods are in the custody of a third party. However, does French law recognize a gift from hand to hand executed *constituto possessorio*? Or would it regard such a tradition as relying on mere words of gift? Would *constitutum possessorium* not conflict with the old adage *donner et retenir ne vaut* (to give and retain is not valid)?

Pre-*Code Civil* law indeed required a *tradition réelle* (real transfer) to perfect a gift from hand to hand. Originally, the maxim *donner et retenir ne vaut* was regarded as insisting on a *tradition réelle*. This requirement would protect the donor's heirs. If

---

159   At p. 844.
160   (1809) 1 Taunt. 458.
161   Note that in these old cases, such as *Dublin City Distillery* and *Elmore v. Stone*, delivery, though not necessary for the passing of ownership, was still important because of section 17 of the Statute of Frauds 1677. This and almost all other sections of the statute have now been repealed.
162   [1963] 3 All ER, p. 433, at p. 435(i).
163   For the requirement of *traditio* to perfect a *don manuel* see Cass req 23 June 1947, D. 1947 J 463.
164   F. Terré and Ph. Simler, Droit civil, les biens, 4th ed., Paris 1992, p. 399; Mazeaud/Breton, Leçons de droit civil, IV, 2, Successions, libéralités, 4th ed., Paris 1982, p. 672.

the donor were able to make a gift while retaining a usufruct for life (*traditio ficta* using *constitutum possessorium*), he would hardly feel any loss; only his heirs would suffer the loss. By requiring the donor to suffer himself he would be prevented from making gifts too easily.[165]

Apart from requiring a real tradition the maxim had another meaning: it required that the gift should be irrevocable.[166] It was not allowed and rendered the gift invalid if the donor had the right to renege at will. A gift should be binding, otherwise it is no gift.[167] Gradually the requirement of *tradition réelle* was relaxed, and in the *Code Civil* only the second meaning of the adage is preserved.[168] In 1878 the *Chambre des requêtes* of the *Cour de Cassation* recognized the validity of the gift from hand to hand perfected by a clause retaining for the donor a usufruct (*rétention d'usufruit*).[169] Such a transfer is a perfectly valid and irrevocable transfer of the bare ownership (*nue-propriété, nuda proprietas*).

8.6 Donor lost possession

In *Thomas v. The Times Book Co. Ltd*[170] a further exception to the *traditio* requirement was made for a donor who had lost possession of the thing he wanted to give. The author Dylan Thomas had been commissioned by the BBC to write a play. When the manuscript was finished he handed it over to Mr Cleverdon, a BBC producer. It was stencilled and a number of copies were made. After Mr Thomas had been given back the manuscript he lost it. As he was to fly to the United States in a few days to give readings from the manuscript Mr Thomas was quite upset and telephoned Mr Cleverdon about the loss. The latter put him at ease saying that the manuscript had been stencilled and that he would give him some copies at the airport. Thomas was very grateful for this and when Mr Cleverdon gave him the copies Thomas told him that if Cleverdon could find the manuscript he could keep it. Thomas mentioned several places where he might have left it. A few days later Cleverdon found the manuscript at one of these places. Many years later, after Thomas' death, his administratrix sued the defendants for the return of the manuscripts, which in the meantime had been sold to them.

Counsel for the plaintiff contended that there had been no delivery to perfect the gift. Yet, Plowman J. did not agree: 'The fact is that Mr Cleverdon got possession of this manuscript from the Soho public house in which it had been left by Dylan Thomas, and he got that possession with the consent of Dylan Thomas. That, in my

---

165 See J. Brissaud, Manuel d'histoire du droit privé, Paris 1935, p. 671-672.
166 See Merlin, Répertoire universel et raisonné de jurisprudence, vol. 8, 5th ed., Brussels 1826, at *donation*, section V, § II, p. 490; Brissaud, p. 670. See also two official letters of Chancellor d'Aguesseau, published in: Pardessus, Œuvres complètes du Chancelier d'Aguesseau, Paris 1819, vol. 12, p. 308 (a letter of 22 May 1731) and p. 315 (a letter of 25 June 1731).
167 Article 2, § II.
168 F. Terré and Ph. Simler, p. 351.
169 Cass req. 5 August 1878, D 1879,1,253. See also Planiol and Ripert, vol. V, nr. 401 bis and nr. 443-447.
170 [1966] 2 All ER 241.

judgment, is sufficient delivery to perfect a gift in Mr Cleverdon's favour.' He continued '...that when Mr Cleverdon got possession of the manuscript with the consent of Dylan Thomas, the gift was perfected.'

So, a gift may be perfected without a transfer of possession, where the donor has lost possession of the thing. It cannot be perfected, however, without the donee acquiring possession of it. As Plowman J. clearly said, the gift was perfected when Mr Cleverdon got possession of the manuscript.

The requirement of the donee having to acquire possession is similar to the rule of the German *gemeines Recht*. There the owner who had lost possession of the object he wished to transfer, had to assign his action of revindication, so that the future acquirer could claim the thing back in case someone wrongfully refused to turn it over. Ownership passed only when the acquirer got possession of the thing.

9 Causal or abstract transfer?

As we have seen before, it is possible to demonstrate that a transfer under the Sale of Goods Act needs a valid legal ground. Yet, it cannot be ascertained whether transfers outside the scope of this act need a valid *causa traditionis* as well. It seems that a transfer based on a deed is abstract.[171] Yet, as to the ancient common law requirement of delivery it is even more difficult to answer our question: the requirement of delivery is based purely on case law. Consequently, it is impossible to draw conclusions from the system of a statute. Some cases might, at first instance, seem to give some clue, but when examining them carefully it appears that they do not offer a solid proof. Below we will have a look at some of these cases.

Having seen that acceptance of the gift is essential, the judgment in *Dewar v. Dewar*[172] might at first sight look surprising. It is a classic case of disagreement about the *causa traditionis*. A mother gave £500 to one of her sons telling him she intended it to be a gift. The son accepted the money, yet he accepted it as a loan, not as a gift, and made this clear to her.

After the mother had died another son of hers claimed part of the £500, or the proceeds of it, contending that the money was a loan and that in consequence it formed part of their mother's estate.[173] He started proceedings against his brother who now regarded the money as a gift.

Goff J., who had to determine whether it was a loan or a gift, was unable to rely on any precedent. He held that the defendant's acceptance of the money, together with his mother's intention to make a gift, sufficed to constitute a gift. Goff J. clearly stated that there was a valid gift: 'The passages to which I have referred [passages from case law] lead me to the conclusion that where a person intends to

---

171 Of course, if the deed itself has been made under the influence of a defect of will, the deed is void or voidable.

172 [1975] 2 All ER 728.

173 The term 'estate' here means the deceased's patrimonium.

make a gift and the donee receives the thing given, knows that he has got it and takes it, the fact that he says: "Well, I will only accept it as a loan, and you can have it back when you want it", does not prevent it from being an effective gift. Of course, it does not turn it into a loan unless the donor says: "Very well, let it be a loan." He could not force the donor to take it back, but the donee, having transferred it to him effectively and completely, intending to make a gift, and he – so far from repudiating it – having kept it, it seems to me that that is an effective gift and, accordingly, I hold that the defendant has established that the mother's contribution was a gift.'[174]

The gift was complete the moment he accepted the money. So, the fact that the defendant accepted the money saying he regarded it as a loan did not prevent it from being a gift. This is a rare case of a gift valid despite the donee's express non-acceptance. The judgment is difficult to reconcile with the other authorities on gift, where acceptance, express or deemed, is regarded as essential.

Looking at the famous antinomy between Julianus and Ulpianus[175] one might think that *Dewar v. Dewar* demonstrates that the transfer of ownership, at least in certain instances, is abstract rather than causal. Julianus says in D. 41,1,36 that if there is agreement about the thing to be transferred but disagreement about the *causa traditionis*, ownership still passes. He gives an example similar to the case in *Dewar v. Dewar*: someone pays coined money to another as a gift whereas the latter accepts the money as a loan for consumption (*mutuum*). Julianus then continues saying that it is settled law that ownership passes even though the parties do not agree about the *causa traditionis*. In chapter 7 we will see that Savigny used this passage as one of the arguments to support his theory of the abstract transfer system in German law.

Yet, for two reasons *Dewar v. Dewar* cannot be considered as an example of an abstract transfer. First, although there was disagreement about the *causa traditionis* in *Dewar v. Dewar*, it was held that nonetheless an effective gift had been made. So, despite the disagreement there was a valid *causa traditionis*: the *causa donandi*. As a result, *Dewar v. Dewar* is not an example of a transfer lacking a valid *causa*.

Secondly, cases in which money is transferred are commonly unsuited to demonstrate whether a transfer system is causal or abstract. Where money is paid there is a transfer of ownership only if coins or banknotes are transferred to the acquirer. If, on the other hand, money is paid by crediting the payee's bank account, by a transfer from one account to another or by paying cash into an account or otherwise, the concept of ownership does not apply.

Moreover, even when coins and banknotes are used we should keep in mind that usually the money will be mixed by the payee with his own money. If the money is so mixed it can no longer be ascertained whether the payee got ownership of the money because of a valid transfer of ownership or because of original acquisition as a result of the mixing. If in such a case the underlying contract or

---

174   See p. 733.
175   See chapter 7, § 2.1.

other *causa* is void and the payee nonetheless becomes owner of the money, one could feel inclined to say that the transfer is abstract. Yet, one could also contend that the transfer was invalid and the payee received ownership because of the mixing rather than the transfer. In short, instances where generic goods are transferred and then mixed are unable to prove either contention.

Westdeutsche Landesbank Girozentrale v. Islington London Borough Council[176] is an example of a case in which money was transferred under a void contract. In this case the bank and the local authority entered into an interest rate swap agreement. Similar agreements had been entered into by several other local authorities before. In one of these interest swap cases, a case not related to the present case in *Westdeutsche*, the House of Lords held such interest swaps void for the reason that it is *ultra vires* (outside the legal power) of a local authority to make these contracts. After this decision it was clear that also in *Westdeutsche* the money had been paid on the basis of a void contract. The bank demanded repayment of the moneys paid to the local authority. It was granted an action for money had and received, a personal claim ex unjustified enrichment[177], rather than a legal or equitable proprietary claim.[178] However, from the judgment it does not follow that the transfer of money is abstract, because the money was mixed with other money belonging to the local authority. As Lord Goff said: 'on receipt of the money by the payee it is to be presumed that (as in the present case) the identity of the money is immediately lost by mixing with other assets of the payee...'.[179,180]

---

176 [1996] 2 All ER 961.
177 The action for money had and received is often called a personal claim in restitution at common law; see Lord Goff's judgment, p. 967(f).
178 The bank had asked for an equitable proprietary claim because this claim would have entitled the bank to compound interest on the moneys paid, rather than simple interest it would get on a personal action.
179 P. 973(h). See also Lord Browne-Wilkinson's judgment, p. 986(d) and p. 998.
180 By the way, even if the action the bank had asked for had been granted (an equitable proprietary claim based on a resulting trust) this would not have been evidence for a causal transfer. For, a beneficial interest under a trust, such as the interest *Westdeutsche* asserted to have, survives mixing of the trust assets, whereas legal ownership will fall away in the case of mixing.

5 Transfer of movables in Dutch law

1 Introduction

Unlike German, French and English law the Dutch civil code of 1992, the *Burgerlijk Wetboek*, contains a general article about the transfer of *goederen*. The Dutch term *goederen* covers *zaken* (movable and immovable tangible property) and *vermogensrechten* (personal and real rights that represent a certain money value). It could therefore best be translated with 'assets'.[1] The provision, article 3:84 BW[2], applies to all transfers whatever the object or the legal ground of the transfer (sale, gift, unjustified enrichment etc). Article 3:84 subs. 1 provides that the transfer of an asset requires *levering* on the basis of a valid legal ground executed by a person privileged to dispose of the thing.[3] In the next section we shall see what the concept of *levering* means and how to translate it. As a rule *levering* requires that the transferor should provide the acquirer with possession of the thing. In most cases the requirement is comparable to the Roman *traditio*. For that reason we can say that Dutch law has a tradition system.

Under the old civil code of 1838 it was disputed whether the Dutch transfer system was abstract or causal. Only in 1950 did the Dutch Supreme Court, the *Hoge Raad*, decide the question in favour of the causal system. The new 1992 civil code codified this choice.[4] In art. 3:84 it unequivocally requires that a transfer should be based on a valid *causa traditionis*, a valid legal ground.

2 Real agreement

2.1 A controversial notion

Traditionally the concept of *levering* is regarded as consisting of two elements: a real agreement, called *goederenrechtelijke overeenkomst*[5], and in most cases, certain additional formalities which vary according to the kind of asset to be transferred. Where movables are transferred the formality will normally consist in providing the acquirer with possession of the thing. The formalities required to transfer immovable property, to give another example, are a notarial deed and registration.

---

1   Covering *Sachen* as well as *Rechte* the German equivalent of *goederen* is *Gegenstände*, a term rarely used in German law. Cf. Motive III, p. 33, Mugdan III, p. 18; Windscheid/Kipp, Lehrbuch des Pandektenrechts, vol. 1, p. 694.
2   The abbreviation '3:84' refers to article 84 of Book 3. Unless stated otherwise the articles mentioned in this chapter refer to the *Burgerlijk Wetboek* of 1992.
3   For the meaning of the term 'privileged to dispose' see chapter 2, § 5.
4   For this historical development see chapter 7, § 6.
5   Some prefer the old term *zakelijke overeenkomst*, the term used under the old civil code. In this code the umbrella term to denote all assets, movable, immovable and intangible, was *zaak*. As in the new civil code the umbrella term was changed into *goed* the term *zakelijke overeenkomst* was accordingly changed into *goederenrechtelijke overeenkomst*.

Unlike in Germany the concept of real agreement[6] is not undisputed in Dutch law. Whereas the different formalities required are clearly laid down in the civil code the real agreement is mentioned neither in the old nor in the new civil code. Nonetheless the concept is acknowledged by a majority of Dutch legal authors. Moreover, it can be found in the *Parlementaire Geschiedenis*[7] and in several decisions of the *Hoge Raad*.[8]

A number of authors doubt the usefulness of the concept and claim that in certain cases the concept is superfluous.[9] The dispute about its usefulness is normally confined to the transfer of movables. For it is generally accepted that, to give some examples, the notarial deed required for the transfer of immovable property[10] and the deed needed for the transfer of a claim (*cessie*, assignment)[11] should be regarded as containing a real agreement:[12] it is an instrument in which the transferor declares to transfer and the transferee declares to acquire the object involved; it is the agreement about the transfer of the object.

2.2 Arguments against the real agreement[13]

The parties' will to make a transfer
Take the following example. I sell a book or a painting to another person and hand it over to him. According to the advocates of the real agreement there are two legal acts here: a contract of sale, which in Dutch law does not suffice to let ownership pass, and an agreement about the transfer of ownership. In addition there is a transfer of possession of the book, in this instance the handing over. Concentrating on this example the opponents of the real agreement argue that a real agreement is superfluous because the will to transfer ownership has been expressed already in the contract of sale. Normally the real agreement is defined as an agreement in which the parties agree about the passing of ownership; it expresses their mutual will to transfer ownership. Is not this will expressed already by the contract of sale? There cannot be any misunderstanding about the seller's and buyer's willingness

---

6 For a definition of the concept see chapter 2, § 2.2.
7 Literally it means 'Parliamentary History'. It indicates a collection of official documents relating to a statute presented to Parliament, and the parliamentary debates about the statute. The most important documents are the draft articles and official comments and explanations by the drafter(s) or the Minister of Justice. These are used as one of the means to interpret the statute involved.
8 See O.K. Brahn and W.H.M. Reehuis, Overdracht, Monografieën nieuw BW, nr. B6a, 3rd ed., Deventer 1997, p. 51.
9 In varying degree among others: Brahn and Reehuis, Overdracht, p. 49-62; J.H.A. Lokin, Traditio; de verschaffing van het bezit, in: R. Feenstra, J.H.A. Lokin and N. van der Wal (eds.), Flores Legum, Groningen 1971, p. 121-132; J.L. den Dulk, De zakelijke overeenkomst, (thesis Groningen 1979) Alphen a/d Rijn 1979; R.D. Vriesendorp, Het eigendomsvoorbehoud, (thesis Groningen 1985) Deventer 1985, p. 23; Reehuis and Heisterkamp, Goederenrecht 1994, nr. 131-134.
10 Art. 3:89 BW.
11 Art. 3:94 BW.
12 The same applies to the deed mentioned in art. 3:95 BW, as we shall see below.
13 In describing the arguments *pro* and *contra* I will focus on the most important arguments.

to transfer ownership of the book. Of course an additional agreement about the transfer of ownership would be unnecessary.

Legal consequences of the real agreement

In the traditional view the legal act of transfer consists of two elements: the real agreement, and in most cases, certain additional formalities. Where movables are transferred these formalities in principle consist in the transferor providing the acquirer with possession of the thing. It may be thought that in this case the real agreement has no legal consequences and is therefore superfluous. In this instance the passing of ownership could be seen to be brought about solely by the providing of possession. The thought is based on the following reasoning. In order to transfer movables a providing of possession is needed. So, the real agreement cannot in itself pass ownership. It passes ownership only if accompanied by a providing of possession. Therefore the real agreement itself has no legal consequences.

Such a reasoning is obviously false. It is incorrect to say that an act which cannot in itself attain the result it aims at and must be accompanied by another act has no consequences and is therefore superfluous. In many cases the law requires certain formalities for a legal act to be valid or fully effective. These formalities do not take away the importance of the legal act itself.

The problem can lucidly be explained by making use of the German legal term *condicio iuris* (a condition required by the law).[14] The nucleus of a legal act consists in the declaration of will of one or more parties. Yet, in many cases the legal consequences intended by the declaration cannot be attained unless certain additional requirements are met, such as the capacity to make legal acts[15], consent of a third party or drawing up a deed. Such conditions required by the law should be distinguished from conditions agreed upon by the parties to the legal act themselves. For that reason they are called *condiciones iuris*.

Now, for a valid transfer of movables it is required, among other things, that the transferor have the privilege to dispose of the thing, that there be a valid legal ground for the transfer, and in most cases, that certain formalities be fulfilled, such as the drawing up of a deed or providing of possession. The nucleus of the transfer, though, is the transferor's and acquirer's declaration that ownership of the thing involved should pass from the former to the latter, that is, the real agreement. Of course this declaration has no effect unless all additional requirements[16], the *condiciones iuris*, have been met. But it would be wrong to say that as a consequence the real agreement in itself has no legal effects and cannot be regarded as a legal

14 See for this concept in general: P. Oertmann, Die Rechtsbedingung, Leipzig/Erlangen 1924 and Von Tuhr, Allgemeiner Teil II, p. 147-152 and III, p. 282.

15 Called *handelingsbekwaamheid* in Dutch and *Geschäftsfähigkeit* in German.

16 Or their substitutes, such as third party protection where the transferor has no privilege to dispose, or the parent's permission where the transfer is executed by a minor.

act.[17] On the contrary, the real agreement should be seen as the core of every transfer of ownership. It *is* the legal act of transferring ownership. As a result the terms transfer and real agreement are in reality synonymous.[18]

As to the Dutch terminology there is quite some confusion.[19] The term *overdracht*, for example, has a double meaning. We can read in the *Parlementaire Geschiedenis*[20] that the legislator intended the term to denote the result of a valid act of transfer: the passing of ownership accomplished by a valid transfer.[21] At the same time, however, there are certain articles where the word *overdracht* is undoubtedly used to denote the legal act of transfer rather than its result. The best example is art. 3:86,[22] the article protecting third party acquirers against a transferor lacking the privilege to dispose. It provides that a transfer (*overdracht*) by a person who is not privileged to dispose is nonetheless valid if certain requirements are fulfilled. A result of a legal act (the passing of ownership) cannot be valid or void, only the legal act itself can (the legal act of transfer). Consequently the word *overdracht* here denotes the legal act of transferring ownership.

To complicate things even further Dutch law has a third notion: the *levering*, mentioned above. As previously said it is usually defined as consisting of two elements: the real agreement, and in certain cases, additional formalities. Since we have seen that the formalities are merely *condiciones iuris* accompanying a legal act it appears that the legal act in question, the real agreement, is in fact equal to the term *levering*. They both denote the legal act of transferring ownership. As a result we can say that Dutch law has three terms to indicate the same legal act: *overdracht*, *levering* and *goederenrechtelijke overeenkomst*.

Having seen this we could try to translate article 3:84 subs. 1 as follows: 'For the passing of ownership of an asset ['passing' referring to the *result*] a transfer is needed ['transfer' indicating the *cause*, i.e. the legal act] which is based on a valid legal ground and which is executed by a person privileged to dispose.'

2.3 Arguments in favour of the real agreement

Above I have said that often a very simple example such as the sale and transfer of a book or painting is used to demonstrate that a real agreement is superfluous. In the real agreement seller and buyer of the painting agree about the transfer of

---

17 Cf. Oertmann, Die Rechtsbedingung, p. 10 and 64; Von Tuhr, Allgemeiner Teil II, p. 148-150. See also Beekhuis in Asser/Beekhuis, Zakenrecht, vol. 1, 9th. ed., Zwolle 1957, p. 151. This view can be found already in Savigny, System des heutigen römischen Rechts, vol. 3, p. 312-313.

18 *Mutatis mutandis* the same goes for the creation of a limited real right and for the transfer of a limited real right or a personal right. Here the real agreement is the legal act of creation or transfer.

19 F.H.J. Mijnssen and G.H.A. Schut, Bezit, levering en overdracht, p. 36 et seq.; Schut, Het nieuwe 2014, WPNR 1972, p. 255.

20 Parl. Gesch. Boek 3, p. 308 (Memorie van Antwoord II).

21 The passing of ownership which is not brought about by a legal act of transfer *inter vivos* is called *overgang* rather than *overdracht*. Examples are the passing of ownership from the deceased to the heir or the acquisition of property as a result of marriage.

22 Cf. A.S. Hartkamp, Compendium, nr. 89.

ownership of the thing. But, did not they agree about this already in the contract of sale? They most certainly did.

However, this is true only in the above example, one of the simplest instances of a transfer. Only a slight complication of the example is needed to demonstrate that a real agreement is indispensable. For that reason some opponents of the real agreement stress that their arguments and objections against the concept apply only to the straightforward example of a transfer of a specific movable thing. Yet, a legal concept, such as the transfer of ownership, must be as complicated as necessary to deal with the most demanding situation. It cannot be simplified just because in some instances some of its elements are superfluous.

Below I will describe a number of situations in which the real agreement is indispensable for a clear analysis of the transfer. The arguments have been used previously in chapter 3 and 4 in relation to French and English law.

traditio ficta

It may be thought that the concept of *traditio ficta* proves the existence of the real agreement. In the case of *traditio ficta* ownership of a thing is transferred by mere agreement. No physical act is needed, like handing over the object. It is tempting to conclude that this agreement must be the real agreement.

However, the argument is wrong. As we have just seen in § 2.2 the *condiciones iuris* should be distinguished from the legal act itself. The *condicio iuris* of providing possession should be distinguished from the legal act of transfer, the real agreement, whether the providing of possession takes place by way of *traditio vera* or *traditio ficta*. True, the transfer of possession, *vera* or *ficta*, needs an agreement. Yet, this agreement is solely about the transfer of possession and it is therefore not identical with the real agreement, which is an agreement about the transfer of *ownership* rather than *possession*. So, *traditio ficta* cannot be used to prove the real agreement.[23]

retention of ownership

As shown already in chapter 3, § 2.2 the retention of ownership clause cannot support the real agreement. Unlike in German law it is unclear whether the suspensive condition[24] is attached to the transfer itself or rather to the obligation to transfer. The text of art. 3:92 BW is ambiguous.[25]

---

23 So, the agreement mentioned in art. 3:115 BW (*tweezijdige verklaring*) is not the real agreement but simply the agreement about the transfer of possession. It is comparable to the *Einigung* in § 854 subs. 2 BGB. Cf. chapter 2, § 3.4.

24 Note, however, that the retention of ownership clause may also take the form of a resolutive condition. Here ownership passes immediately to the buyer but reverts to the seller if the goods have not been paid for in time.

25 'Heeft een overeenkomst de strekking dat de een zich de eigendom van een zaak die in de macht van de ander wordt gebracht, voorbehoudt totdat een door de ander verschuldigde prestatie is voldaan, dan wordt hij vermoed zich te verbinden tot overdracht van de zaak aan de ander onder de opschortende voorwaarde van voldoening van die prestatie.' ('If a contract intends one party to retain ownership of a thing the control over which is given to the other party, until the latter's

transfer without prior contract

For the transfer of ownership *inter vivos* it is indispensable that both transferor and acquirer agree to the transfer. Where there is a contract obliging to transfer ownership, a contract of sale for instance, the contract may be enough to demonstrate the parties' will to transfer ownership. Yet, a transfer is not necessarily preceded by a contract. Let us have a look at a few examples.

A transfer may be based on an obligation ex unjustified enrichment[26]. If a contract for the sale of generic goods, wheat for example, is void or has been avoided ownership in principle does not pass to the buyer. However, if the wheat is physically delivered to the buyer, stored in a silo and mixed with the buyer's own wheat the seller nonetheless loses ownership as a result of the buyer's original acquisition. As the buyer is thus unjustly enriched he is under a duty to return the amount of wheat bought from the seller. This entails an agreement about the passing of ownership of the wheat. It is obvious that here the agreement cannot be regarded to be part of a contract but should be seen as a separate agreement aimed solely at the transfer of ownership.

Another example is a transfer based on delict. In exceptional cases damages should be paid in kind rather than in money.[27] A classic illustration is the case in *Pos/Van den Bosch*[28]. A landlord had granted his tenant in the contract of lease[29] an option to buy the leased land. The option could be exercised only after the landlord and his sisters had died. However, one of the landlord's sisters, Neeltje Brouwer, who outlived her brother and sisters, made a gift of the land to her great-nephew Pos. As it frustrated the lessee's option to buy the land her gift constituted

---

obligation is performed, the first person is deemed to bind himself to make a transfer of the thing under the suspensive condition of performance of that obligation').

Note that in the original text as well as the translation it is ambiguous whether the condition is attached to the transfer or to the contractual obligation to transfer. Despite that, it is generally accepted that the *transfer* is made under a condition, rather than the obligation. See Asser/Mijnssen/De Haan, nr. 267 and 270. This interpretation corresponds with § 455 BGB, which reads: 'Hat sich der Verkäufer einer beweglichen Sache das Eigentum bis zur Zahlung des Kaufpreises vorbehalten, so ist im Zweifel anzunehmen, daß die Übertragung des Eigentums unter der aufschiebenden Bedingung vollständiger Zahlung des Kaufpreises erfolgt und daß der Verkäufer zum Rücktritte von dem Vertrage berechtigt ist, wenn der Käufer mit der Zahlung in Verzug kommt' ('Where the seller of a movable has retained ownership until full payment of the purchase price, it should, provided there is any doubt, be assumed that the transfer of ownership is performed under the suspensive condition of full payment of the purchase price and that the seller has the right to terminate the contract for breach of contract when the buyer defaults on payment of the price').

26 Dutch law distinguishes between two kinds of unjustified enrichment: an enrichment caused by a certain undue performance (*onverschuldigde betaling*, art. 6:203-211 BW) and enrichment arisen otherwise (*ongerechtvaardigde verrijking*, art. 6:212 BW). The distinction is comparable to the German distinction between *Leistungskondiktion* on the one hand and *Nicht-Leistungskondiktion* or *Eingriffskondiktion* on the other hand, which both belong to the concept of *ungerechtfertigte Bereicherung* (§ 812 BGB).

27 See art. 6:103 BW.

28 Cf. HR 17 November 1967, NJ 1968, 42 (*Pos/Van den Bosch*).

29 It was a contract of *huur* (*locatio conductio*) which unlike the common law lease creates only personal rights and duties.

a breach of contract. When the lessee, Van den Bosch, heard of her death and the gift of the land he started judicial proceedings against Pos. He contended that in this particular case (Pos administered his great-aunt's finances and knew of the lessee's option) Pos' accepting the gift amounted to a delict against him. In addition he said that damages in money would not be an appropriate compensation. In the circumstances of the case (Van den Bosch owned adjoining land) the only suitable compensation would be to force Pos to transfer the land to Van den Bosch for the estimated value. The *Gerechtshof* (Court of Appeal) agreed and the *Hoge Raad* approved of this decision. So, in the above case a transfer was based on an obligation ex delict.[30]

A third example can be found in the termination of contracts. If ownership has been transferred under a voidable contract the avoidance will revest ownership in the seller automatically. For avoidance of a contract has retroactive effect, that is to say, after avoidance it is deemed that the contract, which formed the legal ground of the transfer, has never existed (art. 3:53 subs. 1 BW). Yet, in the 1992 civil code the termination[31] of a contract has no retroactive effect. Any transfer of ownership executed before the termination remains valid, as the legal ground of the transfer does not lapse. Still, the transfer should be undone. Accordingly, the termination gives rise to an obligation for the acquirer to retransfer the object to the seller.[32] Also here the transfer is not preceded by a contract.

transfer of generic goods

As we have seen in chapter 4 a real right such as ownership cannot exist unless it is known to which specific object the right relates. The reason is that a real right forms a relationship between a person and a specific object. This principle of specificity applies to Dutch law as well.[33] According to art. 6:227 BW contractual obligations should be determinable (*bepaalbaar*), that is to say, it should be possible to determine without the parties' aid the contents of each party's obligations. Where there is a contract for the sale of a quantity of oil the quantity and quality should be determinable. Yet, this degree of identification does not suffice for a transfer of ownership (or the creation of a limited real right such as pledge). Ownership can pass to the buyer only when it is known which specific object (i.e. which identified amount of oil in the above example) is to be transferred to the buyer.[34]

---

30 There is no reason to think that the decision was confined to immovable property.
31 *Ontbinding*, art. 6:265 et seq. BW.
32 The *verbintenis tot ongedaanmaking* (obligation to undo) ex art. 6:271 BW.
33 Cf. HR 12 January 1968, NJ 1968, 274 (*Teixeira de Mattos*) and more clearly HR 10 February 1978, NJ 1979, 338 (*Nieuwe Matex*).
34 It is unclear whether the requirement of specificity is codified in the new Dutch civil code. According to Mijnssen the requirement is laid down in art. 3:84 subs. 2 BW, but many authors disagree. See H.J. Snijders, De titel van art. 3:84 lid 2 BW, in: M.H. Claringbould (et al.), Van beheering, 'goederenrechtelijke beschouwingen', twaalf opstellen bij het zestiende lustrum van Societas Iuridica Grotius en de vierhonderdenvijftigste geboortedag van Hugo de Groot, Deventer 1998, p. 163 et seq. The debate is of no importance: it is unquestioned that for a valid transfer of ownership the goods should be identified.

Normally, it is true, the requirement of specificity will not create any problem. For, unless the parties have agreed otherwise, a *traditio vera* is needed in order to transfer ownership to the buyer. That is to say, a physical delivery (*aflevering*)[35] of oil is needed. Such a delivery necessarily involves a separation of a certain quantity of oil so that the requirement of specificity will be met.

However, when the parties agree that *levering* should take place *constituto possessorio* a separation is not self-evident. Commonly, for practical reasons, the oil sold ex bulk will remain in the same container until delivery to the buyer. Eventually physical delivery will entail separation and thus individualisation, but *constitutum possessorium* is intended to give the buyer ownership before any physical delivery. In such a case ownership passes only when a certain amount of oil has been separated from the bulk and appropriated to the buyer.[36] As the separation and appropriation to the contract requires consent of both the seller and the buyer the appropriation should be regarded as a real agreement.

Undoubtedly, in the case of *traditio ficta* a real agreement is needed. Yet, it would be wrong to infer that in the case of physical delivery of generic goods a real agreement is superfluous. Physical delivery cannot pass ownership to the buyer against his will. If he refuses to accept the goods because of poor quality ownership remains with the seller, even if they have already been physically delivered to him. There should always be agreement about the passing of ownership.

article 3:95

In order to transfer a movable art. 3:90 subs. 1 requires the transferor to provide the acquirer with possession of the thing. The article, however, applies only where the transferor has power (*macht*) over the thing. Here the term power (*macht*) covers direct possession (actual physical power) as well as indirect possession (power via a *detentor*).[37] It is said that the transferor cannot provide possession when the thing is not within his power, for example as a result of theft or loss.

Still, there is a practical need to be able to transfer ownership in these instances. Commonly an insurance policy will as a condition for payment demand the owner to transfer ownership to the insurance company, so that if the object is found the company can sell it to compensate some of its payments. In these cases art. 3:95 enables the owner to transfer ownership by drawing up a deed. This deed contains the mutual will to transfer ownership of the thing, that is, the real agreement.

---

35 Art. 7:9 BW.
36 As we have seen in chapter 4, § 3 no separation and appropriation is needed where the buyer is given a co-ownership share in an identified bulk. See for Dutch law: HR 10 February 1978, NJ 1979, 338 (*Nieuwe Matex*).
37 Regrettably, the term *macht* (power) does not have a standardised meaning in the Dutch civil code. To give an example, in art. 3:90 subs. 2, as we will see, the word *macht* excludes indirect possession.

2.4 Indispensable element

As a conclusion we can say that the real agreement is an indispensable element within any transfer of ownership. What is more, the real agreement forms the nucleus of every transfer.[38] It *is* the legal act of transferring ownership. The additional formalities that are often attached to this legal act are merely *condiciones iuris*. So, as said before, the terms 'real agreement' and *levering* express the same notion: the legal act of transfer.[39]

However, it should be noted that the concept of real agreement is not confined to the transfer of ownership. As in German law the real agreement is needed for the transfer of any real right (ownership or limited real rights), and also for the granting of a limited real right.[40] As to the transfer of ownership the concept may be defined as an agreement in which the transferor declares to transfer ownership of a specific asset and in which the acquirer declares to accept ownership of it.

3 Providing possession (*bezitsverschaffing*)

For the transfer of movables[41] which are in the power of the transferor art. 3:90 subs. 1 requires that the transferee be provided with possession of the thing. Below we will see the different ways in which possession may be provided.

3.1 *Traditio vera*: art. 3:114

The simplest way to provide possession is a handing over of the object or any other act which gives direct possession over the object, such as the handing over of keys.[42] As 'handing over' is not really the most appropriate expression for the *traditio* of bulky goods art. 3:114 BW defines the *traditio vera* as giving the acquirer

---

38 Cf. Schut in: Ars Aequi 1970, p. 152 et seq., at p. 155.
39 Hence I will translate *levering* with (legal act of) transfer.
40 Although art. 3:84 is applicable also to the release of a limited real right (see art. 3:98) it should not be inferred that also the release contains a real agreement. The release is a legal act performed by the holder of a right aiming at terminating the right in question. Where someone's right of ownership has been burdened with a limited real right the holder of this right may release the owner of the burden by 'abandoning' his right. As the release of the right is detrimental to the holder of the right and favourable to the party released of his burden this legal act in principle does not require the consent of the released party. It is a unilateral legal act. See Von Tuhr, Allgemeiner Teil II, p. 204 and 269. Therefore it would be pointless to require a real agreement here.
41 The provision does not apply to movables which are *registergoederen* (registered objects) such as certain ships and aircraft. For the transfer of these objects special rules apply which I shall leave out in this chapter.
42 The handing over of keys (to a car, a safe etc.) is often called *traditio symbolica*. However, as explained in chapter 4, § 8.2. it should not be regarded as a separate kind of *traditio ficta*. Since it gives the acquirer direct control over the object in question it is simply *traditio vera*. See L.C. Hofmann, Het Nederlandsch zakenrecht, 3rd. ed., Groningen/Batavia 1944, p. 235.

the opportunity to exercise the power the transferor himself could exercise over the object.[43]

3.2 *Traditio ficta*: art. 3:115

Art. 3:115 provides that in three instances a 'mutual declaration', that is agreement, suffices to transfer possession to the acquirer. In sub a, b and c it defines the *constitutum possessorium* (sub a), the *traditio brevi manu* (sub b) and *traditio* where a third party stays in possession of the thing (sub c).

Constitutum possessorium is defined as the form of *traditio* where the transferor is *possessor* of the thing and the parties agree that the transferor will henceforth hold the thing for the transferee as a *detentor*. By doing so the transferor's *possessio* (*bezit*) is transferred to the acquirer and the transferor retains physical power over the object as a *detentor* (*houder*). As in German law it is unknown whether the *constitutum* should be concrete or abstract. A concrete *constitutum* should always be based on a specific legal ground such as loan, hire or custody. If, on the other hand, the *constitutum* is allowed to be abstract it is not necessary to be able to indicate the exact legal ground. But, unlike in German law the question is not even discussed. For the reasons set out in chapter 2, § 4.3 I see no reason why the *constitutum* should be based on a concrete legal ground. True, it normally will, but to my mind it is not essential.

In the case of *brevi manu* the reverse happens. Whereas *constitutum possessorium* turns the *possessor* (transferor) into a *detentor*, *brevi manu* turns the *detentor* (the acquirer) into a *possessor*. As a result possession is transferred from the transferor to the transferee. If someone wishes to buy the car he has been leasing for three years the *traditio* can be made *brevi manu*, without any physical delivery being needed.

As the third kind of *traditio* mentioned in sub c was unknown to Roman law and accordingly unknown to the learned law since the rediscovery of Justinian's Digest no special term had been developed for it. For some strange reason Dutch law uses the term *traditio longa manu* to indicate this form of *traditio*.[44] The term *traditio longa manu* as well as the terms *traditio brevi manu* and *constitutum possessorium* are names created by medieval jurists or jurists of later generations to denote instances of *traditio* recognized already in Roman law. Now, the modern use Dutch law makes of the term *traditio longa manu* does not correspond at all with the term's original meaning. For that reason the term may cause some confusion among non-Dutch lawyers who know the original meaning of the term.

---

43 Cases falling within the scope of § 854 subs. 2 BGB (agreement suffices where the acquirer is able to exercise power over the object) are in Dutch law covered by art. 3:114. In Dutch law the possessor may transfer possession by giving the acquirer permission to collect the thing at a certain place. See Asser/Mijnssen/De Haan, Zakenrecht I, 13th ed., Zwolle 1992, nr. 194.

44 For the possible origin of this inappropriate use of the term *traditio longa manu* see W.J. Zwalve, Hoofdstukken uit de geschiedenis van het Europese privaatrecht, vol. 1 (Inleiding en zakenrecht), Groningen 1993, p. 79, fn. 78.

An example of genuine *traditio longa manu* can be found in Jav. D. 46,3,79.[45] The passage by Javolenus about the payment of money is actually the only passage in the Digest where the expression *longa manu* is used. According to Javolenus a payment can be made by laying down the money before the eyes of the creditor. Another instance recognized as *traditio longa manu* is mentioned in Cels. D. 41,2,18,2. The seller and buyer of a plot of land are standing on a tower overlooking the land. From the tower the seller shows the buyer the boundaries of the land he declares to transfer to the buyer. Such an act suffices for a valid *traditio* of the land. In both examples, it is true, the transfer of possession is somewhat less physical than walking over the ground or putting money into the creditor's hands, but they are still forms of *traditio vera*.

The Dutch *'longa manu'*, on the other hand, is a form of *traditio* in which a third party before and after the *traditio* is *detentor* of the thing. Movables given in custody to a third party, a warehouseman for example, may be transferred without the things leaving the warehouse or the parties being in the neighbourhood of the warehouse. Similarly a thing lent to someone may be transferred to a third person while the borrower is still using it. The English equivalent is the attornment of a bailee mentioned in *Re Hamilton Young* and *Dublin City Distillery*.[46] Yet, unlike in English law the third party does not have to agree with the change in possession. To be valid the *traditio 'longa manu'* should either be assented to by the *detentor* or notified to him. As notification suffices the third party is unable to block the transfer of possession. Without or even against his will his *detentio* for the transferor will be changed into *detentio* for the acquirer.[47] In Germany the same function is fulfilled by § 931 BGB (*Abtretung des Herausgabeanspruchs*). However, § 931 has a broader function: it is used also for the transfer of things that are stolen or lost, and thus is also the equivalent of art. 3:95 BW.

So, the new Dutch meaning of *longa manu* differs completely from the original meaning of the term. Dutch law needed a name for a new kind of *traditio*, a *traditio* where a third party is in possession as *detentor*. Apparently Dutch lawyers have contended themselves with redefining a romanistic term rather than taking the effort to create a new term.

Apart from these forms of *traditio ficta* sometimes a fourth form of *traditio* is recognized: *traditio sine manu*. The term, which is not mentioned in the civil code, is used to indicate the *traditio* between two people living together, married or unmarried. In chapter 4 we have seen the example of a husband making a gift of furniture to his wife.[48] Any physical act of moving the furniture is, of course, unnecessary. The definition of art. 3:114 does not really fit the situation. The husband does not provide his wife with the power he previously had over the

---

45 Since money (coins) was regarded as movable property the payment should be regarded as a transfer of movables.

46 *In Re Hamilton Young*, [1905] 2 KB, at p. 786; *Dublin City Distillery v. Doherty*, [1914] AC, at p. 847-848 and 852. See chapter 4, § 8.4.

47 He will, however, keep all contractual rights he had against the transferor.

48 Chapter 4, § 8.2.

furniture: his physical power over the things remains intact and his wife had the same physical power already before the transfer of possession.

It is important to note that all forms of *traditio* involve a transfer of possession and accordingly a derivative acquisition of possession. On the other hand, a transfer by a deed as mentioned in art. 3:95 is not regarded as involving a transfer of possession. Consequently it is seen not as form of *traditio ficta* but rather as an exception to the requirement of *traditio*.[49]

3.3 Is the transfer of possession a legal act?

Some jurists, mostly opponents of the concept of real agreement, maintain that the transfer of possession is not a legal act but rather a factual act.[50] This is wrong. As said in chapter 2, § 3.3, possession should be seen not only as a fact but also as a right. Where the holder of this right transfers the right to another there is agreement about the transfer of a right. This is undoubtedly a legal act, whether or not it is accompanied by a physical act, the handing over of the object.

The transferee, the subsequent possessor, does not acquire a new right of possession but acquires the right that before belonged to the transferor; it is therefore a derivative acquisition. On the other hand, where a *detentor*, who after all does not have *possessio*, hands the thing over to another the latter acquires possession originally, as a result of *occupatio*.[51] If in the first example a prescription period was running in favour of the transferor the transferee continues this period; yet the possessor who acquired possession originally has to start a new prescription period.[52]

Having seen this we can have a look at a very peculiar reasoning by Den Dulk. He denies that the transfer of possession should be seen as a legal act. In addition he denies the usefulness or even the existence of the real agreement. This inevitably means that according to Den Dulk the transfer of ownership does not contain any legal act whatever. Consequently, in Den Dulk's view the transfer of ownership is not a legal act. As a result the transfer of ownership cannot be void, nor can it be avoided. After all, only legal acts can be void or voidable. Factual acts cannot. What is more, in Den Dulk's view a transfer cannot be made under a condition. Clearly this conclusion is untenable.

A necessary conclusion of the above is that where a thing is sold and possession is transferred to the buyer three legal acts should be distinguished: the contract of sale (although it is not part of the transfer itself), the real agreement (the core of the

---

49 The reason for this is the following. If a thing is stolen or lost otherwise it is commonly said that the owner has lost possession. As a result he is unable to transfer possession to the acquirer. To enable the owner to transfer ownership an exception to the *traditio* requirement had to be made. Yet, again the double meaning of possession causes misunderstanding. The owner has lost only possession as a fact, not possession as a right.
50 See for instance Den Dulk, p. 88.
51 J. Drion, annotation to HR 22 May 1953 (*Sio/De Jong*), NJ 1954, 189, at p. 360.
52 See chapter 2, § 3.3 *in fine* and § 3.5, fn. 91.

transfer) and in addition the transfer of possession (which is not always needed). Although it may be impossible to distinguish these legal acts in practice the fine distinctions are needed for the analysis of more complicated transfers.

3.4 Relativity of *constitutum possessorium*

As the object remains in the hands of the transferor a transfer *constituto possessorio* is invisible to third parties. It may seem as if the transferor is still owner of the asset. For that reason the effect of such a transfer is somewhat weakened: until the transferee has acquired actual control[53] over the thing, the transfer does not work as against persons having an older right in the thing (art. 3:90 subs. 2)[54] such as ownership (if the transferor was a non-owner) or a limited proprietary right.[55] So, the transfer works only relatively.

When, to give an example, a possessor who is a non-owner sells a thing to a bona fide purchaser and possession is transferred by way of *constitutum possessorium* ownership passes to the purchaser provided all requirements of art. 3:86 are fulfilled, the article protecting the purchaser against the transferor lacking the privilege to dispose. However, the transfer does not work as against the true owner: he may still revindicate the thing from any possessor. True, the purchaser meets all requirements for protection mentioned in art. 3:86. Yet, art. 3:86 protects the purchaser only against the transferor lacking the privilege to dispose of the thing. In this case the transfer suffers two concurrent defects: the transferor is not privileged to dispose and, in addition, the act of transfer (*levering*) is weakened: it works as against everyone except third parties having an older right in the thing, such as the owner. The second defect cannot be healed by art. 3:86, nor by any other provision.[56]

In an official comment on art. 3:90 BW we can read what motivated the legislator to weaken a transfer *constituto possessorio*. A transferee who does not insist on acquiring actual power over the object involved, is considered not to deserve any protection against the transferor lacking the privilege to dispose.[57] The true owner should not be able to lose his right as a result of a transfer that is invisible to him.[58] This argument could be seen as an application of the principle of publication.

---

53 Similar to what in French law is called *possession réelle*.
54 Under the 1838 civil code the relativity of *constitutum possessorium* was first acknowledged by the Hoge Raad's decision in *Sio/De Jong*, 22 May 1953, NJ 1954, 189.
55 Memorie van Antwoord II, Parl. Gesch. boek 3, p. 385. Note that the category of persons having an older right in the thing covers also certain personal rights which give its holder priority over general creditors in case of insolvency (*voorrecht*): Nota van Verbetering, Parl. Gesch. Inv. boek 3, p. 1236.
56 *Mutatis mutandis* the same reasoning applies where before the transfer the object has been burdened with a limited real right unknown to the purchaser. Here the purchaser cannot rely on the protection against unsuspected limited real rights given by art. 3:86 subs. 2.
57 This function is highlighted in the Memorie van Antwoord II, Parl. Gesch. boek 3, p. 386. For the same reason the acquirer's protection against limited rights is postponed.
58 See Memorie van Antwoord II, in Parl. Gesch. boek 3, p. 384-385.

In Dutch law a similar protection can be found in art. 3:237. The article introduced into the new civil code an invisible pledge. To create a right of pledge the 1838 civil code required that the security object should be brought into the hands of the creditor or a third party. The debtor was not allowed to keep or regain actual control of the thing.[59] However, there was a practical need for a security right on movables which allowed the debtor to remain in actual control of the asset. It would enable a debtor to raise capital on the security of assets which he needed to run his business, such as machines, trucks and trading stock. As a result case law introduced the concept of *fiducia cum creditore* into Dutch law. In the new civil code *fiducia cum creditore* has been abolished and replaced with the new invisible pledge, which has the same function. To create an invisible pledge a deed suffices so that the object can stay in the power of the debtor (art. 3:237). As this kind of pledge is invisible to third parties it is somewhat weaker than the visible pledge. If the debtor appears not to be privileged to dispose, or if the object has been burdened with a limited real right, the creditor who receives an invisible pledge is not protected against this.[60]

3.5 Prohibition of interversion

The modern interpretation and its main consequences

Article 3:111 provides: 'If a person has started to hold a thing for another under a certain legal relation he shall continue to do so under the same legal ground, until it appears that this has changed either because of an act by the person for whom he is holding or because of a denial of the latter's right.' According to the current explanation of the provision a *detentor* of a thing in principle cannot turn or intervert his *detentio* into *possessio*, nor can he turn his *detentio* for a certain person into *detentio* for another person.[61]

One of the consequences of the rule most frequently discussed is the fact that a *detentor* cannot transfer possession. Sometimes reference is made to the Roman adage *nemo plus iuris ad alium transferre potest quam ipse haberet* (no one can transfer to another more right than he himself has): as a *detentor* has no possession he is not able to transfer possession.

This in turn has consequences for the transfer of ownership, more precisely for the *detentor*'s power to transfer ownership. Normally, it is true, a non-owner, such as a *detentor* or *possessor*, will not be privileged to dispose of the asset. Yet, as we have seen in chapter 2, § 5.3 he will in principle have the power to transfer ownership of a movable to a bona fide third party, provided the latter has acquired

---

59 Art. 1198 BW 1838.
60 *Mutatis mutandis* the same applies to the so-called silent pledge on personal claims, a pledge which is not notified to the debtor of the claim (art. 3:239).
61 The exceptions mentioned in the article will be illustrated below. The rule that a *detentor* cannot turn himself into a *detentor* for a third person has been expressed clearly in HR 22 May 1953, NJ 1954, 189 (*Sio/De Jong*), HR 29 September 1961, NJ 1962, 14 (*Smallingerland/Picus*) and HR 8 June 1973, NJ 1974, 346 (*Nationaal Grondbezit/Kamphuis*).

the thing for a consideration. The protection given by art. 3:86 BW to the bona fide purchaser entails a power of the non-owner to transfer ownership to the purchaser. We should bear in mind, however, that art. 3:86 protects the bona fide party only against a transferor not being privileged to dispose of the movable. All other requirements for a valid transfer should be fully met, such as the requirement of a valid legal act of transfer (*levering*). In order to meet this requirement a transferor who has actual power over the object (*macht*) has to provide the acquirer with possession (art. 3:90 subs. 1). Where the non-owner is *possessor* he will be able to transfer possession to the acquirer. If, on the other hand, he is a *detentor* a transfer of possession will be impossible.

In the latter instance the transfer of ownership has two concurring defects: the transferor has no privilege to dispose, and in addition the transferor is not able to transfer possession to the acquirer. The first problem is solved by art. 3:86. The second, however, cannot be solved. Now, would the *detentor* be able to alter his *detentio* into *possessio*? If he were, this would enable him to transfer possession after all. Yet art. 3:111, the prohibition of interversion, prevents such a change.

Still, in many cases the *detentor* will be able to transfer ownership to the bona fide third party. For art. 3:90 subs. 1 does not require the transferor to *transfer* possession but rather to *provide* possession. There is a subtle but very important difference between these terms. *Providing possession* covers all instances of *transfer* of possession (*traditio vera* as well as *traditio ficta*) but it is a broader expression: it includes also cases in which a *detentor* provides another with the actual power over a thing[62]. Since in the latter case the transferee will acquire possession of the thing originally, as a result of *occupatio*, he is said to have been *provided* with the possession of the object, although there has been no transfer of possession in the strict sense of the word. Thus a factual handing over of the thing suffices for the *detentor* to meet the requirement of art. 3:90 subs. 1.[63] Strictly speaking forms of fictitious tradition are not available to a *detentor*, as they are forms of transferring possession. Nonetheless, he may also provide possession in a way resembling *traditio brevi manu* or *traditio 'longa manu'* provided that it gives the acquirer the power over the object that art. 3:90 demands. *Constitutum possessorium*, or better, something resembling this, does not suffice: here the actual power over the object remains with the transferor.

The usual explanation

In the official comment on his draft of the new civil code Meijers (1880-1954) explains the prohibition of interversion by saying that it should be impossible for someone to lose possession without being aware of it or without the factual situation changing.[64] If a *detentor* wishes to hold the thing henceforth for himself

---

62 Similar to what French law calls *possession réelle*.
63 This handing over differs from the handing over mentioned in art. 3:114 in that the latter act constitutes a transfer of possession, that is to say, in art. 3:114 the transferee acquires possession derivatively rather than originally. Cf. fn. 51 *supra*.
64 Toelichting Meijers (Meijers' commentary) on art. 3.5.5. (= 3:111), Parl. Gesch. boek 3, p. 432.

he ought to notice the person for whom he is holding. The loss of possession should thus be 'publicized'. In this requirement one could see an application of the principle of publication.

Does this offer the possessor any useful protection? Take the example of an owner/possessor who has lent a thing to another. The *detentor* (the borrower) sells the thing to a third party. For the transfer of ownership to be valid it is needed that all requirements of art. 3:86 should be met and, in addition, that there should be a valid providing of possession by the *detentor*. As we have seen he is able to provide possession in many ways. Only one possible way is barred by the prohibition of interversion: a providing of possession resembling *constitutum possessorium*. The prohibition does not prevent a factual handing over or other ways of giving the purchaser actual control over the thing.

In the requirement that the *detentor* should provide the acquirer with actual control and in the rule that interversion is possible only by noticing the original possessor one could see a form of publication. Yet, what is the use of publication? Commonly the principle of publication aims at warning third parties that a certain right which works as against them has originated, changed or lapsed so that third parties can in future take account of this.

However, the person said to be protected here is not a third party but the owner of the asset. In such a case the principle of publication obviously does not fulfil its warning function. The publication is of no use to the owner: the moment he learns of the loss of possession the loss has already become irreversible.

So, when applying the prohibition of interversion to a *detentor* selling to a third party it creates an exception to the rule that the *detentor* is able to deprive the owner of his ownership. Yet it is an exception which cannot be logically explained by referring to the principle of publication. To understand the purpose of the prohibition we should have a look at Roman law, where the rule has been developed. We shall then see that the way in which modern Dutch law interprets the rule, inspired by German law, differs a lot from the use the prohibition originally had in Roman law. The historical survey will also clarify the difficult relationship between the prohibition of interversion and art. 3:90 subs. 2, the relativity of *constitutum possessorium*.

Historical background

The modern Dutch prohibition of interversion has its historical roots in the ancient Roman adage *nemo sibi ipse causam possessionis mutare potest*, which means 'no one can for himself change the legal ground of his possession'. The adage is attributed to the *veteres*,[65] the old Roman jurists, that is to say, the jurists of the pre-classical era of the 2nd and 1st century B.C. It is no longer possible to ascertain all different

---

65 Paul. D. 41,2,3,19 and Marc. D. 41,2,19,1.

uses the adage may have had originally: it seems that even the classical jurists did not understand the full impact of it.[66]

There is, however, one clear case where the classical jurists still apply the adage: *usucapio* (acquisitive prescription). As a result of *usucapio* a possessor who holds a thing for himself may after a certain period (2 years for land and 1 year for other assets)[67] become its owner. For a valid *usucapio* classical Roman law requires, among other things, that the possessor have acquired possession on the basis of a *iusta causa*[68] (legal ground) and that he be *bonae fidei* (in good faith). Still, acquisitive prescription is not available where the object in question has been stolen, robbed or lost otherwise, even if the possessor was in good faith and acquired the thing under a legal ground. These restrictions aim at limiting the scope of *usucapio* to those cases in which it is regarded as just.

The *iusta causa* will often be a legal act aiming at the transfer of ownership, such as a sale or a gift. Prescription is then called *usucapio pro emptore* and *usucapio pro donato* respectively. If in such a case one of the requirements of a valid transfer is not met, for example because the seller does not own the object, or because the seller is a minor, the sale nonetheless offers a legal ground for acquisitive prescription (*iusta causa usucapionis*). If in our example the seller or his *tutor* does not revindicate the object within one or two years the buyer, being possessor of the object, acquires ownership provided that at the moment he acquired possession he did not know of the defect in the transfer.

In Roman law the concept of *usucapio* was of great importance for a transfer by a non-owner because there was no protection of bona fide third parties in the modern sense of the word, that is, a provision giving the bona fide transferee ownership at the moment of the transfer. The transferee could nevertheless receive ownership as a result of *usucapio*, not immediately, of course, but only after one or two years. Thus the concept of acquisitive prescription had *inter alia* the function of protecting certain third parties.

Now, in pre-classical Roman law there was a peculiar case in which a possessor could usucapt although he knew from the beginning that he was not entitled to the object whatsoever. It was an instance of *usucapio pro herede*, acquisitive prescription

---

66 F.B.J. Wubbe, Nemo sibi causam possessionis mutare potest, in: J.E. Spruit and M. van de Vrugt (eds.), Brocardica in honorem G.C.J.J. van der Bergh, 22 studies over oude rechtsspreuken, Deventer 1987, p. 129 et seq., at p. 131. Marcellus is openly in doubt as to the right application of the adage: D. 41,2,19,1.

67 These periods can be found already in the Twelve Table Statute, the *Lex XII Tabularum* (6,3). See M. Kaser, Eigentum und Besitz im älteren römischen Recht, 2nd ed., Cologne/Graz 1956, § 11.

68 This requirement, the *iusta causa usucapionis* (legal ground for acquisitive prescription) should not be confused with the requirement of *iusta causa traditionis*, the legal ground of the transfer of ownership. The requirements have a lot in common but should nonetheless be distinguished. See H.R. Hoetink, Justus titulus usucapionis et justa causa tradendi, TR vol. 29 (1961), p. 230 et seq.; F. Wubbe, Die Interessenlage bei traditio und usucapio, TR vol. 32 (1964), p. 558 et seq. and E.H. Pool, Een kwestie van titels, Causa van bezit, verjaring en eigendom naar klassiek Romeins recht, (thesis Amsterdam) Amsterdam 1995, p. 23 et seq.

as heir.[69] If after the owner's death someone who was not his heir took possession of certain objects of the deceased's estate he could usucapt even though he knew that he was not entitled to the estate. Apparently this was not seen as unjust in this period.[70] Oddly, the requirement of *bona fides* did not prevent this form of *usucapio*: the requirement did not apply here.[71] Nor was taking possession of things belonging to a deceased's estate regarded as *furtum* (theft), which would have excluded *usucapio*.[72] In this pre-classical time it was considered more important that the deceased's estate be accepted soon so that the family rites would be observed and the deceased's creditors would know who to address to realize their claims.[73]

In the classical era, however, this opinion had changed: the above instance of acquisition was now called *lucrativa* (profitable)[74] and *inproba* (unjust)[75]. This undesirable effect of *usucapio pro herede* was somewhat limited by the adage *nemo sibi ipse*. A mere *detentor*, someone holding the object for another, a lessee or borrower for example, cannot usucapt the thing he has leased or borrowed because the legal ground of his possession is not regarded as a *iusta causa* for acquisitive prescription. If the *detentor* were able to change the legal ground of his possession[76] into one of the recognized *iustae causae*, such as *pro herede*, he would start a short prescription period without the owner (the heir) being aware of it. True, usually such a prescription will be barred by the requirement of good faith. Yet, as we have just seen, the requirement of good faith was no impediment in this case. The *detentor* would be able to deprive the true heirs of their property within one year.[77] But *usucapio* is excluded here by the adage 'no one can himself change the legal ground of his possession': it prevents the *detentor* from changing the legal ground of his 'possession' (i.e. lease or loan) into a *iusta causa usucapionis*.

Later a *senatus consultum* (senate's decision) initiated by emperor Hadrian offered the true heirs an action to claim back the objects involved from any wrongful

---

69 Gai. 2,52 et seq.

70 E.H. Pool, Een kwestie van titels, Causa van bezit, verjaring en eigendom naar klassiek Romeins recht, thesis Amsterdam, Amsterdam 1995, p. 100.

71 F. Wubbe, Usureceptio und relatives Eigentum, TR 28 (1960), p. 15-16.

72 D. 47,19,6; Jörs/Kunkel/Wenger, Römisches Recht, 4th ed. by Honsell, Mayer-Maly and Selb, Berlin etc. 1987, p. 471.

73 Gai. 2,55.

74 Gai. 2,56.

75 Gai. 2,55.

76 Note that the terms *detentor* and *detentio*, legal concepts used in the 19th century *gemeines Recht*, were not used in Roman law as technical terms. Roman law does distinguish between *naturalis possessio* (natural possession), holding a thing for another, and *possessio civilis* (possession according to *ius civile*), holding a thing for oneself, but often the equivocal term *possessio* is used to denote both types of possession. See Kaser I, § 94, I and II.

   In the adage the word *possessio* refers to all sorts of possession and thus includes *possessio naturalis*: see Jul. D. 41,5,2,1 and M. Kaser, Eigentum und Besitz im älteren römischen Recht, p. 335-336 and 339-340.

77 Gai. 2,54.

possessor as if they had not been usucapted.[78] As a result the adage *nemo sibi ipse* was no longer needed to bar this prescription. As far as we know the *usucapio pro herede* was one of only two cases where the adage was still important.[79] In the Digest the adage is cited also in relation to other instances, but merely to say that the adage is no impediment in the case involved, that it does not apply there.[80] The adage had now lost an important part of its function.

The Dutch civil code of 1992

Referring to classical Roman law Pothier explains that the adage *nemo sibi ipse* is needed to prevent a *detentor* from acquiring ownership by way of prescription.[81] Articles 2236, 2237 and 2240 of the French civil code, in which this rule is laid down, are clearly derived from Pothier's analysis;[82] so are articles 592, 1996 and 1997 of the Dutch civil code of 1838, which are based on the *Code Civil*. Apart from art. 592 all these articles, the French as well as the Dutch, are part of the law about prescription.[83]

For the short acquisitive prescription the old Dutch civil code of 1838 required a *iusta causa* (*wettige titel*: art. 2000 BW). Yet, in the new Dutch civil code this was abolished as a requirement for acquisitive prescription.[84]

In Roman law the *nemo sibi ipse* adage was used to prevent acquisitive prescription in favour of possessors who knew they were not entitled to the things involved. For some strange reason Roman law did not take the straightforward path of calling them possessors in bad faith thus barring them from acquisitive prescription. Yet, in modern law such possessors are without exception called possessors in bad faith. They would never be able to rely on art. 3:99 BW, as it requires good faith. Consequently, it may now seem as if the adage no longer applies to prescription. Yet, as we shall see below, in modern Dutch law the adage

---

78 Gai. 2,57. The senate's decision cannot be dated: see J.E. Spruit and K. Bongenaar, De Instituten van Gaius, 2nd ed., Zutphen 1994, p. 173, fn. 8.

79 The other instance being *usureceptio*, see Gai 2,59.

80 See Wubbe, Nemo sibi causam possessionis mutare potest, p. 129.

81 Pothier, Traité de la possession, ch. 2, Œuvres, vol. 9, Paris 1846, p. 275 et seq.

82 However, the explanation of these articles given by Bigot-Préameneu is far from lucid. See Locré, Législation, vol. 8, Brussels 1836, p. 347, nrs. 9-13.

83 As to the French civil code and the old Dutch civil code there seems to be a case in which acquisitive prescription against an unknowing owner is possible. Here interversion is allowed if based on *une cause venant d'un tiers* (art. 2238 CC), *eenen oorzaak die van een derde afkomt* (art. 1997 old BW). It seems to be based on an example given by Julian in D. 41,3,33,1. In the new Dutch civil code this rather strange example has been removed. See Toelichting Meijers ad art. 3.5.5. (= 3:111), Parl. Gesch. boek 3, p. 432.

84 See Ontwerp Meijers, Toelichting Meijers and the Memorie van Antwoord II, Parl. Gesch. boek 3, p. 408-409. Unfortunately, the exact reason for abolition is unknown. It may have been the purely logical reasoning that next to the requirement of good faith the requirement of a legal ground would have been superfluous. The Memorie van Antwoord II seems to indicate this. See Parl. Gesch. boek 3, p. 409. It may also have been the result of German influence. In his draft Meijers mentions that the German civil code (see § 937 BGB) abolished the requirement of a *iusta causa*. See Parl. Gesch. boek 3, p. 408, fn. 1.

is still important both for the short prescription of art. 3:99 BW and for the long prescription of art 3:105 j° 3:306 BW.

The traditional use of the adage in modern Dutch law

In modern Dutch law the prohibition of interversion is still used to prevent a prescription period from running against an unsuspecting owner. Art. 3:111 BW does not forbid interversion altogether, as Roman law seems to have done: it provides that interversion is possible only when the person for whom the *detentor* holds the thing agrees to it or when the *detentor* openly and in good faith denies the right of the person for whom he held the thing.

If for example the owner[85] who has lent a thing to another sells and transfers the thing to the borrower he may use a *traditio brevi manu* to transfer his possession. If he does so the borrower's *detentio* is turned into *possessio*, or, as the Romans would have said, the legal ground of his 'possession'[86] has changed. Here the interversion of the legal ground is justified by the possessor's consent.

In the second instance mentioned in art. 3:111 (denial of the other party's right) interversion is also possible without the owner's consent. Yet, it is possible only if the person for whom the *detentor* held the thing is informed of the change. Let us take the following example: a borrower who suddenly has a good reason to believe that he is the real owner of the thing and wishes to become its possessor. If he were able to change his *detentio* into *possessio* without informing the lender a prescription period would start to run without the lender knowing this. If the borrower were in good faith the prescription period would be 3 years for movables. Being unsuspecting the lender would not think of revindicating the thing, whereas a revindication would be needed to prevent acquisitive prescription by the borrower. So, a formal denial informs the lender of a possible future loss of his right which he can then try to prevent.

As a result of long prescription a mala fide possessor may acquire ownership of a thing. When the owner's action of revindication has lapsed (extinctive prescription of the right of action) the then possessor of the object will acquire ownership.[87] In principle it will take 20 years for the revindication to lapse.[88] Yet, due to the *nemo sibi ipse* adage the *detentor* is able to turn himself into possessor and thus start a prescription period only if he informs the possessor.

As shown above the prohibition of interversion was never intended to prevent a *detentor* from transferring possession and thus encumber him in transferring ownership, which is nowadays the most prominent function of *nemo sibi ipse*. Before the Senate's decision under emperor Hadrian its function was to prevent a *detentor* from usucapting *pro herede* (as heir). In modern Dutch law it has a function within the field of prescription as well. Because of the *nemo sibi ipse* adage in its modern

---

85 Here I take the example of a possessor who is also owner of the asset. Yet, the same applies to a possessor who has no ownership.
86 Note that in this expression 'possession' consists of *possessio* and *detentio*.
87 Art. 3:105 subs. 1 BW.
88 Art. 3:306 BW.

form a prescription period cannot run against an unsuspecting owner and thus deprive him silently of his ownership. The adage protects the owner against both forms of prescription, the long as well as the short prescription period.

What inspired Dutch law to a broader use of the adage?

In addition to the traditional use the *nemo sibi ipse* adage obtained another function. In its second function the adage prevents a *detentor* from transferring ownership to a third party without bringing the thing in the physical power of the latter. What led Dutch law to use the adage to this effect?

Art. 592 of the old Dutch civil code, in which the *nemo sibi ipse* adage was laid down, was placed in the title on possession. As we can read in the *Parlementaire Geschiedenis* (Parliamentary History) published by Voorduin the Dutch legislator rejected the French legislator's decision to treat the concept of possession in the title on prescription. The Dutch legislator preferred a separate title on possession within the book on property law. It was decided that also the prohibition of interversion, the Dutch equivalent of the French article 2240 should be placed in the general title on possession rather than in the title on prescription. It gives the impression that the prohibition of interversion is a rule applying to possession in general and that its use is not limited to prescription. Yet, in the Parliamentary History the broader use of the adage, that is to say, the use beyond the concept of prescription, is not illustrated by any example.[89] In textbooks of the 19th century and the beginning of the 20th century the rule is explained only by referring to the concept of prescription.

However, when a practical need arose to weaken or even nullify invisible transfers executed by *constitutum possessorium*, the position of the rule in the title on possession led Dutch law to stretch the rule beyond its original scope. Scholten (1875-1946) proposed to use the prohibition of interversion to prevent a *detentor* from transferring possession *constituto possessorio*[90] and his reasoning, based on art. 592 old BW, was adopted by the *Hoge Raad* in *Sio/De Jong* in 1953.[91]

The modern third party protection of art. 3:86 BW is largely based on a theory developed by Scholten in the first half of the 20th century.[92] As one of the requirements for third party protection Scholten put forward that the transferee should have acquired *reëel bezit*[93] (lit.: 'actual possession', that is, possession giving actual power over the object). In his view a transfer by way of *constitutum possessorium* did not meet this requirement. As a consequence a person who had acquired *constituto possessorio*, whether from a *possessor* or from a *detentor*, could not

---

89 J.C. Voorduin, Geschiedenis en beginselen der Nederlandsche wetboeken, Utrecht 1838, vol. 3, p. 346-347 and vol. 5, p. 556-557.

90 Scholten, WPNR 1906, p. 569; Zakenrecht, 7th ed. (1933), p. 65 and 99; more clearly 8th ed. (1945), p. 67 and 100.

91 HR 22 May 1953, NJ 1954, 189. The decision was affirmed by the *Hoge Raad* in *Smallingerland/Picus*, HR 29 September 1961, NJ 1962, 14.

92 Like the French civil code the old Dutch civil code did not have a clear concept of third party protection against a transferor lacking the privilege to dispose.

93 Comparable with the French term *possession réelle*.

invoke third party protection as long as he had not acquired actual possession. To support his view he referred to § 933 of the *Bürgerliches Gesetzbuch*, in which a similar rule was laid down.[94]

As Dutch law lacks an umbrella term covering *possessio* and *detentio* two separate rules are needed to weaken the *constitutum*: art. 3:90 subs. 2, which applies where the *constitutum* is made by a possessor, and the prohibition of interversion which applies to a *detentor* trying to transfer possession by way of *constitutum possessorium*. Both provisions express the thought that someone who intends to acquire ownership or a limited real right does not deserve the normal third party protection as long as he leaves the thing involved in the hands of the transferor or grantor.[95]

In German law the weakening of the *constitutum possessorium* could be united in a single paragraph (§ 933 BGB) as the term *Besitz* covers *possessio* as well as *detentio*.[96] The paragraph is placed among provisions which protect a third party against a transfer by a non-owner. It provides that where a thing has been transferred *constituto possessorio* the transferee can invoke the third party protection only from the moment he has acquired actual control over the thing, provided he is still in good faith at that moment. If, to give an example, a non-owner sells and transfers the thing to a bona fide purchaser by way of *constitutum possessorium* the latter will not be protected by § 932 BGB (protection against the transferor being a non-owner) until he has acquired actual control over the thing.[97]

The reason for the German legislator to defer third party protection in the case of *constitutum possessorium* is equal to the reason mentioned in the official comment on art. 3:90 BW. Paragraph 933 BGB intends to protect the owner of a movable against being deprived of his ownership without noticing it. Moreover, the transferee who does not insist on acquiring actual control and leaves the thing with the transferor is considered as not deserving any protection.[98,99]

---

94   Scholten, Zakenrecht, 7th ed. 1933, p. 99; see also Salomons, 2014 tot 1950, De geschiedenis tot 1950 van de vertrouwensbescherming bij overdracht van roerende zaken door een beschikkings-onbevoegde, (thesis Amsterdam, UvA 1997) s.l. 1997, p. 297-305.

95   Yet, there is a slight difference between the prohibition of interversion and article 3:90 subs. 2 in that the first nullifies the transfer of possession altogether, whereas the second nullifies the transfer by way of *constitutum possessorium* only as against third parties having an older right in the thing.

96   The relation between these provisions would be clearer if the prohibition of interversion in its second function and the provision in art. 3:90 subs. 2 were placed among the provisions about third party protection.

97   A similar deferring of third party protection can be found in § 936 BGB. This paragraph protects the acquirer of a thing against the thing being burdened with limited real rights unknown to him (cf. art. 86 subs. 2 BW). If the thing is transferred *constituto possessorio* the protection is deferred until the transferee has acquired actual control from the transferor.

98   See Motive III, p. 345 (Mugdan vol. 3, p. 192) and Protokolle III, p. 3704 (Mugdan, vol. 3, p. 632).

99   These two arguments apply only if the transferor has transferred possession *constituto possessorio* holding the object in direct possession. However, a transfer *constituto possessorio* is possible also when the possessor has indirect possession. If B, for instance a warehouseman, is holding the object as a *detentor* the possessor (A), who has indirect possession, may transfer his possession *constituto possessorio* turning himself into a *detentor* for the acquirer (C). As a result B is now a *sub-detentor* holding the object for A, and A a *detentor* for C. As to publication of the transfer, that is,

Regrettably, in Dutch law the weakening of *constitutum possessorium* is oddly scattered over two different provisions:[100] on the one hand art. 3:90 subs. 2, and, on the other hand, the prohibition of interversion. It obscures the strong relation between both provisions in deferring third party protection. After all, both provisions have been developed by Scholten as consequences of his *reëel bezit* requirement.[101]

4 The privilege to dispose (*beschikkingsbevoegdheid*)

Also Dutch law requires that the transferor should have the privilege to dispose of the asset involved. The term *beschikkingsbevoegdheid* is based on the German equivalent *Verfügungsbefugnis*. The verb *beschikken*, like the German verb *verfügen*, is an umbrella term covering the alienation of assets (such as ownership, limited real rights and claims) and the creation of limited real rights. It derives from German pandectism of the late 19th century.

The privilege to dispose may be based on ownership[102], a legal act or the law. An example of a statutory provision giving a privilege to dispose is art. 68 *Faillissementswet* which provides that the trustee in bankruptcy (the *curator*) is privileged to dispose of the insolvent's assets.[103] Also the pledgee has the privilege to dispose of another's assets, provided, of course, that all requirements for execution are fulfilled (art. 3:248 BW).[104]

As in German law (§ 185 BGB) a privilege to dispose can be based on a legal act. The owner may permit another person to dispose of his asset. If he orders a *commissionair* (undisclosed commercial agent) to sell and transfer an asset the legal acts of sale and transfer will be made in the agent's name. It is an example of indirect agency. By ordering the transaction the owner gives the agent a privilege to dispose of the asset.[105] Another important example is the sale and transfer of goods under a retention of ownership clause. If there is a practical need for the buyer to resell the goods before full payment of the price the seller, who is still

---

visibility, the practical result equals a *traditio 'longa manu'*. As in the case of *'longa manu'* there is no reason to weaken this kind of *constitutum possessorium*. Cf. J. Drion in the annotation to the *Hoge Raad*'s judgment in *Sio/De Jong*, NJ 1954, p. 363, 1st col.

100 Leaving out of consideration art. 3:237 BW.

101 Scholten, Zakenrecht, 7th ed. 1933, p. 99.

102 Or from being the 'holder' of a right (*rechthebbende*). In English law the holder of a right is simply called the owner of the right. Yet, because of the limited definition of *zaken* (movable or immovable tangibles) Dutch law does not use the term ownership in regard to rights. There is no material difference, though.

103 When the debtor is declared insolvent he loses the privilege to dispose of his assets (art. 23 *Faillissementswet*).

104 Cf. Groefsema, § 6.2.

105 In the case of direct agency the agent has no privilege to dispose; he does not need it because the principal is deemed to have made the transfer himself. It suffices if the agent has the privilege to represent. See chapter 2, § 5.2.

owner, may allow the buyer to sell and transfer his goods. The permission gives the buyer a privilege to dispose of the seller's goods.[106]

---

106 Similarly the pledgee of goods may permit the pledgor to sell and transfer the goods free of the right of pledge. It gives the pledgor a privilege to dispose of the pledgee's right of pledge. The moment the pledgor transfers the goods he releases the right of pledge.

6 Gift from hand to hand

1 Introduction

The gift from hand to hand gives a good example of the importance of the real agreement. It raises dogmatic problems that are common to German, Dutch, French and English law, problems that can be solved only by a proper understanding of the role of the real agreement. Nineteenth century German literature, especially, paid a lot of attention to the nature of the gift from hand to hand. Is it a contract at all? If so, is it a consensual or a real contract? As we shall see in the next chapter, Savigny used the example of the gift from hand to hand to support the abstract transfer theory.

2 Executed and executory gifts

Within the law of gifts of England, France, The Netherlands and Germany a distinction can be made between executed and executory gifts. The first category consists in gifts that are directly performed without any preceding obligation to make the gift. An executory gift, on the other hand, is a binding promise to make a gift in future.

The gift from hand to hand, on its turn, is a subcategory of executed gifts. Originally it was confined to the transfer of ownership of movable property, usually including sums of money and claims to bearer.[1] Yet, nowadays the gift from hand to hand is no longer confined to the transfer of ownership in the strict sense: an executed gift of a sum of money may be made by a transfer from one bank account to the other.[2] However, since such a transfer is not a transfer of ownership it is outside the scope of my book. I will therefore, when speaking about gifts from hand to hand, concentrate on gifts consisting in the transfer of movable property.

3 Conferred enrichment and the *causa donandi*

A distinction should be made between enrichment and gift. In order to make a gift it is first of all needed for the donor to enrich the donee in some way. Yet, the enrichment in itself does not suffice to constitute a gift. In addition both parties, donor and donee, should agree that the enrichment is without recompense, that is to say, that the enrichment is *causa donandi*: intended as a gift. It is an agreement about the legal ground of the enrichment. So, the concept of 'gift' consists of the enrichment on the one hand, and the agreement that it be a gift on the other hand.

It is not feasible to give a description of all the different enrichments that could be the subject matter of a gift. However, it should be noted that the subject matter

---

1   See for example art. 7A:1724 of the Dutch BW. The article will be abolished in 2001.
2   See for example the decision of the Dutch *Hoge Raad* 7 April 1978, NJ 1978, 624.

of a gift, executory or executed, is not limited to the transfer of ownership of movable or immovable property. To give an example, a gift may also consist in the grant or transfer of a limited real right, assignment of a claim to the donee, release of a real right burdening the donee's property, release of a personal claim against him and paying a debt due by the donee to a third party. Already in classical Roman law these forms of enrichment could be the subject matter of gifts.[3] Modern Dutch, French and German law also allow such enrichments to be conferred as a gift.[4]

German and Swiss law developed a concept to describe all these different forms of enrichment: the concept of *Zuwendung*.[5] It would be misleading to translate the concept simply with 'enrichment', since enrichments by coincidence, for example original acquisition of ownership as a result of mixing, does not amount to a *Zuwendung*. Nor does a unilateral act by the enriched party, such as a deliberate mixing by the latter of another's goods with his own goods. The enrichment should be based on the will of the enrichor, it should be conferred by him to the enriched. Accordingly, it would be more appropriate to translate *Zuwendung* with 'conferred enrichment'.

Both the German *Bürgerliches Gesetzbuch* and the Swiss *Obligationenrecht*[6] use the term *Zuwendung* in their general definition of the gift.[7] Only because of the broad concept of *Zuwendung* was it possible to draft a provision containing a general definition applying to executed as well as executory gifts. The executed gift forms a *Zuwendung* because it consists in a transfer of ownership, the assignment of a debt, the payment of the donee's debt etc., which are all cases where the enrichment is directly perfect. However, also the promise to make a gift in future constitutes a *Zuwendung*. This may seem odd, since the promise, for example to transfer a car, has yet to be followed by the transfer itself. Only then will the donee be owner of the car. Still, even before the transfer to him, the donee is enriched: not

---

3   Kaser I, p. 601.

4   As to French and Dutch law the meaning of the concept of gift as laid down in the French and Dutch civil codes (art. 931 CC and art. 7A:1719 BW respectively) is quite narrow. The above forms of gift are acknowledged either as falling within the narrow concept of gift as laid down in civil codes (called *donation directe* or *formele schenking*) or as being a *donation indirecte* or a *materiële schenking*. See Mazeaud/Breton, Leçons de droit civil, vol. II,2, Successions, Libéralités, 4th ed., Paris 1982, p.681 et seq.; Gr. van der Burght and J.P. Penders, Schenking, Deventer 1989, p. 68 et seq. and p. 117 et seq.

5   The term *Zuwendung* was hardly ever used in the *Pandektenrecht*. As a *terminus technicus* it was introduced into German law by the *Bürgerliches Gesetzbuch*. In modern German literature the concept of *Zuwendung* is somewhat neglected. For a very extensive treatment of the concept see Von Tuhr, Allgemeiner Teil III, § 71 et seq. (more than 100 pages).

6   The 1881 code on the law of obligations.

7   See § 516, subs. 1 BGB: 'A conferred enrichment through which someone enriches another at the expense of his patrimony constitutes a gift when both parties agree that the enrichment be without recompense.' ('Eine Zuwendung, durch die jemand aus seinem Vermögen einen anderen bereichert, ist Schenkung, wenn beide Teile darüber einig sind, daß die Zuwendung unentgeltlich erfolgt.').

   Art. 239 OR: 'Every conferred enrichment *inter vivos* through which someone at the expense of his patrimony enriches another without corresponding performance in return, constitutes a gift.' ('Als Schenkung gilt jede Zuwendung unter Lebenden, womit jemand aus seinem Vermögen einen andern ohne entsprechende Gegenleistung bereichert.').

with ownership of a car, but with an enforceable personal claim against the donor, which has a certain value in itself. By making a binding promise to give the donor confers on the donee a personal right *causa donandi*.[8]

4 The requirement of notarization for executory gifts

For various reasons the executory gift, the promise to give, has been subject to certain formalities, such as a deed in English law and a notarial deed in Germany[9], France[10] and the Netherlands[11]. The main reason for German law to insist on notarization seems to have been to protect the donor against instantaneous and ill-considered gifts, though other reasons such as evidential problems are mentioned as well.[12]

The French requirement of notarization was imposed for very different reasons. The requirement which is laid down in art. 931 CC is part of a long-standing French tradition of protecting heirs. To ensure that the heirs would receive a reasonable portion of the deceased's estate ancient French law devised various means to limit the owner's power to make gifts. The limitations applied to gifts by will, and in some regions also to gifts *inter vivos*. In the South of France, in the *pays de droit écrit*, the forced heirship was called the *légitime*, a right to a certain fraction of the inheritance.[13] Here the *légitime* was accepted in many districts already around 1100,[14] though in varying form.[15] Gradually the principle began to be

---

8 Next to the general definition of gift there are special provisions for the executed gift in § 516, subs. 2 BGB and for the executory gift in § 518 BGB. The latter paragraph contains the requirement of notarization of the promise to give. A similar ordering can be found in Swiss law. Art. 239 OR contains the general definition of gift, art. 242 and 243 OR are provisions specially for the gift from hand to hand, respectively the promise to give. Art. 243 OR requires a written instrument for the promise to give.

   Oddly, modern German authors contend that § 516, subs. 1 BGB contains a definition of the gift from hand to hand only. See for example Münchener-Kollhosser, § 516, Rdnr. 1 and Staudinger-Cremer, 1995, § 516, Rdnr. 2 (although the latter is not really unequivocal). In the parliamentary history of the paragraph we can read that this view is wrong. See Mugdan, vol. 2, p. 158 et seq., at pp. 160, 162 and 163 (Motive) and p. 738 (Protokolle). Most probably this mistake originates in a disregard of the extent of the concept of *Zuwendung*. Often it is, without much further thought, regarded as equivalent to a transfer, whereas a transfer is merely one of many forms a *Zuwendung* may take. Cavin, for instance, claims that the text of art. 239 OR is 'unfortunate, as the gift is a contract by which an obligatory relationship is constituted, not a *Verfügung* which transfers ownership.' ('...wenig glücklich, denn die Schenkung ist ein Vertrag, mit dem ein Schuldverhältnis begründet wird, nicht eine Verfügung, mit welcher Eigentum zugewendet wird.'). See P. Cavin, in: M. Gutzwiller et al. (eds.), Schweizerisches Privatrecht, vol. VII, 1, p. 183, fn. 1.
9 § 518 BGB.
10 Article 931 CC.
11 Article 7A:1719 BW.
12 Mugdan, Motive, vol. 2, p. 162-163.
13 See for modern French law: art. 913 et seq. CC.
14 J.P. Dawson, Gifts and promises, Continental and American law compared, New Haven/London 1980, p. 41.

accepted in the North as well.[16] It was accepted by the *Parlement de Paris* and codified in the revised version of the *Coutumes de Paris* in the 16th century.[17] In the 17th century it was generally accepted in the North of France, the regions of customary law.[18]

This *légitime* received support from a series of Royal Ordinances requiring notarization of gifts *inter vivos*. For the notarization requirement in these ordinances no official reason was ever given. The reasons may have been diverse. The requirements may have been imposed to help collect taxes on gifts, and to protect creditors of the donor against a lessening of the donor's creditworthiness. Still, the main reason was, most probably, to discourage making gifts (notarization was a time-consuming and costly process) and thus protect the wealth and power of the influential families.[19] The first of these Royal Ordinances dates back to 1539, the last and most famous is the ordinance of 1731 by the hand of chancellor d'Aguesseau.[20] The *Code Civil*'s requirement of notarization of gifts is directly based on d'Aguesseau's ordinance: the text of art. 931 CC has been taken almost literally from art. 1 of the 1731 ordinance.[21]

The requirement of notarization in the Dutch *Burgerlijk Wetboek* (art. 7A:1719) is due to direct influence of the French *Code Civil*. The requirement did not exist in the *Rooms-Hollands recht* (the Roman-Dutch law of the 17th and 18th centuries).[22] So, via article 931 of the *Code Civil* the Dutch requirement originated in the French Royal Ordinances of the 16th, 17th and 18th century. However, returning to Roman-Dutch law on this point, the new Dutch provisions on gift abolish the requirement of notarization, as it is thought unnecessary to protect the donor against his own impulsive conduct.[23]

---

15 Coing, Europäisches Privatrecht, vol. 1, § 130, III.

16 Next to the *réserve*: see Viollet, Histoire du droit civil français, p. 933. The *réserve* is a somewhat different form of forced heirship.

17 Viollet, p. 933.

18 Dawson, p. 41.

19 Dawson, p. 43-45.

20 See Dawson, p. 43. The full text of d'Aguesseau's ordinance has been published in: J.-M. Pardessus, Œuvres complètes du Chancelier d'Aguesseau, Paris 1819, vol. 12, p. 265 et seq.

21 The text of art. 1 of the ordinance reads: 'Tous actes portant donation entre-vifs, seront passés par-devant notaires, et il en restera minute, à peine de nullité.' See Pardessus, p. 167. In requiring notarization also the drafters of the *Code Civil* aimed at protecting the heirs' *légitime*, although for different reasons: not to protect influential families but to ensure equality among heirs. See Dawson, p. 45-48.

22 C. Asser and J. Limburg, Handleiding tot de beoefening van het Nederlandsch burgerlijk recht, vol. 3, 1st part, Zwolle 1905, p. 394 et seq.

23 The provisions about gift are part of the 1838 civil code. They are planned to be replaced by new provisions in 2001. Art. 7.3.1. BW abolishes the requirement of notarization. See Toelichting op het voorontwerp, p. 896. As a result of this change a special provision on gifts from hand to hand is no longer needed. Note that the article number (7.3.1.) is only provisional.

5 Gift from hand to hand exempt from notarization

However, despite the insistence on notarization of executory gifts all of these countries allow an informal unnotarized form of gift: the gift from hand to hand. In the Dutch *Burgerlijk Wetboek* of 1838 the gift from hand to hand was codified in art. 7A:1724. The German definition of gift in § 516 subs. 1 BGB has been drafted so as to comprise the executory as well as the executed gift. Also the French *Code Civil* recognizes the validity of the gift from hand to hand, the *don manuel*. In doing so it continues the pre-*Code Civil* law. The ordinance of 1731, which restated the requirement of notarization, was not intended to obstruct gifts from hand to hand. Chancellor d'Aguesseau, the draftsman of the ordinance, made clear that the notarization requirement did not apply to this category of gifts.[24] The *Code Civil*, it is true, does not mention the gift from hand to hand, but it has never been the intention of the draftsmen to abolish the *don manuel* and extend the formality of a notarial deed to all gifts.[25]

6 The true nature of the gift from hand to hand

We have seen that the subject matter of a gift is not limited to the transfer of ownership of movable or immovable property. It may also consist for example in the grant or transfer of a limited real right, release of a real right burdening the donee's property, assignment of a claim to the donee, or release of a personal claim against him and paying a debt due by the donee to a third party.

Since the gift is such a broad concept Von Savigny[26], following his pupil Puchta[27] on this point, proposed to place the gift in the *Allgemeiner Teil*, the general part, of the civil law. Savigny emphasized that gift is 'a general character which different legal acts may take.'[28] Over the years this view became the prevailing one in German law.[29]

Windscheid, however, did not agree to this approach and saw the law of contract as the proper place for the concept of gift.[30] Probably due to Windscheid's influence on the drafting of the *Bürgerliches Gesetzbuch* - he was a member of the first drafting commission - the gift was placed in Book 2 of the civil code, the book

---

24 D'Aguesseau wrote this in an official letter from 25 June 1731. It has been published in Pardessus, Œuvres complètes du Chancelier d'Aguesseau, Paris 1819, vol. 12, p. 310 et seq. The remark in question is on p. 312.

25 Merlin, Répertoire, vol. 8, 5th ed., Brussels 1826, *donation*, section II, § VII; see also the *Rapport* by Jaubert of 29 April 1803, in: Locré, Législation civile, vol. 5, ch. 15, nr. 45. Cf. Cass req 23 June 1947, D. 1947 J 463.

26 Savigny describes a large variety of gifts. See System, vol. IV, p. 1-156.

27 See Savigny, System, vol. IV, p. 3, fn. c.

28 System, vol. IV, p. 3.

29 Windscheid/Kipp, Lehrbuch des Pandektenrechts, vol. 3, § 365, fn. 18.

30 In his Lehrbuch he placed the gift in the book on obligations, in a part on obligations ex contract. See § 365.

on obligations, rather than in Book 1, the general part. Naturally, though, it did not lose anything of its 'general character'. In the *Motive* and *Protokolle*, part of the German Parliamentary History, it is emphasized that the gift is a true *Vertrag*.

Indeed there cannot be a gift without the donor's and donee's consent.[31] Yet, does this entail that every gift is by definition an *obligatory* contract? The position of the gift in Book 2 of the *Bürgerliches Gesetzbuch* seems to indicate this. It is beyond any doubt that executory gifts are obligatory contracts. A binding promise to give creates a duty to make a gift in future, an obligation emanating from the agreement between donor and donee. In the case of an executed gift, on the other hand, there is no such obligation to make a gift. It is the very definition of the executed gift. Here the conferred enrichment (*Zuwendung*) is accompanied by an agreement that the enrichment should be a gift (*Schenkung*). The agreement may even follow some time after the *Zuwendung*, for example where the donor pays a debt due by the donee to a third party. The *Motive* and *Protokolle* rightly state that every gift is a true *Vertrag*, but the tacit inference, made by many German authors, that therefore every gift is an *obligatory* contract (*Schuldrechtlicher Vertrag*) is obviously wrong. *Vertrag* simply means 'agreement'; the obligatory contract is no more than a subcategory of 'agreement'. Puchta already warned against this common mistake. In a paragraph about *donatio inter vivos* he said: 'The current method of placing the gift with the obligations...is very suitable to obscure the correct understanding of it; in the very case of the simplest and most natural way of giving, the immediate transfer of ownership, there is no obligation. Ultimately this placing most probably originates in the misunderstanding of assuming every agreement to be an obligatory relationship.'[32]

7 Real and consensual contracts

In the second half of the 19th century the category of real contracts began to be questioned by some authors,[33] Koeppen[34], Bruns[35] and Stobbe[36], among others.

---

31 Note that the donee's acceptance need not be explicit: he is presumed to accept the gift until the contrary appears. Nonetheless agreement is essential.

32 G.F. Puchta, Pandekten, 2nd ed. Leipzig 1844, p. 96-97, 7th ed., ed. by A. Rudorff, Leipzig 1853, § 69, footnote d): 'Die jetzt gewönliche Methode, die Lehre von den Schenkungen zu den Obligationen zu stellen...ist ganz geeignet, den wahren Begriff der Sache zu verdunkeln; gerade bey der einfachen und natürlichsten Art zu schenken, die im sofortigen Hingeben zu Eigenthum besteht, kommt gar keine Obligatio vor. Zuletzt läßt sich jene Stellung wohl auf den Irrthum, bey jedem Vertrag an ein obligatorisches Verhältnis zu denken...als ihre eigentliche Veranstaltung zurückführen.'

33 In the *Motive* at § 453 of the first draft (the predecessor of § 607 BGB, the paragraph on *Darlehen* (*mutuum*)) it is said that 'among legal authors there is a controversy whether modern law should stick to the Roman distinction between consensual and real contracts...' As for modern law quite a number reject the distinction contending that all real contracts have become consensual contracts. This is being contended especially for the *Darlehen*.' ('In der Theorie herrscht Streit, ob für das moderne Recht an der römischrechtlichen Unterscheidung zwischen Konsensual- und Realkontrakten festzuhalten sei... Nicht wenige verwerfen diese Unterscheidung für das heutige Recht, wonach alle Realverträge zu Konsensualverträgen geworden seien. Insbes. auch für den Darlehensvertrag wird

This viewpoint was to acquire more and more adherents in the course of the 20th century. A number of authors claim that in modern German law all contracts are consensual contracts[37] and that the category of real contracts is no longer relevant. Some even express relief saying that at last the theory of the real contract is now overcome. The drafting commissions of the *Bürgerliches Gesetzbuch* expressly left this controversy to legal science and chose neutral formulations to describe the contracts in question.[38] So, to attack or support the category of real contracts a reference to the text of the German civil code cannot be convincing.

The main argument against the real contract is that consensus should suffice to create a contract. Roman law, where our concept of real contract originated, did not have the principle of freedom of form. To be valid and enforceable a contract had to be clothed in one of the recognized forms. Classical Roman law did have a small number of contracts that could be created by mere consensus, but it did not recognize consensualism as a principle. A *nudum pactum*, an agreement not clothed in one of the authorized forms, was unenforceable.

Only much later was it gradually acknowledged that in principle any agreement should be enforceable. From the Middle Ages the canon lawyers had developed the adage *pacta sunt servanda* (agreements should be adhered to). However, this adage applied to canon law only. As it overtly conflicted with Roman law, the adage was not accepted as applying in the field of civil law. Yet, when the school of natural law began to emphasize the power of the human will to create legal

---

dies behauptet.'). See Mugdan, vol. 2, p. 169.

34 A. Koeppen, Der obligatorische Vertrag unter Abwesenden, Jher. Jahrb., vol. 11 (1871), p. 139 et seq., at p. 352 et seq.

35 F. von Holtzendorff (ed.), Encyklopädie der Rechtswissenschaft in systematischer Bearbeitung, 4th ed., vol. 1, Leipzig 1882, p. 491.

36 O. Stobbe, Handbuch des deutschen Privatrechts, vol. 3, 2nd ed., Berlin 1885, p. 70.

37 See for example W. Fikentscher, Schuldrecht, 9th ed., Berlin/New York 1997, § 12 and the authors mentioned there.

38 As to *Leihe* (*commodatum*) the second drafting commission said that 'the question whether the loan for use should be seen as a real contract in the Roman sense cannot be settled in the Code, but should be left to science.' ('Die Frage, ob der Leihvertrag als ein Realvertrag im römischrechtlichen Sinne anzusehen sei, könne im Gesetzbuche nicht entschieden werden, sondern müsse der Wissenschaft überlassen bleiben.'). See Mugdan, vol. 2, p. 895.

As to *Darlehen* (*mutuum*) the first drafting commission made a similar though less explicit statement. 'There is no need to end the academic controversy by characterizing the loan for consumption as a normal consensual contract. Rather, we should choose a formulation which makes clear that the duty to return [goods of the same quality and quantity] necessarily presupposes a receipt of the loan.' ('Es besteht aber auch kein Bedürfnis in Erledigung des wissenschaftlichen Streites den Darlehensvertrag als einen gewöhnlichen Konsensualvertrag zu bezeichnen. Es ist vielmehr eine Fassung zu wählen, welche zum Ausdrucke bringt, daß die Erstattungspflicht nothwendig den vorhergehenden Empfang des Darlehens voraussetzt.'). The passage, however, shows a preference for regarding the loan for consumption as a real contract. See Mugdan, vol. 2, p. 170.

consequences[39] the canon law adage, which was often referred to by the natural lawyers, gained influence on the civil law. Gradually in the course of the 16th and 17th century the adage *pacta sunt servanda* was recognized as governing the civil law of contract.[40]

Yet, despite this development many continental civil codes made in the 18th and 19th century maintained, knowingly or not, the character of the real contracts: here consensus between the parties does not suffice to create the contract. Real contracts come into being only when a certain thing (*res*) has been transferred.

Is there any practical need for a 'real' moment?

When the loan is gratuitous the requirement of a transfer is justified because it protects the lender against being bound by his own impulsive behaviour. Yet, if it is for consideration, if the lender receives a recompense, for example in the form of interest, there is no reason why a pre-contract in which someone promises to make a loan, should not be binding. In the German *gemeines Recht* of the 19th century such a pre-contract was enforceable.[41] Also in modern German,[42] Dutch,[43] French[44] and English law such a promise is indeed binding. It gives the future borrower a personal claim against the future lender for the transfer of the money. Often the binding promise will be part of a *Krediteröffnungsvertrag* (opening of credit).

Where there is a binding pre-contract obliging to make a *mutuum*, a binding *pactum de mutuo dando*, it does not make sense to see *mutuum* as a real contract. The pre-contract and the main contract are in practice one and the same legal transaction, a transaction that is binding upon both parties as a result of mere consensus. Accordingly, it is by many authors called a consensual contract.[45] For

---

39 Grotius compared the freedom to create contracts by mere will to the freedom to transfer ownership by mere will. See De iure belli ac pacis, 2,11,1,3, Amsterdam 1712; in § 3 he says: 'Moreover, as we have said before [in 2,6,1] ownership of a thing can be transferred when the will has been expressed sufficiently. Why then would it not be possible to confer a personal right [in this manner] as well, either a claim for the transfer of ownership (which is less than ownership itself) or a claim for a certain act, for indeed we are as much entitled to our *actiones* as to our things?' ('Adde quod, voluntate sufficienter significata, transferri rei dominium potest, ut ante diximus. quid ni ergo possit transferri & jus in personam, aut ad transferendum dominium (quod jus ipso dominio minus est) aut ad aliquid agendum, quippe cum in actiones nostras par jus habemus atque in res nostras?'). See R. Feenstra and M. Ashmann, Contract, aspecten van de begrippen contract en contractsvrijheid in historisch perspectief, 2nd ed., Deventer 1988, p. 18.

40 See Feenstra and Ashmann, p. 6; Zimmermann, The law of obligations, p. 537-545.

41 Windscheid/Kipp, Lehrbuch des Pandektenrechts, vol. 2, § 371.

42 Staudinger-Hopt and Mülbert, 12th ed., Vorbem. § 607 ff, Rdnr. 254 d) and § 607, Rdnr. 15 and 25.

43 Asser/Kleijn, Bijzondere overeenkomsten, vol. 4, 4th/5th ed., Zwolle 1988, nr. 97; Hoge Raad 26 March 1958, NJ 1958, 399.

44 Mazeaud/Chabas, Principaux contrats, 2e partie, p. 909.

45 The case law on *Darlehen*, however, is equivocal: no clear choice can be found whether *Darlehen* is a real or a consensual contract. See Staudinger-Hopt and Mülbert, 12th ed., § 607, Rdnr. 13b.

the same reason Swiss law[46] and the new Dutch law[47] have characterized *mutuum* as a consensual contract. True, the *mutuum* is not yet complete before the money or other fungibles are handed over: the borrower's duty to return a similar amount of money etc. arises only when he receives the money. So, one of the essential obligations arising from *mutuum* depends on the transfer of credit. But this is not a distinguishing feature: also in the case of hire the hirer's duty to return the object arises only the moment he receives the object. This does not turn hire into a real contract.

As said before, many modern German authors claim that in German law all contracts are consensual: offer and acceptance suffice to create a contract. They contend that the category of real contracts no longer exists. Yet, such a statement is too absolute. A distinction should be made as to whether real contracts are for consideration or gratuitous.[48] Most probably all pre-contracts involving a real contract for consideration are binding. At any rate, a pre-contract in which a lender promises to give a loan for interest will be binding upon him. However, there are real contracts that do not tolerate a binding promise preceding it. A good example is the gift from hand to hand. A promise is binding only if laid down in a notarial deed. But then it is no longer a gift from hand to hand. It is the very characteristic of the executed gift that it is not preceded by a binding promise to make the gift. The requirement of transferring the object protects the donor; it is a sign of seriousness.[49] Those real contracts that are not preceded by a binding promise have not lost their 'real' character.[50]

Unfortunately, however, no such distinction is being made. The reason may be that the authors denying the existence of real contracts commonly use the example of a commercial loan of money, that is, a contract for consideration. Without any further reasoning they then suppose that all real contracts have lost their 'real' nature.[51]

As a result of their statement that all contracts are consensual and that a gift is a contract German and Swiss authors have difficulties in explaining the executed gift. To force this kind of gift into the category of obligatory contract they maintain that the performance of the gift from hand to hand is logically preceded by an

---

46 See article 312 OR, the text of which clearly speaks of the lender's obligation to transfer the subject matter of the loan. See also B. Christ, in: M. Gutzwiller et al. (eds.), Schweizerisches Privatrecht, vol. VII: Obligationenrecht, zweiter Halbband: besondere Vertragsverhältnisse (ed. by F. Vischer), Basel/Stuttgart 1979, p. 226.

47 Article 7.2.1.1. BW (not yet in force; the numbering of the article is only provisional).

48 It should be borne in mind that in Roman law *mutuum*, *commodatum*, and *depositum* were gratuitous contracts.

49 A. Wacke, Das Besitzkonstitut als Übergabesurrogat in Rechtsgeschichte und Rechtsdogmatik, Cologne 1974, p. 87.

50 See also Windscheid/Kipp, Lehrbuch des Pandektenrechts, vol. 2, § 371, fn. 6. Here Windscheid says that the loan for consumption can be regarded as a consensual contract only if the transfer of the objects lent is preceded by an obligation for the lender to make the transfer and an obligation for the borrower to accept the loan and pay interest. Cf. also A. Wacke, Das Besitzkonstitut, p. 87.

51 See for example Staudinger-Hopt and Mülbert, 12th ed., § 607, Rdnr. 12 et seq.; Münchener-Westermann, Vorbem. § 607, Rdnr. 7.

obligation. In their theory the obligation exists only for an imaginary second: it is immediately executed so that it lapses the moment it comes into being. It is a very artificial way of interpreting the gift from hand to hand needed only to uphold their theory that all contracts are consensual.

As Von Tuhr clearly described their view is wrong. Von Tuhr[52] compared the gift from hand to hand with the so-called *Handkauf* (literally 'sale from hand to hand', a contract of sale that is immediately executed by both parties). An example of sale from hand to hand is buying a magazine in a newsstand or buying stamps from a machine (the so-called *Automatenkauf*). Here the making of the contract and its performance coincide. As a result it seems as if no obligations have ever existed. Yet, this is not true: obligations have arisen on both sides. They become visible when one or both parties' performances are defective. If the machine gives you the wrong stamps or no stamps at all, the seller is in principle obliged to give you the right stamps. If you manage to fool the machine by throwing false coins into the slot you will still have to pay for the stamps. So, obligations do arise, as in every contract of sale. What makes a sale from hand to hand look special is the fact that the obligations normally disappear as soon as they arise: they exist only for an imaginary second (*juristische Sekunde*). Nonetheless, as Von Tuhr stressed, in the contract of sale the seller's obligation to transfer is an essential part of the contract.

The gift from hand to hand, he continued, is different. It would be incorrect to regard the gift from hand to hand as containing an obligation to transfer an object, an obligation which is then immediately fulfilled the moment it arises.[53] Only the executory gift, the binding promise, is an obligatory contract, because it creates an obligation to perform the gift. The gift from hand to hand, however, is not an obligatory contract.

The true character of the gift from hand to hand
It is certain that agreement between donor and donee is needed. Where the executed gift consists in transferring a movable, the real agreement required for the transfer could at the same time contain the agreement about the *causa* of the transfer, the agreement that the enrichment should be a gift (*causa donandi*). Yet, it would be more accurate to see the agreement about the *causa* as a separate agreement accompanying the real agreement.[54] For, one should always distinguish the transfer (or other conferred enrichment) from the gift. The difference is apparent when the agreement follows some time after the enrichment, for example if the donor has paid a debt due by the donee to a third person and later informs the donee of it. The payment itself is not a gift; it is a mere enrichment of the donee conferred on him by the donor unilaterally without the donee's will. The enrichment becomes a gift only when the donor and donee agree that it be a gift. In German law it is called the 'agreement about the legal ground' (*Abrede über den*

---

52 Von Tuhr, Allgemeiner Teil III, p. 75.
53 Von Tuhr, Allgemeiner Teil III, p. 75. The same view can be found in Larenz, Schuldrecht II,1, 13th ed., Munich 1986, p. 200.
54 Von Tuhr, Allgemeiner Teil III, p. 82, fn. 126.

Rechtsgrund).[55] Without such an agreement the enrichment would be without *causa* and therefore unjustified. It would in principle give the 'donor' a restitutionary claim for the return of the enrichment. How are we to regard this agreement in the different countries we are examining?

As to English law there is no choice between an obligatory contract and a mere agreement. For a contract to be valid English law requires some form of consideration. It should therefore be regarded as an agreement to be perfected by delivery.[56] Dutch, German and French law, on the other hand, do not have a consideration requirement. In these systems of law there is no reason why the gift from hand to hand should not be a contract. Since the gift from hand to hand is a contract created by conferring an enrichment on the donee, French and Dutch law (the latter until 2001) have traditionally regarded this gift as a real contract.[57] Also for German and Swiss law this would be a better characterization.

8 Dogmatic importance of the gift from hand to hand

The gift from hand to hand demonstrates the existence and importance of the real agreement. As to French law it illustrates, together with all other real contracts, that, unlike art. 1138 CC suggests, the *solo consensu* rule does not apply to every transfer of property. According to the *solo consensu* rule an obligation ex contract to transfer ownership is immediately and automatically executed. However, in the case of a gift from hand to hand there is no such obligation ex contract: the contract is created only as a result of the transfer of ownership. To this transfer the ancient *traditio* requirement still applies. In addition a real agreement is needed. This requirement can never be omitted.

Also as to English law the gift from hand to hand demonstrates the importance of the real agreement. Since here a gift cannot be regarded as a contract the gift from hand to hand should in English law be seen as a real agreement accompanied by an agreement that the enrichment should be *causa donandi*.

---

55 Larenz, Schuldrecht, II,1, p. 200.
56 Or by deed.
57 Mazeaud/Chabas, II,1, Obligations, théorie générale, 9th ed., Paris 1998, nr. 80; Asser/Kleijn, nr. 262.

7 *Iusta causa traditionis*

1 Introduction

In this chapter we shall examine the history of the causal and abstract transfer theories. We shall see that in their modern form the two systems were both created only in the beginning of the 19th century. The causal system was introduced into French law by the *Code Civil* of 1804. The concept of real agreement (*dinglicher Vertrag*) and the abstract transfer system as applied in German law up to the present day have been introduced into German law by F.C. von Savigny and his followers in the first decades of the 19th century. The origin of these systems, however, is much older and we will see that they both developed from a common base: Roman law. Accordingly, the modern dichotomy cannot be appreciated properly without analysing these developments. To give an example, both in creating the real agreement and in developing the abstract system Savigny was influenced considerably by Donellus and the theories of the medieval glossators and commentators. The main argument put forward by Savigny to defend his abstract system can be found already in the writings of the glossators.

To understand how the modern transfer systems came into being we should analyse in rough the transfer theories of the glossators, commentators and later generations of jurists. We will then see that the abstract transfer system is based on certain texts from the so-called learned law, that is Roman law as explained by the learned jurists from the time of the rediscovery of the Digest.

In the learned law before Savigny we will not find any consistent transfer theory in the modern sense of the word. There seems to be no *communis opinio* and, what is more, even statements of one and the same author are often in conflict. Yet, these statements, however conflicting and vague, have in common that they are the result of a controversy over how the opaque and confusing Roman law sources should be interpreted, a debate which has been going on for centuries. One thing was clear: for a transfer of ownership to be valid Roman law required a *iusta causa traditionis*. This requirement could not be denied. The controversy was about the meaning of the term *iusta causa*.

2 The root of the problem

2.1 The confusing Roman basis[1]

In D. 41,1,31, pr. Paulus says: '*Traditio* alone will never pass ownership; it will, however, if a sale or another sufficient ground has preceded on the basis of which *traditio* has followed.'[2]

---

1   I will discuss only the main passages which played a vital role in the controversy.
2   Numquam nuda traditio transfert dominium, sed ita, si venditio aut aliqua iusta causa praecesserit, propter quam traditio sequeretur.

The controversy was fuelled especially by the well-known antinomy in the Digest between Julianus and Ulpianus. They both commented on the following case. Someone transfers money to another with the intention of making a gift; the other party, however, accepts the money as a loan rather than as a gift. Thus, there is no agreement about the *causa traditionis*, the legal ground why ownership should pass. On the other hand, there is agreement about the fact that ownership should be transferred. Both parties intend ownership to pass, but for different legal reasons. As there is no agreement about the gift or the loan there is no contract between the parties. According to Julianus (D. 41,1,36, pr.) ownership passes nonetheless: 'When we agree on the thing that is transferred, though disagree about the legal ground of the transfer, I see no reason why the transfer should be ineffective, for example when I think that under a will I am bound to you to transfer land while you think it is due to you under a stipulation. For, also if I give you coined money as a gift and you accept it as a loan for consumption, it is certain that the passing of ownership is not impeded by us disagreeing about the legal ground of the transfer.'[3] Ulpianus, on the other hand, referring to the same example, disagrees and claims that ownership does not pass (D. 12,1,18, pr.): 'If I have given you money as a gift and you accept it as a loan for consumption there is no gift according to Julianus. But it is yet to be seen whether it is a loan. I think that there is no loan, and, what is more, that ownership of the coins does not pass to the recipient, because the latter has accepted them with a different intention.'[4]

For centuries, since the rediscovery of the Digest in the 12th century, jurists have been trying, unsuccessfully though, to explain this contradiction. Yet, it is important to realize that the Roman jurists did not know any consistent transfer theory. They were not interested in dogmatics and building theories. Therefore any attempt to reconcile these conflicting statements in the Roman sources is doomed to fail.

2.2 Justinian's interpolation

Justinian is partly to blame for the confusion. In classical Roman law there were three methods of transferring ownership: the ancient *in iure cessio*, *mancipatio* and a relatively new form called *traditio*. As *in iure cessio* had already become obsolete in the classical period[5] I will concentrate on *mancipatio* and *traditio*. Assets valuable to agriculture such as immovables within the Italic region, slaves, large cattle and rural servitudes could be transferred only by way of *mancipatio* (they were therefore called *res mancipi*).[6] For that reason *mancipatio*, an abstract form of transfer,[7] was the most

---

3 Cum in corpus quidem quod traditur consentiamus, in causis vero dissentiamus, non animadverto, cur inefficax sit traditio, veluti si ego credam me ex testamento tibi obligatum esse, ut fundum tradam, tu existimes ex stipulatu tibi eum deberi. nam et si pecuniam numeratam tibi tradam donandi gratia, tu eam quasi creditam accipias, constat proprietatem ad te transire nec impedimento esse, quod circa causam dandi atque accipiendi dissenserimus.

4 Si ego pecuniam tibi quasi donaturus dedero, tu quasi mutuam accipias, Julianus scribit donationem non esse: sed an mutua sit, videndum. et puto nec mutuam esse magisque nummos accipientis non fieri, cum alia opinione acceperit.

5 Kaser I, p. 415.

6 Kaser I, p. 414.

important method of transferring ownership. For the transfer of other assets, which were often less valuable, *traditio* sufficed.

In Justinianian law *traditio* had become the general form of transfer: its scope was extended to cover the *res mancipi* of classical Roman law. By this time *mancipatio* itself had fallen into disuse.[8] Yet, the change created a problem in composing the Digests or Pandects, a compilation of the texts by classical jurists made in the 6th century by order of emperor Justinian. As the classical texts were to receive force of law, they had to be updated to reflect the modern Roman law of Justinian's time. Accordingly the word *traditio* was interpolated for *mancipatio*, that is to say, *mancipatio* was replaced with *traditio*.[9] Many of these interpolated texts, originally written specially for the abstract *mancipatio*, could thus easily give the impression of *traditio* being abstract. Moreover, Justinian's jurists failed to make clear whether or not the transfer of ownership should be regarded as abstract or causal.

Since Justinian's order to interpolate *traditio* for *mancipatio* was published in his *Codex*[10] it was known to the glossators and later generations that some passages containing the word *traditio* might be corrupt. Yet, it was unknown exactly which texts had been interpolated. Only at the end of the 19th century was it discovered that one of the texts of our famous antinomy, Jul. D. 41,1,36, pr., had been interpolated. So, this was unknown to the glossators, commentators and subsequent generations, including Savigny.[11] They trusted these texts to reflect genuine classical and Justinianian Roman law. It is therefore not at all surprising that many of them thought the classical *traditio* to be an abstract form of transfer. Their view seemed to accord rather well with the classical texts as interpolated by Justinian's jurists.

2.3 Three different theories

From the time of the glossators the requirement of *iusta causa* has been explained in many different ways. The explanations tend to vary from jurist to jurist, and even within the writings of one and the same jurist inconsistent explanations may be found, so that the jurist in question seems to hover between two different lines of thought. A transfer theory was created only by Savigny and his pupils in the beginning of the 19th century. The learned law of the Middle Ages, humanists and later generations of jurists did not bother to create any transfer theory.

Still, to analyse their statements I will make use of three main types of transfer system as a reference point. As we will see in chapter 8 these types may be relevant also for future attempts at harmonizing European private law. I will call these transfer theories the *causa vera* theory, the *animus dominii transferendi* theory and the

---

7 Kaser I, p. 414.
8 Kaser II, p. 282.
9 C. 7,31,1,5.
10 See previous fn.
11 It was discovered by Lenel. See O. Lenel, Quellenforschungen in den Edictcommentaren, ZSS Rom, vol. 3 (1882), p. 179-80; See also J.C. van Oven, Praeadvies over causa en levering, The Hague 1924, p. 29, fn. 1.

abstract theory. It should be noted, however, that there is no proof that any of these systems has ever been in existence before the 19th century.

The *causa vera*[12] theory requires a valid legal ground. When, for instance, a thing is being transferred on the basis of a contract of sale whereas in reality the contract has never existed, ownership does not pass. Such a contract, which exists only in the minds of the parties, is often called a putative contract, or a putative legal ground (*causa putativa*) in contrast with a valid or true legal ground (*causa vera*). Similarly, ownership cannot pass under a void contract.

According to the *animus dominii transferendi*[13] theory, or short the *animus* theory, ownership may pass even though the contract is void or merely putative, provided there is genuine consensus between the parties that ownership should pass. A contract of sale, to take an example, is not entirely unimportant, as it is an indication that the parties intend to transfer ownership. Yet, the essential requirement is the parties' will to transfer ownership. And this will can be present even if the contract is void or merely putative.

Now, a contract may be void for various reasons, illegality, for example, or a defect of will such as fraud (*dolus*). In some of these instances the voidness of the contract does not entail that there is no mutual will to transfer ownership. Where a contract is void for illegality the parties' will to transfer ownership will normally not be affected by the contract being illegal. On the other hand, where there is a defect of will there is no true consensus between the parties that ownership should pass. As we shall see in this chapter, within the group of jurists who hold that ownership may pass under a putative or invalid *causa* we can make a further distinction according to their opinion on the consequences of defects of will.

A true respect for the parties' will should involve acknowledging that a defect of will in the underlying contract affects both the contract and the transfer. If one of the contracting parties has entered into a sales contract under the influence of a defect of will, the contract does not accord with his true will. Nor does the transfer of ownership made to execute the contract. I will call this transfer theory which respects the true will of the parties the *animus* theory. On the one hand, the theory recognizes that a putative or invalid *causa* suffices to transfer ownership, on the other hand, defects of will affect both the contract and the transfer.

To other jurists a transfer may be valid even if the underlying contract has been entered into under the influence of a defect of will. In their theory the transfer of ownership and thus the parties' will to transfer ownership is abstracted from any underlying *causa traditionis*. This theory is called the abstract theory. It is the theory which has been introduced into German law by Savigny and his followers.

---

12 Lit.: real legal ground.
13 Lit.: the will to transfer ownership.

3 The *iusta causa traditionis* before Savigny

3.1 The glossators and commentators[14]

causa putativa

In a gloss on D. 41,1,31, pr. (Paulus' remark on the *iusta causa* requirement), Rogerius (?-1170?[15]) writes that the *iusta causa* is needed only as an indication of the transferor's will to transfer. 'This is said [i.e. that a *iusta causa* is required] so as to facilitate proving that the person who has transferred possession had the will to transfer ownership, but not in order that ownership will not pass whenever the *traditio* is not preceded by a *iusta causa*, as when you pay, wrongly believing you are obliged to.'[16] This opinion necessarily entails that *iusta causa* is no longer a requirement for a valid transfer. Yet, Rogerius does not expressly draw this conclusion.

Martinus Gosia (?-1150s?[17]) and Accursius (among 1182/85-1260/63[18]) both emphasize the importance of the transferor's will to transfer.[19] Martinus Gosia, and in his footsteps Accursius, try to reconcile the Julianus/Ulpianus antinomy by distinguishing two cases, a technique often used by the glossators to solve contradictions.[20] After all, if Julianus and Ulpianus are talking of different cases, their solutions need not be conflicting. The two glossators consider the possibility that in Jul. D. 41,1,36 ownership passes because in this example the transferor does not care on which legal ground ownership passes to the acquirer, whereas in Ulp. D. 12,1,18 ownership does not pass because here the transferor insists on making a gift and consequently does not want ownership to pass on another legal ground.[21] In short, ownership may in certain instances pass without there being

---

14 See in general: J.G. Fuchs, Iusta causa traditionis in der Romanistischen Wissenschaft, Basel 1952 and J.H. Dondorp and E.J.H. Schrage, Levering krachtens geldige titel, enige grepen uit de geschiedenis van de vereisten voor eigendomsoverdracht, Amsterdam 1991. See for the influence of fraud on the transfer of ownership: J.E. Scholtens, Justa causa traditionis and contracts induced by fraud, SALJ vol. 74 (1957), p. 280 et seq. I will confine myself to only a small number of jurists.

15 Hermann Lange, Römisches Recht im Mittelalter, vol. 1, Die Glossatoren, Munich 1997, p. 192-94.

16 Gloss *propter quam traditio sequeretur* on Paul. D. 41,1,31, pr., in: G. Dolezalek, Der Glossenapparat des Martinus Gosia zum Digestum Novum, ZSS Rom vol. 84 (1967), p. 245-349, at p. 304: 'Hoc ideo dicit, quoad eum, qui tradidit dominium transferre volisse facilius probari possit, non autem ideo quod dominium non transferatur quandoque, quamquam tradendi causa iusta non precesserit, veluti si te obligatum putans indebitum solueris.'

17 Lange, Die Glossatoren, p. 170-71.

18 Lange, Die Glossatoren, p. 335-337.

19 Dondorp and Schrage, p. 47-48.

20 Martinus Gosia and Accursius also make other distinctions to explain the antinomy: see Dondorp and Schrage, p. 47-48; Fuchs, p. 39-41.

21 Martinus Gosia, gloss on Jul. D. 41,1,36 (ed. Dolezalek, ZSS Rom vol. 84 (1967)), p. 308: '...Vel hic voluit dominium transferri omnino quacumque causa obligationis, sive ea qua putavit sive alis...' (...Or, here [i.e. in Julianus' example] he wanted to transfer ownership anyway on the basis of whichever obligation, either the obligation he had in mind or any other...).

Accursius, gloss *non fieri* on Ulp. D. 12,1,18, pr.: '...Hic erat certa causa ex qua volebat dominium transferre, scilicet donatio, nec ex alia causa volebat rem ad alium pertinere; ibi etiam aliter volebat

a valid underlying contract, namely where despite disagreement about the legal ground there is agreement that ownership should pass.

Many of the commentators, such as Jacques de Révigny (?-1296[22]), Bartolus de Saxoferrato[23] (1313-1357[24]) and Baldus de Ubaldis (1320/27-1400[25]) shared their views. Jacques de Révigny[26] and Baldus[27] claim that it is not the contract which forms the basis of the passing of ownership but rather the owner's will to transfer.

To defend his point of view that a putative *causa* sufficed to pass ownership Accursius referred to the *condictio indebiti* of Roman law, an argument used frequently in the following centuries and which in the 19th century was to be used by Savigny to defend his abstract transfer system. If a thing had been transferred without *causa* a *condictio indebiti* was available to claim the thing back, a personal action ex unjustified enrichment. According to Accursius this can be explained only when a transfer without *causa* is valid. For, if the transfer were invalid the transferor would not need a *condictio* as he still had ownership and thus an action of revindication. In order to prevent any contradiction with Paulus' requirement of *iusta causa* Accursius had to say that *iusta causa* does not necessarily mean a *valid causa* and that a putative *causa* sufficed to meet the requirement.[28] As a result, for a valid transfer of ownership the *Glossa Ordinaria* required agreement between the transferor and transferee that ownership should pass, and in addition a transfer of possession.[29]

As many other glossators and commentators shared the views of the quoted jurists we can say that during the period of the glossators and commentators in principle a *causa putativa* or an invalid contract sufficed to let ownership pass.[30]

---

fieri rem accipientis.' (Here [i.e. in Ulpianus' example] he wanted to transfer ownership on the basis of a certain legal ground, namely a gift, and he objected to the thing belonging to the other party on another legal ground. There [i.e. in Julianus' example] he accepted the thing to become the acquirer's also on any other legal ground.).

22 H. Coing (ed.), Handbuch der Quellen und Literatur der neueren europäischen Privat-rechtsgeschichte, vol. 1 (Mittelalter), Munich 1973, p. 281.

23 Comment on Afr. D. 12,1,41, Venice 1585, fo. 21, 3rd col.

24 J.L.J. van de Kamp, Bartolus de Saxoferrato, 1313-1357, Amsterdam 1936, p. 4 and 148; Coing, Handbuch, vol. 1, p. 269.

25 Coing, Handbuch, vol. 1, p. 269.

26 Lectura super Codice, lecture on C. 4,50,6, Paris 1519 (repr. Bologna 1967), fo. 205, 2nd col.

27 Comment on C. 4,50,6, Venice 1577, fo. 127, 4th col.-fo. 128, 1st col. (nrs 32-35); comment on C. 2,3,20, Venice 1577, fo. 114, 2nd and 3rd col.

28 Gloss *iusta causa* on Paul. D. 41,1,31: '...vera vel putativa: alioquin si dicas ex putativa non transferri dominium, totus titulus de condictione indebiti obstaret; qui titulus habet locum, quando transfertur dominium alicuius rei ex putativa causa...' (real or putative: otherwise if you say that ownership cannot be transferred on the basis of a putative legal ground, the entire title on the action ex unjustified enrichment would be contrary to this; this title is applied where ownership of a thing is transferred on the basis of a putative legal ground...).

29 E. Landsberg, Die Glosse des Accursius, Leipzig 1883, p. 106.

30 There were, however, instances in which, according to some of these jurists, a *causa putativa* did not suffice. See Dondorp and Schrage, p. 62-63 and Fuchs, p. 42.

defects of will

The above makes clear that in the period of the glossators and commentators most jurists in principle did not insist on a valid legal ground. Yet, we cannot infer from these passages which of them followed the *animus* theory and which the abstract theory. To ascertain this we should do an extra test.

As I have said before, the sole difference between the *animus* theory and the abstract theory consists in their treatment of defects of will. In an abstract system the fact that one of the parties entered into the contract under the influence of a defect of will cannot automatically hamper the passing of ownership.[31] In the *animus* theory, on the other hand, such a defect prevents ownership from passing. So, in order to find authors who endorse the abstract theory rather than the *animus* theory we should focus on their opinion about the consequences a defect of will has on the passing of ownership. For the following reasons, however, such an enquiry is very difficult.

First, the modern sharp distinction between void and voidable has fully developed only in the late 18th[32] and 19th century. True, in Roman law, and accordingly, in the learned law after the rediscovery of the Digest, there were cases of nullity *ipso iure*, i.e. nullity working automatically and, on the other hand, cases in which nullity could be achieved only by judicial decision at the request of the person entitled to plead nullity.[33] Yet, void and voidable as legal concepts were created only in the 19th century by German legal science, by Savigny among others.[34] What is more, there was hardly any consensus among medieval jurists which defects of will entailed voidability and which voidness of the contract.

Secondly, to make things worse, there was no agreement about the legal consequences of voidability. Naturally, after the contract had been avoided, the transaction had to be undone. Where an object had been handed over, the thing had to be returned. The claim to have the transaction undone was often called *restitutio in integrum*. Yet, it is unclear whether it was a personal or a real action. Nor was it known whether or not *restitutio* had retroactive effect.

But only where avoidance has retroactive effect can examples of avoided contracts be used to demonstrate which of the three transfer systems was

---

31 In some cases, though, it may be held that the act of transfer itself is also executed under the influence of the same defect of will (in modern German law this is called *Fehleridentität* (identity of defect), see chapter 2, § 2.2).

32 Although Pothier does not use the terms 'void' and 'voidable' he makes a clear distinction of the two cases. See: Traité des obligations, part 1, ch. 1, sect. 1, art. 3; Traité du contrat de vente, part 5, ch. 2, Œuvres de Pothier, vol. 2, Paris 1848, p. 13 et seq. and vol. 3, Paris 1847, p. 139 et seq.

33 Kaser I, § 60; H. Kantorowicz, Studies in the glossators of the Roman law, Cambridge 1938, p. 76.

34 See M. Harder, Die historische Entwicklung der Anfechtbarkeit von Willenserklärungen, AcP 173 (1973), p. 209 et seq. This creation was made possible by the development in the 18th and early 19th century of the concept of legal act. See Harder, p. 216 et seq. See also H. Hammen, Die Bedeutung Friedrich Carl v. Savignys für die allgemeinen dogmatischen Grundlagen des Deutschen Bürgerlichen Gesetzbuches, Berlin 1983, p. 123 et seq. Kantorowicz seems to suggest, however, that the distinction between void and voidable can already be found in Bulgarus' *De dolo summula*: see Kantorowicz, Studies, p. 76.

supported. If a jurist says that avoidance of the contract does not affect the passing of ownership this could be an indication that the jurist supported the abstract theory. However, it is also possible that in his view the passing of ownership is not affected because of the avoidance having no retroactive effect. For this reason we should use examples of avoidance only if we know that the jurist in question holds that avoidance has retroactive effect. I have not yet found any unequivocal instance.

As a result, to ascertain which transfer system the glossators and commentators and later generations of jurists adhered to we should examine cases where the contract is void rather than voidable. As for void contracts the best example is the *dolus causam dans contractui*. It indicates a form of fraud so serious that it has induced the victim to entering into the contract.[35] By many Italian glossators and commentators it was accepted that this kind of fraud rendered certain kinds of contract, namely the *contractus bonae fidei*[36] void *ab initio,* or void *ipso iure,* as it was then called.[37] Yet, to be certain which transfer theory an individual jurist followed we have to check if he indeed acknowledges that fraud turns the contract void.[38]

Applying this '*dolus* test' it turns out that a number of important glossators and commentators assert that in the case of *dolus causam dans contractui* a *contractus bonae fidei* is void but that it passes ownership nonetheless, if followed by *traditio.* Such a statement is an unequivocal indication for the abstract theory. The view is lucidly expressed by Rogerius in the following words: 'If someone has been induced to sell as a result of fraud, the transfer of possession following the sale passes ownership to the acquirer, although the sale is void *ipso iure.*'[39] Other advocates of this view

---

35 It was distinguished from *dolus incidens,* a less severe form of fraud. Here it was assumed that without fraud the defrauded party would still have entered into the contract, though under conditions more favourable to him.

36 Contracts which require both parties to act in good faith. All consensual contracts such as sale belonged to this category. Here the judge has to consider not only duties that flow from the words of the contract but also duties based on *bona fides* (good faith). In the case of a *contractus stricti iuris,* on the other hand, the judge was in principle unable to take into account good faith. The unclassical terms *contractus bonae fidei* and *contractus stricti iuris* derive from the classical distinction between *bonae fidei iudicia* (good faith judgments) and judgments in which good faith was of less importance. See Kaser I, p. 485 et seq. and Schulz, Classical Roman law, p. 35-36. It should be noted, however, that even in classical law the distinction was quite blurred. Moreover, in the post-classical era the distinction gradually faded away: in Justinianian law the distinction can still be found, but, at the same time, it was acknowledged that all contracts had to be made and executed in good faith. See Kaser II, p. 333-34.

37 See for example Azo, Lectura super Codicem, on C. 2,20 and C. 2,54, ed. Paris 1577 (repr. Turin 1966), p. 116 and 155; Azo, Summa super Codicem, de dolo malo rubrica, ed. Pavia 1506 (repr. Turin 1966), p. 41.

38 *Metus* (duress) does not offer a good test because in Roman law there was controversy about the consequences of duress. According to Paulus (D. 4,2,21,5) a contract made under the influence of duress was nonetheless valid. The opposite view that such a contract is void can be found for example in Ulp. D. 50,17,116, pr. See A.S. Hartkamp, Der Zwang im römischen Privatrecht, (thesis Amsterdam 1971) Amsterdam 1971, § 14 and 15 (p. 102-126).

39 Enodationes quaestionum super Codice: 'Si enim quis, ut venderet, dolo fuerit inductus, licet ipso iure venditio non valeat, traditio tamen, que ex ea sequitur, dominium ad accipientem transfert.' Published in: Kantorowicz, Studies, p. 289.

I have found are Accursius[40], Bartolus[41], Baldus[42] and Jacques de Révigny[43].[44] However, we should always bear in mind that these jurists were not yet thinking in general rules and abstract concepts intending to build a flawless and consistent legal system: they have not been trying to design a general theory about the transfer of (certain kinds of) property. Consequently, even though in the case of fraud the transfer is clearly abstract we cannot conclude that the abstract theory applied to other defects in the *causa* as well. We should not be surprised to find in the writings of the very same jurists statements that are inconsistent with the abstract system. Bartolus and Martinus Gosia, for example, stress that if one of the parties has transferred ownership under the influence of a mistake, the transfer is void if as a result of the mistake there is no genuine will to transfer.[45] Furthermore, in Baldus' comment on C. 4,44,2 we can read that when a contract of sale is avoided because of *laesio enormis*[46] the avoidance annuls a right of *pignus* (pledge) or *hypotheca* (hypothec) granted by the buyer to a third party prior to the avoidance.[47] Baldus' explanation strongly suggests that to his mind the third party's real right lapses because the buyer's right of ownership reverts to the seller with retroactive effect. Undoubtedly, it is impossible to reconcile such a statement

---

40 Gloss *locum habere* on Ulp. D. 4,3,7, pr.: 'Item nonne rei vindicatio locum habet cum dolus dedit causam contractui? Respondeo non. quia ex inutili contractu transit dominium...'. (Moreover, is not a revindication available where the contract has been induced by fraud? My answer is no, because ownership passes on the basis of an ineffective contract...).

41 Comment on C. 2,4,19, Venice 1585, fo. 55, 4th col.-fo. 56, 2nd col.

42 Comment on C. 2,4,19, Venice 1577, fo. 129, 1st col.: 'Respondeo, quod in bonae fidei contractibus [dolus causam dans contractui] excludit qualitatem substantialem: quae inest a propria & speciali natura contractus, & ideo vitiat...sed quando ratio ordinata ad impediendam obligationem, & non dominium impediendum, ibi impeditur obligatio, sed non dominium...nam obligatio non potest esse sine vero & efficaci contractu, sed dominium potest transferri ex causa putativa: unde non requirit efficaciam precedentis contractus. Fundatur enim solum in quadam sua immediata causa, scilicet in consensu transferendi dominii, & non in robore contractus,...' (My answer is that in the case of contracts *bonae fidei* [*dolus causam dans contractui*] excludes an essential characteristic which originates in the proper and special nature of the contract, and for that reason it vitiates the contract... However, as the reason is to impede the obligation, and not the [passing of] ownership, the obligation is impeded, but not [the passing of] ownership... For an obligation cannot exist without a true and effective contract; ownership, on the other hand, may pass on the basis of a putative legal ground: hence the validity of the preceding contract is not required. [The transfer of] (O)wnership namely is based merely on its immediate cause, which is the agreement about the transfer of ownership, rather than the validity of the contract...).

43 Lectura super Codice, on C. 4,44,2, Paris 1519 (repr. Bologna 1967), fo. 201, col. 4.

44 Other commentators sharing this view are mentioned in: Scholtens, Justa causa traditionis and contracts induced by fraud, SALJ vol. 74 (1959), p. 284, fn. 18.

45 Martinus' gloss on Jul. D. 41,1,36 as edited by Dolezalek in ZSS Rom vol. 84 at p. 308) and Bartolus' comment on Afr. D. 12,1,41, Venice 1585, fo. 21, 3rd col. Cf. Dondorp and Schrage, p. 46-47.

46 Lit.: severe impairment. It indicates the situation in which the price of a thing sold is less than half its market value at the time of the sale. It developed in post-classical Roman law. See Kaser II, § 264 III.

47 Baldus on C. 4,44,2, Venice 1577, fo. 118, co. 4.

with an abstract transfer theory.[48] It is clearly in contradiction with his own statement about the consequences of fraud.[49]

Bulgarus' (before 1100?-?[50]) account on fraud does not fit the abstract transfer theory. In a *summula* on the subject he claims the following: 'Although the transfer of possession has passed ownership to the buyer, justice, which is done when the judgment about the fraud is passed, discovers the transfer of possession to have been, as it were, void.'[51] The first subordinate clause (Although...to the buyer/*licet...transtulit*) may give the impression of Bulgarus adhering to an abstract transfer system. Nonetheless, I think that Bulgarus regards the contract as voidable rather than void. It would explain why in his opinion ownership initially passes to the buyer.[52] It then revests in the seller upon avoidance of the contract.

Another indication for a non-abstract view is to be found in Baldus' passage on fraud. It discloses that as to fraud the so-called *Ultramontani*, the commentators from the South of France, do not agree with Baldus' view. They do accept that in the case of *dolus causam dans contractui* ownership may pass to the acquirer. Yet from the transfer being valid they draw the conclusion that the contract affected by fraud should be considered valid as well because a void legal ground cannot have

48 See Baldus on C. 4,44,2, Venice 1577, fo. 118, col. 4: '...resoluto iure pignorantis resolvitur ius recipientis,' (when the pledgor's right has been rescinded, the acquirer's right [i.e. the third party's right of security] is rescinded,...). Baldus' explanation reads as follows: '...quia res non erat pignorantis iure perpetuo, & irrevocabili, sed erat revocationi subiecta. Et ideo finito iure creditoris, quod non erat perpetuum, nec efficaciter radicatum, finitur ius acceptoris,...' (...because the thing did not belong to the pledgor in perpetuity and irrevocably but was subjected to revocation. And for that reason, when the creditor's right [i.e. the buyer's right] has been ended, which was not perpetual and had not rooted effectively, the acquirer's right [i.e. the third party's right] ends...). Although Baldus does not use the term 'retroactivity' nor states that the security right is deemed to have been granted by a non-owner, which would be a clear indication for ownership reverting to the seller retroactively, the above passage is hard to explain in a different sense. If this is right, the passage accords only with a causal system, or, as the passage is about a defect of will, the *animus* theory.

49 See fn. 42 *supra*.

50 Lange, Die Glossatoren, p. 162-163.

51 In his *De dolo summula*: 'Cum enim nulla sit venditio, cui dolus causam dederit,... Cum ergo venditio suo effectu destituitur, sequens traditio rescinditur, que, licet dominium in ementem transtulit, equitate tamen illa, que expeditur, cum iudicium de dolo ventilatur, quasi nulla fuisse detegitur.' Published in: Kantorowicz, Studies, p. 243. (For, as a sale induced by fraud is void,... As then the sale is without any effect, the subsequent transfer of possession is rescinded. Although the transfer of possession has passed ownership to the buyer, justice, which is done when the judgment about the fraud is passed, discovers the transfer of possession to have been, as it were, void.).

52 If, on the other hand, Bulgarus really had in mind voidness *ab initio* his statement that ownership passes would accord only with an abstract transfer theory. Still, in that case the last sentence saying that the *traditio* is deemded to be void would be discordant. In an abstract system the voidness of the contract would never be able to affect the passing of possession and/or ownership as well.

legal effects.[53] Clearly this reasoning is consistent only with a causal transfer theory.

When focusing on their views about the meaning of *iusta causa traditionis* it seems as if the glossators and the commentators we have examined all adhere to one and the same transfer theory; for they all agree that a putative legal ground suffices to transfer ownership. Still, the *dolus* test demonstrates that there is no such unanimity. It shows that in this period of legal history elements of all three theories, the *animus* theory, the abstract and the causal theory can be found, at least in an undeveloped form.

3.2 Donellus, Duarenus and Cuiacius

As did some of the glossators and commentators Donellus (Doneau, 1527-1591), who was influenced considerably by the *Glossa Ordinaria*[54], emphasized the vital importance of the *animus dominii transferendi*, the will to transfer ownership. He wrote that the *causa* merely confirms and shows the transferor's will to make a transfer.[55] From this Donellus draws the following conclusion: if the *causa* is merely an indication for the transferor's will to transfer ownership, a *causa* is not essential for the transfer, provided the transferor's will to transfer can somehow be ascertained.[56] Consequently, only two requirements are vital for a transfer of ownership: transfer of possession and the transferor's and acquirer's will to transfer ownership.[57] Explaining this Donellus recalls that Accursius used the example of an undue payment to prove that the *causa* may be either real or putative, and he adopts the reasoning.[58]

In itself the above passage does not yet determine whether Donellus adheres to the *animus* theory or to the abstract theory. Both theories emphasize the importance of the parties' will to make a transfer. To ascertain which transfer theory Donellus advocates we should examine his treatment of defects of will, as we have done before with the glossators and commentators. We should find out whether in his view ownership may pass under a contract that is void for a defect of will. Unfortunately this is quite difficult to ascertain.

In a paragraph on the general requirements for the validity of contracts Donellus writes that *error* (mistake), *metus* (duress[59]) and *dolus malus* (fraud) render a

---

53 See Baldus, on C. 2,4,19, Venice 1577, fo. 128, 4th col., nr. 9, and Vinnius, Selectarum iuris quaestionum libri duo, I, XII, Rotterdam 1685, p. 64-65; Bachoven, in: M. Wesenbeck, Commentarii in Pandectas juris civilis et Codicem Justinianeum olim dicti paratitla (with notes and observations by Bachoven), Leiden 1649, p. 137 (Wesenbeck's comment on D. 4,3 [De dolo malo]), fn. 1. Regrettably the *Ultramontani* are merely referred to as a group; no individual names are mentioned.
54 Landsberg, Die Glosse des Accursius, p. 111, fn. 3. The *Glossa Ordinaria* has had an enormous influence on jurists of later centuries.
55 Cf. Rogerius in fn. 16 *supra*.
56 Commentarii de iure civili, 4,16, Hannover 1612 (ed. by Scipio Gentilis), p. 141.
57 Ibidem.
58 Ibidem.
59 Literally *metus* means fear, whereas duress indicates the reason of the fear: the violence.

contract void because they take away the consensus which is a vital requirement for the validity of any contract.[60] From his treatment of *metus* we can infer, although with some difficulty, that where the owner of a thing makes a transfer under the influence of duress ownership passes to the acquirer despite the contract being void.[61] As to *dolus malus* Donellus is even less clear. Yet, notwithstanding the lack of lucid statements about the passing of ownership and the use of indefinite terms we can say that also in the case of fraud ownership passes.[62]

From these passages it can be inferred that Donellus advocated what was later to be called the abstract transfer theory. In § 4.1 we will see that Savigny in his turn refers to Donellus to support the abstract theory. He was influenced substantially

60 Commentarii de iure civili, 12,6 and 7, Opera omnia, vol. 3, Lucca 1763, p. 471 et seq., especially p. 481-482. On p. 483 he refers to the adage *coactus volui, tamen volui* (he consented under duress, still he consented) based on Paul. D. 4,2,21,5. Yet, this does not change his view that in the case of a contract *bonae fidei* the consent and thus the contract is void. He uses the reference only to explain why a contract *stricti iuris*, such as a *stipulatio*, made under the influence of duress is not void *ipso iure*.

61 Commentarii de iure civili, 15,39,22-26, Opera omnia, vol. 4, Lucca 1764, p. 373-375. For instance p. 373: 'Nam dominus qui rem suam tradidit alienandi caussa, dominium amisit translatum in alienum... Nec obstat, quod metu coactus dominus...id fecit. Nam ut dixi initio, etsi nisi cogeretur nollet, tamen coactus voluit.' (For the owner who transfers the possession of his thing in order to alienate it, passes ownership to the other party. And it is no obstacle that the owner did this because of duress. After all, as I have said in the beginning, although without the duress he would not have intended, because of it he nonetheless did intend). P. 375: 'Res ablata sic restituitur, si ut tradita est, ita veteri domino retradatur... Scilicet ut traditione nova recipiat vetus dominus dominium & possessionem, quae per metum amiserat. Traditione enim dominia transferuntur' (A thing taken away is restituted if it is retransferred to the former owner in the state in which it was transferred... Undoubtedly, in order that through a new *traditio* the former owner regains the ownership and possession which he transferred because of duress. After all, ownership is transferred by *traditio*.).

I have translated the verb *amittere* with 'to pass [ownership]' because from his chapter on *metus* it appears that Donellus uses the verb to indicate a transfer of ownership or possession: he uses *alienare* and *amittere* as synonyms. From the Middle Ages the word *amittere* is used also to denote a transfer, a meaning that cannot be found in classical Latin. See O. Prinz (ed.), Mittellateinisches Wörterbuch, bis zum ausgehenden 13. Jahrhundert, vol. 1, Munich 1967, col. 570.

However, on p. 373 Donellus oddly relies on the adage *coactus volui, tamen volui* to explain why ownership passes. I assume that, like in 12,7 (see previous fn.), Donellus does not mean that the contract is valid despite *metus*, as this would not accord with his lengthy and clear treatment of the general requirements for the validity of contracts (12,7).

62 Commentarii de iure civili, 15,41, Opera omnia, vol. 4, p. 391 et seq. Here evidence is indirect only. In many passages, e.g. on p. 391-392, p. 428-429, Donellus speaks about an owner who has transferred his thing under the influence of duress. He does not add whether the transfer is valid, thus conveying the impression it is.

by Donellus' thoughts.[63] It is known that he admired Donellus and read his works thoroughly.

However, we cannot say that Donellus' view evidently prevailed in the period of the humanists. Among Donellus' most famous contemporaries we can find one jurist, Duarenus, who gives equivocal support to Donellus, and one jurist who clearly disagrees with him, Cuiacius.

Duarenus (Duaren, 1509-1559) gives an inconsistent analysis of the matter. In his treatment of the *condictio indebiti* he states that if someone pays money or transfers a thing[64] without being obliged to, ownership passes to the recipient. The payor is given a personal action for the return of the thing.[65] Furthermore Duarenus writes that *dolus causam dans contractui* renders a contract of sale void *ipso iure*,[66] but that ownership nonetheless passes to the recipient.[67] The defrauded party may be given a remedy, *restitutio in integrum*, to claim the thing back. These passages seem to be an unequivocal confirmation of the abstract transfer theory. However, in the treatment on acquisition of ownership Duarenus contradicts himself saying that when as a result of mistake the owner transfers an asset which he did not intend to transfer, ownership does not pass. This passage is incompatible with an abstract theory.

Cuiacius (Cujas, 1522-1590), one of Donellus' most important contemporaries, undoubtedly disagreed with Donellus view. In a very lucid exposition he asserted that for a transfer of ownership the underlying contract had to be valid.[68]

---

63 See for example Chr. Bergfeld, Savigny und Donellus, in: H. Coing (ed.), Vorträge zum 200. Geburtstag von F. C. von Savigny, Ius commune, Veröffentlichungen des Max-Planck-Instituts für Europäische Rechtsgeschichte, vol. 8, Frankfurt a/M 1979, p. 24 et seq., especially p. 25, fn. 8.

   Felgenträger notes that often through Savigny's words Donellus is speaking directly to us. See: Friedrich Carl v. Savignys Einfluß auf die Übereignungslehre, Leipzig 1927, p. 38. Yet, Savigny may also have been influenced directly by Accursius' *Glossa Ordinaria*, as in the years in which he developed the abstract transfer system he was intensively studying Accursius' Gloss for his book *Geschichte des römischen Rechts im Mittelalter* (see Felgenträger, p. 38).

64 Duarenus uses the term payment, but note that the term comprises a money payment as well as a transfer of other kinds of property.

65 F. Duarenus, De condictione indebiti, cap. I, Opera omnia, vol. 3, Lucca 1766, p. 319.

66 De dolo malo, cap. I, Opera omnia, vol. 1, Lucca 1765, p. 146.

67 De in integrum restitutionibus, cap. I, Opera omnia, vol. 1, p. 135.

68 Cuiacius, Commentarius ad titulos quosdam digestorum, comment on the title *de dolo malo*, Opera omnia, Napels 1722, vol. 1, p. 975b: 'Restat igitur, dolo ab emptore adhibito, ut ipso iure venditio nulla sit. Ubi autem ob eam causam nulla venditio est, quod dolo emptoris circumscriptus venditor servum vendiderit, & nulla manumissio est quasi facta a non domino: ex nullo enim contractu dominium non transfertur, licet possessio transferatur,...' (So, the conclusion is that if fraud is committed by the buyer the sale is *ipso iure* void. Furthermore, where for this reason the sale is void, because the seller defrauded by the buyer sells a slave, the act of freeing the slave is also void, as if it were done by a non-owner: after all, ownership cannot be transferred on the basis of a void contract, even if possession is transferred,...).

   Cuiacius, In libros IV priores Codicis Justiniani, on C. 4,50, Opera omnia, Napels 1722, vol. 10, p. 1017: '...: falsum est enim, quod tentat Accursius ex inutili contractu dominium adquiri per traditionem: nam si inutilis est contractus, ergo & nuda traditio.' (...: namely, Accursius' view that by means of *traditio* ownership may be acquired on the basis of a void contract is wrong: for when the contract is void, the mere *traditio* is void as well.).

3.3 The Roman-Dutch law

Legal historians usually call the transfer system of Roman-Dutch law (17th-18th century) abstract.[69] Yet, to my mind this qualification is misleading. It is the result of applying the modern distinction between causal and abstract transfer systems to a period in which the distinction had not yet developed. In such a classification there is no room for midway solutions. As a result a transfer system that suffices itself with a putative legal ground, a system in between the causal and the abstract system, is often regarded as an abstract system thus obscuring the difference between the *animus* theory and the true abstract system as applied in modern German law.

Many statements by Roman-Dutch jurists can be found which do not fit into a causal transfer system. From this many legal historians seem to draw the conclusion that because the transfer system is not causal it must be abstract, wrongly making the impression that a third system cannot exist. In fact, most of the passages quoted to demonstrate that the Roman-Dutch transfer system was abstract are no proof at all for an abstract system in the modern sense of the word, that is, an abstract system as applied in German law. On the contrary, several statements can be found that fit into the *animus* theory better than into an abstract theory.

Paulus Voet[70], for instance, states that the *causa traditionis* need not be valid and that it may even be putative, provided the parties both intend ownership to pass.[71] It is a statement that in itself fits perfectly into the *animus* theory.

However, to find out whether certain Roman-Dutch jurists may be regarded as adhering to the *animus* theory or rather to the abstract theory, we should scrutinize what they write about the consequences of defects of will, as we have done in the analysis of the glossators, commentators and humanists. Here we will encounter the same difficulties: there is no clear distinction between void and voidable, and there was hardly any consensus among Roman-Dutch jurists which defects of will

---

69 See E.M. Meijers, Levering en rechtstitel, Verzamelde privaatrechtelijke opstellen, vol. 2, Leiden 1955, p. 80 et seq.; L.J. van Apeldoorn, Levering en titel van eigendomsovergang in het oude Nederlandsche recht, WPNR 1929, p. 711-714 and 723-725; A.S. de Blécourt and H.F.W.D. Fischer, Kort begrip van het oud-vaderlands recht, 7th ed., Groningen 1959, p. 153; C.G. van der Merwe, Sakereg, 2nd ed., Durban 1989, p. 307-308; C.G. Van der Merwe and M.J. de Waal, The law of things and servitudes, Durban 1993, p. 152; D.L. Carey Miller, Transfer of ownership, in: R. Feenstra and R. Zimmermann (eds.), Das römisch-holländische Recht, Fortschritte des Zivilrechts im 17. und 18. Jahrhundert, Berlin 1992, p. 521 et seq., at pp. 537-539, and Carey Miller, The acquisition and protection of ownership, Cape Town/Wetton/Johannesburg 1986, p. 125-127; De Vos, UCT Lecture Notes, p. 60, as referred to in Carey Miller, The acquisition, p. 127.

70 Paulus Voet, In quatuor libros Institutionum Imperialium Commentarius, vol. 1, comment on Inst. 2,1,41-43, nr. 3, Utrecht 1668, p. 466: 'Traditio enim sine causa ad effectum dominii transfferendi pro nulla habetur... Nec interest causa sit vera, modo habilis & justa, an putativa, cum & haec ad dominium transfferendum sufficat.' (For *traditio* without a legal ground aiming at the transfer of ownership is held ineffective... It is also irrelevant whether the legal ground be valid, merely appropriate and *iusta*, or putative, since the latter also suffices to transfer ownership.)

71 Other, less important authors holding the same opinion are mentioned by Van Apeldoorn at p. 724.

entailed voidability and which ones voidness of the contract.[72] In addition, it was not settled whether avoidance had retroactive effect. Of course, the party who had acted under the influence of a defect of will could claim that the transaction should be undone. The claim was called *restitutio in integrum* or *relief*. However, there was controversy about whether it was a personal or a real action.[73]

In Roman-Dutch law it was generally accepted that *dolus causam dans contractui* rendered a *contractus bonae fidei* void *ipso iure*. Still, for every individual jurist we need to check if he indeed follows this line. I have found four jurists who expressly say that *dolus causam dans contractui* indeed makes a contract *bonae fidei* void *ipso iure* and who, in addition, draw the conclusion that as a consequence the transfer of ownership based on the contract is void as well. These jurists are Huber[74], Bronchorst[75], Wissenbach[76] and Johannes Voet. It is lucidly brought forward by Johannes Voet saying: 'If a *contractus bonae fidei* has been made as a result of fraud, it is *ipso iure* void, so that *restitutio* is not necessary... And since something which is void cannot have any consequences, it follows that neither ownership nor any other right can be held to have passed to the buyer on the basis of the *traditio* following the transaction. For, never a bare *traditio* transfers ownership; it does so only if the *traditio* has been preceded by a sale or another legal ground *which is valid.*'[77] Moreover, their views accord with a decision of the Court of Holland, Zeeland and Friesland affirmed by the Supreme Court of Holland, Zeeland and Friesland.[78] The texts clearly do not fit into an abstract transfer system. When

---

72 Cf. L. Winkel, Die Irrtumslehre, in: Feenstra and Zimmermann (eds.), Das römisch-holländische Recht, Fortschritte des Zivilrechts im 17. und 18. Jahrhundert, Berlin 1992, p. 225-244.

73 According to Vinnius, who describes the controversy, *restitutio* was a personal action. See: A. Vinnius, Selectarum iuris quaestionum libri duo, I,XI, Rotterdam 1685.

74 U. Huber, Praelectionum juris civilis tomi tres, Louvain 1766, on the title *de dolo malo* (D. 4,3), vol. 2, p. 169-170: 'Ni per textus legum sit, vereor, ut ratio juris cogat, ei quod nullum, quod nihil est, τῶ μὴ ὄντι, tam notabilem effectum tribuere, qualis est dominii translatio.' (Unless it is on the basis of a legal text, I fear that the legal system does not require one to attribute to something which is void, which is nothing, the non-existing, so notable an effect as the transfer of ownership). Note that τῶ should be τῷ.

75 E. Bronchorst, Enantiophanon centuriae quatuor, cent. I, assertio 57, Leiden 1598, p. 73-75: 'Ex nullo enim et inutili contractu dominium non transfertur.' (For, on the basis of a void and ineffective contract ownership does not pass).

76 J.J. Wissenbach, Excercitationum ad quinquaginta libros pandectarum partes duae, Lib. IV, disputatio XIII (nr. 34), Franeker 1661, p. 107-108: 'Dolus dans causam contractui bonae fidei, hunc vitiat ipso iure, ita ut ex eo nulla detur actio... Ex nullo enim contractu non transfertur dominium.' (Fraud which has induced a bona fide contract annuls the contract *ipso iure*, so that it [i.e. the contract] does not give any action... For ownership cannot be transferred on the basis of a void contract).

77 Commentarius ad Pandectas, vol. 1, comment on D. 4,3: 'Si dolus causam dederit contractui bonae fidei, is ipso iure nullus est, ut restitutione opus non sit... Cumque id quod nullum est, nullum possit effectum producere; consequens est, ut neque dominium neque jus ullum aliud ex subsecuta ad negotium nullum traditione possit videri in emtorem translatum: nunquam enim nuda traditio dominium transfert: sed ita, si venditio aut alia justa causa *eaque valida* praecesserit.' (italics mine)

78 The undated decision has been reported in: C. Neostadius, Utriusque Hollandiae, Zelandiae, Frisiaeque curiae decisiones, in the chapter decisiones Supremi Senatus Hollandiae, Zelandiae et Frisiae, decisio V, The Hague 1667, p. 137. The core of both courts' reasoning has been summarized in the heading: 'Emptionem, cui causam dolus dedit, adeo, ipso jure, nullam esse, ut venditori,

assuming that the Roman-Dutch transfer system was abstract, as do most legal historians, these passages can be explained only by calling them exceptions to the general rule. On the other hand, when distinguishing three transfer systems rather than two, it appears that the passages about fraud are not at all inconsistent with the statements that ownership may pass under a putative contract. When explaining the Roman-Dutch transfer system as adhering to the *animus* theory both groups of statements are consistent without the need of describing the fraud cases as exceptions. For, fraud, a defect of will, eliminates one of the parties' will to transfer ownership, which in the *animus* theory is fatal to a valid transfer.

On the other hand, there are also jurists who evidently adhere to the abstract transfer theory, at least as regards fraud. In a text about fraud Vinnius says that *dolus causam dans contractui* renders the contract void but that the voidness of the contract does not affect the passing of ownership.[79] Here Vinnius refers to the controversy between the *Ultramontani* and the *Citramontani*, the Italian commentators, about the consequences of *dolus causam dans contractui*, and joins Baldus' view (i.e. the abstract transfer). Also Noodt adheres to the abstract transfer system.[80]

Apparently Roman-Dutch jurists were divided over how to interpret the *iusta causa* requirement. Some jurists maintain that despite the contract being void ownership still passes to the acquirer. Others refuse to acknowledge that a contract which is void *ipso iure* may pass ownership.

---

traditae rei vindicatio, etiam adversus tertium possessorem, competat.' (That the contract of sale, which has been entered into as a result of fraud, is void *ipso iure*, so that the seller is given an action to revindicate the thing of which possession has been transferred, even against a third party possessor). Johannes Voet refers to the case approving of the judgment: see Commentarius ad Pandectas, IV,III,3.

79 Vinnius, Selectarum iuris quaestionum libri duo, I, XII.

80 G. Noodt, De forma emendandi doli mali, Opera omnia, Leiden 1767, vol. 1. In chapter 3 et seq. Noodt extensively describes that fraud renders *contractus bonae fidei* void. In chapter 15, p. 317 he mentions the consequences for the transfer of ownership: 'Altera difficultas est, quod ex contractu in quo apparet dolus malus, dominium traditione transferri potest: cum ex regula juris nuda traditio numquam transferat dominium: nisi venditio aut alia justa causa praecedat, propter quam traditio sequatur... Sed nec objectio facit moram judicio meo. non enim vult illa regula, ut dominium traditione mutetur, utique praecedere causam veram ac jure firmam: sed praecedere venditionem, aut similem causam, ob quam dominium transferri solet: sive re vera praecedat, sive praecedere tradentis spe aut opinione praesumatur... nec semper veram quaerit causam. satis ei est, aliquam tradentis opinione subesse. Nam & indebitum per errore solutum, dominium in accipientem transfert...' (The other difficulty is that on the basis of a contract in which there is fraud ownership can be transferred, despite the legal rule that *traditio* alone will never pass ownership unless a sale or another legal ground precedes after which *traditio* follows... But in my considered judgement the objection does not stand in the way. For this rule does not require that in order to exchange ownership by *traditio* a true and valid legal ground should precede in any case. Rather it requires that a sale or a similar legal ground precede on the basis of which ownership is usually transferred, a legal ground which either precedes in reality or is assumed to precede in the transferor's expectation or opinion... It [i.e. the law] does not always require a valid legal ground; it suffices if some legal ground exists in the mind of the transferor. For, also what has been paid by mistake and was not due passes ownership to the acquirer).

3.4 A fragmentary image

From the preceding we can learn that the history of the *iusta causa* requirement renders a highly fragmented and inconsistent picture. The different texts making up the Digest were ambiguous and even inconsistent. Being directly based on these texts the learned law, not unexpectedly, was hardly more consistent. In the period from the rediscovery of the Digest up to the beginning of the 19th century we can find fragments of all three transfer theories. Neither in the Middle Ages nor in the humanist period nor in Roman-Dutch law can we find any majority view about the interpretation of the *iusta causa* requirement.

What is more, even within the writings of one and the same jurist we may often find conflicting statements, especially among medieval jurists: they felt themselves strongly bound to the texts of the *Corpus Iuris Civilis* and were not yet concerned in building a consistent legal system.

True, already the commentators have started to structure some parts of law.[81] Yet, the building of a consistent legal system began only in the period of the humanists[82] and especially in the period of natural law.[83] Nonetheless, even in this period or in Roman Dutch law jurists do not normally develop a general transfer theory. They tend to treat the question only, or at least mainly, in comments about fraud. Still, in many instances their arguments are laid down in very general formulations and are not at all limited to fraud cases. They are often based on reasons that may claim general application, such as the opinion that a void contract cannot have any legal consequences, or that it cannot transfer ownership. It seems that in these cases the concept of fraud merely functioned as the *sedes materiae*[84] for general remarks about the validity of a transfer. Yet, the authors usually did not indicate unequivocally whether or not their remarks applied also to other defects in the underlying contract.

Having seen the division of opinion in all these periods I think the traditional view that in the learned law of these centuries the abstract theory dominated is not tenable.[85] It is true, within these periods elements may be found that fit into an abstract theory. Still, the picture is not that clear.

The passages I have quoted before inevitably lead to the conclusion that in the period before the beginning of the 19th century no transfer theories existed. We do find a lot of statements about the meaning of *iusta causa traditionis* but no general

---

81 P. Koschaker, Europa und das römische Recht, 4th ed., Munich/Berlin 1966, p. 90-94.

82 G.C.J.J. van den Bergh, Geleerd recht, 3rd ed., Deventer 1994, p. 49 et seq., at p. 55-57.

83 Koschaker, ch. 14 and 15; H. Coing, Europäisches Privatrecht, vol. 1, § 9 (p. 67-72).

84 Lit.: place of the subject, i.e. the place in a book where a certain subject-matter is treated. Justinian's Digest or Codex, to take an example, are not at all systematically arranged. Comments on these texts usually follow the structure of the text commented upon, somewhat like the German comments on the German civil code. When the author wants to give a more general account of a legal problem he still needs some title in the Digest or Codex as a peg to hang his account on. It is obvious that in such a book the accounts are not always limited to the title in question.

85 The view that the abstract theory dominated is generally accepted. The view is supported by for example Meijers, Van Oven, Fuchs, Dondorp and Schrage.

theory in the modern sense of the word: a theory applicable to all possible defects in the underlying *causa traditionis*. Moreover, in none of the periods analysed can we find a majority view. It would be anachronistic and therefore wrong to use the divide causal/abstract to analyse transfer 'theories' from a period before the divide had originated.

4 The German abstract system

4.1 Its origin: Savigny

Savigny and the *titulus and modus* theory

From the second half of the 18th century the so-called *titulus and modus*[86] theory began to prevail in Germany. It was the period of the late *Usus Modernus Pandectarum* and the late *Vernunftrecht*, the synchronous natural law movement. According to this theory a transfer of ownership requires a *titulus* and a *modus*. Here *titulus* is the equivalent of *causa*, and *modus* (lit. manner[87]) indicates the requirement of *traditio*. When confined to the voluntary transfer of ownership the theory is nothing new: just a new name for a well-established theory. Yet, the theory was new in that some authors extended the two requirements of *titulus* and *modus* to cover other acquisitions of real rights as well, for example original acquisition.[88] The *titulus and modus* theory is important only in that Savigny dissociated himself from this theory in developing the abstract transfer system.

A new theory emphasizing the requirement of *titulus* next to *modus* might give the impression of demanding a valid legal ground.[89] Still, it is not simple to answer the question whether it indeed required a *causa vera* or whether a *causa putativa* sufficed: within the *titulus and modus* theory both opinions were put forward.[90] Thus the new word *titulus* is no more revealing than the old term *iusta causa traditionis*. It would therefore be misleading to associate the term *titulus* with

---

86 See Coing, Europäisches Privatrecht, vol. 1, § 30; vol. 2, § 72. The theory was incorporated into the Prussian codification of 1794, the *Allgemeines Landrecht für die Preußischen Staaten*, in I, 9, § 1 and 2, and into the Austrian codification of 1811, the *Allgemeines Bürgerliches Gesetzbuch*, in § 380. See also Fuchs, p. 70-81.

87 I.e. the manner in which ownership had to be transferred.

88 Cf. Fuchs, p. 77 et seq.; Johow, Entwurf eines bürgerlichen Gesetzbuches für das Deutsche Reich, Sachenrecht, Begründung, erster Band, Berlin 1880, p. 628 et seq., published in: Die Vorlagen der Redaktoren für die erste Kommission zur Ausarbeitung des Entwurfs eines Bürgerlichen Gesetzbuches, Sachenrecht, vol. 1, Allgemeine Bestimmungen, Besitz und Eigentum, ed. by W. Schubert, Berlin/New York 1982.

89 The theory is often seen as a causal transfer system. See for instance Coing, Europäisches Privatrecht, vol. 1, p. 180; Brandt, Eigentumserwerb und Austauschgeschäft, Leipzig 1940, p. 52.

90 According to Ranieri the opinion that a *causa putativa* sufficed prevailed. See F. Ranieri, Die Lehre der abstrakten Übereignung in der deutschen Zivilrechtswissenschaft des 19. Jahrhunderts, in: H. Coing and W. Wilhelm (eds.), Wissenschaft und Kodifikation des Privatrechts im 19. Jahrhundert, vol. 2, Frankfurt a/M 1977, p. 90 et seq., at p. 91; Ranieri, Brevi note sull'origine della nozione di negozio reale ed astratto, TR vol. 38 (1970), p. 315 et seq., at p. 327-328.

a causal system in the modern sense of the word, that is, with the *causa vera* theory. On the contrary, the distinction between causal and abstract transfer theories and accordingly the dilemma of choosing between them was unknown before Savigny's abstract transfer system became generally accepted. In this time one does not find any consistent and elaborate theories about whether the transfer needs a valid *causa*.[91]

Now, in the early 19th century Savigny began to challenge the then prevailing *titulus and modus* theory.[92] From lecture notes made by various students we know that already in the winter of 1815/1816 he had rejected the *titulus and modus* theory and had developed the concept of real agreement.[93] Savigny published his new ideas only much later, in 1840[94], yet many of his pupils had already disseminated the new theory from the 1820s onwards.[95]

Savigny's main arguments

The most important arguments Savigny used in developing the abstract transfer system were the gift from hand to hand (*Handschenkung*) and the *condictio indebiti* (claim ex undue payment). These arguments can be regarded as both systematic and historical: they are based on the system of Roman law. Like the learned jurists of the preceding centuries the Historical School was founded on the interpretation of classical and Justinianian Roman law. Historical arguments were of great importance, and for that reason Savigny stressed that his theory accorded with the true nature of Roman law. At the same time, though, the Historical School had to adapt Roman law to the modern requirements of the time, because in 19th century Germany Roman law applied as a secondary source of law. As a result, the Historical School was in fact not primarily historical, that is, concerned in reconstructing genuine Roman law. It transformed Roman law into a logical system of concepts and thus continued the efforts at systematization of its predecessor, the school of natural law,[96] which the Historical School attacked so fiercely for deviating from the true nature of Roman law in order to build a logical system of law. So, in its approach towards Roman law two opposing viewpoints were vying for prominence: historical and systematic arguments. This conflict had existed ever

---

91 A.F.J. Thibaut, System des Pandektenrechts, 7th ed., Jena 1828, vol. 1, § 148-152 and vol. 2, § 592. C.F. Mühlenbruch, Doctrina Pandectarum, vol. 2, 4th ed., Halle 1839, § 246.

92 As we have just seen, the *titulus and modus* theory was extended beyond its original scope of application. The extension was unnecessary and complicated. Savigny was therefore right in rejecting this extension. Yet he overreacted by rejecting the theory altogether, not only its extension to other forms of acquisition but also its original field of application: the voluntary transfer. Of course his argument was unconvincing. Savigny used the aberrations of the theory as an argument to repudiate the theory itself.

93 Felgenträger, p. 32-34. First steps towards this rejection can be found already in his lectures of the winter of 1803-1804 (see Felgenträger, p. 27-31).

94 System des heutigen römischen Rechts, vol. 3, Berlin 1840, p. 312 et seq.; Das Obligationenrecht, vol. 2, Berlin 1853 (repr. Aalen 1987), p. 254 et seq.

95 Felgenträger, p. 37 and 41-45.

96 See Koschaker, Europa und das römische Recht, ch. 14 and 15, esp. p. 250-251, 270, 275, 278-279.

since Roman law was applied in practice, but it became all the more notable when the pandectist movement began to stress the historical argument, thus wrongly suggesting the predominance of history over systematics. Even so, in some instances practicality seems to have been of lesser importance than authenticity, that is, what was then thought to be true Roman law.

In D. 41,1,31, pr., quoted above, Paulus seems to require that the *iusta causa* precede the *traditio* (...si venditio aut aliqua iusta causa *praecesserit*...). Accordingly, the *iusta causa* requirement was often, also during the *Usus Modernus*, called *iusta causa praecedens* (preceding legal ground). Commonly, the requirement was illustrated with the example of a preceding contract obliging to make a transfer. Using the example of giving a coin to a beggar Savigny attacked this interpretation of *iusta causa* demonstrating that in the case of a gift from hand to hand there is no preceding contract. According to notes students made of Savigny's lectures he said the following: 'But what about the gift? Here there is no obligatory relation at all, here the mere factual transfer of possession is the transfer of ownership, as a result of which their opinion [i.e. the opinion of jurists who require a preceding obligatory relation] has been completely disproved; for it is the donor's will that makes the donee owner, nothing else. So, we should use the term *iusta causa* only to denote the owner's will to transfer ownership through *traditio*.'[97] To support his theory he then referred to Donellus.[98]

Later he slightly changed his definition of *iusta causa*. In a lecture held in 1827[99] and subsequently in his *Obligationenrecht* (1853)[100] he said that, although *iusta causa* and the will to transfer are closely related concepts, it would be wrong to say that *iusta causa* is the will to transfer. Rather, *iusta causa* is the legal relationship from which the will to transfer can be inferred. Savigny thus joins Donellus in regarding the *iusta causa* as an indication of the owner's will to transfer, an opinion which was brought forward already by Rogerius.

So, from the fact that the gift from hand to hand is not preceded by any obligation Savigny deduces that *iusta causa* is not necessarily a preceding contract, that the *iusta causa* may consist also in the transferor's intention to make a gift. As an example he added the loan for consumption, another instance where the transfer is not necessarily preceded by an obligation to make the transfer.

As we have seen in chapter 6, it is indeed true that a gift from hand to hand is not preceded by an obligation to make the transfer. It is the very definition of a gift from hand to hand. Yet, the particular *causa* in question should be defined more

---

97 Lecture notes from 1815/16 cited by Felgenträger, p. 33-34: 'Aber wie steht es mit der Schenkung? Da ist ja gar kein obligator. Verhältnis, hier ist ja die bloße factische Tradition der Übergang des Eigenthums, wodurch nun ganz die Ansicht jener umfällt; denn die Absicht des Gebers macht den Beschenkten zum Eigenthümer, nichts anderes. Iusta causa müssen wir also nur nennen, die Absicht des Eigenthümers mit der Tradition das Eigenthum zu übertragen.' See also the lecture notes from 1820/21 cited by Felgenträger on p. 35-36. See also Das Obligationenrecht, vol. 2, p. 256-257.

98 Felgenträger, p. 34. The lecture notes refer to Donellus' comment on C. 4,50,6.

99 Felgenträger, p. 36.

100 Das Obligationenrecht, vol. 2, p. 258.

accurately. As demonstrated in chapter 6, § 7 *in fine*, a gift from hand to hand involving a transfer of ownership entails two different agreements: a real agreement, in which the parties agree about the transfer of ownership, and in addition the agreement that the transfer should be a gift. The real agreement is needed only when the gift consists in transferring ownership, or in the creation or transfer of a limited real right. The latter agreement, on the other hand, is always needed. In a causal transfer system it is this agreement which forms the *iusta causa* of the transfer. Von Tuhr summarizes both elements defining the gift from hand to hand as an 'enrichment conferred by way of gift' (*Zuwendung causa donandi*).[101]

Savigny is right in saying that the gift from hand to hand is not preceded by an obligation. Still, the example does not compel us to adopt the *animus* or the abstract theory. In fact, it was fit only to demonstrate that the traditional definition of *iusta causa* was too strict: that the *iusta causa* may consist in something other than a preceding contract, for example the agreement that the transfer should be a gift. Yet it does not prove that the transfer may be valid even if the underlying contract (here the agreement about the transfer being a gift) is not.

As a second argument Savigny referred to the Roman actions ex unjustified enrichment, especially the *condictio indebiti*. We have seen that Accursius used the same argument in the *Glossa Ordinaria*. The argument was to be used for centuries since. It became one of the core arguments against requiring a valid *causa*. The reasoning is as follows. Where possession of a thing has been transferred to another person without a legal ground, for instance because the underlying contract is void or has been avoided, Roman law offers a *condictio*. This is a personal claim rather than a real claim based on ownership. It aims at undoing the unjustified enrichment.[102] Due to the Roman principle of *condemnatio pecuniaria* the claim is for the return of the thing or its value.[103] From a personal action being available it is then concluded that ownership nonetheless passed to the other person. Had it not passed, the claimant would not have needed this *condictio* as he could still make use of the *rei vindicatio*.

The argument is unpersuasive: it is wrong to say that because a *condictio indebiti* is available the transferor must have lost ownership. It is not superfluous for a causal transfer system to give the transferor two remedies: a *rei vindicatio* and in addition a *condictio indebiti*. True, normally the owner will rely on his revindication as it is an action which works as against everyone. Yet, the object transferred may be lost, consumed or sold to a bona fide third party. Moreover, the transferee may have acquired ownership of the thing as a result of original acquisition. The transferor will then have to resort to the *condictio* because it is the only remedy left to him. For that reason a causal system offers both actions. The *rei vindicatio* and the *condictio indebiti* are two parallel actions which amplify one another. As a

---

101   Von Tuhr, Allgemeiner Teil III, § 72, especially p. 74 et seq.
102   Kaser I, p. 592 et seq.
103   See chapter 4, fn. 109.

consequence, the fact that the transferor is given a *condictio* does not lead to the conclusion that he has lost ownership: he may have more than just one remedy.[104]

Still, if in classical Roman law the owner had in principle two actions, the *rei vindicatio* and the *condictio indebiti*, it is remarkable that none of the classical texts mentions the availability of the *rei vindicatio* in these instances. Clearly this gives strength to the *condictio indebiti* argument, especially in a movement involved in the reconstruction of true Roman law. Van Oven has explained this peculiarity of the Roman texts as follows. When *traditio* was introduced into Roman law as a means of transferring ownership the system of *condictiones* had already fully developed. The system had been created to fit the abstract *mancipatio*, which was the oldest form of transfer. And, even after *traditio* had been introduced *mancipatio* remained the most important form of transfer: it dominated the minds of classical jurists. This may explain why the availability of the *rei vindicatio* alongside the *condictio indebiti* cannot be found in the classical texts.[105]

Savigny's role
The abstract theory was not entirely new: significant fragments of the theory can be found already in for example Baldus' and Donellus' writings. Still, Savigny's role in developing the abstract system should not be underestimated. First of all, he created a new concept, the real agreement. Since the rediscovery of the Digest, it is true, many jurists have claimed that agreement between the transferor and acquirer should suffice to let ownership pass. But Savigny seems to have been the first to regard the agreement as a separate legal act, distinct from the underlying contract. He calls it *dinglicher Vertrag* (real agreement).[106] Second, he and his followers developed the existing fragments into a consistent theory and gradually turned it into the prevailing theory in Germany. This is the importance of Savigny for the German transfer theory.

abstraction from the *causa traditionis*
In Savigny's theory the transfer is independent of any possible *causa traditionis*. Defects in the underlying contract do not affect the validity of the transfer of ownership. That is to say, if there is no valid *causa* ownership nevertheless passes to the acquirer. And if ownership has been transferred on the basis of a voidable contract, avoidance of the contract does not invalidate the transfer. Savigny himself mentioned only the influence of mistake (*Irrtum*) on the transfer of ownership. He wrote that if the owner is induced to transfer ownership as a result of mistake, he may undo the transfer with one of the *condictiones* offered by Roman law. Here

---

104 See P. Scholten, Zakenrecht, 7th ed., Zwolle 1933, p. 153. Note that even Meijers, an advocate of the abstract theory, rejected the *condictio indebiti* argument for this reason: E.M. Meijers, Levering en rechtstitel, Verzamelde privaatrechtelijke opstellen, p. 80 et seq., at p. 81.

105 Van Oven, Praeadvies over causa en levering, p. 15 and 33-35.

106 See Felgenträger, p. 34; Savigny, System des heutigen römischen Rechts, vol. 3, Berlin 1840, p. 312-313; Savigny, Das Obligationenrecht, vol. 2, p. 257, fn. (m).

Savigny refers to the *condictio indebiti*, among other things.[107] His followers then applied the same principle to all other defects of will and formed it into the abstract transfer system that we can now find in modern German law. Still, the vital step was taken by Savigny himself in the above example of mistake.

In itself Savigny's creation of the real agreement was not yet decisive for the development of the abstract system. Certainly, it would have been impossible for Savigny to develop the abstract system without the concept of real agreement. Without distinguishing the legal act of transfer from the underlying *causa* it is impossible to regard the transfer as abstracted from the *causa*. But, as such the latter concept does not yet determine the question whether the transfer is causal or abstract. The existence of a real agreement does not exclude that the transfer system is causal. What is more, to my mind the concept is indispensable even to consensual transfer systems, which do not know the real agreement as a concept.

protection of third parties?

In modern German law it is often said that the principle of abstraction has the effect of protecting third parties. A defect in the contract rendering it void or voidable does not automatically affect the validity of the transfer. As a result the acquirer, who has become owner, is able to transfer ownership to a third party. Thus, the third party cannot be affected by a defect in the contract between the second transferor and his predecessor. Such a protection of third parties was useful in the 19th century because Roman law and, accordingly, the German *gemeines Recht* knew only a very limited protection of third parties in the form of acquisitive prescription (*usucapio*).[108] Savigny, however, did not use this argument to support the abstract transfer system.[109] Apparently, the protection of third parties did not play any role in the creation of the new transfer system. The argument was advanced only much later, when the abstract system was generally accepted.[110]

---

107 Das Obligationenrecht, vol. 2, p. 261: 'Wenn das Eigenthum auf eine, an sich gültige Weise freiwillig übertragen wird (durch Mancipation, Tradition u.s.w.), der vorige Eigenthümer aber zu dieser Uebertragung bestimmt wird durch mangelhafte Beweggründe, insbesondere durch Irrtum, so ist die Uebertragung an sich gültig und wirksam, sie kann aber hinterher angefochten und entkräftet werden durch eine Reihe sorgfältig ausgebildeter Condictionen...' (If ownership is transferred voluntarily in a way that is in itself valid (through *mancipatio, traditio* etc.), but the owner is induced to transfer by flawed motives, especially mistake, the transfer is in itself valid and effective, yet it can afterwards be challenged and neutralized by a number of carefully drafted *condictiones*...).

108 See chapter 2, § 1.3.

109 Ranieri, Die Lehre der abstrakten Übereignung, p. 103.

110 H. Dernburg, Beitrag zur Lehre von der justa causa bei der Tradition, AcP 40 (1857), p. 1 et seq., at p. 2.; R. von Jhering, Geist des römischen Rechts auf den verschiedenen Stufen seiner Entwicklung, vol. 3, 3rd ed., Leipzig 1877, p. 207-208.

4.2 Modern German law

codification of the principle of abstraction

When in 1874 the first drafting commission started to make preliminary drafts for a German civil code it codified the principle of abstraction with only little debate.[111] In addition to using the *condictiones* argument[112] it emphasized that the principle of abstraction was needed to make a sharp distinction between the law of obligations and the law of property.[113] Furthermore, it was stressed that the real agreement was by definition an abstract legal act.[114] These are clearly non-arguments. In reality no valid argument was brought forward to support the choice. It is striking to see that the codification of the abstract transfer system was explained only so briefly, because from the preliminary discussions of the first drafting commission we can learn that among the draftsmen there was no unanimity in favour of the abstract system. Far from it: some of the draftsmen had proposed to adopt the French consensual system for the transfer of movable property. The proposal was rejected by 6 members to 5.[115] Although after the first draft was published in 1888 the principle of abstraction was criticized by some jurists,[116] the second drafting commission maintained the principle,[117] despite serious opposition within the commission.[118]

subsequent developments in the 20th century

In the 1930s and 40s criticism of the principle of abstraction showed a huge increase. Many jurists, especially the nazi jurists, argued for the abolition of this principle.[119] As to the transfer of movables they proposed either a consensual transfer system or a causal tradition system. The Nazi Party, who despised the *Bürgerliches Gesetzbuch* as a product of a liberal and individualistic era, prepared a

---

111   See Schubert, Die Entstehung der Vorschriften, p. 101.

112   See Motive, vol. 3, p. 7-9 (Mugdan, vol. 3, p. 4-5).

113   Motive, vol. 3, p. 7 (Mugdan, vol. 3, p. 4). See also Johow, Entwurf eines bürgerlichen Gesetzbuches für das Deutsche Reich, Sachenrecht, Begründung, erster Band, Berlin 1880, p. 629-630, published in: W. Schubert (ed.), Die Vorlagen der Redaktoren für die erste Kommission zur Ausarbeitung des Entwurfs eines Bürgerlichen Gesetzbuches, Sachenrecht, vol. 1, Allgemeine Bestimmungen, Besitz und Eigentum, Berlin/New York 1982. This is the explanation added to the preliminary draft of the law of property made by Johow. It was the basis for deliberations of the first drafting commission. The commission finished its work publishing the first draft (*Erster Entwurf*) and the *Motive*, the explanation to it.

114   Motive, vol. 3, p. 8 (Mugdan, vol. 3, p. 5).

115   See Schubert, Die Entstehung der Vorschriften, p. 144.

116   Schubert, Die Entstehung der Vorschriften, p. 118 et seq.

117   Schubert, Die Entstehung der Vorschriften, p. 131 and 161.

118   From O. von Gierke and E. Strohal. See U. Eisenhardt, Die Entwicklung des Abstraktionsprinzips im 20. Jahrhundert, in: G. Köbler and H. Nehlsen (eds.), Wirkungen europäischer Rechtskultur, Festschrift für Karl Kroeschell zum 70. Geburtstag, Munich 1997, p. 215 et seq., at p. 217.

119   Among others Ph. Heck, Heinrich Lange, H. Krause, J. Hedemann, W. Felgenträger, H. Brandt and Th. Süß. See Eisenhardt, Die Entwicklung des Abstraktionsprinzips im 20. Jahrhundert, p. 218-228.

draft for a new civil code, the *Volksgesetzbuch* in which the principle of abstraction was to have been abolished. Yet, in 1943 the project was discontinued and the new civil code was never promulgated.[120] After the Second World War criticism largely disappeared in West-Germany. In East-Germany it continued and led to the adoption of the causal system for the transfer of movables in the 1975 civil code (*Zivilgesetzbuch*) of the German Democratic Republic.[121] Since the reunification of Germany the principle of abstraction applies to all states of the Federation again.[122]

5 French law

We have just seen that Savigny and his pupils developed the abstract system into a general transfer theory which at the end of the 19th century was adopted by the draftsmen of the German civil code. To find out how the causal system in its modern form has originated we should examine French law.

According to Pothier, whose writings have had an enormous influence on the draftsmen of the *Code Civil*, a putative legal ground suffices to transfer ownership.[123] In his treatment of the *condictio indebiti* he writes that someone who transfers a thing wrongly believing he is under an obligation to do so has the will to transfer ownership. And if the acceptant has the will to acquire ownership of the thing, there is a mutual intention to transfer ownership. To Pothier this suffices to let ownership pass. The transferor, though, is given a personal remedy to claim the thing back. In short, *error in causa*, mistake about the legal ground of the transfer, does not bar the passing of ownership.[124]

Pothier's treatment of the defects of will makes clear that he does not adhere to the abstract theory. He gives a very lucid exposition about the consequences defects of will have on the passing of ownership. Avoidance (*rescision*) of the contract has retroactive effect, that is to say, the contract is deemed never to have existed. Consequently, ownership, which has been transferred to the acquirer, reverts

---

120   Eisenhardt, p. 221-228.

121   Par. 25 and 26 *Zivilgesetzbuch* (1975). Although the paragraphs themselves are far from clear, the official comment on § 26 makes clear that the transfer needs a valid underlying contract obliging to make the transfer. See Kommentar zum Zivilgesetzbuch der Deutschen Demokratischen Republik vom 19. Juni 1975 und zum Einführungsgesetz zum Zivilgesetzbuch der Deutschen Demokratischen Republik vom 19. Juni 1975 (edited by the Ministry of Justice), 2nd ed., Berlin 1985, p. 59.

122   Art. 8 of the Treaty between the Federal Republic of Germany and the German Democratic Republic of 31-8-1990 taking effect from 3-10-1990, the so-called *Einigungsvertrag*. Cf. J. Isensee and P. Kirchhof (eds.), Handbuch des Staatsrechts der Bundesrepublik Deutschlands, vol. 9 (Die Einheit Deutschlands, Festigung und Übergang), Heidelberg 1997, § 209, Rdnr. 6 et seq.

123   Traité du droit de domaine de propriété, part 1, ch. 2, sect. 4, art. 2, § 3, Œuvres de Pothier, vol. 9, Paris 1846, p. 180.

124   Traité du contrat de prêt de consumption et des matières qui y ont rapport, part 3 (traité du quasi-contrat appelé promutuum et de l'action condictio indebiti), sect. 2, art. 7, Œuvres de Pothier, vol. 5, Paris 1847, p. 118.

automatically to the transferor with retroactive effect, because the legal ground on the basis of which the acquirer holds the asset has been avoided. The transferor is deemed always to have been owner of the asset. Being owner he may revindicate the asset.[125] If before avoidance of the contract the acquirer has transferred the asset to a third party or burdened it with a limited real right, the rights acquired by these third parties lapse when the contract between the first and second party is avoided. As the second party is deemed never to have become owner, he has never been able to transfer the asset or grant a limited real right, for no one may transfer more right than he himself has.[126,127] Now, such automatic revesting of ownership in the first party is unthinkable in an abstract transfer system. On the other hand, where in Pothier's view a putative legal ground suffices to transfer ownership his transfer 'theory' cannot be causal. His thoughts would, however, be compatible with the *animus* theory.

When in 1804 the *Code Civil* introduced the consensual transfer system there was no longer any choice whether to adopt the abstract, *animus*, causal theory or any other theory. A *traditio* system, which applied in pre-*Code Civil* law,[128] in principle allows for the adoption of any of these transfer theories. However, when ownership passes on the basis of the contract, that is, when the contract itself is said to pass ownership, the contract must be valid in order to transfer ownership. So, by opting for a consensual transfer system the French *Code Civil* automatically ruled out the abstract and the *animus* theory.

Probably the draftsmen did not realize at the time. As we have seen in chapter 3 the draftsmen of the *Code Civil* regarded the introduction of the consensual system as a mere codification of a long-standing practice: since it was usual in old French law to insert in contracts for the sale of immovables a clause that possession was transferred, ownership normally passed at the time the contract was made. They seem to have overlooked that in the new transfer system a putative legal ground no longer suffices to transfer ownership. An explanation may be that there were hardly any practical consequences. As to avoidance of contracts nothing had changed: also in the new French legal system avoidance has retroactive effect and causes ownership to revert to the transferor, avoiding not only the acquirer's right of ownership, but also any real rights (ownership or limited rights) given to third parties.

Toullier, who wrote one of the first comments on the *Code Civil*, adopts Pothier's reasoning about the consequences of avoidance. Yet, here, in a section on *rescision*,

---

125   Traité du contrat de vente, part 5, ch. 2, sect. 2, art. 1, § 1, Œuvres de Pothier, vol. 3, Paris 1847, p. 139.
126   Ibidem, § 2, Paris 1847, p. 148; ibidem, § 4, Paris 1847, p. 154.
127   Pothier illustrates it by giving an example of *lésion* (*laesio enormis*: severe impairment of the seller caused by the thing being sold for an extremely low price). Yet it is clear that according to Pothier the same reasoning applies to other defects of will which turn the contract voidable: *violence* (duress) and *dol* (fraud). See: Traité des obligations, part 1, ch. 1, sect. 1, art. 3, § 2 and 3, Œuvres de Pothier, vol. 2, Paris 1848. In his view, by the way, a contract entered into under influence of mistake (*erreur*) is void rather than voidable. See ibidem, § 1.
128   See chapter 3, § 2.1.

he does not explain that in the new consensual transfer system avoidance of the contract *necessarily* entails avoidance of the passing of ownership.[129] In his treatment of the *condictio indebiti*, however, Toullier does make this link. He stresses that a mere transfer of possession does not suffice to pass ownership, that always a *iusta causa* is needed, especially under the *Code Civil* in which *traditio* is no longer a way of transferring ownership. The passage is not entirely unambiguous, but if I understand Toullier correctly he means that in a system in which the contract itself transfers ownership the *iusta causa* must be valid *by definition*. He rejects Pothier's opinion that in the case of *error in causa* ownership passes, saying that there is no true will to transfer where the will is a result of a mistake.[130]

Still, apart from this very brief remark by Toullier, thrown in as an *obiter dictum*, the question whether the legal ground of the transfer should be valid seems to be hardly discussed in 19th century French law books. Of course you cannot expect these authors to use the terms 'causal transfer system' or 'abstract transfer system'. The terms 'causal' and 'abstract' used to denote different transfer systems were not yet known at the time. Even in Germany the term 'abstract transfer', mentioned by Savigny and his pupils, became part of the jurist's vocabulary only from the 1840-50s.

Nonetheless, from a systematic point of view we can say that the question whether the transfer system should be causal or abstract had been decided by the *Code Civil*. Whether we should regard the French causal system as based on Roman law or on writings of the learned jurists is difficult to say. Although there was an eminent French jurist in the humanist period who adhered to the causal theory, Cuiacius, neither the draftsmen of the *Code Civil* nor the early 19th century French authors refer to Cuiacius' theory. The draftsmen do not even discuss the meaning of the *iusta causa* requirement in Roman law. This all demonstrates that the choice

---

129   C.B.M. Toullier, Le droit civil français, 5th ed., vol. 7, Paris 1830, nr. 549-550. Cf. also C.-S. Zachariae, C. Aubry and C. Rau, Cours de droit civil français, 2nd ed., Brussels 1842, vol. 1, § 336; F. Laurent, Principes de droit civil français, 2nd ed., Brussels/Paris 1878, vol. 19, nr. 72 et seq., vol. 17, nr. 78 et seq., at nr. 81. See for modern French law: Cour de Cassation 6 Dec. 1967 (Bull. Civ. 1967, I, n° 358, p. 269) discussed by J. Chevallier in Rev. trim. dr. civ. 1968, p. 708-709.

130   Toullier, vol. 11, nr. 58 and nr. 95, 5th ed., Paris 1830, p. 71-72 and 119-120. At p. 123-124, by the way, Toullier seems to contradict himself. If someone erroneously transfers a thing to another without there being any obligation to do so he may claim the thing back from the recipient. But what if the latter transfers it to a third party before the owner claims the thing back? Does the owner have an action as against the third party? According to Toullier the third party is protected against such an action provided he is in good faith. Oddly, however, Toullier seems to explain this by saying that as against the third party the second party has become owner because despite the *error in causa* the owner was truly willing to transfer ownership. A remarkable revival of the analysis Pothier used under pre-civil code law to explain the same case. See: Traité du contrat de prêt de consomption et des matières qui y ont rapport, part 3 (traité du quasi-contrat appelé promutuum et de l'action condictio indebiti), section 2, article 7.

     This strange passage by Toullier seems to have led Ranieri to claim, wrongly to my mind, that during the first decades after the promulgation of the *Code Civil* a putative legal ground sufficed to transfer ownership. See Ranieri, Die Lehre der abstrakten Übereignung, p. 109-111.

for a causal system was not made deliberately. Far from this, the causal system is merely a logical consequence of the consensual transfer system.[131]

6 Dutch law

Understandably, the same terminological problem applies to 19th century Dutch law: the terms 'causal' and 'abstract' were unknown for the larger part of the century. What is more, as in France there was no discussion about whether or not a transfer needs a valid legal ground.

As to the first half of the 19th century research in Dutch law is hampered by the lack of extensive and authoritative legal literature. In addition, it seems that in this period there has been no case law relevant to our question. In order to ascertain which transfer theory dominated we should rely on the various civil codes and draft civil codes made in this period. Unfortunately these texts do not offer a clear answer: they are often indefinite.

In article 589 beginning and subs. 3 and 4 the *Wetboek Napoleon* of 1809 requires for a transfer to be valid 'that it be executed on the basis of some legal ground fit to transfer ownership' (subs. 3) and 'that it be executed with the apparent intention to let ownership pass' (subs. 4).[132] According to Van Oven, a view I share, the provision seems to require a valid legal ground, thus adhering to the causal transfer theory. If the term 'legal ground' in subs. 3 were to include a putative legal ground, the provision would suffice itself with the parties' will to transfer and acquire ownership. The legal ground would be no more than an indication for the parties' will. If this reading were true subs. 4 requiring the parties' will to transfer would obviously be a duplication. So, if the draftsmen had wished to codify the abstract theory, they would most probably have left out the third subsection.[133]

The *Wetboek Napoleon*[134] was an adapted version of the French *Code Civil* specially made for the Kingdom of Holland; it was in force only for a very short period: a few months after its promulgation at 1 May 1809 the Kingdom of Holland was dissolved and annexed to the French empire, and 1 March 1811 the French civil code was introduced in the Netherlands. This brought into Dutch law the causal

---

131 The causal system, it is true, might be said to be based indirectly on Roman law; for the consensual transfer system is in its turn a consequence of the frequent use of *constitutum possessorium* in the transfer of immovables.

132 Om levering bestaanbaar te doen zijn, is het noodig:
   (...)
   3. dat zij gedaan worde op grond van eenigen titel, geschikt om eigendom over te dragen; en
   4. dat zij gedaan worde met het blijkbaar oogmerk, om den eigendom te doen overgaan.
   The text of the provision is almost identical to the preceding draft by Van der Linden (1807-1808). See J. van der Linden, Ontwerp burgerlijk wetboek 1807/1808, book 2, title 2, section 2, article 23, ed. by J.Th. de Smidt, Amsterdam 1967, p. 80.

133 Van Oven, praeadvies, p. 93-94.

134 Full title: *Wetboek Napoleon ingerigt voor het Koningrijk Holland* (lit: 'Code of Napoleon written for the Kingdom of Holland').

and consensual transfer system of the *Code Civil*. After the Netherlands had regained independence in 1813 the *Code Civil* was not immediately abolished. It was intended to be replaced in due time with a Dutch civil code. Eventually the *Code Civil* was to have force of law until 1838, when the Dutch civil code was promulgated.

The draft civil codes of 1816 and 1820, which never became law, codified a transfer system that was certainly not causal. Article 1129 of the 1816 draft, which article is identical to art. 1018 of the 1820 draft, provides that ownership passes when the transferor and acquirer agree about the passing of ownership, even if there is a misunderstanding between the parties about the legal ground of the transfer (*error in causa*).[135] It is not evident whether in these provisions the modern abstract theory is laid down. The last part of the section (after the semicolon) suggests that in the case of other kinds of mistake the passing of ownership is hampered.[136,137] If this is correct the 1816 and 1820 drafts had a transfer system more akin to what I call the *animus* theory.[138]

The 1838 civil code is even less clear. As to the transfer of ownership article 639 of the *Burgerlijk Wetboek* provides that ownership may be acquired through transfer on the basis of a legal ground fit to pass ownership, executed by a person

135   ... Wanneer echter de overdrager en de aannemer het ten aanzien van den eigendoms-overgang eens zijn, gaat de eigendom over, al ware het ook dat er ten aanzien van den eigenlijken regtsgrond eene dwaling bij eene der partijen had plaats gehad; behoudens hetgeen hieronder nader omtrent de gevolgen van dwaling in overeenkomsten, zal gezegd worden.

      (Where, however, the parties agree about the passing of ownership, ownership passes, even if one of the parties is mistaken about the true legal ground; except for what will be further said hereunder about the consequences of mistake in contracts).

136   Nothing is explicitly said about the consequences of mistake on the passing of ownership. The provision on mistake which art. 1018 of the 1820 draft refers to is art. 2278, reading: 'Dwaling maakt geene overeenkomst nietig, dan wanneer men gedwaald heeft in het wezen der zaak, die het onderwerp der overeenkomst uitmaakt. Dwaling maakt mede geene overeenkomst nietig, wanneer men alleenlijk gedwaald heeft in den persoon, met wien men meende te handelen, ten zij de overeenkomst voornamelijk uit aanmerking van dezen persoon is aangegaan.' (Mistake renders a contract void only if one was mistaken about the substance of the thing which is the subject-matter of the contract. Furthermore, mistake does not render a contract void if one was mistaken only about the person one was thinking to deal with, unless the contract was made especially for this person).

      Most probably *wezen der zaak* was intended to denote the physical object that had to be transferred. As a result it may be translated with *substance of the thing*. The wording seems to derive from Pothier, via art. 1110 *Code Civil*. Illustrating the meaning of *substance de la chose* Pothier gives examples about the sale of physical objects. See Traité des obligations, part 1, ch. 1, sect. 1, art. 3, § 1, Œuvres de Pothier, vol. 2, Paris 1848, p. 13-14.

137   Oddly neither Meijers nor Van Oven pays attention to this part of the provision. See Meijers, levering en rechtstitel, p. 84-86; Van Oven, praeadvies, p. 94-95.

138   Van Oven, on the other hand, who does not distinguish between the abstract and *animus* theory, says that the 1820 draft undoubtedly adhered to the abstract theory. See praeadvies, p. 95.

privileged to dispose of the thing.[139] Regrettably, the article does not indicate whether the legal ground should be valid. Accordingly, the omission prolonged an ambiguity that had been in existence for hundreds of years in the learned law based on the *Corpus Iuris Civilis*.

The question whether the legal ground should be valid was discussed in Dutch legal literature only from the second half of the 19th century. Writing about undue payment Diephuis said that a putative legal ground does not suffice to let ownership pass, a view that is undoubtedly causal.[140] Opzoomer, on the other hand, an author strongly influenced by German legal literature, adhered to the abstract theory, referring to Windscheid, Puchta, and to Donellus as well.[141]

Whereas for the larger part of the 19th century Dutch law was under a strong influence of French law, in the last decades of the century the influence of the German pandectistic school was growing rapidly. When in 1899 part of a draft for a new Dutch civil code was published, the so-called *Ontwerp 1898* (the 1898 draft), it proposed to codify the abstract transfer theory.[142] Yet the draft never became law.

In the beginning of the 20th century more and more authors joined the causal/abstract debate and, as a result, it developed into a famous controversy among Dutch jurists.[143] The abstract theory was defended by among others Suijling[144], Hofmann[145] and Meijers[146], the man that was to become the father of the new civil code. Advocates of the causal theory were among others Scholten[147] and Van Oven[148]. In this period the *Hoge Raad*, the Dutch Supreme

---

139 Art. 639 BW 1838: 'Eigendom van zaken kan op geene andere wijze worden verkregen, dan door...opdragt of levering, tengevolge van eenen regtstitel van eigendoms-overgang, afkomstig van dengenen die geregtigd was over den eigendom te beschikken.' At the dotted place the article deals with other means of acquiring ownership.

140 Diephuis, Het Nederlandsch burgerlijk regt, vol. 11, Groningen 1888, p. 68-70.

141 C.W. Opzoomer, Het burgerlijk wetboek verklaard, vol. 3, 2nd ed., Amsterdam 1876, p. 258-259. Here we can find Savigny's unconvincing argument of the gift from hand to hand, and the equally weak reference to the *titulus and modus* theory (for these arguments see § 4.1 *supra*). Cf. Opzoomer, vol. 6, 2nd ed., The Hague 1891, p. 223 et seq.: on p. 225-226 he refers to Donellus.

142 See article 105, Ontwerp tot herziening van het burgerlijk wetboek, tweede boek, The Hague 1899, p. 156; see also the comment on this article, Ontwerp tot herziening van het burgerlijk wetboek, tweede boek, toelichting, The Hague 1899, p. 373. The official comment refers to the German civil code. In the comment the abstract theory is regarded as generally accepted. No evidence is quoted, however.

143 See about this debate: A.F. Salomons, 2014 tot 1950, De geschiedenis tot 1950 van de vertrouwensbescherming bij overdracht van roerende zaken door een beschikkingsonbevoegde, (thesis Amsterdam, UvA), s.l. 1997, ch. 9, § 1.

144 J.Ph. Suijling, Inleiding tot het burgerlijk recht, vol. 5 (Zakenrecht), Haarlem 1940, nr. 245 et seq.

145 L.C. Hofmann, Het Nederlandsch zakenrecht, Groningen/Batavia 1944, p. 227.

146 Levering en rechtstitel, Verzamelde privaatrechtelijke opstellen, vol. 2, p. 80 et seq.; Levering en onderliggende rechtsverhouding (causa), Verzamelde privaatrechtelijke opstellen, vol. 2, p. 131 et seq.

147 C. Asser, Handleiding tot de beoefening van het Nederlandsch burgerlijk recht, vol. 2, 4th ed., ed. by P. Scholten, Zwolle 1905, p. 97-99, and all subsequent editions edited by him.

148 J.C. van Oven, praeadvies, p. 106 et seq.

Court, was unable to make up its mind and, accordingly, it gave a number of vague and inconsistent judgments some of which could be regarded as adhering to the causal theory, others as opting for an abstract theory.[149]

In 1939 the *Hoge Raad* accepted the causal transfer system in a case about the assignment of claims.[150] Since the decision was confined to assignment of claims it was still unsettled whether the causal system applied also to the transfer of other assets. As to movable property the debate was finally settled in 1950 in favour of the causal theory by the *Hoge Raad*'s judgment in *Damhof/de Staat*.[151]

When after the Second World War Meijers was appointed to draft a new civil code he codified the causal system, despite having been one of the most prominent advocates of the abstract transfer system.[152] In what would later become article 3:84 subs. 1 Meijers unequivocally laid down that the *causa*, called *titel* in Dutch, should be valid.

149   See Asser-Beekhuis, Zakenrecht, vol. 1, 11th ed., Zwolle 1980, p 180-181; Salomons, 2014 tot 1950, ch. 10, § 2.2.
150   HR 9 February 1939, NJ 1939, 865 (*Woldijk/Nijman*).
151   HR 5 May 1950, NJ 1951, 1.
152   Parl. Gesch. Boek 3, p. 316-317.

8 The three systems compared
A common core?

1 The first dividing line:
tradition systems and consensual systems

1.1 Mitigation of the *traditio* requirement

As we have learnt from the history of French law the *Code Civil*'s consensual system was not a sudden break with the Roman tradition system. On the contrary, it slowly developed from the Roman transfer system as a result of the widespread use of forms of fictitious tradition. As to the sale of land conveyancing practice had reversed rule and exception: in a large part of France, in the South as well as in the North, it was standard practice to include in contracts for the sale of land a clause declaring that possession was or had been transferred to the buyer. As a result *constitutum possessorium*, a form of fictitious tradition which originally was allowed only as an exception to the requirement of a real tradition, had gradually become the rule. So, in most of France ownership of land passed at the time the contract of sale was made. Later, in the *Code Civil* this reversal of rule and exception was formally acknowledged and extended to all sorts of property.

Notwithstanding the contrasting starting-points there is no great discrepancy between a consensual system and a tradition system that allows *traditiones fictae*. True, in a consensual system ownership in principle passes when the contract is made, whereas in a tradition system it passes only when possession is transferred. Yet the difference appears quite insignificant when considering that these principles are merely *ius dispositivum*. In both transfer systems the moment when ownership should pass may be altered by the parties to the contract. In a consensual system the parties can opt for ownership to pass at a later time, or they can make the passing of ownership depend on a certain condition such as full payment of the purchase price. In a tradition system the parties may opt to advance the passing of ownership by using a fictitious transfer. Using a *traditio ficta* they are able to let ownership pass when the contract is made, before any physical transfer of possession has taken place.

In the case of *traditio ficta* the transfer of ownership is brought about by mere agreement without any physical act being needed, a striking similarity between the consensual and tradition system.[1] For that reason Grotius referred to the *traditiones fictae* to support his view that agreement alone sufficed to transfer ownership. In *De iure belli ac pacis* he wrote the following: 'Yet, above we have said that according to natural law *traditio* is not required for the transfer of ownership; this is also acknowledged by the Roman lawyers in some instances, as in the case of a gift performed with retention of a usufruct [a form of *constitutum possessorium*], or the

---

1   Dogmatically, there is of course the difference that the tradition system requires an extra element: the agreement about the transfer of possession.

transfer of a thing to someone who is already in possession of it or someone who has borrowed the thing [i.e. *brevi manu*];...'.[2]

One could object, however, that the acknowledgement of fictitious tradition has not taken away all practical differences. After all, as a consequence of abolishing the *traditio* requirement a consensual system allows ownership to be transferred even when the owner is not in possession of the object, for example because the thing has been stolen or lost. In contrast, a pristine, unmitigated tradition system cannot let ownership pass in such a case, even if it allows forms of *traditio ficta*. For, tradition, whether real or fictitious, constitutes a transfer of possession. And, although a *traditio ficta* is made simply by agreement without any physical handing over of the object, it still requires the owner to be in possession. Without possession there is no transfer of possession.

In a tradition system such as German and Dutch law this practical difficulty can be solved only by accepting that in these instances no form of tradition is required, not even a *traditio ficta*. In German law this step was taken in 1900 (§ 931 BGB);[3] in Dutch law it was acknowledged only in 1979 by the *Hoge Raad*.[4] The rule has now been codified in article 3:95 of the *Burgerlijk Wetboek*.

As a result of these mitigations of the *traditio* requirement almost all practical differences between the consensual system and the tradition system have disappeared: in both systems the parties are able to let ownership pass at the moment of their choice. The difference between the two systems is a difference only of starting-points, and these are *ius dispositivum*.

1.2 The specificity principle

However, there is no unlimited freedom for the parties in choosing the time when ownership should pass. The principle of specificity prevents ownership from passing before it is known exactly which specific assets should be transferred to the acquirer. Where a certain amount of generic goods is sold ownership will pass only after specific assets have been identified as the goods to be transferred to the buyer. Yet, what is important to our comparison: the consequences of the principle of specificity are exactly the same in both systems, so that the principle does not cause the systems to diverge. The reason for this is quite simple: the principle of specificity flows from the definition of ownership, and this definition is equal in every legal system described here. Ownership, like any other right *in re*, forms a relationship between a person and a certain identified asset. Consequently, in order for ownership to be transferred it must be known which specific asset is to be transferred.

---

2 Grotius, De iure belli ac pacis, 2,8,25, Amsterdam 1712: 'Atqui supra diximus, ad dominii translationem naturaliter traditionem non requiri; quod & ipsi Jurisconsulti in quibusdam casibus agnoscunt, ut in re donata usufructu retento, aut in eum collata qui possideat, aut commodatam servet;...'.

3 See chapter 2, § 4.4.

4 HR 27 April 1979, NJ 1981, 139; restated in HR 1 February 1980, NJ 1981, 140.

1.3 The minimum requirements

The absolute minimum requirements for a voluntary transfer of movables are twofold. First, the transferor and transferee should agree about the passing of ownership,[5] and, second, this agreement should be related to identified assets. In short, the parties should agree to the transfer of identified assets.

Traditio is not essential to the transfer itself and tolerates to be set aside. The original function of the *traditio* requirement has long ago become obsolete the moment indirect possession was acknowledged. In primitive legal systems handing over of physical power makes public the transfer of ownership. But, from the moment a legal system acknowledges indirect possession, that is possession without physical power over the object, possession can no longer be relied on as a means of publication. A person may have physical power without having ownership or, reversely, he may have ownership without having physical power. In the case of *traditio ficta* the passing of ownership is invisible to third parties. Moreover, there may be a transfer of physical power without a transfer of ownership, as in the case of a loan or lease. And even where *traditio* involves a transfer of ownership the transfer may be made under a suspensive condition so that the buyer receives physical power without becoming owner at the same time.

So what difference is left when we acknowledge that *traditio* is no longer essential to a tradition system? Is it the real agreement, the separate legal act to transfer ownership? Is this the feature distinguishing the consensual systems from the tradition systems? The notion of real agreement was introduced into German law by Von Savigny and was subsequently adopted by Dutch law. It has developed into a concept characteristic to many tradition systems. Yet, although the concept is unknown to French and English legal theory an analysis of the French transfer system and the system of the Sale of Goods Act has demonstrated that also these consensual systems can be said to contain a real agreement. We can therefore conclude that the consensual and the tradition system have a very important element in common: the agreement about the transfer of identified assets. This is not surprising considering that the real agreement is in fact the legal act of transfer.[6]

1.4 The relation between consensual and causal

It seems as if the decision whether to adopt a causal or an abstract transfer system will be influenced by the choice between a consensual and a tradition system. Yet, the argument that a consensual system is necessarily causal no longer applies when acknowledging that also in these systems the transfer contains a real agreement. In

---

5   This requirement does not entail that the will of each party as expressed by him should correspond to his true will. In many legal systems a declaration of will that does not correspond with the declaror's true will is nonetheless binding on him, provided the declaree did not know nor should have known that the declaror made a mistake.

6   See chapter 5, § 2.2.

a consensual system, it is true, the real agreement may coincide with the contract obliging to make the transfer, but it should nonetheless be seen as a distinct element. If the contract itself passed ownership the transfer would inevitably be causal. Yet, it is not the contract that passes ownership; it is the real agreement. Therefore the transfer might be abstract even in a consensual system.

2 The second dividing line: causal and abstract systems

2.1 Choosing between causal and abstract?

Unlike the dividing line between tradition and consensual systems the dividing line between causal and abstract systems has not been mitigated and is as real as ever.[7] It seems as if harmonization here means choosing either the causal or the abstract system.

The most important practical consequence of such a choice will undoubtedly be the different protection of the parties to the transfer against insolvency of the other party. Yet, as I have said in chapter 1 a satisfactory protection against insolvency cannot be obtained merely by opting for a certain transfer system. For that reason insolvency arguments should not be decisive in making this choice. We should concentrate on systematic, that is dogmatic, arguments. In doing so it should be possible to opt for a transfer system that is consistent in its treatment of defects of will.[8]

2.2 Internal inconsistency of the abstract theory

When confining oneself to systematic arguments it is to my mind obvious that the abstract transfer system has inconsistencies. Like the adherents of the causal system also Savigny and his followers stress the importance of consensus for the passing of ownership. However, according to the abstract theory the transfer of ownership is valid even when one of the contracting parties has entered into the contract under the influence of mistake, fraud, or any other defect of will. Clearly there is no real consensus here. That is the very reason why the party who acted under the influence of a defect of will is given the power to avoid the contract.[9] He should be able to undo the entire transaction. Yet the abstract theory is far from consistent here: the victim, it is true, has the power to avoid the contract, but the avoidance does not affect the transfer based on this contract. The transfer is regarded as a neutral legal act uninfluenced by any possible defects in the parties' will. In doing so the abstract system in reality disregards the parties' will. By ignoring the true

---

7   Note, however, that the abstract transfer is no more than *ius dispositivum*. See chapter 2, § 1.3.
8   See chapter 7, § 2.3.
9   Note that in Savigny's time a sharp distinction between void and voidable legal acts had not yet been fully developed. As a result the terminology was unsettled. Here I use modern terminology.

will of the parties where there is a defect of will Savigny negates the importance of the parties' will and negates one of the foundations of his own theory.

The principle of abstraction makes an artificial segregation between two legal acts which economically and in the mind of the parties are part of one and the same transaction. The transfer takes place for a certain reason, to make a gift, a loan, or to fulfil some obligation. These legal motives cannot be disregarded. When a party in reality did not consent to the contract in question, he certainly did not want the transfer of ownership based on it.[10]

2.3 A midway solution

As we have seen in chapter 7 we are not forced to choose between two extremes: causal and abstract. The division into these two uncompromising transfer theories is of relatively recent date: the beginning of the 19th century. In the period before the 19th century the learned law had no transfer theories whatever. When examining the different interpretations of the *iusta causa* requirement proposed in this period it appears that these do not fit into the division causal/abstract. So, from a historical point of view there is no valid reason to confine our choice to the extremes of causal and abstract. Nor is there any dogmatic argument for doing so.

Several learned jurists in the period before 1800 seem to opt for some midway solution: their statements fit into a theory which I have called the *animus* theory. Now, although it is very unlikely that such a theory has ever been current, the *animus* theory may be a useful compromise for future law to bridge the gap between causal and abstract transfer systems.

In such a theory all defects of will are treated equally. Avoidance of the contract for a defect of will nullifies the transfer as well. To use German terminology, as regards defects of will there should always be *Fehleridentität*, identity of defect. In the *animus* theory ownership passes only if there is a genuine will to make the transfer. A valid contract is not needed, however. Where for example the contract is void for illegality ownership nonetheless passes to the acquirer because there is a true will to make the transfer. From a systematic point of view I should say that the *animus* theory is certainly more consistent than the abstract theory. And, although no transfer theory can claim any convincing historical justification it must be said that the *animus* theory accords well with many statements quoted in the preceding chapter.

---

10 Cf. Stadler, who acknowledges this relation between the contract and the transfer. She nonetheless remains faithful to the abstract system. See A. Stadler, Gestaltungsfreiheit und Verkehrsschutz durch Abstraktion, Tübingen 1996, p. 179.

Summary

The subject-matter of this book is the transfer of movable property in German, French, English and Dutch law. The transfer using negotiable instruments and the transfer by way of security will not be considered. Nor will transfers which require registration.

Of particular importance is the division into the three main types of transfer system: the causal consensual system, the causal tradition system and the abstract tradition system. Here two dividing lines intertwine: the distinction between causal and abstract systems and the distinction between consensual and tradition systems.

Chapter 1

In chapter 1 the above-mentioned transfer systems will be considered in the abstract. Furthermore, a few principles of property law will be explained. A causal transfer system demands that the transfer be based on a valid legal ground, i.e. a legal reason justifying the passing of ownership (*iusta causa traditionis*). In an abstract system, on the other hand, the transfer is valid even if it is not based on a valid legal ground. Under the influence of Savigny and his pupils, German law opted for the abstract system. In a consensual system a valid transfer of ownership in principle does not require any transfer or providing of possession. In the current view ownership passes simply as a result of entering into a contract which imposes an obligation to make a transfer. A tradition system, on the other hand, distinguishes between the underlying contract and the legal act of transfer. Notwithstanding these differences in theory, in the chapters on German, French, English and Dutch law we shall see that the distinction between causal and abstract, and the distinction between consensual and tradition, are not as sharp as might appear at first glance.

Chapter 2

In chapter 2 the German transfer system, the only abstract system to be treated in this research, will be discussed. As said before, an abstract system distinguishes between the contract obliging to make the transfer (*Verpflichtungsgeschäft*) and the transfer itself (*Übereignung, Veräußerung*). The transfer is valid even if the preceding contract is void or has been avoided with retroactive effect. If ownership has been transferred under a voidable contract avoidance will not automatically revest ownership in the transferor.

Yet, there are several exceptions to the abstraction (§ 2.2). First of all, fraud and duress (*Täuschung* and *Drohung*) will in principle affect the validity of both the contract and the transfer. Such a common defect of will is called *Fehleridentität* (identity of defect). Second, the abstraction is merely *ius dispositivum*: the parties may, expressly or tacitly, make the transfer depend on the validity of the underlying contract.

The German transfer system is a tradition system: apart from *Einigung* (real agreement) § 929 BGB requires *Übergabe* (a transfer of possession) (§ 3). The transfer of possession needs the will of the transferor to make the acquirer possessor, and the corresponding will of the transferee to acquire possession from the transferor. It is an act aiming at the passing of possession. As possession is not only a fact but also a right, the transfer of possession can be regarded as a legal act (§ 3.1-3.5). Still, in German law this is recognized only in regard to the transfer of possession mentioned in § 854 subs. 2 BGB, a transfer of possession by mere agreement. On the other hand, the transfer of possession by providing actual power (§ 854 subs. 1 BGB) is seen as no more than a factual act. For practical reasons German law provides that in some instances no transfer of actual power is needed as between the transferor and transferee. The instances are *Geheißerwerb* (§ 3.6), *traditio brevi manu*, *constitutum possessorium* and the assignment of the *Herausgabeanspruch* (§ 4).

As a rule a valid transfer also demands that the transferor should be privileged to dispose (*Verfügungsbefugnis*) (§ 5). Yet, in certain cases a person who is not privileged to dispose is nonetheless able to make a valid transfer. For, if the acquirer is in good faith, and if all other requirements for third party protection are met, the transfer is regarded as valid. A non-owner is thus able to transfer a thing belonging to another. Here the transferor is the non-owner, yet the bona fide third party succeeds in a right (i.e. ownership) which previously belonged to the owner. I have called this ability to transfer 'the power to dispose' (§ 5.3).

The concept of agency demonstrates that the current German view, according to which the transfer of possession under § 854 subs. 1 BGB is not a legal act, leads to inconsistency. The German point of view has led to the opinion that the concept of agency cannot be applied to the transfer of actual power (*traditio vera*). At the same time, however, for practical reasons, forms of transfer are recognized which in reality amount to agency.

Chapter 3

Chapter 3 treats the French causal and consensual transfer system, which does not require a transfer of possession. Here consensus between the parties suffices. Traditionally in this system the contract itself is held to pass ownership. Ownership passes at the moment the contract is made. Yet, there are some very important exceptions to this principle. As a result of the principle of specificity, ownership of generic goods can pass only when certain goods are separated and appropriated for delivery to the acquirer (§ 1.2-1.3). And, where there is a contract for the transfer of future goods, ownership can pass only after the goods have come into existence. Furthermore, it is often overlooked that in the case of sale the 'translative effect of obligations' applies only to the passing of ownership of the thing, not the transfer of the money due in exchange (§ 1.1).

The French consensual system originated in a frequent use of *constitutum possessorium* and similar forms of *traditio* in contracts for the sale of land. In pre-*Code civil* law the requirement of *traditio* was deprived of all practical consequences as a result of notaries enclosing in contracts for the sale of land a standard clause that possession was transferred by way of *constitutum possessorium* or otherwise. Thus, in practice ownership of land passed when the contract was made (§ 2.1).

In spite of the French legislator's choice to let ownership pass when the contract is made, I believe that for a proper understanding of the French transfer system the concept of real agreement is indispensable (§ 2). In § 2.2 examples will be treated which demonstrate that the real agreement exists also in French law. The concept should be distinguished from the *traditio* and may therefore play a role in a system which abolished *traditio* as a requirement for the transfer of ownership.

Chapter 4

Chapter 4, in which English law is analysed, divides into parts A and B. The division was necessitated by the presence in English law of two different transfer systems: the ancient common law system which requires a transfer of possession, and the consensual system of the Sale of Goods Act 1979. In part A (Transfer based on sale) we shall see that also in the consensual system of the Sale of Goods Act immediate passing of ownership is possible only as regards specific existing (in contrast to future) things. As in French law the purchase price will not pass to the seller when the contract is made. The rule that ownership of generic goods cannot pass to the buyer before certain goods have been appropriated to the buyer has led to an amendment of the Sale of Goods Act. Where the contract stipulates that the goods should be taken from a specified bulk the buyer will under certain conditions (among which payment) become co-owner in the bulk.

It is likely that the English consensual system originated in a way similar to the development of the consensual system on the continent. Originally the common law requirement of *traditio* applied to every transfer of movables. However, it was gradually held that, when a contract for the sale of a movable was made, it immediately passed constructive possession to the buyer, making the seller a bailee for the buyer. As a consequence ownership passed when the contract was made, before any physical handing over had taken place. It involved a fictitious *traditio* similar to the continental *constitutum possessorium* (§ 6.1).

It can be proven that, like French law, the English consensual system contains a real agreement (§ 4). The systematic arguments are comparable to the ones mentioned in chapter 3. The question whether the tradition system of the Sale of Goods Act is causal or abstract is not discussed in English law. Still, on systematic grounds, it can be demonstrated that the system is causal (§ 5).

Part B will describe the ancient common law system of transfer which requires a transfer of possession (*traditio*). An important instance to which the ancient requirement still applies is the gift from hand to hand (in contrast with the gift by deed). Here *traditio* may take the form of providing actual power, but in some cases a fictitious transfer of possession will suffice (§ 8). It is difficult to ascertain whether transfers outside the scope of the Sale of Goods Act need a valid legal ground. Most probably a transfer by deed is abstract, but as to the ancient common law transfer by *traditio* no conclusion is possible: there is no legislation, case law or literature which could give us any clue whatever.

Chapter 5

For a valid transfer of movables Dutch law in principle requires the providing of possession to the acquirer. Furthermore, unlike the old civil code the new 1992 code expressly provides that every transfer needs a valid legal ground. As a result the transfer system may be classified as a causal tradition system.

There is some controversy whether the transfer of ownership needs a real agreement. I think that the majority of the authors are right in asserting that a real agreement is essential to any transfer. In Dutch law the term transfer (*overdracht*) indicates not only the result (the passing of ownership) but also the act to attain the result: the transferring of ownership. This act aiming at the passing of ownership to the acquirer should be regarded as a legal act the nucleus of which is formed by the real agreement. Any formalities required in addition to the real agreement should be seen as *condiciones iuris* (conditions required by the law rather than conditions stipulated by the parties). They suspend the effect of the legal act until certain additional requirements, such as *traditio*, have been met. In reality, the concepts of *levering*, the real agreement and the act of *overdracht* are synonymous (§ 2).

Possession may be provided by giving actual power or by using a form of fictitious *traditio* (§ 3). In one instance, article 3:95, not even a fictitious *traditio* is needed. The peculiarity of *constitutum possessorium* is that it does not work as against persons having an older right in or over the thing until the transferee has acquired actual power over the thing. So, until that moment the transfer of ownership works only relatively. The reason is to postpone third party protection until the third party has acquired actual power. For the same reason it is held that a *detentor* cannot transfer possession by way of *constitutum possessorium*. To achieve this result an ancient adage is used: *nemo sibi ipse causam possessionis mutare potest* (no one can for himself change the legal ground of his possession).

Chapter 6

The gift from hand to hand, which will be analysed in chapter 6, is a good illustration of the importance of the real agreement. In the case of a gift from hand to hand ownership passes only when actual power over the thing is given to the donee. It is an executed gift, that is, a gift which is not preceded by an obligation to transfer the thing by way of gift. If, on the other hand, the transfer is preceded by a binding promise to make the gift it is called an executory gift.

A consensual system in which the obligation is said to transfer ownership ('translative effect of obligations') cannot satisfactorily explain the gift from hand to hand: there is no obligation to make the transfer. Accordingly, when the gift involves a transfer of ownership a real agreement is needed to accomplish the transfer. The gift from hand to hand consists of two elements: an enrichment conferred to the acquirer and an agreement that the enrichment should be a gift.

Chapter 7

The gift from hand to hand was one of the arguments with which Savigny and his pupils developed the German abstract system. The division causal/abstract originated in the beginning of the 19th century and is therefore of relatively recent date. Neither in Roman law nor in the learned law after the rediscovery of the Digest has one ever tried to make a general theory about the consequences of defects in the legal ground of the transfer. Although it is nowadays acknowledged that in classical Roman law *traditio* was a causal form of transfer the evidence is somewhat blurred. Partly due to interpolations the Digest contains inconsistencies which influenced the interpretation of the *iusta causa* requirement since the Middle Ages. Legal historians generally hold that in the time of the glossators, commentators, humanists and in Roman-Dutch law the transfer system was abstract. Yet, when we examine what authors of the time write about the consequences of voidness or avoidance no abstract system appears to have existed. What is more, in this period no transfer system existed whatsoever.

The abstract theory was developed by Savigny and his pupils from 1815/1816. In the case of defects of will the theory involves an artificial distinction between contract and transfer. In principle a defect of will is taken to affect the contract only, not the transfer as well. Yet, if in reality one did not want the contract, this applies all the more to the transfer executing the contract.

The causal system originated in the consensual system of the *Code Civil*: where the contract itself passes ownership a valid transfer necessarily depends on the contract being valid. Even so, the choice for a causal system was not deliberate: it was merely a logical consequence of opting for a consensual system, a consequence one did not realize when the *Code* was enacted.

Chapter 8

In conclusion it turns out that the division between consensual systems and tradition systems and the division between causal and abstract systems are not unbridgeable. As regards the first divide the existence of fictitious *traditio* and exceptions to the requirement of *traditio* have reduced the difference between consensual and tradition systems to a distinction only of *ius dispositivum*. In both systems parties are able to let ownership pass when they think fit, provided the principle of specificity is met. Both systems have in common that every transfer of movables requires a real agreement. The acknowledgment that also consensual systems have a real agreement entails that consensual systems are no longer causal of necessity.

The historical survey in chapter 7 shows us that the sharp distinction between the extremes of causal and abstract has been in existence only from the beginning of the 19th century. Moreover, the chapter demonstrates that a transfer system may be created which lies in between causal and abstract, for example a system in which defects of will always affect the transfer whereas other defects do not.

Samenvatting

Onderwerp van dit boek is de overdracht van roerende zaken in het Duitse, Franse, Engelse en Nederlandse recht. Hierbij blijft de overdracht door middel van handelspapieren buiten beschouwing, evenals de overdracht tot zekerheid en de overdracht van registergoederen. Van groot belang is de onderscheiding binnen de overdrachtsstelsels van drie hoofdtypen, namelijk het causale consensuele stelsel, het causale traditiestelsel en het abstracte traditiestelsel. Hierbij komen twee scheidslijnen samen, het onderscheid tussen het causale en abstracte stelsel, en het onderscheid tussen het consensuele stelsel en het traditiestelsel.

Hoofdstuk 1

In hoofdstuk 1 worden de bovengenoemde overdrachtssystemen in abstracto uitgelegd en worden tevens enkele beginselen van het goederenrecht uiteengezet. Een causaal overdrachtssysteem stelt als voorwaarde dat de overdracht gebaseerd moet zijn op een geldige titel, dat wil zeggen, een geldige reden voor overdracht (*valid legal ground, iusta causa traditionis*). In het abstracte stelsel is een overdracht zelfs geldig wanneer er geen geldige rechtsgrond aanwezig is. De overdracht wordt hier geabstraheerd van haar eventuele rechtsgrond. Onder invloed van Savigny en zijn leerlingen heeft het Duitse recht voor dit systeem gekozen.

In een consensueel stelsel is voor een geldige eigendomsoverdracht in beginsel geen bezitsoverdracht of bezitsverschaffing nodig. Volgens de heersende leer gaat eigendom in dit systeem reeds over door het enkele sluiten van een overeenkomst die tot eigendomsoverdracht verplicht. In een traditiestelsel wordt evenwel een onderscheid aangebracht tussen de onderliggende overeenkomst en de overdracht.

In de hoofdstukken over het Duitse, Franse, Engelse en Nederlandse recht zal echter blijken dat deze tegenstellingen tussen causaal en abstract en tussen consensueel en traditie, die vaak gezien worden als onoverbrugbaar, veel minder scherp zijn dan ze op het eerste gezicht lijken.

Hoofdstuk 2

In hoofdstuk 2 wordt het Duitse overdrachtsstelsel besproken, het enige abstracte stelsel in dit onderzoek. In een abstract stelsel als het Duitse wordt onderscheid gemaakt tussen de overeenkomst die tot overdracht verplicht (*Verpflichtungsgeschäft*) en de overdracht zelf (*Übereignung, Veräußerung*) (§ 1.2). De overdracht is geldig ook al is de voorafgaande overeenkomst nietig of met terugwerkende kracht vernietigd. Wanneer eigendom is overgegaan op grond van een vernietigbare overeenkomst leidt de vernietiging van de overeenkomst niet tot een automatisch terugvallen van de eigendom naar de vervreemder (§ 1.3).

Er zijn echter enkele belangrijke uitzonderingen op deze abstractheid (§ 2.2). Allereerst zullen de wilsgebreken bedrog en bedreiging (*Täuschung* en *Drohung*: § 123 BGB) in beginsel zowel de overeenkomst als de overdracht aantasten. Er is dan sprake van *Fehleridentität* (gemeenschappelijk wilsgebrek). Bovendien is de abstractheid slechts van regelend recht: partijen kunnen uitdrukkelijk of stilzwijgend de overdracht afhankelijk maken van de geldigheid van de onderliggende overeenkomst.

Tegelijkertijd is het Duitse overdrachtsstelsel een traditiestelsel: § 929 BGB eist naast *Einigung* (de goederenrechtelijke overeenkomst) *Übergabe* (bezitsoverdracht) (§ 3). Deze bezitsoverdracht vereist de wil van de vervreemder om de verkrijger tot bezitter te maken en de overeenstemmende wil van de verkrijger bezit van de vervreemder te ontvangen. Het is een handeling gericht op het overgaan van bezit. Omdat bovendien bezit niet alleen een feit is maar ook een recht, is de bezitsoverdracht een rechtshandeling (§ 3.1-3.5). In het Duitse recht wordt dit echter alleen erkend voor de bezitsoverdracht op grond van § 854 Abs 2 BGB (bezitsoverdracht door tweezijdige verklaring), niet voor de overhandiging genoemd in § 854 Abs 1 BGB (verschaffing van de feitelijke macht, *traditio vera*). Uit praktische overwegingen staat het Duitse recht toe dat in bepaalde gevallen geen macht over de zaak wordt overgedragen van de vervreemder naar de verkrijger. Deze gevallen zijn *Geheißerwerb, traditio brevi manu, constitutum possessorium* en *Abtretung des Herausgabeanspruchs*.

In beginsel is voor een geldige overdracht tevens vereist dat de overdrager beschikkingsbevoegd is (*Verfügungsbefugnis, privilege to dispose*) (§ 5). Maar ondanks dit vereiste is in bepaalde gevallen iemand die niet bevoegd is over een goed te beschikken toch in staat een rechtsgeldige overdracht tot stand te brengen. Wanneer namelijk de verkrijger te goeder trouw is en aan de overige vereisten van derdenbescherming is voldaan, wordt de overdracht als geldig beschouwd. Een niet-eigenaar kan op deze manier het goed van een ander overdragen. De vervreemder is de niet-eigenaar, maar de rechtsvoorganger van de derde te goeder trouw is de eigenaar. Deze macht om over te dragen heb ik beschikkingsmacht genoemd (*power to dispose*) (§ 5.3).

Het leerstuk van de vertegenwoordiging laat zien dat de heersende opvatting in Duitsland dat de bezitsoverdracht van § 854 Abs 1 BGB (verschaffen van feitelijke macht) geen rechtshandeling is tot tegenstrijdigheid leidt. Op basis van deze opvatting wordt namelijk aangenomen dat vertegenwoordiging bij deze vorm van bezitsoverdracht niet mogelijk is (§ 6). Om praktische redenen worden echter rechtsfiguren toegelaten die in feite neerkomen op vertegenwoordiging.

Hoofdstuk 3

Hoofdstuk 3 behandelt het Franse causale consensuele overdrachtssysteem waarin de eis van bezitsoverdracht niet geldt. Volgens de traditionele opvatting doet in dit consensuele systeem de overeenkomst zelf de eigendom overgaan: wilsovereenstemming (consensus) volstaat. Eigendom gaat over op het moment dat de overeenkomst wordt gesloten. Op dit beginsel zijn echter belangrijke uitzonderingen: door de werking van het specialiteitsbeginsel kan eigendom van generieke goederen pas overgaan wanneer bepaalde goederen zijn afgescheiden en bestemd voor aflevering aan de verkrijger. Ook bij een overeenkomst die verplicht tot overdracht van toekomstige zaken kan eigendom pas overgaan na het sluiten van de overeenkomst. Bovendien wordt vaak voorbij gegaan aan het feit dat het *effet translatif des obligations* bij de koopovereenkomst alleen geldt voor de eigendomsoverdracht van de zaak, en niet voor de overgang van de koopprijs.

Het Franse consensuele systeem is ontstaan door een veelvuldig toepassen van het constitutum possessorium en andere vergelijkbare vormen van bezitsoverdracht bij de verkoop van onroerende zaken. Onder het recht van voor de *Code Civil* werd bij de verkoop van onroerende zaken de eis van bezitsoverdracht van zijn praktische waarde beroofd doordat het notariaat de gewoonte overnam om in koopovereenkomsten de clausule op te nemen dat bezit werd overgedragen door constitutum possessorium of op een andere vergelijkbare wijze. In de praktijk ging eigendom van onroerende zaken daardoor over op het moment van het sluiten van de koopovereenkomst.

Ondanks de keuze van de Franse wetgever om de eigendom in beginsel over te laten gaan bij het sluiten van de overeenkomst ben ik van mening dat het begrip goederenrechtelijke overeenkomst onontbeerlijk is voor een goed begrip van het Franse overdrachtssysteem. De gevallen die aantonen dat ook het Franse recht een goederenrechtelijke overeenkomst kent worden weergegeven in § 2.2. Het begrip goederenrechtelijke overeenkomst moet worden onderscheiden van de bezitsoverdracht en kan ook een rol spelen in een stelsel dat bezitsoverdracht als vereiste voor eigendomsoverdracht heeft geschrapt.

Hoofdstuk 4

Hoofdstuk 4, waarin het Engelse recht aan de orde komt, is onderverdeeld in delen A en B. Deze splitsing is nodig omdat het Engelse recht twee verschillende overdrachtssytemen kent: het oude common law stelsel waarin bezitsoverdracht vereist is, en het consensuele stelsel van de *Sale of Goods Act 1979.*

In onderdeel A (*Transfer based on sale*) blijkt dat ook in het consensuele stelsel van de Engelse *Sale of Goods Act* onmiddellijke eigendomsovergang op het moment van het sluiten van de koopovereenkomst slechts mogelijk is bij de koop van een tegenwoordige (i.t.t. toekomstige) specifieke zaak. En, evenals in het Franse recht zal ook hier de koopprijs niet op de verkoper overgaan bij het sluiten van de overeenkomst. De regel dat eigendom van generieke zaken niet op de koper kan overgaan voordat bepaalde zaken zijn afgescheiden en zijn bestemd voor levering aan de koper (appropriation) heeft geleid tot een wijziging van de *Sale of Goods Act.* Wanneer in het contract bepaald is dat de zaken uit een door koper en verkoper aangewezen partij (bulk) genomen moeten worden, krijgt de koper onder bepaalde voorwaarden (waaronder betaling) een mede-eigendomsaandeel in deze partij.

Het is aannemelijk dat de wijze waarop het Engelse consensuele stelsel is ontstaan vergelijkbaar is met de ontwikkeling van het consensuele stelsel op het continent. Oorspronkelijk gold het common law vereiste van bezitsoverdracht voor iedere overdracht van roerende zaken. Maar langzamerhand ontstond de opvatting dat een koopovereenkomst met betrekking tot een roerende zaak meteen indirect bezit aan de koper gaf, waardoor de verkoper houder voor de koper werd. Hierdoor ging eigendom over bij het sluiten van de overeenkomst, voordat enige fysieke overhandiging had plaatsgevonden. De overeenkomst bevatte een fictieve bezitsoverdracht vergelijkbaar met het continentale constitutum possessorium (§ 6.1).

Niet alleen van het Franse maar ook van het Engelse consensuele stelsel kan aangetoond worden dat zij een goederenrechtelijke overeenkomst bevat (§ 4). De systematische argumenten zijn vergelijkbaar met de gronden genoemd in hoofdstuk 3. De vraag of het overdrachtsstelsel van de *Sale of Goods Act* causaal of abstract is wordt in het Engelse recht niet besproken. Toch kan op systematische gronden worden aangetoond dat het systeem causaal is (§ 5).

In onderdeel B wordt het oude common law stelsel van overdracht beschreven, waarin overdracht van bezit vereist is. Een belangrijk geval waarvoor de oude overdrachtseisen nog gelden is de schenking van hand tot hand (i.t.t. de schenking op basis van een akte, de zogenaamde *deed*). De bezitsoverdracht kan hier de vorm aannemen van reële machtsverschaffing, maar in bepaalde gevallen kan aan het vereiste ook worden voldaan door een fictieve bezitsoverdracht (§ 8). Of overdrachten die niet onder de *Sale of Goods Act* vallen een geldige titel nodig hebben is moeilijk vast te stellen. Waarschijnlijk is een overdracht op basis van een *deed* abstract, maar voor de oude common law overdracht met bezitsoverdracht is geen conclusie mogelijk: er is geen wetgeving, rechtspraak of literatuur waaruit ook maar iets kan worden afgeleid over deze vraag.

Hoofdstuk 5

In het Nederlandse recht is voor de eigendomsoverdracht van roerende zaken in beginsel bezitsverschaffing nodig. Bovendien bepaalt het Burgerlijk Wetboek van 1992, anders dan het oude wetboek, dat elke overdracht op een geldige titel gebaseerd moet zijn. Het is dus een causaal traditiesysteem.

Of voor eigendomsoverdracht een goederenrechtelijke overeenkomst is vereist is niet onomstreden. Toch meen ik met de meerderheid der auteurs dat de goederenrechtelijke overeenkomst essentieel is voor elke overdracht. De term overdracht duidt niet alleen een resultaat aan (de overgang van eigendom) maar ook de handeling waarmee dit resultaat bereikt wordt: het overdragen van de eigendom. Deze handeling, die gericht is op het doen overgaan van eigendom op de verkrijger, is te beschouwen als een rechtshandeling. De goederenrechtelijke overeenkomst is de kern van deze rechtshandeling. Eventuele formaliteiten die vereist zijn naast de goederenrechtelijke overeenkomst moeten gezien worden als *condiciones iuris* (rechtsvoorwaarden). Zij stellen de werking van de rechtshandeling uit totdat aan bepaalde aanvullende eisen, zoals bijvoorbeeld bezitsverschaffing, is voldaan. In wezen zijn de begrippen levering, goederenrechtelijke overeenkomst en overdracht (als handeling) synoniem (§ 2).

De bezitsverschaffing (§ 3) kan geschieden door feitelijke machtsverschaffing of door verschillende vormen van fictieve bezitsoverdracht. In een enkel geval, art.

3:95, is zelfs geen fictieve bezitsoverdracht vereist. De leveringsvorm *constitutum possessorium* heeft de eigenaardigheid dat zij niet werkt tegenover oudere gerechtigden op de zaak totdat de verkrijger de feitelijke macht over de zaak heeft verkregen. Tot dit moment werkt de eigendomsoverdracht dus slechts relatief. De reden is dat hierdoor de derdenbescherming wordt uitgesteld totdat de derde feitelijke macht over de zaak heeft verkregen. Om dezelfde reden wordt gezegd dat de houder niet door middel van *constitutum possessorium* bezit kan overdragen. Om dit laatste resultaat te bereiken wordt het aloude adagium *nemo sibi ipse causam possessionis mutare potest* gebruikt (niemand kan voor zichzelf de rechtsgrond van zijn bezit veranderen).

Hoofdstuk 6

De schenking van hand tot hand, beschreven in hoofdstuk 6, vormt een goed voorbeeld van het belang van de goederenrechtelijke overeenkomst. Bij de schenking van hand tot hand gaat eigendom pas over wanneer de feitelijke macht over een zaak aan de begiftigde wordt verschaft. Het is een vorm van *executed gift* (let.: uitgevoerde schenking), een schenking die niet vooraf wordt gegaan door een verplichting tot het overdragen van een zaak bij wege van schenking. Wanneer de overdracht wel vooraf wordt gegaan door een verplichting (bindende schenkings-belofte) heet zij *executory gift* (nog uit te voeren schenking).

Een consensueel systeem waarin men zegt dat de overeenkomst zelf eigendom overdraagt (*effet translatif des obligations*) kan de schenking van hand tot hand niet op bevredigende wijze verklaren. Er is namelijk geen verbintenis tot overdracht. Wanneer de schenking de vorm aanneemt van eigendomsoverdracht is daarom een goederenrechtelijke overeenkomst nodig om de overdracht van eigendom te bereiken. De schenking van hand tot hand bestaat uit twee elementen: de aan een ander verleende verrijking (*conferred enrichment, Zuwendung*) en de overeenkomst dat deze verrijking bij wege van schenking is verricht.

Hoofdstuk 7

De schenking van hand tot hand was een van Savigny's argumenten waarmee hij en zijn leerlingen het abstracte systeem hebben ontwikkeld. De tweedeling causaal/abstract is ontstaan in het begin van de 19e eeuw en is hiermee relatief recent. In het Romeinse recht noch in het geleerde recht van na de herontdekking van de Digesten heeft men zich ooit bekommerd een algemene leer te ontwikkelen over de invloed van gebreken in de titel voor de overdracht. Hoewel tegenwoordig wordt aangenomen dat *traditio* in het klassieke Romeinse recht een causale vorm van overdracht is geweest is het bewijs hiervoor niet erg duidelijk. De Digesten bevatten, mede door interpolaties, tegenstrijdigheden die ook na de middeleeuwen hun invloed bleven uitoefenen op de interpretatie van het titelvereiste. Volgens de heersende leer onder rechtshistorici was het overdrachtssysteem ten tijde van de glossatoren, commentatoren, humanisten en het oud-vaderlandse recht abstract. Wanneer men beziet wat volgens de verschillende auteurs uit deze periodes de gevolgen zijn van nietigheid of vernietiging van de overeenkomst blijkt echter dat er geen abstract overdrachtssysteem bestond. Sterker nog, er bestaat helemaal geen overdrachtssysteem in deze periodes.

De abstracte leer is door Savigny en zijn leerlingen ontwikkeld vanaf de jaren 1815/1816. De leer leidt bij wilsgebreken tot een onnatuurlijk onderscheid tussen overeenkomst en overdracht. Een wilsgebrek wordt geacht in beginsel alleen de overeenkomst aan te tasten, niet ook de eigendomsoverdracht. Echter, wanneer men de overeenkomst niet werkelijk heeft gewild, geldt dit a fortiori voor de eigendomsoverdracht ter uitvoering van deze overeenkomst.

De causale leer komt voort uit het consensuele systeem van de *Code Civil*: wanneer de overeenkomst zelf eigendom overdraagt, gaat eigendom alleen over als de overeenkomst geldig is. De keuze voor een causaal systeem is overigens niet bewust gebeurd: het was slechts een logisch uitvloeisel van de keuze voor een consensuele overdracht, een gevolg dat men zich bij de invoering van de *Code* niet heeft gerealiseerd.

Hoofdstuk 8

In de conclusie blijkt dat de twee belangrijke onderscheidingen, de scheidslijn tussen consensuele en traditiestelsels en die tussen causale en abstracte stelsels, geen onoverbrugbare barrières vormen. Wat de eerste scheidslijn betreft is door het toelaten van fictieve bezitsoverdracht en uitzonderingen op het vereiste van bezitsoverdracht het onderscheid tussen consensuele stelsels en traditiestelsels een onderscheid van regelend recht geworden. In beide stelsels zijn partijen in staat de eigendom te laten overgaan op het moment van hun keuze zolang maar voldaan is aan het specialiteitsbeginsel. De twee systemen hebben gemeenschappelijk dat een goederenrechtelijke overeenkomst vereist is voor elke eigendomsoverdracht van roerende zaken. Het aannemen dat ook consensuele stelsels een goederenrechtelijke overeenkomst kennen heeft overigens tot gevolg dat consensuele stelsels niet langer noodzakelijkerwijs causaal zijn.

De historische uiteenzetting in hoofdstuk 7 laat zien dat het scherpe onderscheid tussen de extremen causaal en abstract pas bestaat sinds het begin van de 19e eeuw. Uit dit hoofdstuk blijkt tevens dat tussenvormen tussen causaal en abstract mogelijk zijn, bijvoorbeeld in de vorm dat wilsgebreken altijd doorwerken in de overdracht, maar andere gebreken niet.

Curriculum vitae in breve coactum

Lars van Vliet was born on the 28th March 1970. After his final examination *gymnasium* α he studied Dutch law at Maastricht University from 1988-1992 and graduated *cum laude*. In 1992-1993 he studied tax law at this university. From September 1993 until January 1998 he was a research assistant (*assistent in opleiding*) of Maastricht University, and since 1998 he has been a university lecturer (*universitair docent*) at the same university.

Bibliography[*]

Literature before 1500

Azo, Lectura super Codicem, Paris 1577 (repr. Turin 1966).

Azo, Summa super Codicem, Pavia 1506 (repr. Turin 1966).

Baldus de Ubaldis, 10 vols (Venice 1577): In primum, secundum et tertium Codicis libros commentaria; in quartum & quintum Codicis libros commentaria; in sextum Codicis librum commentaria; in VII, VIII, IX, X & XI Codicis libros commentaria; in primam Digesti Veteris partem commentaria; in secundum Digesti Veteris partem commentaria; in primam et secundam Infortiati partem commentaria; in Digestum Novum commentaria; Praelectiones in quatuor Institutionum libros (Venice 1576); in Decretalium volumen commentaria (Venice 1580).

Bartolus de Saxoferrato, 11 vols (Venice 1585): In primam Digesti Veteris partem; in secundam Digesti Veteris partem; in primam Infortiati partem; in secundam Infortiati partem; in primam Digesti Novi partem; in secundam Digesti Novi partem; in primam Codicis partem; in secundam Codicis partem; Super Authenticis, & Instit.; Consilia, quaestiones et tractatus; Repertorium locupletissimum in omnes Lecturas Bartoli a Saxoferrato (general register vol.).

Bulgarus, De dolo summula, Published in: Kantorowicz, Studies, p. 243-244.

Jacques de Révigny, Lectura super Codice, Paris 1519 (repr. Bologna 1967).

Martinus Gosia, see: Der Glossenapparat des Martinus Gosia zum Digestum Novum, ed. by Dolezalek, G., ZSS Rom vol. 84 (1967), p. 245-349.

Rogerius, Enodationes quaestionum super Codice, published in: Kantorowicz, Studies, p. 281-293.

Socinus, Bartholomaeus, Consiliorum seu potius responsorum Mariani Socini ac Bartholomaei filii senensium..., 4 vols, Venice 1579.

Literature from 1500 to 1800

Bronchorst, E., Enantiophanon centuriae quatuor, Leyden 1598.

Cuiacius, J., Opera omnia, 10 vols + 1 register vol., Napels 1722-1727.

Domat, J., Les loix civiles dans leur ordre naturel, Paris 1723.

Donellus, H., Opera omnia, 12 vols, Lucca 1762-1770.

Donellus, H., Commentarii de iure civili, ed. by Scipio Gentilis, Hannover 1612.

Duarenus, F., Opera omnia, 4 vols, Lucca 1765-1768.

Grotius, H., De iure belli ac pacis, 2,6,1 and 2,8,25, Amsterdam 1712.

Huber, U., Praelectionum juris civilis tomi tres, Louvain 1766.

---

[*]   Included in this list is all literature referred to in the footnotes and a number of other books and articles consulted which are related to the subject matter of the book.

Neostadius, C., Utriusque Hollandiae, Zelandiae, Frisiaeque curiae decisiones, The Hague 1667.

Noodt, G., Opera omnia, Leyden 1767, vol. 1.

Pothier, R.J., Œuvres de Pothier, annotées et mis en corrélation avec le Code Civil et la législation actuelle, ed. by Bugnet, 10 vols + register vol., Paris 1845-1862.

Pufendorf, S. von, De iure naturae et gentium, Amsterdam 1704.

Tiraquellus, Andreas (1488-1558), De iure constituti possessorii Tractatus, Paris 1549.

Vinnius, A., Selectarum iuris quaestionum libri duo, I, XII, Rotterdam 1685.

Voet, Johannis, Commentarius ad Pandectas, 2 vols, Geneva 1778.

Voet, Paulus, In quatuor libros Institutionum Imperialium Commentarius, vol. 1, Utrecht 1668.

Wesenbeck, M., Commentarii in Pandectas juris civilis et Codicem Justinianeum olim dicti paratitla (with notes and observations by Bachoven), Leyden 1649.

Wissenbach, J.J., Excercitationum ad quinquaginta libros pandectarum partes duae, Lib. IV, disputatio XIII (nr. 34), Franeker 1661.

Literature after 1800

Adam, J.H., Longman dictionary of business English, 2nd ed., Beirut-Harlow 1989.

Apeldoorn, L.J. van, Levering en titel van eigendomsovergang in het oude Nederlandsche recht, WPNR 1929, p. 711-714 and 723-725.

Arndts von Arnesberg, L., Lehrbuch der Pandekten, 10th ed. (by Pfaff, L. and Hofmann, F.), Stuttgart 1879.

Asser, C. and Limburg, J., Handleiding tot de beoefening van het Nederlandsch burgerlijk recht, vol. 3, 1st part, Zwolle 1905.

Asser/Beekhuis: C. Asser's Handleiding tot de beoefening van het Nederlands burgerlijk recht, Zakenrecht, 9th ed., by Beekhuis, J.H., Zwolle 1957 (vol. 1) and 1963 (vol. 2); 12th ed., Zwolle 1985 (vol. 1) by Beekhuis, J.H., Mijnssen, F.H.J. and De Haan, P.

Asser/Kleijn: C. Asser's Handleiding tot de beoefening van het Nederlands burgerlijk recht, Bijzondere overeenkomsten, vol. 4, 4th-5th ed., by Kleijn, W.M., Zwolle 1988.

Asser/Mijnssen/De Haan: C. Asser's Handleiding tot de beoefening van het Nederlands burgerlijk recht, Zakenrecht, 13th ed., vol. 1 (Algemeen goederenrecht), by Mijnssen, F.H.J. and Haan, P. de, Zwolle 1992; vol. 2 (Zakelijke rechten) by Davids, W.J.M., Mijnssen, F.H.J. and Velten, A.A. van, Zwolle 1996.

Baker, J.H., An introduction to English legal history, 3rd ed., London 1990.

Baker J.H. and Milsom, S.F.C., Sources of English legal history, Private law to 1750, London 1986.

Baron, J., Pandekten, 6th ed., Leipzig 1887.

Battersby, G. and Preston, A.D., The concepts of 'property', 'title' and 'owner' used in the Sale of Goods Act 1893, MLR 1972, p. 268 et seq.

Bauer, K., Ersitzung und Bereicherung im klassischen römischen Recht, und die Ersitzung im BGB, (*Dissertation* Freiburg im Breisgau) Berlin 1988.

Baur, F., Baur, J.F. and Stürner, R., Sachenrecht, 17th ed., Munich 1999.

Beatson, J., Anson's law of contract, 27th ed., Oxford 1998.

Bekker, E.I., Das Rechts des Besitzes bei den Römern, Festgabe an Johann Caspar Bluntschli, Leipzig 1880.

Bell, A.P., Modern law of personal property in England and Ireland, London 1989.

Bénabent, A., Droit civil, Les contrats spéciaux, civils et commerciaux, 3rd. ed., Paris 1997.

Benjamin's Sale of Goods, ed. by Guest, A.G. et al., 5th ed., London 1997.

Bergfeld, Chr., Savigny und Donellus, in: H. Coing (ed.), Vorträge zum 200. Geburtstag von F. C. von Savigny, Ius commune, Veröffentlichungen des Max-Planck-Instituts für Europäische Rechtsgeschichte, vol. 8, Frankfurt a/M 1979, p. 24 et seq.

Bergh, G.C.J.J. van der, Geleerd recht, 3rd ed., Deventer 1994.

Biermann, J., Traditio ficta. Ein Beitrag zum heutigen Civilrecht auf geschichtlicher Grundlage, Stuttgart 1891 (repr. Amsterdam 1968).

Birks, P., Mixtures, in: N. Palmer and E. McKendrick (ed.), Interests in goods, London/New York/Hamburg/Hong Kong 1993, p. 449-468.

Blackburn, C., A treatise on the effect of the contract of sale: on the legal rights of property and possession in goods, wares and merchandize, 1st ed., London 1845.

Blécourt, A.S. de, Fischer, H.F.W.D., Kort begrip van het oud-vaderlands recht, 7th ed., Groningen 1959.

Brahn, O.K., Levering, beschikkingsonbevoegdheid, Monografiën Nieuw BW, nr. B6b, 2nd. ed., Deventer 1992.

Brahn, O.K. and Reehuis, W.H.M., Overdracht, Monografiën Nieuw BW, nr. B6a, 3rd. ed., Deventer 1997.

Brandt, H., Eigentumserwerb und Austauschgeschäft: der abstrakte dingliche Vertrag und das System des deutschen Umsatzrechts im Licht der Rechtswirklichkeit (*Habilitation* Leipzig) Leipzig 1940.

Bridge, M.G., The Sale of Goods, Oxford 1997.

Bridge, M.G., Personal property law, 2nd ed., London 1966.

Brinz, A., Lehrbuch der Pandekten, vol. 1, 3rd ed., Erlangen 1884.

Brissaud, J., Manuel d'histoire du droit privé à l'usage des étudiants en licence et en doctorat, nouvelle édition, Paris 1935.

Brunner, C.J.H., review of Nieuwenhuis' book 'Uit de ban van hier en nu', RM Themis 1982, p. 36 et seq.

Bruns, C.G., Das Recht des Besitzes im Mittelalter und in der Gegenwart, 1848 (repr. Osnabrück 1965).

Bruns, V., Besitzerwerb durch Interessenvertreter, Tübingen 1910.

Buchholz, S., Abstraktionsprinzip und Immobiliarrecht. Zur Geschichte der Auflassung und der Grundschuld, Ius Commune Sonderhefte nr. 8, Frankfurt a/M 1978.

Buchka, G. von, Vergleichende Darstellung des Bürgerlichen Gesetzbuches für das Deutsche Reich und des Gemeinen Rechts, Berlin 1897.

Buckland, W.W., McNair, A.D., Roman law and common law. A comparison in outline, 2nd ed., by Lawson, F.H., Cambridge 1974.

Bufnoir, C., Propriété et contrat, 2nd ed., Paris 1924.

Burght, Gr. van der, and Penders, J.P., Schenking, Deventer 1989.

Caemmerer, E. von, Rechtsvergleichung und Reform der Fahrnisübereignung, in: Gesammelte Schriften, ed. by Leser, H.G., vol.. 1, Tübingen 1968, p. 146-186.

Caemmerer, E. von, Übereignung durch Anweisung zur Übergabe, JZ 1963, p. 586 et seq.

Caenegem, R.C. van, An historical introduction to private law, Cambridge 1992.

Carey Miller, D.L., Transfer of ownership, in: R. Feenstra and R. Zimmermann (eds.), Das römisch-holländische Recht, Fortschritte des Zivilrechts im 17. und 18. Jahrhundert, Berlin 1992, p. 521 et seq.

Carey Miller, D.L., The acquisition and protection of ownership, Cape Town/Wetton/Johannesburg 1986.

Chevallier, J., discussion of Cass civ 6-12-1967 (Bull. 1967, I, p. 269, nr. 358), Rev. trim. dr. civ. 1968, p. 708-709.

Chitty on Contract, by Guest, A.G. et al. (eds.), vol. 1 (General principles), vol. 2 (Specific contracts), 27th ed., London 1994.

Coing, H., Europäisches Privatrecht, vol. 1 (Älteres gemeines Recht), Munich 1985; vol. 2 (19. Jahrhundert), Munich 1989.

Coing, H. (ed.), Handbuch der Quellen und Literatur der neueren europäischen Privatrechtsgeschichte, vol. 1 (Mittelalter, 1100-1500), Munich 1973; vol. 2 (Neuere Zeit, 1500-1800), part 1 (Wissenschaft), Munich 1977.

Coing, H., Zur Geschichte des Begriffs 'subjektives Recht', in: H. Coing, Zur Geschichte des Privatrechtsystems, Frankfurt a/M. 1962.

Cosack, K., Lehrbuch des bürgerlichen Rechts, vol. 1 (Die allgemeinen Lehren und das Schuldrecht), 7th ed., Jena 1922; vol. 2 (Sachenrecht. Recht der Wertpapiere. Gemeinschaftsrecht. Familienrecht. Erbrecht.), by Cosack, K. and Mitteis, H., 7th-8th ed., Jena 1924.

Cornil, G., L'évolution historique de la vente consensuelle et la loi 50, D. de actionibus empti et venditi, Nouvelle Revue historique de droit Français et étranger, vol. 25 (1901), p. 136 et seq.

Crome, C. System des deutschen bürgerlichen Rechts, vol. 1 (Einleitung und Allgemeiner Theil), Tübingen/Leipzig 1900.

Crossley Vaines' Personal property, 5th ed., by Tyler, E.L.G. and Palmer, N.E., London 1973.

Davenport, B.J., Ownership of bulk cargoes, LMCLQ 1986, p. 4-7.

Dawson, J.P., Gifts and promises, Continental and American law compared, New Haven/London 1980.

Dernburg, H., Beitrag zur Lehre von der justa causa bei der Tradition, AcP 40 (1857), p. 1 et seq.

Dernburg, H., Das bürgerliche Recht des deutschen Reichs und Preußens, vol. 1 (Die allgemeinen Lehren des bürgerlichen Rechts des Deutschen Reichs und Preußens), Halle 1902.

Dernburg, H., Pandekten, 7th ed. (with assistance of J. Biermann), Berlin 1902 (vol. 1), Berlin 1903 (vols 2 and 3).

Diephuis, G., Het Nederlandsch burgerlijk regt naar de volgorde van het burgerlijk wetboek, 1st ed., 9 vols, Groningen 1844-1855.

Diephuis, G., Het Nederlandsch burgerlijk regt, 13 vols, Groningen 1869-1890.

Dolezalek, G., Der Glossenapparat des Martinus Gosia zum Digestum Novum, ZSS Rom vol. 84 (1967), p. 245-349.

Dondorp, J.H. and Schrage, E.J.H., Levering krachtens geldige titel, enige grepen uit de geschiedenis van de vereisten voor eigendomsoverdracht, Amsterdam 1991.

Drion, H., De betekenis van het bezit voor ons huidige recht, WPNR 1967, p. 109-113, p. 121-127 and p. 133-137.

Drion, J., annotation to Hoge Raad 22 May 1953 (Sio-De Jong), NJ 1954, 189, p. 360-364.

Dulk, J.L. den, De zakelijke overeenkomst, (thesis Groningen 1979) Alphen a/d Rijn 1979.

Dutilleul, F.C. and Delebeque, Ph., Contrats civils et commerciaux, 3rd. ed., Paris 1996.

Eisenhardt, U., Die Entwicklung des Abstraktionsprinzips im 20. Jahrhundert, in: Köbler, G. and Nehlsen, H. (eds.), Wirkungen europäischer Rechtskultur, Festschrift für Karl Kroeschell zum 70. Geburtstag, Munich 1997, p. 215 et seq.

Endemann, F., Lehrbuch des bürgerlichen Rechts, vol. 1 (Einleitung, Allgemeiner Teil, Recht der Schuldverhältnisse), 9th ed., Berlin 1903; vol. 2 (Sachenrecht, Familienrecht), 7th ed., Berlin 1900.

Enneccerus, L., Lehrbuch des bürgerlichen Rechts, vol. 1.1, (Erster Band, erste Abteilung: Einleitung, Allgemeiner Teil), 6th-8th ed., Marburg 1911.

Enonchong, N., Title claims and illegal transactions, LQR 1995, p. 135 et seq.

Esser, J., Einführung in die Grundbegriffe des Rechtes und Staates, Vienna 1949.

Esser, J., Schuldrecht, vol. 2 (Besonderer Teil), 6th ed., by Weyers, H.-L., Heidelberg 1984.

Exner, A., Die Lehre vom Rechtserwerb durch Tradition, Vienna 1867.

Feenstra, R., Ius in re. Het begrip zakelijk recht in historisch perspectief, Leiden/Zwolle 1979.

Feenstra, R., Reclame en revindicatie, (thesis Amsterdam, G.U.) Haarlem 1949.

Feenstra, R. and Ashmann, M., Contract, aspecten van de begrippen contract en contractsvrijheid in historisch perspectief, 2nd ed., Deventer 1988.

Feenstra, R. and Zimmermann, R. (eds.), Das römisch-holländische Recht, Fortschritte des Zivilrechts im 17. und 18. Jahrhundert, Berlin 1992.

Felgenträger, W., Friedrich Carl v. Savigny's Einfluß auf die Übereignungslehre, Leipzig 1927.

Ferid, M. and Sonnenberger, H.J., Das französische Zivilrecht, vol. 2 (Schuldrecht, die einzelnen Schuldverhältnisse; Sachenrecht), 2nd ed., Heidelberg 1986.

Ferrari, F., Vom Abstraktionsprinzip und Konsensualprinzip zum Traditionsprinzip, ZEuP 1993, p. 52 et seq.

Fikentscher, W., Schuldrecht, 9th ed., Berlin/New York 1997.

Flume, W., Allgemeiner Teil des Bürgerlichen Rechts, vol. 2, Das Rechtsgeschäft, 4th ed., Berlin/Heidelberg 1992.

Fuchs, J.G., Iusta causa traditionis in der Romanistischen Wissenschaft, Basel 1952.

Gierke, O. (von), Der Entwurf eines bürgerlichen Gesetzbuchs und das deutsche Recht, Leipzig 1889.

Gierke, O. (von), Deutsches Privatrecht, vol. 2 (Sachenrecht), Leipzig 1905.

Goode, R.M., Proprietary rights and insolvency in sales transactions, London 1985.

Goode, R.M., Commercial law, London 1995.

Goode, R.M., Ownership and obligation in commercial transactions, LQR 1987, p. 433 et seq.

Gordley, J. and Mattei, U., Protecting possession, AJCL 1996, p. 293 et seq.

Gordon, W.M., Studies in the transfer of property by traditio, Aberdeen 1970.

Groefsema, L., Bevoegd beschikken over andermans recht, (thesis Groningen) Deventer 1993.

Guisan, F., La protection de l'acquéreur de bonne foi en matière mobilière, (thesis Lausanne) Lausanne 1970.

Gutzwiller, M. et al. (eds.), Schweizerisches Privatrecht, Basel/Stuttgart 1967-.

Haab, R. et al., Kommentar zum schweizerischen Zivilgesetzbuch, Band IV (Das Sachenrecht), erste Abteilung (Das Eigentum, art. 641 bis 729), Zurich 1977.

Haan, C.J. de, Eigendomsovergang van roerende zaken, The Hague 1946.

Hall, F.A. van, Dertig vragen omtrent bezit en bezitregt, volgens het nieuwe Nederlandsche Burgerlijke Wetboek, Bijdragen tot Regtsgeleerdheid en Wetgeving, 1828, p. 118 et seq.

Halsbury's Laws of England, 4th ed., vol. 9(1), Reissue 1998, Contract, section 6 (Void and illegal contracts, by Bragg, R.J.).

Hammen, H., Die Bedeutung Friedrich Carl v. Savignys für die allgemeinen dogmatischen Grundlagen des Deutschen Bürgerlichen Gesetzbuches, Berlin 1983.

Harder, M., Die historische Entwicklung der Anfechtbarkeit von Willenserklärungen, AcP 173 (1973), p. 209 et seq.

Harris, D.R., The concept of possession in English law, in: A.G. Guest (ed.), Oxford essays in jurisprudence, Oxford 1961.

Hartkamp, A.S., Compendium van het vermogensrecht volgens het nieuwe burgerlijk wetboek, 5th ed., Deventer 1999.

Hartkamp, A.S., Der Zwang im römischen Privatrecht, (thesis Amsterdam, UvA 1971) Amsterdam 1971.

Hartkamp, A.S., Het begrip leveringstitel, WPNR 1974, p. 375-383 and 393-399.

Hazewinkel-Suringa, D., De rechtstitel bij de eigendomsoverdracht, in: Rechtsgeleerde opstellen van de hand van oud-leerlingen aangeboden aan Prof. Mr. Paul Scholten ter gelegenheid van zijn 25-jarig hoogleeraarschap, Haarlem 1932, p. 168 et seq.

Heck, Ph., Das abstrakte dingliche Rechtsgeschäft (in the series 'Schriften der Akademie für Deutsches Recht'), Tübingen 1937.

Heck, Ph., Grundriß des Sachenrechts, 3rd ed., Tübingen 1930 (repr. Aalen 1994).

Hedinger, M.P., Über Publizitätsdenken im Sachenrecht, Bern 1987.

Heemskerk, W.H., Vorderingsrecht en rechtsvordering, Deventer 1974.

Heilfron, E., Grundriß des bürgerlichen Rechts, Mannheim/Berlin/Leipzig, vol. 1 (Allgemeiner Teil), 6th ed., 1927; vol. 2 (Recht der Schuldverhältnisse), 6th ed., 1930; vol. 3 (Sachenrecht), 5th ed., 1930; vol. 4 (Familienrecht und Erbrecht), 4th ed., 1933.

Heumann, H. and Seckel E., Handlexikon zu den Quellen des römischen Rechts, 11th ed., Jena 1907 (repr. Graz 1971).

Hellwig, K., Lehrbuch des deutschen Civilprozeßrechts, vol. 1, Leipzig 1903.

Hellwig, K., Wesen und subjektive Begrenzung der Rechtskraft. Eine prozessuale Abhandlung mit Beiträgen zum bürgerlichen Recht, insbesondere zur Lehre von der Rechtsnachfolge und der Verfügungsmacht des Nichtberechtigten, Leipzig 1901.

Higgins, M.J., The transfer of property under illegal transactions, MLR 1962, p. 149 et seq.

Hoetink, H.R., Justus titulus usucapionis et justa causa tradendi, TR vol. 29 (1961), p. 230 et seq.

Hoetink, H.R., Nemo plus iuris ad alium transferre potest quam ipse habet, in: Rechtskundige opstellen op 2 november 1935 door oud-leerlingen aangeboden aan Prof. Mr. E.M. Meijers, Zwolle 1935, p. 474 et seq.

Hofmann, F., Die Lehre vom titulus und modus adquirendi, und von der iusta causa traditionis, Vienna 1873.

Hofmann, L.C., Het Nederlandsch zakenrecht, 3rd ed., Groningen/Batavia 1944.

Hohfeld, W.N., Fundamental legal conceptions as applied in judicial reasoning, New Haven 1964 (repr. Westport, Connecticut 1978).

Holdsworth, W., A history of English law, 7th ed., ed. by Goodhart, A.L. and Hanbury, H.G., 16 vols + register vol. (by Burke, J.), London 1956-1972.

Holmes, O.W., The common law, Boston 1881 (repr. New York 1991 with introduction by S.M. Novick).

Holmes-Pollock Letters, The correspondence of Mr Justice Holmes and Sir Frederic Pollock 1874-1932, 2 vols., ed. by Howe, M. de Wolfe, Cambridge (Massachusetts) 1941.

Holtzendorff, F. von (ed.), Encyklopädie der Rechtswissenschaft in systematischer Bearbeitung, 4th ed., vol. 1, Leipzig 1882.

Honoré, A.M., Ownership, in: A.G. Guest (ed.), Oxford essays in jurisprudence, Oxford 1961, p. 107 et seq.

Houin, R., Sale of goods in French law, in: Some comparative aspects of the law relating to sale of goods, International and Comparative Law Quarterly Supplementary Publication nr. 9, London 1964, p. 16 et seq.

Huet, J., Traité de droit civil, Les principaux contrats spéciaux, Paris 1996.

Ibbetson, D., From property to contract: the transformation of sale in the Middle Ages, The Journal of legal history, vol. 13 (1992), p. 1-22.

Ibbetson, D., Sale of goods in the fourteenth century, LQR 107 (1991), p. 480-499.

Isensee, J. and Kirchhof, P. (eds.), Handbuch des Staatsrechts der Bundesrepublik Deutschlands, vol. 9 (Die Einheit Deutschlands, Festigung und Übergang), Heidelberg 1997.

Jahr, G., Romanistische Beiträge zur modernen Zivilrechtswissenschaft, AcP vol. 168 (1968), p. 9 et seq.

Jhering, R. von, Der Besitzwille. Zugleich eine Kritik der herrschenden juristischen Methode, Jena 1889, repr. Aalen 1968.

Jhering, R. von, Geist des römischen Rechts auf den verschiedenen Stufen seiner Entwicklung, vol. 3, 3rd ed., Leipzig 1877.

Jobard-Bachellier, M.-N., Existe-t-il encore des contrats réels en droit Français? Ou la valeur des promesses de contrat réel en droit positif, Rev. trim. dr. civ. 1985, p. 1 et seq.

Johow, R., Entwurf eines bürgerlichen Gesetzbuches für das Deutsche Reich, Sachenrecht, 4 vols, vol. 1 (text of the draft), Berlin 1880; 3 vols 'Begründung' (Explanation), Berlin 1880. The full text of the draft and the explanation on 'Besitz' and 'Eigentum' published in: Die Vorlagen der Redaktoren für die erste Kommission zur Ausarbeitung des Entwurfs eines Bürgerlichen Gesetzbuches, Sachenrecht, vol. 1 (Allgemeine Bestimmungen, Besitz und Eigentum), ed. by Schubert, W., Berlin/New York 1982.

Jörs, P., Kunkel, W., Wenger, L., Römisches Recht, 4th ed. by Honsell, H., Mayer-Maly, Th., Selb, W., Berlin etc. 1987.

Kamp, J.L.J. van de, Bartolus de Saxoferrato, 1313-1357, Amsterdam 1936.

Kantorowicz, H., Studies in the glossators of the Roman law, Cambridge 1938.

Kaser, M., Das Geld im römischen Sachenrecht, TR vol. 29 (1961), p. 169-229.

Kaser, M., Das römische Privatrecht, 2nd ed., vol. 1, Das altrömische, das vorklassische und klassische Recht, Munich 1971; vol. 2, Die nachklassischen Entwicklungen, Munich 1975. Cited as Kaser I and II.

Kaser, M. and Hackl, K., Das römische Zivilprozeßrecht, Munich 1997.

Kaser, M., Der römische Anteil am deutschen bürgerlichen Recht, JS 1967, p. 337-344.

Kaser, M., Eigentum und Besitz im älteren römischen Recht, 2nd ed., Cologne/Graz 1956.

Kaser, M., Römisches Privatrecht, 16th ed., Munich 1992.

Koeppen, A., Der obligatorische Vertrag unter Abwesenden, Jher. Jahrb., vol. 11 (1871), p. 139 et seq.

Kohler, J., Bürgerliches recht, in: Kohler, J. Enzyklopädie der Rechtswissenschaft in systematischer Bearbeitung (begründet von Franz von Holtzendorff), vol. 2, Munich/Leipzig/Berlin 1914.

Kohler, J., Der dingliche Vertrag, in: Gesammelte Abhandlungen aus dem gemeinen und französischen Civilrecht, entnommen den Annalen der badischen Gerichte und der Zeitschrift für französisches Civilrecht, Mannheim 1883, p. 1 et seq.

Kohler, J., Substanzrecht und Wertrecht, AcP 91 (1901), p. 155 et seq.

Kolb, F.-J., Geheißerwerb. Eine Positionsbestimmung im Spannungsfeld zwischen Traditionsprinzip und Verkehrsbedürfnis, (Dissertation Mainz) Frankfurt a/M 1997.

Kolbe, K.W., Die Wirksamkeitsvoraussetzungen des constitutum possessorium nach der Pandektistik, (Dissertation Frankfurt a/M) s.l. 1957.

Kommentar zum Zivilgesetzbuch der Deutschen Demokratischen Republik vom 19. Juni 1975 und zum Einführungsgesetz zum Zivilgesetzbuch der Deutschen Demokratischen Republik vom 19. Juni 1975 (ed. by the Ministry of Justice), 2nd ed., Berlin 1985.

Kooiker, H., Lex scripta abrogata, De derde Renaissance van het Romeinse recht, Deel I, De uitwendige ontwikkeling, (thesis Groningen 1996) Nijmegen 1996.

Koschaker, P., Europa und das römische Recht, 4th ed., Munich/Berlin 1966.

Kümpel, S., Der Bestimmtheitsgrundsatz bei Verfügungen über Sammeldepotguthaben. Zur theorie des Bruchteilseigentums sui generis, WM 1980, p. 422 et seq.

Landsberg, E., Die Glosse des Accursius, Leipzig 1883.

Lange, Hermann, Römisches Recht im Mittelalter, vol. 1 (Die Glossatoren), Munich 1997.

Larenz, K., Allgemeiner Teil des deutschen bürgerlichen Rechts, 7th ed., Munich 1989.

Larenz, K., Lehrbuch des Schuldrechts, vol. 2, 1, 13th ed., Munich 1986.

Larroumet, annotation on Cour d'Appel de Paris, 14 October 1997, D 1998 J p. 91 et seq.

Laurent, F., Principes de droit civil français, 2nd ed., vol. 19, Brussels/Paris 1878.

Law Commission Working Paper No. 112, Rights to Goods in Bulk; Scottish Law Commission Discussion Paper No. 83, Bulk Goods: Section 16 of the Sale of Goods Act 1979 and Section 1 of the Bills of Lading Act 1855, London 1989.

Law Commission No. 215, Scottish Law Commission No. 145, Sale of goods forming part of a bulk, London 1993.

Lawson, F.H., A common lawyer looks at the civil law. Five lectures delivered at the University of Michigan, November 16, 17, 18, 19, and 20, 1953, Ann Arbor 1953 (repr. Westport (Connecticut) 1977).

Lawson, F.H., The passing of property and risk in sale of goods - a comparative study, LQR 1949, p. 352 et seq.

Lawson, F.H., Rights and other relations in rem, in: Festschrift für Martin Wolff, ed. by E. von Caemmerer et al., Tübingen 1952, p. 103 et seq.

Lawson F.H. and Rudden, B., The law of property, 2nd ed., Oxford 1982.

Lenel, O., Quellenforschungen in den Edictcommentaren, ZSS Rom, vol. 3 (1882), p. 177 et seq.

Linden, J. van der, Ontwerp burgerlijk wetboek 1807/1808, ed. by J.Th. de Smidt, Amsterdam 1967.

Liver P., Das Eigentum, in: Gutzwiller, M., Schweizerisches Privatrecht, Sachenrecht, Erster Halbband, ed. by A. Meier-Hayoz, Basel/Stuttgart 1977.

Locré, J.G., Législation civile, commerciale et criminelle, ou commentaire et complément des codes Français, 16 vols, Bruxelles 1836-1838.

Lokin, J.H.A., Prota, Vermogensrechtelijke leerstukken aan de hand van Romeinsrechtelijke teksten uitgelegd, 4th ed., Groningen 1995.

Lokin, J.H.A., Traditio; de verschaffing van het bezit, in: Feenstra, R., Lokin, J.H.A. and Wal, N. van der, Flores Legum, Groningen 1971, p. 121-132.

Malaurie, Ph. and Aynès, L., Cours de droit civil, Les contrats spéciaux, 10th ed. Paris 1996.

Martinek, M., Traditionsprinzip und Geheißerwerb, AcP 188 (1988), p. 573-648.

Marty, G. and Raynaud, P., Droit civil, les biens, ed. by Jourdain, P., Paris 1995.

Mazeaud, H. and L, Mazeaud, J., Chabas, F., Leçons de droit civil, vol. II, 2, Biens: droit de propriété et ses démembrements, Paris 1989.

Mazeaud, H. and L, Mazeaud, J., Chabas, F., Leçons de droit civil, vol. III, 2, Principaux contrats, Vente et échange, by Juglart, M. de, 7th ed., Paris 1987.

Mazeaud, H. and L, Mazeaud, J., Breton, A., Leçons de droit civil, IV, 2, Successions, libéralités, 4th ed., Paris 1982.

Mazeaud, H. and L, Mazeaud, J., Chabas, F., Leçons de droit civil, vol. II, 1, Obligations, théorie générale, 8th ed., Paris 1991.

McCormack, Geoffrey, Nemo sibi ipse causam possessionis mutare potest, Bullettino dell'Instituto di Diritto Romano, vol. 75 (1972), p. 71-96.

McCormack, Gerard, Proprietary claims and insolvency, London 1997.

McCormack, Gerard, Proprietary claims and insolvency in the wake of Westdeutsche, JBL 1997, p. 48 et seq.

McCormack, Gerard, The eye of Equity: identification principles and equitable tracing, JBL 1996, p. 225 et seq.

Medicus, D., Anspruch und Einrede als Rückgrat einer zivilistischen Lehrmethode, AcP 174 (1974), p. 313 et seq.

Medicus, D., Martin Wolff (1872-1953), Ein Meister an Klarheit, in: H. Heinrichs, H. Franzki, K. Schmalz and M. Stolleis (eds.), Deutsche Juristen jüdischer Herkunft, Munich 1993.

Meier-Hayoz, A., Berner Kommentar, Band IV (Sachenrecht), 1. Abteilung (Das Eigentum), 1. Teilband (Systematischer Teil und Allgemeine Bestimmungen, Art. 641-654 ZGB), Bern 1981.

Merlin, P.-A., Répertoire universel et raisonné de jurisprudence, 36 vols, 5th ed., Brussels 1825-1828.

Merwe, C.G. van der, Sakereg, 2nd ed., Durban 1989.

Merwe, C.G. van der, and Waal, M.J. de, The law of things and servitudes, Durban 1993.

Meijers, E.M., Eigendomsoverdracht van roerende lichamelijke zaken, Verzamelde privaatrechtelijke opstellen, vol. 2, Leiden 1955, p. 27 et seq.

Meijers, E.M., Levering en onderliggende rechtsverhouding (causa), Verzamelde privaatrechtelijke opstellen, vol. 2, Leiden 1955, p. 131 et seq.

Meijers, E.M., Levering en rechtstitel, Verzamelde privaatrechtelijke opstellen, vol. 2, Leiden 1955, p. 80 et seq.

Mijnssen, F.H.J., review of Den Dulk's book 'De zakelijke overeenkomst', RM Themis 1982, p. 68 et seq.

Milsom, S.F.C., Historical foundations of the common law, 2nd ed., London 1981.

Milsom, S.F.C., Sale of goods in the fiftienth century, LQR 77 (1961), p. 257 et seq.

Motive zu dem Entwurfe eines Bürgerlichen Gesetzbuches für das Deutsche Reich, vol. 3 (Sachenrecht), Amtliche Ausgabe, Berlin/Leipzig 1888.

Mugdan, B., Die gesammten Materialien zum Bürgerlichen Gesetzbuch für das Deutsche Reich, Berlin 1899 (repr. Aalen 1979), vol. 1 (Einführungsgesetz und Allgemeiner Teil), vol. 2 (Recht der Schuldverhältnisse), vol. 3 (Sachenrecht), cited as Mugdan, vol. 1, 2 or 3.

Müller-Freienfels, W., Die Abstraktion der Vollmachtserteilung im 19. Jahrhundert, in: Coing, H. and Wilhelm W. (eds.), Wissenschaft und Kodifikation des Privatrechts im 19. Jahrhundert, vol. 2, p. 144 et seq.

Münchener Kommentar zum Bürgerlichen Gesetzbuch, 3rd. ed., Munich 1992-. The author in question is cited as follows: Münchener-author.

Muther, Th., Zur Lehre von der römischen Actio, dem heutigen Klagrecht, der Litiscontestation und der Singularsuccession in Obligationen, eine Kritik des Windscheid'schen Buchs 'Die Actio des römischen Civilrechts vom Standpunkte des heutigen Rechts', Erlangen 1857 (repr. Aalen 1984).

Mijnssen, F.H.J. and Schut, G.H.A., Bezit, levering en overdracht, 3rd ed., Zwolle 1991.

Mourik, M.J.A. van, Verstappen, L.C.A. and Schols, F.W.J.M., Schenking en gift naar nieuw recht, Deventer 1999.

Mühlenbruch, C.F., Doctrina Pandectarum, vol. 2, 4th ed., Halle 1839.

Neumayer, K.H., Die sogenannte Vindikationszession (§ 931 BGB) im dogmatischen Spannungsfeld zwischen Übereignung und procuratio in rem, in: Kuchinke, K. (ed.), Rechtsbewahrung und Rechtsentwicklung, Festschrift für Heinrich Lange zum 70. Geburtstag, Munich 1970, p. 305-324.

Neuner, R., Abstrakte und kausale Uebereignung beweglicher Sachen, Rheinische Zeitschrift für Zivil- und Prozeßrecht 1926, p. 9-59.

Nicholas, B., An introduction to Roman law, Oxford 1977.

Nörr, D., Spruchregel und Generalisierung, ZSS Rom, 1972, p. 18 et seq.

Oeckinghaus, A., Kaufvertrag und Übertragung beim Kauf beweglicher Sachen im deutschen und französischen Recht, Berlin 1973.

Oertmann, P., Die Rechtsbedingung, Leipzig/Erlangen 1924.

Oertmann, P., Kommentar zum bürgerlichen Gesetzbuche und seinen Nebengesetzen, Erstes Buch, Allgemeiner Teil, 2nd ed. (by Gareis, K.), Berlin 1908.

Oertmann, P., Kommentar zum bürgerlichen Gesetzbuche und seinen Nebengesetzen, Zweites Buch, Recht der Schuldverhältnisse, 3rd-4th ed., Berlin 1910.

Ontwerp tot herziening van het burgerlijk wetboek, tweede boek, The Hague 1899.

Ontwerp tot herziening van het burgerlijk wetboek, tweede boek, toelichting, The Hague 1899.

Opzoomer, C.W., Het burgerlijk wetboek verklaard, 2nd ed., 16 vols, vols 1-6 (Amsterdam 1874-); vols 7-13 (The Hague 1891-); vols 14-16 by Levy, J.A. (The Hague 1904-1911).

Oven, J.C. van, Bezitsverkrijging door derden, NJB 1934, p. 701 et seq.

Oven, J.C. van, De bezitsbescherming en hare functies, (thesis Amsterdam, GU) Amsterdam 1905.

Oven, J.C. van, Iusta causa usucapiendi, TR 1939, p. 434 et seq.

Oven, J.C. van, Praeadvies over causa en levering. Welk verband bestaat naar ons recht tusschen de eigendomsverkrijging door levering en de onderliggende rechtsverhouding? Is het wenschelijk te dien aanzien wijziging in ons recht aan te brengen? Te behandelen op de algemeene vergadering der Broederschap van Candidaat-Notarissen in Nederland en zijne Koloniën te Groningen 1924, The Hague 1924.

Oven, J.C. van, WPNR 1949, p. 70.

Palandt, O., Bürgerliches Gesetzbuch, 56th ed., by Bassenge et al. (eds.), Munich 1997. The author in question is cited as follows: Palandt-author.

Pardessus, Œuvres complètes du Chancelier d'Aguesseau, vol. 12, Paris 1819.

Parlementaire geschiedenis van het nieuwe burgerlijk wetboek, Boek 3 (Vermogensrecht in het algemeen); Boek 5 (Zakelijke rechten); Boek 6 (Algemeen gedeelte van het verbintenissenrecht), ed. by Zeben, C.J. and Du Pon, J.W., Deventer 1981.

Parlementaire geschiedenis van het nieuwe burgerlijk wetboek, Invoering boeken 3, 5 en 6, Boek 3 (Vermogensrecht in het algemeen); Boek 5 (Zakelijke rechten); Boek 6 (Algemeen gedeelte van het verbintenissenrecht), ed. by Reehuis, W.H.M. and Slob, E.E., Deventer 1990.

Pawlowski, H.-M., Die gewillkürte Stellvertretung. Eine juristische Entdeckung der deutschen Rechtswissenschaft, JZ 1996, p. 125 et seq.

Planiol, M. and Ripert, G., Traité pratique de droit civil français, 13 vols, Paris 1952-1960.

Pollock, F., A first book of jurisprudence, for students of the common law, 5th ed., London 1923.

Pollock, F., Principles of contract, a treatise on the general principles concerning the validity of agreement in the law of England, 6th ed., London 1894.

Pollock, F., Gifts of chattels without delivery, LQR 6 (1890), p. 446 et seq.

Pollock, F. and Wright, R.S., An essay on possession in the common law, Oxford 1888.

Pollock, F. and Maitland, F.W., The history of English law, 2 vols, 2nd ed.,1898 (repr., ed. by S.F.C. Milsom, Cambridge 1968).

Pool, E.H., Een kwestie van titels, Causa van bezit, verjaring en eigendom naar klassiek Romeins recht, (thesis Amsterdam) Amsterdam 1995.

Prinz, O. (ed.), Mittellateinisches Wörterbuch, bis zum ausgehenden 13. Jahrhundert, vol. 1, Munich 1967.

Puchta, G.F., Pandekten, 2th ed., Leipzig 1844, 7th ed. and 11th ed., both ed. by A.F. Rudorff, Leipzig 1853 and 1872.

Raiser, L., Eigentumsanspruch und Recht zum Besitz, in: Festschrift für Martin Wolff, ed. by E. von Caemmerer et al., Tübingen 1952, p. 123 et seq.

Raiser, L., Der Stand der Lehre vom subjektiven Recht im Deutschen Zivilrecht, Juristenzeitung 1961, p. 465 et seq.

Randa, A., Der Besitz nach österreichischem Rechte, mit Berücksichtigung des gemeinen Rechts, des preußischen, französischen und italienischen, des sächsischen und züricherischen Gesetzbuches, 4th ed., Leipzig 1895.

Ranieri, F., Brevi note sull'origine della nozione di negozio reale ed astratto, TR vol. 38 (1970), p. 315 et seq.

Ranieri, F., Die Lehre der abstrakten Übereignung in der deutschen Zivilrechtswissenschaft des 19. Jahrhunderts, in: H. Coing and W. Wilhelm (eds.), Wissenschaft und Kodifikation des Privatrechts im 19. Jahrhundert, vol. 2, Frankfurt a/M 1977.

Rank-Berenschot, E.B., Over de scheidslijn tussen goederenrecht en verbintenissenrecht, (thesis Leiden 1992) Deventer 1992.

Reehuis, W.H.M., Heisterkamp, A.H.T., Maanen, G.E. van, Jong, G.T. de, Goederenrecht, 10th ed., Arnhem 1994. Cited as Reehuis/Heisterkamp, Goederenrecht.

Rehfeldt, B., Einführung in die Rechtswissenschaft, Berlin 1962.

Reuter, D. and Martinek, M., Ungerechtfertigte Bereicherung, Tübingen 1983.

Rey, H., Berner Kommentar, Band IV (Sachenrecht), 2. Abteilung (Die beschränkten dinglichen Rechte; die Dienstbarkeiten und Grundlasten), 1. Teilband (Die Grunddienstbarkeiten), Lieferung 1 (Systematischer Teil und Kommentar zu art. 730 und 731 ZGB), Bern 1981.

Rey, H., Die Grundlagen des Sachenrechts und das Eigentum, Bern 1991.

Riemer, H.M., Die beschränkten dinglichen Rechte, Bern 1986.

Rudden, B, Les biens et le trust, in: Common law d'un siècle l'autre, ed. by Legrand, P., Cowansville, Québec 1992, p. 253-274.

Rudden, B, Things as things and things as wealth, OJLS 1994, p. 81 et seq.

Rutten, L.E.H., De zakelijke overeenkomst, WPNR 1949, p. 67 et seq.

Salomons, A.F., 2014 tot 1950. De geschiedenis tot 1950 van de vertrouwensbescherming bij overdracht van roerende zaken door een beschikkingsonbevoegde, (thesis Amsterdam, UvA 1997) s.l. 1997.

Savigny, F.C. von, Das Recht des Besitzes, 7th ed., ed. by A.F. Rudorff, Vienna 1865.

Savigny, F.C. von, Das Obligationenrecht als Teil des heutigen römischen Rechts, 2 vols, Berlin 1851-1853 (repr. Aalen 1987).

Savigny, F.C. von, Geschichte des römischen Rechts im Mittelalter, 1st ed., 6 vols, Heidelberg 1815-1831.

Savigny, F.C. von, Landrechtsvorlesung 1824, Drei Nachschriften, Erster Halbband, Ius Commune Sonderhefte, vol. 67, 3.1, ed. by Chr. Wollschläger et al., Frankfurt a/M 1994.

Savigny, F.C., System des heutigen römischen Rechts, 8 vols, Berlin 1840-1849, register vol. by Heuser, O.L., 2nd ed, Berlin 1856.

Scheltema, M., De geschiedenis van het constitutum possessorium, Ars Aequi 1964, p. 1-12.

Schirdewahn, G., Kreditsicherung durch Begründung von Miteigentum, in: Zeitgemäße Bankrechtsfragen. Festgabe der Rechtsabteilung der Disconto-Gesellschaft zum 70. Geburtstag des Herrn Doctor Juris Arthur Salomonsohn, Berlin/Leipzig 1929, p. 150 et seq.

Scholten, P., annotation on Arrondissementsrechtbank Utrecht 21 Feb. 1906, WPNR 1906, p. 569.

Scholten, P., Zakenrecht, 4th ed., Zwolle 1905; 7th ed., Zwolle 1933; 8th ed., Zwolle 1945.

Scholtens, J.E., Justa causa traditionis and contracts induced by fraud, SALJ vol. 74 (1957), p. 280 et seq.

Schrage, E.J.H., Actio en subjectief recht, Amsterdam 1977.

Schrage, E.J.H., Vendita e trasferimento della proprietà nella storia del diritto olandese, in: Non quia romanum sed quia ius, Das Entstehen eines europäischen Rechtsbewußtseins im Mittelalter, Goldbach 1996, p. 191-208.

Schubert, W., Die Entstehung der Vorschriften des BGB über Besitz und Eigentumsübertragung. Ein Beitrag zur Entstehungsgeschichte des BGB, Berlin 1966.

Schut, G.H.A., Ars Aequi 1970, p. 152 et seq.

Schut, G.H.A., Het nieuwe 2014, WPNR 1972, p. 253 et seq.

Schuttevâer, H., Het reële element in de verbruiklening en de schenking van hand tot hand, RM Themis 1957, p. 481-515.

Schwab, K.H. and Prütting, H., Sachenrecht. Ein Studienbuch, 25th ed., Munich 1994.

Schwartz, A.B., Andreas Von Tuhr, Vortrag gehalten im Zürcherischen Juristenverein, Zurich 1938.

Smith, R.J., Property law, London 1996.

Smith, T.B., Property problems in sale, Tagore law lectures, London/Calcutta 1978.

Snijders, H.J., De titel van art. 3:84 lid 2 BW, in: Claringbould, M.H. (et al.), Van beheering, 'goederenrechtelijke beschouwingen', twaalf opstellen bij het zestiende lustrum van Societas Iuridica Grotius en de vierhonderdenvijftiende geboortedag van Hugo de Groot, Deventer 1998, p. 163 et seq.

Snijders, H.J. and Rank-Berenschot, E.B., Goederenrecht, Deventer 1996.

Sohm, R., Institutionen des römischen Rechts, 13th ed., Leipzig 1908.

Spruit, J.E., Enchiridium. Overzicht van de geschiedenis van het Romeins privaatrecht, 3rd ed. Deventer 1992.

Spruit, J.E. and Bongenaar, K., De Instituten van Gaius, 2nd ed., Zutphen 1994.

Stadler, A., Gestaltungsfreiheit und Verkehrsschutz durch Abstraktion, (*Habilitationsschrift* Freiburg im Breisgau), Tübingen 1996.

Stark, E.W., Berner Kommentar, vol. IV (Sachenrecht), 3. Abteilung (Besitz und Grundbuch), 1. Teilband (Der Besitz, Artikel 919-941 ZGB), 2nd ed., Bern 1984.

Staub, H., Handelsgesetzbuch, Großkommentar, ed. by Canaris, C., Schilling, W. and Ulmer, P., 4th ed., Berlin/New York 1983-.

Staudinger, J. von, Kommentar zum bürgerlichen Gesetzbuch mit Einführungsgesetz und Nebengesetzen, 12th ed. (Berlin 1978-) and 13th ed. (Berlin 1993-). The author in question is cited as follows: Staudinger-author. If a year is mentioned it refers to the 13th edition, unless stated otherwise.

Staudinger, J. von, Kommentar zum bürgerlichen Gesetzbuch und dem Einführungsgesetze, vol. 3 (Sachenrecht), part 1 (§§ 854-1017), 9th ed., by Kober, K., Munich/Berlin/Leipzig 1926.

Stephen's commentaries on the laws of England, Crispin Warmington, L. (ed.), 4 vols, 21st ed., London 1950.

Stintzing, W., Die Übertragung beweglicher Sachen nach deutschem bürgerlichen Recht mit Heranziehung des gemeinen und römischen Recht, Leipzig 1911.

Stobbe, O., Handbuch des deutschen Privatrechts, vol. 3, 2nd ed., Berlin 1885.

Strohal, E., Der Sachbesitz nach dem BGB, Jher. Jahrb. vol. 38 (1898), p. 1 et seq.

Strohal, E., Succession in den Besitz nach römischem und heutigem Recht, Graz 1885.

Suijling, J.Ph., Inleiding tot het burgerlijk recht, vol. 5 (Zakenrecht), Haarlem 1940.

Süß, Th., Das Traditionsprinzip - ein Atavismus des Sachenrechts, in: Festschrift für Martin Wolff, ed. by E. von Caemmerer et al., Tübingen 1952, p. 141.

Terré, F. and Simler, Ph., Droit civil, les biens, 4th ed., Paris 1992.

Thibaut, A.F.J., System des Pandektenrechts, 7th ed., vol. 1, Jena 1828.

Thornely, J.W.A., Gifts by delivery within a common household, CLJ 1964, p. 27 et seq.

Toullier, C.B.M., Le droit civil français suivant l'ordre du Code, 14 vols + 1 register vol., Paris 1830-1834.

Treitel, G.H., Remedies for breach of contract (courses of action open to a party aggrieved), International Encyclopedia of Comparative Law, vol. VII (Contracts in general, ed. by Mehren, A. von), ch. 16, Tübingen/The Hague/Paris 1976.

Treitel, G.H., The law of contract, 9th ed., London 1995.

Tuhr, A. von, Allgemeiner Teil des schweizerischen Obligationenrechts, 3rd. ed, vol. 1 (by Peter, H.), Zurich 1979; vol. 2 (by Escher, A.), Zurich 1974.

Tuhr, A. von, Der allgemeine Teil des deutschen bürgerlichen Rechts, Leipzig 1910 (vol. 1: erster Band, Allgemeine Lehren und Personenrecht), 1914 (vol. 2: zweiter Band, Die rechtserheblichen Tatsachen, insbesondere das Rechtsgeschäft, erste Hälfte) and 1918 (vol. 3: zweiter Band, zweite Hälfte). Cited as Von Tuhr I, II and III.

Tuhr, A. von, Eigenthumserwerb an Mobilien nach dem Bürgerlichen Gesetzbuch verglichen mit dem Rechte des Code Civil, Zeitschrift für Französisches Civilrecht, vol. 30 (1899), p. 527-549.

Tuhr, A. von, Eigentumserwerb aus unsittlichem Vertrag, AcP 120 (1920), p. 1 et seq.

Tuhr, A. von, Eigentumsübertragung nach schweizerischem Rechte, Zeitschrift für Schweizerisches Recht, 1921, p. 40-74.

Unger, J., Realcontracte im heutigen Recht, Jher. Jahrb. vol. 8 (1868), p. 1 et seq.

Vinding Kruse, Fr., The right of property, vol. 1 (transl. by Federspiel, P.T.), London/New York/Toronto 1939; vol. 2 (transl. by Philip, D.) London/New York/Toronto 1953.

Viollet, P., Histoire du droit civil Français, 3rd ed., Paris 1905 (repr. Aalen 1966).

Voorduin, J.C., Geschiedenis en beginselen der Nederlandsche wetboeken, 11 vols, Utrecht 1837-1840.

Vriesendorp, R.D., Het eigendomsvoorbehoud, (thesis Groningen) Deventer 1985.

Wacke, A., Das Besitzkonstitut als Übergabesurrogat in Rechtsgeschichte und Rechtsdogmatik. Ursprung, Entwicklung und Grenzen des Traditionsprinzips im Mobiliarsachenrecht, Cologne 1974.

Wadle, E., Die Übergabe auf Geheiß und der rechtsgeschäftliche Erwerb des Mobiliareigentums, JZ 1974, p. 689 et seq.

Warnkönig, L., Bemerkungen über den Begriff der iusta causa bei der Tradition, AcP 6 (1823), p. 111 et seq.

Watson, A., The evolution of law, Oxford 1985.

Weir, T., Taking for granted - the ramifications of *nemo dat*, in: M.D.A. Freeman (ed.), Current Legal Problems, vol. 49(II), Oxford 1996, p. 325 et seq.

Wendt, O., Rechtssatz und Dogma. Glossen zum Entwurf des bürgerlichen Gesetzbuches, Jher. Jahrb. 29 (1890) p. 29 et seq.

Wesenberg, G. and Wesener, G., Neuere deutsche Privatrechtsgeschichte, 4th ed., Vienna/Cologne 1985.

Westermann, H.P., Gursky, K.-H., Pinger, W., Sachenrecht. Ein Lehrbuch, vol. 1, Grundlagen und Recht der beweglichen Sachen, 6th. ed., Heidelberg 1990.

Westermann, H.P., Gursky, K.-H., Eickmann, D., Sachenrecht. Ein Lehrbuch, 7th ed., Heidelberg 1998.

Wieacker, F., Privatrechtsgeschichte der Neuzeit, 2nd ed., Göttingen 1967.

Wiegand, W., Die Entwicklung des Sachenrechts im Verhältnis zum Schuldrecht, AcP 190 (1990), p. 112 et seq.

Wiegand, W., Numerus clausus der dinglichen Rechte. Zur Entstehung und Bedeutung eines zentralen zivilrechtlichen Dogmas, in: Köbler, G. (ed.), Wege europäischer Rechtsgeschichte, Frankfurt a/M/Bern/New York/Paris 1987.

Wilhelm, W., Begriff und Theorie der Verfügung, in: H. Coing and W. Wilhelm (eds.), Wissenschaft und Kodifikation des Privatrechts im 19. Jahrhundert, vol. 2, Frankfurt a/M 1977, p. 213 et seq.

Williams, J., Principles of the law of personal property intended for the use of students in conveyancing, 18th ed. (by T.C. Williams and W.J. Byrne), London 1926.

Windscheid, B. and Kipp, Th., Lehrbuch des Pandektenrechts, vols 1-3, 9th ed. Frankfurt a/M 1906.

Windscheid, B., Die Actio des römischen Civilrechts vom Standpunkte des heutigen Rechts, Düsseldorf 1856 (repr. Aalen 1984).

Windscheid, B., Die Actio, Abwehr gegen Dr. Theodor Muther, Düsseldorf 1857 (repr. Aalen 1984).

Winkel, L., Die Irrtumslehre, in: Feenstra and Zimmermann (eds.), Das römischholländische Recht, Fortschritte des Zivilrechts im 17. und 18. Jahrhundert, Berlin 1992, p. 225-244.

Wolf, Ernst, Lehrbuch des Sachenrechts, 2nd ed., Cologne/Bonn/Berlin/Munich 1979.

Wolff, Martin, Das Recht zum Besitze. Sonderausgabe aus der Festgabe der Juristischen Gesellschaft zu Berlin zum 50järigen Dienstjubiläum ihres Vorsitzenden, des Wirklichen Geheimen Rats Dr. Richard Koch, Berlin 1903.

Wolff, Martin, and Raiser, L., Sachenrecht, Ein Lehrbuch, 10th ed., Tübingen 1957.

Wubbe, F., Die Interessenlage bei traditio und usucapio, TR vol. 32 (1964), p. 558 et seq.

Wubbe, F., article on 'ius in re' in: Paulys Realencyclopädie der classischen Altertumswissenschaft, neue Bearbeitung, begonnen von G. Wissowa, Supplementband X, Stuttgart 1965, columns 333-343.

Wubbe, F., Nemo sibi causam possessionis mutare potest, in: Spruit, J.E. and Vrugt, M. van de (eds.), Brocardica in honorem G.C.J.J. van der Bergh, 22 studies over oude rechtsspreuken, Deventer 1987, p. 129 et seq.

Wubbe, F., Usureceptio und relatives Eigentum, TR 28 (1960), p. 13 et seq.

Zachariae, C.-S., Aubry, C. and Rau, C., Cours de droit civil français, 2nd ed., 3 vols, Brussels 1842-1847.

Zimmermann, R., The law of obligations: Roman foundations of the civilian tradition, Deventer/Boston/Cape Town 1990/1992, Oxford 1996 (paperback).

Zimmermann, S., Die Sammelverwahrung von Edelmetallen, (*Dissertation* Zürich) Bern 1981.

Zwalve, W.J., Hoofdstukken uit de geschiedenis van het Europese privaatrecht, vol. 1 (Inleiding en zakenrecht), Groningen 1993.

Zweigert, K., Aspects of the German law of sale, in: Some comparative aspects of the law relating to sale of goods, International and Comparative Law Quarterly Supplementary Publication nr. 9, London 1964, p. 1 et seq.

Index of Roman legal sources

Note that 150[69] refers to page 150, footnote 69.

a) non-Justinianian sources

Gaius, Institutiones

b) Justinianian sources

Institutes

Digest

Codex

Table of cases

Note that 46[71] refers to page 46, footnote 71.

English and Commonwealth cases

German case

French cases

Dutch cases

Index

Note that 115[95] refers to page 115, footnote 95; ch. VII refers to chapter 7; § II 5.2 refers to chapter 2, § 5.2.